FILM

ANNUAL

1993

JIM FREDRICKSON

STEVE STEWART

COMPANION
PUBLICATIONS

COVER PHOTO: *Basic Instinct*, starring Michael Douglas and Sharon Stone was arguably the most controversial film of the year. It was also, according to the studio, the number one film of 1992 at the box office, grossing $353 million worldwide. For her memorable performance, Stone received a Best Actress Golden Globe nomination and a People's Choice Favorite Actress in a Dramatic Motion Picture nomination.

Cover still: From "Basic Instinct" Courtesy of Carolco.
Motion Picture © 1992 Carolco/Le Studio Canal+S.A.
All Rights Reserved.

Companion Publications
PO Box 2575
Laguna Hills, California 92654

Printed in the United States of America

ISBN: 0-9625277-3-4
ISSN: 1061-4214

Contents

Acknowledgements

We would like to express our sincerest thanks to the many distributors and publicity companies who provided press releases, photographs and other vital information necessary to make this the most complete record of the films receiving theatrical release in 1992. Special thanks go to Sharon Stone and Carolco, Inc. for permitting us to use the cover photo. Extra special thanks to Sterlinda Barrett at Carolco, Inc. for her many efforts in obtaining this permission.

In addition we would like to thank: the publicity departments at MGM and TriStar, Terry Saevig at Columbia Pictures, Myriam Estany at The Walt Disney Company, Dave Wong at Morgan Creek Productions, Karen Ray at The Samuel Goldwyn Company, Wil Adams at Shapiro Glickenhaus Entertainment, Eric Bachmann at Castle Hill Productions, Kathy Decker at Cinetel Films, Inc., Beth Conwell at Kings Road Entertainment, Zac Reeder at Pyramid Distribution, Inc., the staffs at I.R.S. Releasing, Trimark Pictures, Streamline Pictures and Warren Miller Entertainment, and Peggy Stuart.

Introduction
To The 1993 Edition

One of the things I enjoy most when watching an old movie, or a new movie for that matter, is the occasional witty or dramatic "classic" line that stays with you long after the closing credits. We all have our favorites—lines like "Frankly, my dear, I don't give a damn," "Here's looking at you kid," or "I want to be alone."

Unfortunately, I often hear critics lament that film dialogue just isn't what it used to be, and while that may be true, it's certainly as memorable and clever as it ever was. "I'll be back," "Go ahead, make my day," and "Who are you? Your worst nightmare," have all entered the "Film Quote Hall Of Fame" in just the last few years.

1992 was no exception, but it *was* exceptional. It gave us some of the most inspired and witty one-liners ever to be uttered on the silver screen. The reason I mention this is that following the publication of last year's *Film Annual,* we realized that any thorough record of the year in film would not be complete without a section devoted to the year's most memorable film quotes. That's why you'll find our favorites (and no doubt, many of yours) beginning on page 15 in the new Year In Film Quotes section.

While we were making improvements, it occurred to us that the Top 10 Films (according to the critics), and the Top 10 Films (at the box-office) were also essential—not to mention fascinating to compare.

Another new section that seemed an obvious omission is titled The Year In Film. It chronicles the year's highs and lows, milestones and memorable moments throughout the year—just to put it all into perspective. After all, looking back years from now, it might be important or helpful to know the name of the only film to be released in 1992 with an NC-17 rating. Or, more importantly, you might need to know who followed Rob Lowe and Pee Wee Herman in the most-talked-about-scandal-of-the-year department. At the very least, it would be worth noting that *Casablanca* celebrated its 50th anniversary during this momentous and memorable year.

Also new this year, in the Films From A to Z section, we've included advertising and promotional tag lines whenever available and trivia about each film when appropriate. We've also expanded the MPAA Ratings to include not only the letter but also the description as well. Whenever possible, we also indicated the presence of male and female nudity, sexuality and violence.

While we've added many new sections and redesigned our basic format to make the previous sections easier to use, we are still devoted to bringing you all of the American and foreign films released theatrically in the U.S. in 1992 from January 1 through December 31. Every effort has been made to contact all studios and distributors, both large and small, to obtain information. We apologize if we have missed anyone and invite filmmakers to send us information on all new releases for future editions.

If it happened in film in 1992, you'll find it in the *Film Annual*. While other annual film books give you just the photos or just the reviews, we offer an annual and video guide, with films, facts and information you won't find in any other guide. As always, we welcome and look forward to your comments and suggestions on improving future editions.

Steve Stewart
December 31, 1992

1992
The Year In Film

Casablanca, arguably America's favorite film, celebrated its 50th anniversary in 1992 and was re-released in theaters around the country. Many things have changed since 1942, but as so often is the case, the more things change, the more they stay the same. Movies are just as popular as they ever were, Disney is still producing modern classics, and celebrity scandals still make headline news.

Each new year, however, brings its share of newcomers and fresh new faces that catch our attention and often our hearts. This year was no exception. Who could forget the performances of Marisa Tomei in *My Cousin Vinny*, Brendan Fraser in *School Ties* or Kathy Najimy in *Sister Act*?

HERE'S LOOKING AT YOU

Then there were the "overnight" sensations who have been around awhile. Chris O'Donnel in *Scent Of A Woman*, David Paymer in *Mr. Saturday Night* and Brad Pitt in *A River Runs Through It*. All turned in performances that catapulted them to stardom. The most memorable of them all was Sharon Stone in *Basic Instinct*.

Yet, for all the new faces that grabbed our attention, it was the perennial favorites who grabbed our hearts—Al Pacino in *Scent Of A Woman*, Clint Eastwood and Gene Hackman in *Unforgiven*, not to mention film legends Donald O'Connor in *Home Alone 2*, Sylvia Sidney in *Used People* and Eddie Bracken in *Toys*—the latter, just newcomers when *Casablanca* premiered.

IN A LEAGUE OF THEIR OWN

According to *Quigley Publications,* commenting on its annual poll of the top-10 box-office draws, Whoopi Goldberg became the first African-American woman ever to make the list. It was no surprise, however, that Tom Cruise, Mel Gibson, Kevin Costner, Jack Nicholson, Macaulay Culkin, Michael Douglas, Clint Eastwood, Steven Seagal and Robin Williams once again rounded it out.

In November, Disney's 1991 hit *Beauty And The Beast* became the best-selling video of all time. A few months later *Aladdin* became the highest-grossing animated feature in film history, earning more than $147 million in its initial release. In addition, it was the only film of the year to appear on both the critics' Top-10 list and the Box-office Top-10 list—and it's a sure bet that 50 years from now it will still be going strong.

WE'RE TALKING SERIOUS MONEY

During the Great Depression the entertainment business thrived. Decades later, Hollywood barely seemed to notice that the country was in the middle of a recession. According to *Daily Variety,* 1992 was the third-best year in box-office history, taking in $4.9 billion at the box-office.

All of this helps to explain why, when moviegoers were forced to tighten their belts, Hollywood paid author John Grisham an estimated $2.5 million for his unpublished novel, *The Client*. Grisham is the author of *The Firm*, currently in production, starring Tom Cruise. It sold for $600,000. The author's other novel, *The Pelican Brief*, sold to Warner Bros. for a reported $1.27 million.

Yet not everyone in the business was recession-proof. Harold Russell, who won two Oscars in 1946 for his performance in *The Best Years Of Our Lives* was forced to auction one of his statues due to financial difficulties. It sold for $65,000. A few months later, in October, Beatle John Lennon's Oscar raised $100,000 on the auction block, creating a stir among Academy members.

THE SCANDAL THAT ROCKED THE CRADLE

Scandals are certainly nothing new to the entertainment business, only the faces and facts are new—sometimes only the faces. Every year seems to have its memorable scandal. It didn't begin with Rob Lowe or Pee Wee Herman, and it probably won't end with Woody Allen. Especially if the outcomes remain so positive. Lowe and Herman appeared separately in two of the year's top-10 films—*Wayne's World* and *Batman Returns*—while the publicity generated by Allen's very public separation from Mia Farrow and child custody battle was a publicity windfall when his film *Husbands And Wives* opened soon after.

The unhappy couple made the cover of *TIME, Newsweek, People* and all of the tabloids, and nearly upstaged the Republican convention in August. Minority Whip Newt Gingrich wasted no time in calling the Democrats' family-values section of thier platform platform the "Woody Allen plank."

The movie, which opened in September, gave Allen his most successful opening ever.

ONE FALSE POLITICAL MOVE

It has often been said that politics makes strange bedfellows. That was never more true than in Hollywood in 1992.

Politically correct groups protested and boycotted everything from homicidal bi-sexuals in *Basic Instinct* to penguin abuse in *Batman Returns*. Fortunately, or unfortunately, depending on your politics, the protests only drew more attention to the films in question and added to their box-office success.

Politically correct message films like *Ferngully,* which tackled environmental issues, were less popular than their politically incorrect counterparts.

Following the spring riots in Los Angeles, a number of films ready for release, including *Unlawful Entry*, were edited or postponed to avoid inciting further violence. The film *Looters* was edited, renamed *Trespass* and only shown in cities outside Los Angeles until the end of the year. Never one to sidestep controversy, however, Spike Lee featured the Rodney King beating that sparked the riots, in the opening shots of *Malcolm X,* and once again, it was difficult to determine where Hollywood ended and real life began.

CAT WOMAN OF THE YEAR

In this "mother of all election years," women took center stage in politics and seemed to declare war in the movies. Considered the "Year Of The Woman" in politics, critics referred to it as the "Year Of The Lethal Woman" in films. In films like *Lethal Weapon 3, Buffy The Vampire Slayer, Aces: Iron Eagle III, Batman Returns, Final Analysis, The Hand That Rocks The Cradle, Consenting Adults* and many others, women either mutilated, humiliated, or protected their male co-stars. Even Freddie's girlfriend in the animated film *Freddie as F.R.O.7.* was a martial-arts specialist. Women flexed their muscles more than ever before and men ran for cover. If women still lacked power in the industry they could at least intimidate the men who held it.

BACK TO BASIC INSTINCTS

Things weren't much safer, for men or women, in the bedroom. Sex on the screen in

1992 was kinky, dangerous and deadly (more so than usual), and sex, more often than not, led to death—in the movies as in real life. The movies simply reflected the ever-present fear and reality of AIDS.

Sex involved ice picks, high heels, whips, handcuffs and blood. Safe sex, in the form of masturbation, also played a part in many films, including the year's only NC-17 rated film *Bad Lieutenant*. In this film Harvey Keitel lets it all hang out and pushes the limits of sexual depravity.

And perhaps more than any other year, films with gay themes or sexual-identity problems proliferated. From *The Crying Game* to *Single White Female* to *Swoon*, sex was often a prelude to a big surprise.

PRELUDE TO A KISS OF DEATH

In a simpler time, a "kiss was just a kiss." But even a kiss could be deadly in 1992.

In *Prelude To A Kiss*, a film one critic described as a metaphor for AIDS, Alex Baldwin is forced to kiss an old man in order to reclaim his wife's soul. In *Bram Stoker's Dracula* it was hard not to make the connection between the kiss of death and the dreaded plague. But the most memorable kiss—uh...lick—was shared by Michelle Pfieffer's lethal Catwoman and Michael Keaton's "Batman."

Old-fashioned, romantic kisses, on the other hand, were in short supply.

AS TIME GOES BY

Finally, 1992 will be remembered as the year Charlie Chaplin graced the silver screen once again in Richard Attenborough's winning film biography; as the year vice president Dan Quayle declared war on Hollywood; as the year Michael Keaton a.k.a. "Batman" left his hand and foot prints in cement at Mann's Chinese theatre; as the year screen siren Madonna exposed herself once again in a book titled "SEX" that topped the *New York Times* best-seller list for weeks; and for being the year actor Paul Henreid, who co-starred with Bogart and Bergman in *Casablanca,* made his final appearance.

Fortunately for us all, the films that reflected and affected our lives in 1942 and in 1992 will be preserved in time forever.

Top 10 Films of 1992
(According to the Critics)

In 1992, *Hoffa* appeared not only on a few critics' top 10 best lists, but on a few 10 worst lists as well. We mention this as a warning and as a reminder; top-10 lists are subjective, to say the least. The only film to appear on nearly *every* list was *Howards End.* That said, we've compiled all of the year-end top-10 lists available to us (over 50 in all) and come up with a comprehensive Top 10 films for 1992. Of the 10 choices, it's interesting to note that all are dramas but one. The opposite is true of the box-office favorites. Here they are in alphabetical order.

1. Aladdin
Last year's *Beauty And The Beast* became the first animated film to be nominated for a Best Picture Oscar. While *Aladdin*, was not nominated for Best Picture it became the studios most successful film at the box office.

2. The Crying Game
The low-budget, unpredictable and intelligent *The Crying Game*, was the biggest surprise hit of the year. It was also the film that offered the biggest surprise on screen.

3. Glengarry Glen Ross
This film elevated the four letter word to an art form. It also celebrated some of the industry's finest actors in their finest performances.

4. Howards End
The filmmaking team of Merchant and Ivory received the highest honors by appearing on more top-10 lists than any other film of the year.

5. Husbands And Wives
The Woody Allen/Mia Farrow separation scandal not only upstaged the Republican convention but managed to generate more press for the film than any army of press agents ever could have hoped for.

6. Malcolm X
Spike Lee's *Malcolm X* was arguably the best film biography of the year. This in a year crowded with bio pics on Chaplin, Hoffa, Columbus, Babe Ruth and Ruby—quite an achievement.

7. One False Move
One of the year's small-budget, powerful films that nearly went directly to video before receiving a tremendous reception from the critics.

8. The Player
Early in the year, critics were nearly unanimous in their praise of this poignant satire of the Hollywood studio system.

9. Raise The Red Lantern
One of only three foreign films to make the list and the only one in a foreign language.

10. Unforgiven
Earning more than any of his previous westerns, Clint Eastwood's *Unforgiven* was one of those rare films that achieved success not only with the critics but with audiences as well.

Top 10 Films of 1992
(At The Box Office)

It was not a surprise that seven of the top-10 films at the box office in 1992 were comedies. Neither was it a surprise that only one of the top-grossing films of the year, *Aladdin*, made it onto the critics' top-10 lists. The only real surprise was that many entering the "$100 million club" did it within days of their release. The following top-10 list, with figures from *Exhibitor Relations*, includes only those films released between January 1 and December 31st, 1992, and only totals through the last day of the year.

1. Batman Returns　　　　　$165,700,000
While it fell short of breaking the original *Batman* box-office records of 1986, it nevertheless became the highest-grossing film of the year.

2. Home Alone 2:
**　Lost In New York**　　　$147,000,000
One of three sequels that made the top-10 list and helped make this the third-best year in movie history at the box office.

3. Lethal Weapon 3　　　　$144,600,000
Mel Gibson and Danny Glover once again proved to be a lethal combination.

4. Sister Act　　　　　　$139,400,000
Disney made the list twice this year. First with this sleeper comedy of the summer and later in the year with *Aladdin*.

5. Wayne's World　　　　$121,600,000
Critics and audiences were in agreement about Wayne's inventive and intelligent humor. It became the first film of the year to earn $100 million.

6. Basic Instinct　　　　$117,200,000
Basic Instinct became one of the most controversial films of the year. Featuring a politically incorrect psycho-killer the film managed to silence the pro-testers and go on to phenomenal box-office success. It was also reportedly the years highest-grossing film worldwide at the box office.

7. Aladdin　　　　　　　$116,000,000
Aladdin was also the only film of the year to make both critics' and box-office top-10 lists. It also topped $100 million in record time for the studio.

8. A League Of Their Own　$107,300,000
Director Penny Marshall hit the "Big" time once again with this film, which naysayers believed would never attract a crossover audience.

9.The Bodyguard　　　　　$88,300,000
Whitney Houston not only made her film debut opposite one of Hollywood's biggest stars but she also went on to have the year's hottest soundtrack.

10. The Hand That Rocks
**　The Cradle**　　　　　　$87,500,000
Cradle's killer nanny was the first in a long line of psycho-killers who found an audience in films like *Basic Instinct, Single White Female, Unlawful Entry* and *Consenting Adults*.

1992
The Year In Film Quotes

When asked during an interview in Los Angeles, "What's your favorite television show," then Vice President Dan Quayle answered in Wayne Campbellese, "Murphy Brown—not!"

Everyone has his or her favorite movie quote. Here are a few of the best, taken from the films of 1992. (See screenwriter credits accompanying the listing for each film for the names of the writers responsible for these memorable lines.)

SEX

"I know this woman in the biblical sense and she ain't no nun."
—Harvey Keitel, *Sister Act*

"You use sex to express every emotion except love."
—Mia Farrow, *Husbands And Wives*

"I'm no hooker—I'm a housewife. We do it for free."
—Cybill Shepherd, *Once Upon A Crime*

"Mrs. Robinson you're trying to seduce me—aren't you?"
—Joe Pantoliano, *Used People*

"There's only two things I do really well sweetheart, and skating's the other one."
—D.B. Sweeney, *The Cutting Edge*

"He got off before he got offed."
—George Dzundza, *Basic Instinct*

"I wasn't dating him, I was fucking him."
—Sharon Stone, *Basic Instinct*

"I don't know anything about you that's not police business."
"You know I don't wear any underwear don't you Nick?"
—Michael Douglas and Sharon Stone,
Basic Instinct

"The cop couldn't find his dick with two hands and a map."
—Ed Harris, *Glengarry Glen Ross*

"If you haven't gotten a blow job from a superior officer, well, you're just letting the best in life pass you by."
—Jack Nicholson, *A Few Good Men*

"On a Hasidic scale of sexiness, how do I rate?"
—Melanie Griffith, *A Stranger Among Us*

"Big things may happen to that little thing of yours."
—Al Pacino, *Scent Of A Woman*

13

LOVE

"Even when you were throwing up, I knew you cared."
—Jaye Davidson, *The Crying Game*

"Marriage is punishment for shoplifting in some countries."
—Mike Myers, *Wayne's World*

VIOLENCE

"I have two rules. One, I do not date musicians. Two, I do not kill people, ok?"
—Erika Eleniak, *Under Seige*

"What would you do if you were me?"
"Kill myself."
—Ernie Lively and Wesley Snipes
Passenger 57

"Killing isn't like smoking, you can quit."
—Sharon Stone, *Basic Instinct*

"Don't make me come get you."
—Jennifer Jason Leigh, *Single White Female*

"People wish to kill you. Anyone who's met you, I imagine."
—Maggie Smith, *Sister Act*

"Stop, or my mom will shoot."
—Sylvester Stallone,
Stop, Or My Mom Will Shoot!

"The hand that rocks the cradle is the hand that rules the world."
—Julianne Moore,
The Hand That Rocks The Cradle

"I don't know whether to shoot you or adopt you."
—Al Pacino, *Scent Of A Woman*

TELEVISION

"Life doesn't imitate art; it imitates bad television."
—Juliette Lewis, *Husbands And Wives*

"Do you know how to turn on the television? I'm 10 years old—TV's my life!."
—Macauley Culkin,
Home Alone 2: Lost In New York

"You can't believe one word you see on TV. Not one word."
—Dustin Hoffman, *Hero*

"You don't have a video camera! Everyone has a video camera!"
—Ray Liotta, *Unlawful Entry*

HUMOR

"What kind of idiots do you have working here?"
"Only the finest in New York City"
—Catherine O'Hara and desk clerk,
Home Alone II: Lost In New York

"Made ya look"
—Robin Williams, *Aladdin*

"I'm about as crazy as a dog in a hubcap factory."
—Eddie Murphy, *The Distinguished Gentleman*

"He's a mechanic who knows as much about

cars as a cheerleader."
—Al Pacino, *Scent Of A Woman*

"I want to take you somewhere special."
"In Queens?"
—Marcello Mastroianni and Shirley MacLaine,
Used People

"Not too spicy, we're Jewish. We take gas very seriously."
—Shirley MacLaine, *Used People*

"You have something against ice cubes?"
—Michael Douglas, *Basic Instinct*

"You better duck and cover."
—Jean-Claude Van Damme,
Universal Soldier

WOMEN

"She's a robo-babe"
—Dana Carvey, *Wayne's World*

"You smell like you've been with a woman."
"No it's vomit."
— Angela Pleasance and Bob Hoskins,
The Favor, The Watch And The Very Big Fish

MEN

"I think you're just jealous that I'm a genuine freak and you have to wear a mask."
—Danny DeVito, *Batman Returns*

"I'm twice the man you are."
" So is she and it's driving me mad."

—John Savident and John Turturro,
Brain Donors

"I can be butch when I have to. I get it from my mother."
—Peter Friedman, *Single White Female*

"What do you say we slip into the backseat and you make a man out of me?"
"What do you say I slap you around for awhile?"
"Can't we do both?"
—Young boy and Geena Davis,
A League Of Their Own

"My son Tony, he got mugged by a gang of transvestites. They pierced his ear. He got away just before they shaved his legs."
—William Petersen, *Passed Away*

"There's no crying in baseball!"
—Tom Hanks, *A League Of Their Own*

"He does look a little soft."
"Soft! He looks like Liberace."
—William Petersen and Bob Hoskins,
Passed Away

"If this turns into a nuns bar, I'm outta here."
—Bar patron, *Sister Act*

"Roy, you have boobs!"
"They're not mine."
—Pam Dawber and John Ritter, *Stay Tuned*

"If we ever get out of this, things are going to be different, I promise you. I'm going to be the man I was when we first met."
"You weren't blonde then and you wore a lot

15

less makeup."
—John Ritter and Pam Dawber, *Stay Tuned*

"He's the boss. If I could find the right doctor I would have my lips permanently sewed to his ass."
—Peter MacNicol, *Housesitter*

"Sometimes I wish I could boldly go where no man has gone before."
—Dana Carvey, *Wayne's World*

"How was jail? Meet anyone?."
—Pauley Shore, *Encino Man*

DEATH AND TAXES

"I fear death terribly don't you?"
"Not as much as I fear my family."
—Tim Curry and Pamela Reed, *Passed Away*

"This is a wake, not a garage sale!"
—Bob Hoskins, *Passed Away*

"I've got cancer of the career. It's inoperable."
—Billy Crystal, *Mr. Saturday Night*

"Somebody has to die."
"Why?"
"Somebody always does."
—Sharon Stone and Michael Douglas,
Basic Instinct

AMERICANS

"We didn't land on Plymouth Rock, Plymouth Rock landed on us."
—Denzel Washington, *Malcolm X*

"You don't have to wear a patch on your arm to have honor."
—Tom Cruise, *A Few Good Men*

"Ask not what your country can do for you. Ask what you can do for yourself."
—Tim Robbins, *Bob Roberts*

LIARS

"You're the Ernest Hemingway of bullshit!"
—Steve Martin, *Housesitter*

"The trouble is you stink at lying."
"Excuse me, O Queen of Crap."
—Steve Martin and Goldie Hawn,
Housesitter

"I lied about everything—you've got to believe me."
—John Candy, *Once Upon A Crime*

"You're lying."
"Of course I am, but hear me out."
—John Savident and John Turturro,
Brain Donors

"We don't need no preacher selling us bunk."
"I'm not selling bunk, friend—I'm giving it away."
—Heckler and Steve Martin, *Leap Of Faith*

"I've never met anyone like you. You're honest even when you're lying."
—Mary Elizabeth Mastrantonio, *White Sands*

"I don't hustle with people who are dishonest."
—Woody Harrelson, *White Men Can't Jump*

DOCTORS AND LAWYERS

"If I were you, I'd get a second opinion."
—Larry Drake, *Dr. Giggles*

"He could use a gift certificate to the Betty Ford clinic."
—John Turturro, *Brain Donors*

AGE

"Do you mind if I sit down? I've been on my feet for the last 56 years."
—Shirley MacLaine, *Used People*

"Who wants to live to be 95?"
"94-year-olds."
—William Petersen and house guest,
Passed Away

"I'm getting too old for this shit."
—Danny Glover, *Lethal Weapon 3*

WE THOUGHT THAT'S WHAT THEY SAID

"No can do. What's that, a Chinese appetizer?"
—Robert De Niro, *Night And The City*

"That means I'm sorry I shot you, but I thought you were robbing my store."
—Halle Berry, *Boomerang*

"Always bet on black."
—Wesley Snipes, *Passenger 57*

"What if my uniform bursts open and oops, my bosom come flying out?"

"You think there are men in this country who ain''t seen your bosom?"
—Madonna and Rosie O'Donnell,
A League Of Their Own

"It's got more plastic than Cher."
—Mel Gibson, *Lethal Weapon 3*

"Do yourself a favor—floss."
—Sydney Walker, *Prelude To A Kiss*

"Yabba Dabba Doo."
—Al Pacino, *Scent Of A Woman*

HOLLYWOOD

"No stars, just talent."
—Tim Robbins, *The Player*

"The scripts will write themselves."
—Peter Gallagher, *The Player*

"Could we talk about something other than Hollywood for a change?"
—Tim Robbins, *The Player*

"Listen babe, there's no one bigger than Wayne Newton in this town."
—Man in crowd, *Honey I Blew Up The Kid*

BEAUTY

"Obviously you're having a bad hair day."
—Kristy Swanson, *Buffy The Vampire Slayer*

"When you've got a hump back, why spend money on a nose job?"
—Shirley MacLaine, *Used People*

REAL LIFE

"Can I go. Is this over?"
—Woody Allen, *Husbands And Wives*

"Do you think we'd ever break up?"
"I'm not planning on it."
—Mia Farrow and Woody Allen,
Husbands And Wives

"I'm afraid that nine times out of ten, nature pulls one way and human nature the other."
—Emma Thompson, *Howards End*

"Excuse me, does the food magically jump from the plate into your mouth?"
—Marcia Gay Harden, *Used People*

WHERE HAVE WE HEARD THAT BEFORE?

"I'll be back."
—Estelle Getty,
Stop, Or My Mom Will Shoot!

"I'll be back."
—Brendan Fraser, *Encino Man*

"Trust me."
—Mel Gibson, *Lethal Weapon 3*

"Trust me, I'm a doctor."
—Larry Drake, *Dr. Giggles*

"Buckle up."
—Jean-Claude Van Damme, *Universal Soldier*

"Fasten your seat belts folks, it's going to be a bumpy ride."
—Jeffrey Jones, *Stay Tuned*

FAMOUS LAST WORDS

"Not!"
—Mike Myers, *Wayne's World*

"Meow."
—Michelle Pfeiffer, *Batman Returns*

"Cosmetics."
—Susan Sarandon, *Light Sleeper*

"Tits."
—Harrison Ford, *Patriot Games*

"Ok, ok, ok."
—Joe Pesci, *Lethal Weapon 3*

Notes To The Reader

Films Alphabetically

All significant films, both U.S. and foreign, released in the U.S. between January 1 and December 31, 1992 are listed alphabetically in the **Films from A to Z** section of this book. All articles such as "A," "An" or "The" follow the main title for alphabetizing purposes.

Distributor

The film's distribution company is identified in parentheses below the film's title.

Critics Rating

Critics ratings are based on critics opinions from across the U.S. and, as such, opinions may vary. In addition, critics ratings do not necessarily indicate a film's popularity with the audience.

In order to be considered representative and assigned a rating, a film must have been reviewed by at least 10 critics. One point is awarded for each favorable review, one-half point for each mixed review and no points for each negative review. Total points are divided by the total number of reviews to determine a percentage. Based on the percentage, the film is assigned a rating. The ratings are determined as follows: ★★★★★ Excellent (90% or greater), ★★★★ Very Good (greater than 75%, but less than 90%), ★★★ Good (greater than 40%, but less than 75%), ★★ Fair (at least 20%, but less than 40%), ★ Poor (less than 20%) and **Not Rated** (less than 10 critics).

Film Genre

Each film in the **Films from A to Z** section has been categorized by genre. Genres used in this book are: Action, Adventure, Animated, Comedy, Documentary, Drama, Fantasy, Horror, Science Fiction and Thriller.

Foreign Films

Foreign films are listed by the title under which they were released in the U.S. The original language or English translation title will appear in parentheses below the released title.

Tag Line

When appropriate, you will find publicity tag lines that were used to promote the film.

Plot

This section is intended to give the reader a very brief overview of the plot and main characters.

Cast

All major cast members and their roles are listed. Supporting cast members and their characters are included when information is available.

Credits

The "credits" section identifies the film's production personnel. The following major categories are included where applicable: executive producer, producer, director, director of photography, sound, editor, production design, set design, set decoration, costume design, screenwriter, music and casting. In addition, several other categories (assistants, special effects, stunts, etc.) are included when information is applicable and available.

MPAA Rating
Each film's listing includes the rating assigned by the Motion Picture Association of America (MPAA). Those not rated by the MPAA are identified as such.

Ratings used by the MPAA are: **G**/General Audiences, **PG**/Parental Guidance Suggested, **PG-13**/Parents Strongly Cautioned (Some material may be inappropriate for children under 13), **R**/Restricted (Under 17 requires accompanying parent or adult guardian), and **NC-17**/No one under 17 admitted.

Trivia
This section includes any additional information of special interest.

Running Time
Running time is the total running time of the film.

Soundtrack
The record label releasing the film's soundtrack.

Academy Awards
All 1991 Academy Award winners and nominees are listed. In addition, you will find a listing of all prior Academy Award winners for Best Picture, Actor, Actress, Director and Song.

Other Awards
Winners of other film awards are also highlighted. These awards include: British Academy of Film and Television Arts, Chicago Film Critics, D. W. Griffith (National Board of Review), Directors Guild of America, Golden Globe (Hollywood Foreign Press Association), Independent Spirit, Los Angeles Film Critics, National Society of Film Critics, New York Film Critics Circle, People's Choice, Saturn Awards (Academy of Science Fiction, Fantasy & Horror Films) and Writer's Guild of America.

Obituaries
A chronological listing of American film actors and actresses, and noteworthy foreign performers who died during 1991. In addition, directors, screenwriters, cinematographers and other members of the film production crew who either won or were nominated for an Academy Award are also included.

Index
The alphabetical **Index** at the end of the book lists all actors, actresses and film production personnel included in the book.

Aces: Iron Eagle III
(New Line Cinema)

Critics Rating: Not Rated.
Genre: Action—Lou Gossett Jr. is joined this time out by bodybuilder Rachel McLish. Together they wind up this action series with ample fireworks and laughs to spare. Action buffs and followers of the series will claim this as an action-packed, final victory.
Tag Line: "Their best and final mission."
Plot: Gossett again plays Chappy, an Air Force pilot, who this time takes a group of veteran fighter aces on a personal rescue mission. It's also about a private war against the drug lords of Peru. While Anna (McLish) turns out to be a potent secret weapon in this explosive and fitting conclusion.
MPAA Rating: R—For war violence.

Cast
Chappy	Louis Gossett, Jr.
Anna	Rachel McLish
Kleiss	Paul Freeman
Leichman	Horst Buchholz
Palmer	Christopher Cazenove
Horikoshi	Sonny Chiba
Tee Vee	Phil Lewis
General Simms	Mitchell Ryan
Stockman	Fred Dalton Thompson

Also with Tom Bower, Rob Estes, Juan Fernandez, J. E. Freeman, Ray Mancini, Inez Perez and Branscombe Richmond.

Credits
Producer	Ron Samuels
Co-Producer	Stan Neufeld
Associate Producer	Michael R. Casey
Director	John Glen
Assistant Director	James M. Freitag
Director of Photography	Alec Mills
Sound	Susumu Tokunow
Editor	Bernard Gribble
Production Manager	Stan Neufeld
Production Design	Robb Wilson King
Costume Design	Lesley Nicholson
Casting	Vicki Huff
Written by	Kevin Elders
Based on Characters Created by	Kevin Elders
	Sidney J. Furie
Music	Harry Manfredini
Model and Special Effects	John Richardson
Stunt Coordinator	Bob Minor
Aerial Unit Director	David Nowell

Film Facts
Running Time	98 minutes
Soundtrack	Intrada Records
Film	CFI Color
Sound	Dolby Stereo
Location	Tucson, Arizona

Adam's Rib
(Rebro Adama)
(October Films)

Critics Rating: ★★★★★
Genre: Comedy—Four women living together in a small Moscow apartment may feel crowded, but in

this case there's plenty of room for warmth and humor. That's the premise of this tragicomedy by the winner of the Directors' Fortnight at the Cannes Film Festival, Vyacheslav Kristofovich.

Tag Line: "A sexy, spicy comedy."

Plot: The four women of this story are a bedridden grandmother; her divorced daughter, Nina; and Nina's two daughters, Lida and Nastia. Lida is unhappily involved with a married man, while Nastia has recently become pregnant by her high-school boyfriend. The real fun begins one evening when all the men involved inadvertently show up at the apartment at the same time.

MPAA Rating: Not Rated.

Cast

Nina.....................................Inna Tchourikova
With Elena Bogdanova, Maria Goloubkina, Svetlana Riabova and Andrei Tolubeyev.

Credits

Director ....Viatcheslav Krichtofovitch
Director of Photography ....Pavel Lebedev
Sound....................................Jan Potocki
Editor ....Inna Brozhovskaya
Art Direction.............................Sergei Khotimsky
............................Alexander Samulekin
Screenplay ....Vladimir Kounine
Based on the Novel *House of Women* by.............................Anatole Kourtchatkine
Music ....Vadim Khrapatchev

Film Facts

Country of Origin.............................Russia
Language ....Russian (subtitled)
Running Time ....75 minutes
Film ....Color
Sound...Stereo
Location...Moscow

The Adjuster
(Orion Classics)

Critics Rating: ★★★

Genre: Drama—Witty, eccentric, perverted, twisted, abstract and visually stunning were words used by critics to describe this highly stylized Canadian film by writer-director Atom Egoyan (*Family Viewing, Speaking Parts*).

Plot: The central character of this film is Noah

(Elias Koteas), an insurance adjuster. While he spends his time sleeping with vulnerable clients, his wife Hera (Arsine Khanjian) spends her days watching porno films. As a film censor, this also happens to be her job. When Noah and Hera cross paths with an even odder couple, Bubba and Mimi, their individual and collective sexual fantasies lead to a disturbing climax.

MPAA Rating: R—For sensuality and language.

Cast

Noah.....................................Elias Koteas
Hera.....................................Arsinee Khanjian
Bubba.....................................Maury Chaykin
Mimi.....................................Gabrielle Rose
Bert (the head censor) ....David Hemblen
Arianne.....................................Jennifer Dale
Sete.....................................Rose Sarkisyan
Simon.....................................Armen Kokorian
Also with Patricia Collins, John Gilbert, Don McKellar, Stephen Ouimette, Gerard Parkes, Jacqueline Samuda and Raoul Trujillo.

Credits

Co-Producer.....................................Camelia Frieberg
Associate Producer.............................David Webb
Director.....................................Atom Egoyan
Assistant Director.............................David Webb
Director of Photography ....Paul Sarossy
Sound ....Steven Munro
Editor.....................................Susan Shipton
Production Design.....................Linda Del Rosario
.....................................Richard Paris
Art Direction.....................Kathleen Climie
Set Decoration.....................Richard Paris
.....................................Linda Del Rosario
Costume Design ....Maya Mani
Written by.....................................Atom Egoyan
Music ....Mychael Dana

Film Facts

Country of Origin.............................Canada
Running Time ....102 minutes
Film ....Cinemascope Color
Sound ....Stereo

Affengeil
(Life Is Like A Cucumber)
(First Run Features)

Critics Rating: Not Rated.

Genre: Documentary—Gay filmmaker Rosa von Praunheim (*An Army Of Lovers*) examines his friendship with the eccentric German actress Lotti Huber in this 1990 film.

Plot: A survivor of a concentration camp, the 76-year-old Huber flees to Israel and becomes a nightclub dancer. In later years she becomes a TV personality and a flamboyant spokesperson for the gay community. Together she and von Praunheim are a bizarre but entertaining twosome, and the film is a warm and witty portrait of a modern-day heroine.

MPAA Rating: Not Rated—Seminude gay bedroom scenes make this a film for a select audience.

Cast

With Lotti Huber, Gertrud Mischwitzky, Frank Schafer, Hans Peter Schwade, Helga Sloop, Rosa von Praunheim and Thomas Woischnig.

Credits

Executive Producer	Elke Peters
Producer/Director	Rosa von Praunheim
Directors of Photography	Mike Kuchar
	Klaus Janschewski
Editor	Mike Shephard
Art Direction	Volker Marz
Written by	Rosa von Praunheim
Music	Maran Gosov
	Thomas Marquard

Film Facts

Country of Origin	Germany
Running Time	87 minutes
Film	Color
Sound	Stereo

Afraid Of The Dark

(Fine Line)

Critics Rating: ★★★

Tag Line: "You can't escape what you can't see."

Genre: Drama—Making his directorial debut, Oscar-winning screenwriter Mark Peploe (*The Last Emperor*) brings to the screen a terrifying psychodrama with a twist.

Plot: The film, set in London, centers on 10-year-old Lucas (Ben Keyworth). Lucas is slowly going blind. Terrified and lonely, the boy's ability to distinguish between fantasy and reality becomes blurred. Peploe straightforwardly explores the depths of this young boy's mind, showing how he deals with his difficult situation.

MPAA Rating: R

Cast

Lucas	Ben Keyworth
Frank	James Fox
Miriam	Fanny Ardant
Rose	Clare Holman
Dan Burns	Robert Stephens
Tony Dalton	Paul McGann
Lucy Trent	Susan Wooldridge

Credits

Executive Producers	Jean Nachbaur
	Sylvaine Sainderichin
Producer	Simon Bosanquet
Director	Mark Peploe
Assistant Director	Jonathan Benson
Director of Photography	Bruno de Keyzer
Sound	Tony Jackson
	Mark Auguste
	Robin O'Donoghue
Editor	Scott Thomas
Production Design	Caroline Amies
Art Direction	Stephen Scott
Costume Design	Louise Stjernsward
Casting	Lucy Boulting
Screenplay	Mark Peploe
	Frederick Seidel
Music	Richard Hartley

Film Facts

Country of Origin	Great Britain/France
Running Time	92 minutes
Film	Technicolor
Sound	Dolby Stereo

Aladdin

(Buena Vista)

Critics Rating: ★★★★★

Genre: Animated—Once again Disney has magically created an entertaining, heartfelt, old-fashioned film, only this time they've taken a few chances and stretched the genre by providing a few daring surprises along the way.

Tag Line: "An adventure beyond your imagination."

Plot: This is a tale about Aladdin (Weinger), a poor young man who falls in love with a princess. The law forces the princess, Jasmine (Larkin), to marry a prince. All is not lost, however, because Aladdin finds a magic lamp and a very imaginative genie (Williams) who grants him any wish. He becomes a prince, but still must battle an evil adviser to the Sultan, who wants Jasmine and the kingdom for himself. Still, like all Disney fairy tales, a happy ending is just a song away.

MPAA Rating: G

Trivia: Tim Rice, Alan Menken and the late Howard Ashman wrote the music score. Ashman, who died March 14, 1991, from AIDS, had received a Best Original Score Oscar, along with Menken, for *Beauty And The Beast.*

Cast
Voices:

Aladdin	Scott Weinger
Aladdin (singing)	Brad Kane
Genie	Robin Williams
Jasmine	Linda Larkin
Jasmine (singing)	Lea Salonga
Jafar	Jonathan Freeman
Abu	Frank Welker
Iago	Gilbert Gottfried
Sultan	Douglas Seale

Credits

Producers/Directors	John Musker
	Ron Clements
Co-Producers	Donald W. Ernst
	Amy Pell
Sound	Terry Porter
	Mel Metcalfe
	David J. Hudson
Editor	H. Lee Peterson
Production Design	R. S. Vander Wende
Art Direction	Bill Perkins
Casting	Albert Tavares
Screenplay	Ron Clements
	John Musker
	Ted Elliott
	Terry Rossio
Music	Alan Menken
Songs	Howard Ashman
	Alan Menken
	Tim Rice
Supervising Animators	Glen Keane
	Eric Goldberg
	Mark Henn
	Andreas Deja
	Duncan Marjoribanks
	Randy Cartwright
	Will Finn
	David Pruiksma
Story Supervisor	Ed Gombert
Layout Supervisor	Rasoul Azadani
Background Supervisor	Kathy Altieri
Clean-up Supervisor	Vera Lanpher
Visual Effects Supervisor	Don Paul
Computer Graphics Imagery Supv.	Steve Goldberg
Artistic Coordinator	Dan Hansen
Computer-generated Imagery	Dan Philips

Film Facts

Running Time	90 minutes
Soundtrack	Walt Disney Records
Film	Technicolor
Sound	Dolby Stereo
Location	Los Angeles (principal animation)

Alan & Naomi

(Triton)

Critics Rating: ★★★

Genre: Drama—Set in 1944, *Alan & Naomi* is a serious drama about the friendship between a teenage boy and girl and is genuinely humorous and touching.

Plot: Lukas Haas plays a Jewish boy growing up in New York City. When Naomi, an unusual girl, moves in next door, Alan's life changes in ways he never expected.

Having escaped with her mother from occupied France (after witnessing the Nazis' murder of her father), Naomi is left unable to speak. In time, Alan provides the catalyst for her healing, and she regains more than just her voice.

MPAA Rating: PG

Cast

Alan Silverman	Lukas Haas
Sol Silverman	Michael Gross
Naomi Kirschenbaum	Vanessa Zaoui
Ruth Silverman	Amy Aquino

Mrs. Kirschenbaum.........................Victoria Christian
Shaun Kelly...Kevin Connolly
Mrs. Liebman ....Zohra Lampert
Also with Charlie Dow.

Credits

Executive Producer.............................Jonathan Pillot
Producers..David Anderson
....Mark Balsam
Co-Producer ....Don Schain
Associate Producers ....Edward M. Grant
....Jordan Horowitz
Director ....Sterling Van Wagenen
Assistant Director.......................................Rip Murray
Director of Photography ....Paul Ryan
Sound ....Rick Waddell
Editor..Cari Coughlin
Production Manager ....David Blake Hartley
Production Design ....George Goodridge
Costume Design ....Alonzo V. Wilson
Casting..Walken-Jaffe
....Fincannon & Associates
Screenplay..Jordan Horowitz
Based on the Novel by ....Myron Levoy
Music ....Dick Hyman

Film Facts

Running Time ....95 minutes
Film..Allied/WBS Color
Sound ....Dolby Stereo

Alberto Express
(MK2)

Critics Rating: ★★
Genre: Comedy—A dark comedy by director (*Harem*) Arthur Joffe.
Tag Line: "All his life his father gave him everything…Then he gave him the bill."
Plot: Sergio Castellito plays Alberto, a poor, out-of-work man with a wife and a child on the way. All of a sudden he remembers an ancient family tradition and curse his father cast upon him when he was still a young man. His father had demanded that he repay every cent spent on raising him before he could start his own family. Otherwise his own marriage would be somehow doomed. Desperate to settle up with his father, he takes a train back home. His journey becomes a misadventure, however, as

he meets numerous comical characters and situations along the way. The events help him find his own way in life.
MPAA Rating: Not Rated.

Cast

Alberto ....Sergio Castellitto
Alberto's father ....Nino Manfredi
Clara ....Marie Trintignant
The controller ....Marco Messeri
The baroness..Jeanne Moreau
Juliette ....Eugenia Marruzzo
Diamond tooth man ....Dennis Goldson
Waiter ....Roland Amstutz
Train conductor ....Dominique Pinon
The grandfather..................................Nanni Tamma

Credits

Executive Producer.............................Alain Centonze
Producer..Maurice Bernart
Director..Arthur Joffe
Director of Photography ....Philippe West
Sound ....Jean-Paul Mugel
Editor....................................Marie Castro-Brechignac
Set Design...Bernard Vezat
Screenplay ....Arthur Joffe
....Jean-Louis Benoit
....Christian Billette
Music ....Angela Nachon
....Jean-Claude Nachon

Film Facts

Country of Origin....................................France
Language...............................French/Italian (subtitled)
Running Time ....98 minutes
Film...Color
Sound ....Stereo

Alex
(A Idade Major)
(Coralie)

Critics Rating: Not Rated.
Genre: Drama—In this intense Portuguese drama, war not only tears apart a country but a family as well. This is primarily a film for a select audience.
Plot: Ricardo Colares stars as Alex, a young boy who, in the early 1970s, watches his father go off to war. Contact through letters stops after some time. Then one day Alex learns that his father has been

back from the war for months. They reunite, but things are not the same, and the family sadly begins to disintegrate.

MPAA Rating: Not Rated.

Cast

Alex	Ricardo Colares
Mario	Vincent Gallo
Manuela	Teresa Roby
Barbara	Maria de Medeiros
Pedro	Joaquim de Almeida

Credits

Producer	Joao Pedro Benard
Director	Teresa Villaverde
Director of Photography	Elfi Mikesch
Sound	Vasco Pimental
Editors	Manuela Viegas
	Vasco Pimental
Art Direction	Miguel Nendes
	Jeanne Waltz
Written by	Teresa Villaverde

Film Facts

Country of Origin	Portugal
Running Time	120 minutes
Film	Color
Sound	Sound

Alien 3
(20th Century Fox)

Critics Rating: ★★★

Genre: Science Fiction—Dark and moody, only the visuals and special sound effects save this sci-fi thriller from run-of-the-mill status.

Plot: As the film opens, Warrant Officer Ripley (Sigourney Weaver) finds herself the only surviving member of her crew following a crash—except for the alien that tagged along. She has landed on a planet that's used to house hardened male prisoners. This small group of men is now locked in a maximum-security prison with an Alien, which they are forced to fight without any weapons. In a twist, Ripley becomes the secret weapon and the only one able to kill it.

MPAA Rating: R—For monster violence and language.

Trivia: Sigourney Weaver's shaved head turned a lot of heads when the film opened but this was not the first time a woman shaved her head for a feature role. In 1971 George Lucas asked the men and women of his sci-fi film *THX 1138* to shave their heads for their roles as well.

Cast

Ripley	Sigourney Weaver
Dillon	Charles S. Dutton
Clemens	Charles Dance
Bishop II	Lance Henriksen
Aaron	Ralph Brown
Rains	Christopher John Fields
Andrews	Brian Glover
Golic	Paul McGann
Morse	Danny Webb
Junior	Holt McCallany

Credits

Executive Producer	Ezra Swerdlow
Producers	Gordon Carroll
	David Giler
	Walter Hill
Co-Producer	Sigourney Weaver
Director	David Fincher
Assistant Director	Chris Carreras
2nd Unit Director	Martin Brierley
Director of Photography	Alex Thomson
Sound	Tony Dawe
Editor	Terry Rawlings
Production Design	Norman Reynolds
Art Direction	Fred Hole
	James Morahan
Set Decoration	Belinda Edwards
Costume Design	Bob Ringwood
	David Perry
Casting (U.S.)	Billy Hopkins
Casting (U.K.)	Priscilla John
Screenplay	David Giler
	Walter Hill
	Larry Ferguson
Story by	Vincent Ward
Based on Characters Created by	Ronald Shusett
	Dan O'Bannon
Music	Elliot Goldenthal
Special Effects Supervisor	George Gibbs
Visual Effects Producer	Richard Edlund
Alien Effects	Alec Gillis
	Tom Woodruff, Jr.
Original Alien Design	H. R. Giger
Stunt Coordinator	Marc Boyle

Film Facts

Running Time ....115 minutes
Soundtrack..MCA Records
Film ....Rank Laboratories Color
Sound ....Dolby Stereo
Location..London

All The Vermeers In New York

(Strand)

Critics Rating: ★★★

Genre: Drama—A complex tale of love and money, *All The Vermeers* won the Los Angeles Film Critics' Award for best independent/experimental feature in 1991.

Plot: Stephen Lack plays Mark, a financial trader on Wall Street. On a visit to the Metropolitan Museum of Art he meets and later becomes involved with Anna (Emmanuelle Chaulet), a French woman staying in the city. Their difficult relationship unfolds in slow, but realistic fashion.

MPAA Rating: Not Rated.

Cast

Mark.......................................Stephen Lack
Anna..............................Emmanuelle Chaulet
Felicity..................................Grace Phillips
Nicole..............................Katherine Bean
Ariel.......................................Laurel Kiefer
Gracie Mansion...............................Gracie Mansion
Max..Roger Ruffin
Gordon ....Gordon Joseph Weiss

Credits

Executive Producer.........................Lindsay Law
Producer.........................Henry S. Rosenthal
Director/Editor ....Jon Jost
Director of Photography ....Jon Jost
Sound..John Murphy
Production Manager ....Molly Bradford
Conceived by...............................Jon Jost
Music..Jon A. English
.......................Bay Area Jazz Composers Orchestra

Film Facts

Running Time ....87 minutes
Film ....Color
Sound ....Stereo

Amazon

(Cabriolet)

Critics Rating: Not Rated.

Genre: Adventure—*Amazon* is an old-fashioned adventure on one level. It's a story of one man's inner conflicts—and how they affect the world around him—on another level.

Plot: Kari Vaananen stars as a Finnish businessman who is forced to flee his home, ending up in Rio de Janeiro. A string of bad luck next finds him losing all his money and stranded in the middle of the Amazon jungle. His luck finally turns around when he is rescued by Dan (Robert Davi), an American pilot. The two eventually go into business together. But again, just as things seem to be going right, he is confronted by the fact that his dream will only add to the destruction of the Amazonian rain forest.

Viewers with a political bent toward saving the rain forest will want to view this film. Those purely interested in adventure and a solid, old-fashioned plot will also find it entertaining and worthwhile viewing.

MPAA Rating: Not Rated.

Cast

Kari ....Kari Vaananen
Dan ....Robert Davi
Paola ....Rae Dawn Chong
Nina...Minna
Julio Cesar ....Rui Polanah
Lea ....Aili Sovio

Credits

Executive Producers ....Klaus Heydemann
....................................Bruce Marchfelder
Producers...Pentti Kouri
....Mika Kaurismaki
Co-Producers ....Diane Silver
....Bruno Stroppiana
....Paivi Suvilehto
Line Producers (Brazil)...........................Telmo Mais
....Pauli Pentti
Director.......................................Mika Kaurismaki
Assistant Director ....Vicente Amorim
Director of Photography ....Timo Salminen
2nd Unit Camera.........................Jacques Cheuviche
Sound ....Jouko Lumme

Editor..............................Michael Chandler
Art Direction ....Tony de Castro
Screenplay ....Mika Kaurismaki
....Richard Reitinger
Music..............................Nana Vasconcelos

Film Facts
Running Time ....93 minutes
Film ....Color
Sound.............................Dolby Stereo
Location......................................Brazil

American Dream
(Prestige)

Critics Rating: ★★★★★

Genre: Documentary—Academy-Award-winning documentary filmmaker Barbara Kopple (*Harlan County U.S.A.*) focuses her lens this time on the plight of unions during the Reagan '80s.

Plot: The drama centers on the Hormel Corporation and its attempt to cut wages in its Austin, Minnesota, plant in the mid-1980s. The union refuses to accept the company's offer, which leads to a strike. Both sides are allowed to voice their points of view, which makes for a balanced story. In the end, however, it is a story about how the power of the unions has been stripped away.

MPAA Rating: Not Rated.

Credits
Producers............................Barbara Kopple
....Arthur Cohn
Coordinating Producers.....................Peter Miller
....Esther B. Cassidy
Associate Producers ....Jonathan House
...........................Molly Ornati, Bill Susman
...................Gail Rosenschein, Ernest Hood
Director..............................Barbara Kopple
Directors of Photography ....Peter Gilbert
.......................Kevin Keating, Hart Perry
.................Mark Petersson, Mathieu Roberts
Editors..............................Cathy Caplan
.......................Tom Haneke, Lawrence Silk
Associate Editor..........................Robert McFalls
Music..............................Michael Small
Sound Recordist ....Barbara Kopple

Film Facts
Running Time ....100 minutes

Film ....Color
Sound ....Stereo

American Fabulous
(First Run Features)

Critics Rating: Not Rated.

Genre: Documentary

Plot: Gay comedian and commentator Jeffrey Strouth plays himself in this humorous, risqué and campy series of colorful personal tales. He tells the tales from the back seat of his car while driving around America's heartland.

Like self-styled homosexual Quentin Crisp, Strouth is proud of his camp-queen, nonconformist status and his ability to survive. He says in one scene, "My very existence is a crime in most people's eyes." His tales are largely about surviving. Strouth explains how he survived the wrath of an alcoholic father, life as a teenage prostitute and finally heroin addiction. He had the courage and tenacity to beat all the odds but one; he dies of AIDS in 1991.

MPAA Rating: Not Rated.

Credits
Producer/Director/Editor ....Reno Dakota
Directors of Photography ....Travis Ruse
....Reno Dakota
Written/Performed by ....Jeffrey Strouth
Song ("Royal Cafe") Written/
   Performed by.........................American Music Club

Film Facts
Running Time ....105 minutes
Film ....Color (Video - 35 mm transfer)
Sound ....Stereo

American Me
(Universal)

Critics Rating: ★★★

Genre: Drama—Edward James Olmos makes a powerful directorial debut with a dramatic film about the brutality and hopelessness of drugs and gang life.

Plot: Olmos stars as Santana, the ruthless boss of the Mexican Mafia—a notorious prison gang with the power to control the Latino community—both inside and outside the prison walls. It's the story of the American Dream gone mad, the hopelessness created by the tragic cycle of violence, and most of all, it's the saga of three generations of lives wasted.

Filmed on location at Folsom Prison, the film is clearly aimed at getting a message across to inner-city youth in a frightening way that will have a lasting impact.

MPAA Rating: R—For strong violence and sensuality; language and drug content.

Cast

Santana	Edward James Olmos
JD	William Forsythe
Mundo	Pepe Serna
Pie Face	Domingo Ambriz
Puppet	Danny De La Paz
Julie	Evelina Fernandez
Pedro	Sal Lopez
El Japo	Cary-Hiroyuki Tagawa
Little Puppet	Daniel Villarreal
Dornan	Tom Bower
Young Mundo	Richard Coca
Young Santana	Panchito Gomez
Huero	Daniel A. Haro
Esperanza	Vira Montes
Cheetah	Vic Trevino
Young JD	Steve Wilcox

Credits

Executive Producers	Irwin Young
	Floyd Mutrux
	Lou Adler
Producers	Sean Daniel
	Robert M. Young
	Edward James Olmos
Co-Producer	Brian Frankish
Associate Producers	Randee Lynn Jensen
	Antoinette Levine
Director	Edward James Olmos
Assistant Director	Richard Espinoza
Director of Photography	Reynaldo Villalobos
Sound	Dennis Jones
Editors	Arthur R. Coburn
	Richard Candib
Production Design	Joe Aubel
Art Direction	Richard Yanez
Set Design	Stephanie Gordon
	Darrell Wight
Set Decoration	Martin C. Price
Costume Design	Sylvia Vega-Vasquez
Casting	Bob Morones
Written by	Floyd Mutrux
	Desmond Nakano
Story by	Floyd Mutrux
Music	Dennis Lambert
	Claude Gaudette

Film Facts

Running Time	126 minutes
Film	Deluxe Color
Sound	Dolby Stereo
Location	Los Angeles, CA

Antarctica

(Heliograph Film)

Critics Rating: Not Rated.

Genre: Drama—Limited to IMAX theater viewing in select locations.

Tag Line: "Join the explorers as they probe the continent's past to discover our future."

Plot: The five-story-high IMAX screen is the only way to view this very big film about the coldest continent in the world. The film follows a group of brave explorers as they capture the immense beauty and power of this frozen land from above and below the sea.

MPAA Rating: Not Rated.

Cast

Capt. Scott	John Mills
"Birdie" Bowers	Reginald Beckwith
Narrator	Alex Scott

Credits

Executive Producer	
	Museum of Science & Industry (Chicago)
Producers	John Weiley
	David Flatman
Director	John Weiley
Directors of Photography	Tom Cowan
	Malcom Ludgate
Sound	Tony Vaccher
	John Dennison
Editor	Nicholas Holmes

Screenplay	Les A. Murray
	John Weiley
	Michael Parfit
Music	Nigel Westlake

Film Facts

Running Time	43 minutes
Film	Color (IMAX)
Sound	Stereo

Article 99

(Orion)

Critics Rating: ★★★

Genre: Drama—*Article 99* refers to a Veteran Administration rule used to deny medical benefits to veterans in need. Based on real-life incidents, this provocative drama takes an inside look at the desperation of both doctors and patients alike that results from dealing with an uncaring bureaucracy.

Plot: Ray Liotta (*Unlawful Entry*) stars as Dr. Sturgess, a cardiologist dedicated to helping deserving veterans. Together with the help of fellow MDs, Kiefer Sutherland and Lea Thompson, he battles the bureaucratic system for those who are no longer able to do battle.

MPAA Rating: R—For language.

Cast

Dr. Peter Morgan	Kiefer Sutherland
Dr. Richard Sturgess	Ray Liotta
Dr. Sid Handleman	Forest Whitaker
Dr. Robin Van Dorn	Lea Thompson
Dr. Rudy Bobrick	John C. McGinley
Dr. Henry Dreyfoos	John Mahoney
Luther Jerome	Keith David
Dr. Diana Walton	Kathy Baker
Sam Abrams	Eli Wallach
Inspector General	Noble Willingham
Amelia Sturdeyvant	Julie Bovasso
Shooter Polaski	Leo Burmester
Pat Travis	Troy Evans
Dr. Leo Krutz	Jeffrey Tambor
Nurse White	Lynne Thigpen

Credits

Producers	Michael Gruskoff
	Michael I. Levy
Associate Producers	Elena Spiotta
	Roger Joseph Pugliese
Director	Howard Deutch
Assistant Director	K. C. Colwell
Director of Photography	Richard Bowen
2nd Unit Camera	John Allen
Sound	C. Darin Knight
Editor	Richard Halsey
Production Design	Virginia L. Randolph
Art Direction	Marc Fisichella
Set Design	Tom Stiller
Set Decoration	Sarah Stone
Costume Design	Rudy Dillon
Casting	Karen Rea
Screenplay	Ron Cutler
Music	Danny Elfman

Film Facts

Running Time	99 minutes
Soundtrack	Varese Sarabande
Film	DuArt Color
Sound	Dolby Stereo
Location	Kansas City, Missouri

The Babe
(Universal)

Critics Rating: ★★★
Genre: Drama—This straightforward nostalgic and affectionate telling of the Babe Ruth story hits a home run. Topnotch technical credits and memorable performances all around will appeal especially to baseball fans and history buffs.
Plot: John Goodman (*Barton Fink, King Ralph*) stars as the legendary baseball hero George Herman Ruth, also known as the Bambino, Babe and the Sultan of Swat. The film follows Ruth's short life and career from the beginning. Focusing on his huge appetites and excesses, both on and off the field, director Arthur Hiller captures the magic of another time and place in this memorable tale.
MPAA Rating: PG

Cast
Babe Ruth ....John Goodman
Claire Hodgson Ruth ....Kelly McGillis
Helen Woodford Ruth ....Trini Alvarado
Jumpin' Joe Dugan............................Bruce Boxleitner
Brother Mathias ....James Cromwell
Harry Frazee ....Peter Donat
Col. Jacob Ruppert ....Bernard Kates
Lou Gehrig ....Michael McGrady
Jack Dunn ....J. C. Quinn
Miller Huggins..Joe Ragno
Guy Bush...Richard Tyson
Johnny Sylvester (age 10) ....Dylan Day
Johnny Sylvester (age 30) ....Stephen Caffrey
Young George H. Ruth ....Andy Voils

Credits
Executive Producers ....Bill Finnegan
....Walter Coblenz
Producer...John Fusco

Co-Producer.......................................Jim Van Wyck
Associate Producer...................................Erica Hiller
Director ....Arthur Hiller
Assistant Director ....Jim Van Wyck
Director of Photography ....Haskell Wexler
Sound ....Dennis Maitland
Editor ....Robert C. Jones
Production Design ....James D. Vance
Art Direction...Gary Baugh
Set Design.......................................Michael Merritt
....Karen Fletcher-Trujillo
....Linda Buchanan
....J. Christopher Phillips
Set Decoration...Les Bloom
Costume Design....................................April Ferry
Casting...Nancy Nayor
....Valerie McCaffrey
Casting (Chicago) ....Jane Alderman
Casting (Indiana) ....Judy Welker
Written by ....John Fusco
Music ....Elmer Bernstein
John Goodman's Makeup/
    Makeup Supervisor ....Kevin Haney
Visual Effects Supervisor ....Chuck Comisky
Matte Paintings..............................Illusion Arts, Inc.
....Syd Dutton
....Bill Taylor
Stunt Coordinator ....Rick LeFevour

Film Facts
Running Time ....115 minutes
Soundtrack.....................................MCA Records
Film ....Deluxe Color
Sound ....Dolby Stereo
Location ....Chicago

The Bachelor
(Greycat)

Critics Rating: Not Rated.
Genre: Drama—This beautifully lensed period piece with fine performances will appeal to both art-house and mainstream audiences alike.
Plot: Set at the turn of the century, Keith Carradine plays Dr. Emil Grasler, a middle-aged physician who lives with his sister Frederica (Richardson). Left alone after her suicide, he is forced out into the world. He falls in love and becomes involved with a

number of women. Instead of happiness, this only leads to anguish and confusion. Grasler is a man who needs stability in and control of his life, and only when his relationships end is he happy. All of this leads up to an ironic climax.

MPAA Rating: Not Rated.

Cast

Dr. Emil Grasler	Keith Carradine
Frederica/Widow	Miranda Richardson
Sabine	Kristin Scott-Thomas
Katharina	Sarah-Jane Fenton
von Schleheim	Max von Sydow

Credits

Executive Producer	Elda Ferri
Producer	Mario Orfini
Director	Roberto Faenza
Director of Photography	Giuseppe Rotunno
Editor	Claudio Cutry
Production Design	Giantito Burchiellaro
Costume Design	Milena Canonero
Casting	Francesco Cinieri
Screenplay	Ennio De Concini
	Hugh Fleetwood
	Roberto Faenza
Music	Ennio Morricone

Film Facts

Running Time	105 minutes
Film	Technicolor
Sound	Stereo

Back In The USSR

(20th Century Fox)

Critics Rating: Not Rated.

Genre: Adventure—Set in present-day Moscow, *Back In The USSR* is a teen adventure film about a young American tourist who turns up at the wrong place at the wrong time. Although the title is misleading, teen audiences will find this energetic romp an enjoyable romantic adventure.

Plot: Frank Whaley (*Career Opportunities*) stars as Archer Sloan, a tourist intent on making his last night in Moscow a memorable one. When he meets Lena (Natalya Negoda), a young local woman who is involved in the black market, he unsuspectingly becomes involved in a theft that sets the scene for a fast-paced, nonstop chase through Moscow.

MPAA Rating: R—For some language and violence; scene of sensuality.

Cast

Archer	Frank Whaley
Lena	Natalya Negoda
Kurilov	Roman Polanski
Dimitri	Andrew Divof
Claudia	Dey Young
Georgi	Ravil Issyanov
Chazov	Brian Blessed
Whittier	Harry Ditson
Stanley	Constantine Gregory
Mikhail	Alexei Yevdokimov

Credits

Executive Producer	Louis A. Stroller
Producers	Lindsay Smith
	Ilmar Taska
Co-Producer	James Steele
Associate Producer	Anatoly Fradis
Director	Deran Sarafian
Assistant Director	Leo Zisman
Director of Photography	Yuri Neyman
Sound	Gary Cunningham
Editor	Ian Crafford
Production Design	Vladimir Philippov
Set Decoration	Nicolai Surovtsev
	Yuri Osipenko
Costume Design	Cynthia Bergstrom
Casting	Jeremy Zimmerman
Screenplay	Lindsay Smith
Story by	Lindsay Smith
	Ilmar Taska
Music	Les Hooper

Film Facts

Running Time	94 minutes
Film	Deluxe Color
Sound	Dolby Stereo
Location	Moscow

Bad Lieutenant

(Aries)

Critics Rating: ★★★

Genre: Drama—Cult filmmaker Abel Ferrara (*Ms. 45*) pushes the graphic limits with this brutally realistic story of redemption.

Plot: Keitel's character, besides being a gambler, junkie, abusive husband and self-destructive all-around bad guy, is a lapsed Catholic and corrupt New York cop whose assignment to investigate the gang rape of a nun leads to his redemption. Keitel, in turn, redeems the film by turning in the performance of a lifetime. Complex, intriguing and mesmerizing, it is nonetheless difficult to view.

MPAA Rating: NC-17—Contains a full-frontal nude shot of Keitel, public masturbation and rape scenes, for starters.

Cast

Lieutenant	Harvey Keitel
Nun	Frankie Thorn
Jesus	Paul Hipp
Bet cop	Victor Argo
Zoe	Zoe Lund
Lite	Anthony Ruggiero
Jersey girl (driver)	Eddie Daniels
Jersey girl (passenger)	Bianca Bakija
Bowtay	Victoria Bastel
Ariane	Robin Burrows
Julio	Fernando Velez

Also with Frank Adonis, Paul Calderone, Joseph Michael Cruz, Bo Dietl, Minnie Gentry, Vincent Laresca, Iraida Polanco and Leonard Thomas.

Credits

Executive Producers	Ronna B. Wallace
	Patrick Wachsberger
Producers	Edward R. Pressman
	Mary Kane
Co-Producer	Randy Sabusawa
Line Producer/Production Manager	Diana Phillips
Director	Abel Ferrara
Assistant Director	Drew Rosenberg
Director of Photography	Ken Kelsch
Sound	Michael Barosky
Editor	Anthony Redman
Production Design	Charles Lagola
Costume Design	David Sawaryn
Casting (New York)	Meredith Jacobsen
Casting (Los Angeles)	Kimba Hills
Screenplay	Zoe Lund
	Abel Ferrara
Music	Joe Delia

Film Facts

Running Time	98 minutes
Film	Foto-Kem Color
Sound	Stereo

Basic Instinct
(TriStar)

Critics Rating: ★★★

Genre: Thriller—Living up to its notoriety, this erotic psycho-thriller is a portrait of sexual obsession. Gay activist groups from around the country, outraged at the film's portrayal of bi-sexuals as maniacal killers, created tremendous publicity for the film's opening by their protests. While politically correct filmgoers may be offended, this is an energetic film that appealed to quite a few viewers earning it over $100 million within a few months of its opening.

Tag Line: "A brutal murder. A brilliant killer. A cop who can't resist the danger."

Plot: Michael Douglas stars as Nick, a San Francisco cop who lives on the edge. While investigating a brutal murder, he becomes sexually involved with the prime suspect. This sets the stage for a chilling game of cat and mouse. Director Paul Verhoeven (*Total Recall*) keeps the pace frantic and the plot twists sharp in this over the top thriller.

MPAA Rating: R—For strong violence and sensuality, drug use and language. Film contains full frontal male and female nudity.

Cast

Nick Curran	Michael Douglas
Catherine Tramell	Sharon Stone
Gus Moran	George Dzundza
Dr. Beth Garner	Jeanne Tripplehorn
Lt. Walker	Denis Arndt
Roxy	Leilani Sarelle
John Correli	Wayne Knight
Hazel Dobkins	Dorothy Malone
Harrigan	Benjamin Mouton
Capt. Talcott	Chelcie Ross
Dr. Lamott	Stephen Tobolowsky
Lt. Nilsen	Daniel von Bargen
Andrews	Bruce A. Young

Credits

Executive Producer	Mario Kassar
Producer	Alan Marshall
Associate Producers	William S. Beasley
	Louis D'Esposito
Director	Paul Verhoeven

Assistant Director ....Louis D'Esposito
2nd Unit Director (S.F.) ....M. James Arnett
Director of Photography ....Jan De Bont
2nd Unit Camera ....Michael Ferris
Sound ....Fred Runner
Editor ....Frank J. Urioste
Production Design ....Terence Marsh
Art Direction (S.F.) ....Mark Billerman
Set Design ....Steve Berger
Set Design (S.F.) ....Barbara Mesney
Set Decoration ....Anne Kuljian
Costume Design ....Ellen Mirojnick
Casting ....Howard Feuer
Written by..Joe Eszterhas
Music..Jerry Goldsmith
Special Makeup Effects ....Rob Bottin

Film Facts
Running Time ....123 minutes
Soundtrack ....Varese Sarabande
Film..Technicolor
Sound ....Dolby Stereo
Location ....San Francisco; Los Angeles;
....Carmel, California

Basket Case 3: The Progeny
(Shapiro Glickenhaus Entertainment)

Critics Rating: Not Rated.
Genre: Horror—In this, the third installment of director Frank Henenlotter's bizarre cult-film series, the horror takes a back seat to slapstick comedy. Although more outrageously funny than its predecessors, there remains enough blood and guts to keep cult followers and unsuspecting horror-genre fans happy.
Plot: The film continues to follow Duane and Belial Bradley, Siamese twin brothers separated in childhood. Duane got the body, while Belial got the short end of the deal, so to speak. Being the loving brother that he is, Duane carries his less ambulatory brother around in a basket. Belial gets lucky and finds a mate, Eve, this time around. They conceive and she gives birth to a litter of mutated offspring. On learning of the event, the sheriff kills Eve and confiscates the mutants. This, of course, is when the real fun and carnage begin.

MPAA Rating: R—For graphic monster violence, sensuality and language.
Cast
Duane....................................Kevin Van Hentenryck
Granny Ruth ....Annie Ross
Uncle Hal ....Dan Biggers
Sheriff..Gil Roper
Opal ....Tina Louise Hilbert
Little Hal................................James O'Doherty
Credits
Executive Producer ....James Glickenhaus
Producer...Edgar Ievins
Director.....................................Frank Henenlotter
Assistant Director ....Eric Mofford
Director of Photography..........................Bob Paone
Sound..Palmer Norris
Editor ....Greg Sheldon
Production Manager ....Bob Baron
Production Design..........................William Barclay
Art Direction ....Caty Maxey
Costume Design ....Carlene Rosado
Casting ....Annette Stilwell
Written by ....Frank Henenlotter
....Robert Martin
Music...Joe Renzetti
Creature and Makeup Effects ....Gabe Bartalos
Film Facts
Running Time ....90 minutes
Film..TVC Color
Sound ....Stereo

Batman Returns
(Warner Bros.)

Critics Rating: ★★★
Genre: Action—While Director Tim Burton's (*Pee Wee's Big Adventure, Beetlejuice, Edward Scissorhands*) 1986 *Batman* was predominantly dark and moody, *Batman Returns* surpassed the original with its richly textured and highly stylized characters and sets. And it came as no surprise that the year's most anticipated film earned nearly $50 million in its 3-day opening. It earned $100 million in only 10 days.
Plot: The plot has an abundance of twists and turns and just as many subplots. A dangerous, decaying Gotham City is being run from high in the sky by

the ruthless Max Shreck (Christopher Walken), operating from behind the scenes. Lurking beneath the city, in the sewers, the Penguin-man (Danny De Vito) has his own plans for running (ruining) the city. As if two villains weren't enough, Michelle Pfeiffer plays a dowdy secretary transformed into the sexy, ferocious Catwoman with a lethal bullwhip. It is, again, left to Bruce Wayne (Michael Keaton), aka superhero Batman, to protect the city from this trio of dangerous but colorful characters.

MPAA Rating: PG-13

Trivia: In his first feature appearance since his highly publicized scandal, Paul Ruebens, aka Pee Wee Herman, makes a cameo as the Penguin's father.

Cast

Batman/Bruce Wayne	Michael Keaton
Catwoman/Selina Kyle	Michelle Pfeiffer
Penguin/Oscar Cobblepot	Danny DeVito
Max Shreck	Christopher Walken
Alfred	Michael Gough
Commissioner Gordon	Pat Hingle
Mayor	Michael Murphy
Chip Shreck	Andrew Bryniarski
Ice Princess	Cristi Conaway
Organ grinder	Vincent Schiavelli
Jen	Jan Hooks
Josh	Steve Witting
Mrs. Cobblepot	Diane Salinger
Mr. Cobblepot	Paul Reubens

Credits

Executive Producers	Jon Peters
	Peter Guber
	Benjamin Melniker
	Michael Uslan
Producers	Denise Di Novi
	Tim Burton
Co-Producer	Larry Franco
Associate Producer	Ian Bryce
Director	Tim Burton
Assistant Director	David McGiffert
2nd Unit Directors	Billy Weber
	Max Kleven
Director of Photography	Stefan Czapsky
2nd Unit Camera	Don Burgess
Additional 2nd Unit Camera	Paul Ryan
Sound	Peter Hliddal
Editor	Chris Lebenzon

Production Design	Bo Welch
Art Direction Supervisor	Tom Duffield
Art Direction	Rick Heinrichs
Set Design	Nick Navarro
	Sally Thornton
Set Decoration	Cheryl Carasik
Costume Design	Bob Ringwood
	Mary Vogt
Casting	Marion Dougherty
Screenplay	Daniel Waters
Story by	Daniel Waters
	Sam Hamm
Based on Characters Created by	Bob Kane
Based on Characters Published by	DC Comics
Creator/Technical Consultant	Bob Kane
Music	Danny Elfman
Key Makeup Artist	Ve Neill
Key Hairstylist	Yolanda Toussieng
Special Visual Effects	Boss Film Studios
Visual Effects Supervisor	Michael Fink
Mechanical Effects Supervisor	Chuck Gaspar
Special Penguin Makeup and Effects Produced by	Stan Winston

Film Facts

Running Time	126 minutes
Soundtrack	Warner Bros. Records
Film	Technicolor
Sound	Dolby Stereo
Location	Los Angeles
Other Working Titles	*Batman 2*

A Beating Heart
(MK2)

Critics Rating: Not Rated.

Genre: Drama

Plot: Dominique Faysse plays Mado, a French actress whose marriage is on the rocks. Looking for excitement and an escape from her troubles, she begins an affair with a nameless stranger (Fortineau), whom she meets one day on the subway. Their impetuous first meeting turns into an ongoing affair that only serves to confuse and complicate her life further. Foreign film fans and art-house audiences will appreciate the intensity of this romantic drama.

MPAA Rating: Not Rated.

Cast

Mado	Dominique Faysse
Yves	Thierry Fortineau
Jean	Jean-Marie Winling

Credits

Director	Francois Dupeyron
Director of Photography	Yves Angelo
Editor	Francoise Collin
Casting	Romain Bremond
Screenplay	Francois Dupeyron
Music	Jean-Pierre Drouet

Film Facts

Running Time	100 minutes
Film	Color
Sound	Stereo

Beautiful Dreamers
(Hemdale)

Critics Rating: ★★★

Genre: Drama—Set in the 1880s, *Beautiful Dreamers* is a dramatic celebration of the life of counter-culture poet Walt Whitman. While the film may only appeal to a select audience, this heartfelt glimpse at a dreamer who made a difference will leave a lasting impression.

Tag Line: "The world changes some people. Some people change the world."

Plot: Rip Torn stars as the free-spirited Whitman. The story centers on Whitman's trip to London, Ontario, and the uproar he caused in the town. Joining Dr. Maurice Bucke (Colm Feore), who was opposed to the psychiatric practices of the time, the two men fight the system that promoted electro-shock treatment and corporal punishment for the insane.

MPAA Rating: PG-13

Trivia: The title of the Bette Davis classic *Now Voyager* was taken from a Whitman poem and is read by the actress during the film.

Cast

Walt Whitman	Rip Torn
Dr. Maurice Bucke	Colm Feore
Jessie Bucke	Wendel Meldrum
Mollie Jessop	Sheila McCarthy
Rev. Haines	Colin Fox
Dr. Lett	David Gardner
Leonard	Tom McCamus
Agatha Haines	Barbara Gordon
Birdie Bucke	Marsha Moreau
Dr. John Burgess	Albert Schultz

Credits

Executive Producer	Stephen J. Roth
Executive Producer for the National Film Board of Canada	Colin Neale
Co-Executive Producer	Sally Bochner
Producers	Michael Maclear
	Martin Walters
Director	John Kent Harrison
Director of Photography	Francois Protat
Editor	Ron Wisman
Production Design	Seamus Flannery
Costume Design	Ruth Secord
Casting	Deidre Brown
Written by	John Kent Harrison
Music	Lawrence Shragge

Film Facts

Running Time	107 minutes
Film	Color
Sound	Dolby Stereo

Bebe's Kids
(Paramount)

Critics Rating: Not Rated.

Genre: Animated—Billed as the first animated film to feature African-American characters in all principal roles. This is an entertaining and charming family film with a few rough edges.

Tag Line: "Animation with an attitude."

Plot: Screenwriter Reginald Hudlin has taken characters from the late African-American stand-up comedian Robin Harris and fashioned it into a full length feature.

Robin Harris, as voiced by Faizon Love, is a divorcee looking for a new relationship. When he meets Jamika, a single mother with a young son, he sets out to impress her. Their first date is a trip to Fun Park. However, this is no tunnel-of-love outing. She brings along not only her son but also the neighbor kids shes caring for. These are Bebes kids. Now the real fun is just about to start. The kids terrorize not only Robin but the entire Fun Park as well.

MPAA Rating: PG-13

Cast

Voices:

Robin Harris	Faizon Love
Jamika	Vanessa Bell Calloway
Vivian	Nell Carter
Leon	Wayne Collins
LaShawn	Jonell Green
Kahil	Marques Houston
Pee Wee	Tone Loc
Dorothea	Myra J.

Credits

Executive Producers	Reginald Hudlin
	Warrington Hudlin
Producers	Willard Carroll
	Thomas L. Wilhite
Co-Producer	David R. Cobb
Associate Producer	Lynne Southerland
Director	Bruce White
Assistant Director	Michael Serrian
Animation Directors	Lennie Graves
	Chris Buck, Frans Vischer
Sound	Robert L. Harman
	Jerry Clemans, Dan Hiland
Editor	Lynne Southerland
Production Design	Fred Cline
Art Direction	Doug Walker
Casting	Eileen Knight
Screenplay	Reginald Hudlin
Based on Characters Created by	Robin Harris
Music	John Barnes

Film Facts

Running Time	73 minutes
Soundtrack	Capitol Records
Film	Deluxe Color
Sound	Dolby Stereo
Location	Los Angeles (principal animation)

Becoming Colette
(Castle Hill)

Critics Rating: ★★

Genre: Drama—A literary-period drama based on the life of renowned French novelist Sidonie Gabrielle Colette. Danny Huston, John Huston's son, directed the film.

Tag Line: "As a writer, she was to become famous. As a lover, she was to become a legend."

Plot: The story is told through an extended flashback beginning with Colette's (May) early days in a French village in the early 1890s. She marries a flamboyant publisher (Brandauer) who takes her to Paris and forces her to write erotic novels under his pseudonym. Theirs is an erotic love affair that, in one scene, includes a *menage a trois* with another woman (Madsen), bordering on soft porn. Unfortunately, this is one of the few lively moments in the film. Eventually she breaks free of the chains of this relationship and in 1916 begins to publish under her own name.

MPAA Rating: R—For strong sexuality.

Cast

Sidonie Gabrielle Colette	Mathilda May
Henri Gauthier-Villars	Klaus Maria Brandauer
Polaire	Virginia Madsen
Chapo	Paul Rhys
Albert	John van Dreelen
Captain	Jean Pierre Aumont
Sido	Lucienne Hamon
Creditor	Georg Tryphon

Credits

Executive Producers	Todd Black
	Kathryn Galan
	Joe Wizan
Producers	Heinz J. Bibo
	Peer J. Oppenheimer
Supervising Producer	Konstantin Thoeren
Director	Danny Huston
Assistant Directors	Eva-Marie Schoenecker
	Simon Moseley
Director of Photography	Wolfgang Treu
Sound	Axel Arft
Editors	Peter Taylor
	Roberto Silvi
Production Design	Jan Schlubach
	Berge Douy
Costume Design	Barbara Baum
Screenplay	Ruth Graham
Screenplay revision	Burt Weinshanker
Music	John Scott
Title Song by	Jackie DeShannon
Choreographer	Andy Lucas

Film Facts

Country of Origin	United States/Germany
Running Time	97 minutes
Film	Technicolor

Sound ....Dolby Stereo
Location ....Berlin, Germany; Bordeaux, France

Bed & Breakfast
(Hemdale)

Critics Rating: Not Rated.
Tag Line: "It's nice to have a man around the house."
Genre: Drama—Director Robert Ellis Miller (*Brenda Starr*), brings to the screen a good, old-fashioned romantic drama with a happy ending.
Plot: Talia Shire plays Claire Wellesley, the owner of a B&B on the coast of Maine. When Roger Moore, playing Adam, washes up on shore one day, her life is turned upside down. Adam, it seems, is a con-artist on the run. Claire is a widow running from the memories of her late husband. When Claire finally lets down her guard and falls for Adam, his past comes knocking at the door. But before long, things are straightened out and the two lovers find happiness.
MPAA Rating: PG-13
Cast

Adam ....Roger Moore
Claire Wellesley ....Talia Shire
Ruth..Colleen Dewhurst
Cassie Wellesley..Nina Siemaszko
Amos McKirdy ....Ford Rainey
Randolph Hyatt ....Stephen Root
Mitch ....Jamie Walters
Hilton ....Cameron Arnett
Julius ....Bryant Bradshaw
Alex Caxton ....Victor Slezak
Bobby ....Jake Webber
Sam the dog ....Samantha Belle
Also with Leila Carlin, Chevi Colton, Frank Dolan, Marceline Hugot, Harriet Rogers, John Savoia and Bronia Stefan Wheeler.

Credits

Producer..Jack Schwartzman
Co-Producer ....Marcus Viscidi
Director..Robert Ellis Miller
1st Assistant Director ....Joel Segal
2nd Assistant Director ....Peter Merwin
Director of Photography..Peter Sova
Sound ....Mike Rowland
Editor..John F. Burnett

Unit Production Manager....................Marcus Viscidi
Production Design ....Suzanne Cavedon
Art Direction....................................Ron Wilson
Set Decoration....................................Tracey Doyle
Costume Design ....Jennifer Von Mayrhauser
Casting..Dianne Crittenden
Written by ....Cindy Myers
Music ....David Shire
Stunt Coordinator ....Cliff Cudney
....Martin Grace

Film Facts

Soundtrack ....Varese Sarabande
Film..Duart Color
Sound..Dolby Stereo
Location..York, Maine

Beethoven
(Universal)

Critics Rating: ★★★
Genre: Comedy—Beethoven is the family dog in this 1960s-style family comedy that offers little in the way of surprises but much in the way of wholesome, good-natured fun and entertainment.
Tag Line: "The head of the family is the one with the tail."
Plot: Charles Grodin plays the goofy father of this all-American family whose life is turned upside down with the arrival of a mischievous Saint Bernard puppy. Beethoven wreaks havoc on the household but manages to provide lots of laughs and win over the entire household in no time.
MPAA Rating: PG
Cast

George Newton ....Charles Grodin
Alice Newton ....Bonnie Hunt
Dr. Varnick ....Dean Jones
Ryce ....Nicholle Tom
Ted ....Christopher Castile
Emily ....Sarah Rose-Karr
Harvey ....Oliver Platt
Vernon ....Stanley Tucci
Brad ....David Duchovny
Brie ....Patricia Heaton
Devonia Peet ....Laurel Cronin

Credits

Executive Producer ....Ivan Reitman
Producers ....Joe Medjuck

....Michael C. Gross
Co-Producer...Gordon Webb
Associate Producer ....Sheldon Kahn
Director ....Brian Levant
Assistant Director ....Jerram A. Swartz
Director of Photography ....Victor J. Kemper
Sound...Charles Wilborn
Editors...Sheldon Kahn
....William D. Gordean
Production Design ....Alex Tavoularis
Art Direction ....Charles Breen
Set Design ....Stan Tropp
....Gary Diamond
Set Decoration..Gary Fettis
Costume Design...................................Gloria Gresham
Casting...Steven Jacobs
Written by ....Edmond Dantes
....Amy Holden Jones
Music...Randy Edelman
Animal Action Coordinator............Karl Lewis Miller

Film Facts

Running Time ....87 minutes
Soundtrack...MCA Records
Film ....Deluxe Color
Sound ....Dolby Stereo
Location ....Los Angeles

The Best Intentions
(Den Goda Viljan)
(Samuel Goldwyn Co.)

Critics Rating: ★★★★
Genre: Drama—Winner of the Palme d'Or at the Cannes Film Festival, Oscar-winning Danish director Bille August brings to the screen a three-hour epic feature based on the early relationship of Ingmar Bergman's parents. (A six-hour version was simultaneously shot for television in Japan and Europe.)
Plot: The film takes place over a ten-year period around the turn of the century. Samuel Froler plays Henrik Bergman, a poor theology student. Pernilla August plays Anna Akerblom, the daughter of a wealthy family. In the beginning these two strong-willed people are united against Anna's parents, who do not approve of their plans to marry. Once married, their relationship is a turbulent one as their

backgrounds, personalities and desires clash. This is tragically a mismatched couple who spend their lives trying to make their relationship work.
MPAA Rating: Not Rated.
Trivia: Director Bille August (Oscar winner for *Pelle The Conqueror*) and actress Pernilla August (named best actress in Cannes for her role in the film) met and married during the filming.
Cast

Henrik Bergman....................................Samuel Froler
Anna Bergman.....................................Pernilla August
Johan Akerblom ....Max von Sydow
Karin Akerblom....................................Ghita Norby
Nordenson ....Lennart Hjulstrom
Alma Bergman...Mona Malm
Frida Strandberg.....................................Lena Endre
Fredrik Bergman ....Keve Hjelm
Ernst Akerblom......................................Bjorn Kjellman
Carl Akerblom.......................................Borje Ahlstedt
Rev. Gransjo ....Hans Alfredson
Queen Viktoria......................................Anita Bjorn

Credits

Executive Producer ....Ingrid Dahlberg
Producer...Lars Bjalkeskog
Director...Bille August
Assistant Director ....Stefan Baron
Director of Photography ....Jorgen Persson
Sound ....Lennart Gentzel
....Johnny Ljungberg
Editor ....Janus Billeskov Jansen
Production Design ....Anna Asp
Costume Design ....Ann-Mari Anttila
Screenplay ....Ingmar Bergman
Music...Stefan Nilsson
Music Conducted by.....................Esa-Pekka Salonen

Film Facts

Country of Origin.......................................Sweden
Running Time ....180 minutes
Film ....Color
Sound ....Stereo
Location...........................Sweden; Italy; Switzerland

Big Girls Don't Cry, They Get Even
(New Line Cinema)

Critics Rating: Not Rated.

39

Genre: Adventure—Directed by Joan Micklin Silver (*Hester Street, Crossing Delancey*), *Big Girls* is a comic adventure about a 13-year-old girl who leaves home and hits the road.
Tag Line: "Watch out. She's seen *Thelma & Louise*."
Plot: Hillary Wolf plays Laura, a rich kid from a dysfunctional family. Feeling ignored, she runs away from home. On the road she has a few misadventures but before long she has brought her family together through their effort to track her down.
MPAA Rating: PG
Cast

David.................................Griffin Dunne
Laura.................................Hillary Wolf
Josh.................................Dan Futterman
Barbara.................................Patricia Kalember
Stephanie.................................Adrienne Shelly
Keith.................................David Straithairn
Melinda.................................Margaret Whitton
Corrine.................................Jenny Lewis
Sam.................................Ben Savage
Kurt.................................Trenton Teigen

Credits

Executive Producers.................................Melissa Goddard
.................................Peter Morgan
Producers.................................Laurie Perlman
.................................Gerald T. Olson
Director.................................Joan Micklin Silver
Assistant Director.................................David Sardi
Director of Photography.................................Theo Van de Sande
Sound.................................Susumu Tokumow
Editor.................................Janice Hampton
Production Design.................................Victoria Paul
Art Direction.................................Brad Ricker
Set Decoration.................................Joyce Anne Gilstrap
Set Design.................................Maya Shimoguchi
Costume Design.................................Jane Ruhm
Casting.................................Linda Lowy
Screenplay.................................Frank Mugavero
Based on a Story by.................................Frank Mugavero
.................................Mark Goddard, Melissa Goddard
Music.................................Patrick Williams

Film Facts

Running Time.................................96 minutes
Film.................................CFI Color
Sound.................................Dolby Stereo

Black To The Promised Land
(Blues Prods.)

Critics Rating: Not Rated.
Genre: Documentary—First-time documentary director Madeleine Ali brings to the screen a humorous and touching film about an unlikely subject.
Plot: Documenting a 1989 trip by taken 11 African-American students from Brooklyn to a kibbutz in Israel, Ali manages to capture the cultural differences with humor and understanding. When the teenage students arrive on the kibbutz, the preconceived stereotypes of both visitors and hosts become evident. Before long, however, their prejudices are replaced by the reality of coming to know one another. When the students return to Brooklyn, the reality of their real lives—faced with few opportunities and having to struggle just to survive—rushes in to greet them.
MPAA Rating: Not Rated.
Credits

Producers.................................Madeleine Ali
.................................Renen Schorr, Schlomo Rogalin
Director.................................Madeleine Ali
Director of Photography.................................Manu Kadosh
Sound.................................Yossi Vanon
.................................Amir Boverman, Danny Natovich
Editor.................................Victor Nord
Music.................................Branford Marsalis
Graphic Design.................................Shai Zauderer

Film Facts

Country of Origin.................................Israel
Running Time.................................75 minutes
Film.................................Color (16 mm)
Sound.................................Stereo
Location.................................Brooklyn, New York; Israel

Blame It On The Bellboy
(Buena Vista)

Critics Rating: ★★★
Genre: Comedy—*Blame It On The Bellboy* is a good, old-fashioned, zany comedy about a triple case of mistaken identity.

Plot: Taking place in Venice, Bronson Pinchot plays a mixed-up bellboy who accidentally mixes up the itineraries of three guests with similar names. This sets the scene for the slapstick comedy that follows, when each of the three hotel guests finds himself in a very confusing situation, to say the least. This short, light, screwball comedy will appeal to an audience looking for light entertainment and an even lighter plot.

MPAA Rating: PG-13

Cast

Melvyn Orton	Dudley Moore
Mike Lawton/Charlton Black	Bryan Brown
Caroline Wright	Patsy Kensit
Bettino Scarpa	Andreas Katsoulis
Maurice Horton	Richard Griffiths
Bellboy	Bronson Pinchot
Mr. Marshall	Lindsay Anderson
Rosemary Horton	Alison Steadman
Patricia Fulford	Penelope Wilton

Credits

Producers	Steve Abbott
	Jennie Howarth
Director	Mark Herman
Director of Photography	Andrew Dunn
Sound	Peter Glossop
Editor	Michael Ellis
Production Design	Gemma Jackson
Art Direction	Peter Russell
Costume Design	Lindy Hemming
Casting	Irene Lamb
Written by	Mark Herman
Music	Trevor Jones
Solo Guitar	John Williams

Film Facts

Country of Origin	U. S./Great Britain
Running Time	77 minutes
Film	Technicolor
Sound	Dolby Stereo
Location	Venice, Italy; Shepperton, England

Blast 'Em

(Cinema Esperanca International)

Critics Rating: ★★★★
Genre: Documentary—Documentary filmmaker Joseph Blasioli follows, or tries to keep up with, celebrity photographer Victore Malafronte and other paparazzi as they aggressively compete for the best pictures.

Plot: To obsessed photographer Malafronte, celebrities are like prey to be ambushed, staked out, stalked and continually harassed. He says at one point in the film, "I don't have any sympathy for a guy who makes 20 or 30 million." This attitude seems to reflect the general attitude of our society and our obsession with our stars. While the film is shot primarily from the photographer's point of view, reactions from nearly every known celebrity from Madonna to Jack Nicholson to John F. Kennedy, Jr., are captured.

MPAA Rating: Not Rated.

Featuring even more stars than Robert Altman's *The Player*, this entertaining and revealing look at a very unflattering American obsession will appeal to a mainstream audience.

Cast

With John Barrett, Randy Bauer, Nick Elgar, Albert Ferreira, Ron Galella, Sally Kirkland, Virginia Lohle, Rick Maiman, Victor Malafronte, David McGough, Queerdonna, Felice Quinto, Steve Sands, Gerardo Somosa, Eugene Upshaw and David Whitehead.

Credits

Executive Producers	Anders Palm
	Lars Ake Johansson
	Johan Sanden
Producer	Anders Palm
Director	Joseph Blasioli
Co-Director	Egidio Coccimiglio
Director of Photography	Robert Garrard
Sound	Antonio Arroyo
	Marty Casparian
Editors	Joseph Blasioli
	Egidio Coccimiglio
Written by	Joseph Blasioli
Music	Yuri Gorbachow

Film Facts

Country of Origin	Canada
Running Time	100 minutes
Film	Color
Sound	Stereo

Bloodfist III: Forced To Fight
(Concorde)

Critics Rating: Not Rated.
Genre: Action—Executive produced by Roger Corman, *Bloodfist* is a kick-boxing action film that takes place in the confines of a prison.
Plot: Don (The Dragon) Wilson stars as Jimmy Boland, a man wrongly convicted and incarcerated in the state penitentiary. The battles inside the prison are between rival black and white gangs. As an Asian, Jimmy is put in the middle and like most heroes, is forced to fight. Since he is the hero, he quickly shows both sides who's boss.
MPAA Rating: R

Cast

Jimmy Boland	Don (The Dragon) Wilson
Samuel Stark	Richard Roundtree
Pisani	Brad Blaisdell
Taylor	Charles Boswell
Diddler	John Cardone
Wheelhead	Rick Dean
Blue	Gregory McKinney
Bill Goddard	Richard Paul
Leadbottom	Stan Longinidus
Champ	Peter (Sugarfoot) Cunningham

Also with Peter DiBenedetto and Laura Stockman.

Credits

Producer	Roger Corman
Co-Producer	Mike Elliott
Associate Producers	Catherine Cyran
	Nancy Gechtman
Director	Francis Sassone
Assistant Director	Juan Mas
Director of Photography	Rick Bota
Sound	Bill Robbins
Editor	Eric L. Beason
Production Manager	Jonathan Winfrey
Production Design	James Shumaker
Casting	Steven Rabiner
Screenplay	Allison Burnett
	Charles Mattera
Music	Nigel Holten
Stunt Coordinator	Patrick Statham
Martial Arts Choreography	Paul Maslak
	Don (The Dragon) Wilson
	Eric Lee

Film Facts

Running Time	88 minutes
Film	Foto-Kem Color
Sound	Ultra-Stereo

Bob Roberts
(Paramount)

Critics Rating: ★★★★
Genre: Comedy—Thirty-three-year-old writer, director and actor Tim Robbins' witty and timely $4 million political satire won praise from the critics.
Tag Line: "Vote First. Ask questions later."
Plot: Presented as a mock documentary, the cameras follow Robbins, who plays Bob Roberts, a right-wing, folk-singing yuppie-turned-senatorial-candidate. Roberts is a charismatic character—promoting family values and a best-selling album—who has been created by the media. Behind the scenes, Roberts is involved in drug deals, mud-slinging and dirty tricks. Exposing the corruption of politics, the film satirizes not only politicians but the media as well.
MPAA Rating: R—For profanity.
Trivia: The film's folk songs were cowritten by Robbins and his father Gil, a popular 1960s folksinger with the *Highwaymen* ("Michael Row The Boat Ashore").

Cast

Bob Roberts	Tim Robbins
Bugs Raplin	Giancarlo Esposito
Chet MacGregor	Ray Wise
Terry Manchestere	Brian Murray
Sen. Brickley Paiste	Gore Vidal
Delores Perrigrew	Rebecca Jenkins
Franklin Dockett	Harry J. Lennix
Clark Anderson	John Ottavino
Bart Macklerooney	Robert Stanton
Clarissa Flan	Kelly Willis
Tawna Titan	Susan Sarandon
Chuck Marlin	James Spader
Lukas Hart III	Alan Rickman
Chip Daley	Fred Ward
"Cutting Edge" host	John Cusack
Rose Pondell	Helen Hunt

Dan Riley ....Peter Gallagher
The mayor's wife ....Anita Gillette
The mayor's son ....Jack Black
Also with Bob Balaban, Pamela Reed, Fisher Stevens and David Strathairn.

Credits
Executive Producers...........................Ronna Wallace
....Paul Webster
....Tim Bevan
Producer..Forrest Murray
Associate Producers ....James Bigwood
....Allan Nichols
Director ....Tim Robbins
Director of Photography ....Jean Lepine
Sound ....Stephen Halbert
Editor...Lisa Churgin
Production Design...........................Richard Hoover
Art Direction................................Gary Kosko
Set Decoration.................................Brian Kasch
Costume Design..............................Bridget Kelly
Casting ....Douglas Aibel
Casting (Los Angeles) ....April Webster
Written by ....Tim Robbins
Music ....David Robbins
Songs by ....David Robbins
....Tim Robbins

Film Facts
Running Time ....105 minutes
Film...Technicolor
Sound..Dolby Stereo
Location ....Pittsburgh, Pennsylvania

The Bodyguard
(Warner Bros.)

Critics Rating: ★★
Genre: Thriller—Pop star Whitney Houston makes her feature-film debut in an old-fashioned, modern-day love story.
Tag Line: "Never let her out of your sight. Never let your guard down. Never fall in love."
Plot: Kevin Costner stars as Frank Farmer, a former Secret Service bodyguard hired to protect pop star Rachel Marron (Houston) who is being stalked. A fish out of water in the glitzy, glamorous music world, Frank assumes an uptight demeanor

that is at odds with Rachel's carefree lifestyle. Eventually, however, the two opposites attract, and the real sparks fly. Acting and musical performances are all first-rate.
MPAA Rating: R—For language.
Trivia: Whitney Houston's song "I Will Always Love You" was the No. 1 hit on the *Billboard* charts November 25th when the film opened. It became the first song in over 20 years to jump from No. 40 to No. 1.

Cast
Frank Farmer ....Kevin Costner
Rachel Marron.....................................Whitney Houston
Sy Spector ....Gary Kemp
Bill Devaney ....Bill Cobbs
Herb Farmer...Ralph Waite
Greg Portman ....Tomas Arana
Nikki Marron ....Michele Lamar Richards
Tony..Mike Starr
Henry ....Christopher Birt
Fletcher Marron....................................DeVaughn Nixon

Credits
Producers..Lawrence Kasdan
....Jim Wilson
....Kevin Costner
Director ....Mick Jackson
Assistant Director................................Albert Shapiro
Director of Photography ....Andrew Dunn
Sound...........................Richard Bryce Goodman
Editors ....Richard A. Harris
....Donn Cambern
Production Design ....Jeffrey Beecroft
Art Direction ....William Ladd Skinner
Set Decoration ....Lisa Dean
Set Design ....Antoinette J. Gordon
....Roy Barnes
Costume Design..............................Susan Nininger
Casting ....Elisabeth Leustig
Screenplay..Lawrence Kasdan
Music ....Alan Silvestri
Stunt Coordinator ....Norman L. Howell

Film Facts
Running Time ....129 minutes
Soundtrack ....Arista Records
Film...Technicolor
Sound..Dolby Stereo
Location ....Florida; Los Angeles;
....Northern California

Boomerang
(Paramount)

Critics Rating: ★★

Genre: Comedy—In one of a number of twists, this romantic comedy reverses the sexual roles, so that the womanizing man, for a change, is the one being strung along by a man-using woman.

Plot: Eddie Murphy plays Marcus Graham, a hotshot marketing executive of a cosmetics firm. His real profession, however, is looking for the perfect woman—perfect from head to beautiful toes. When the company is taken over, he gets more than a new boss. Robin Givens plays Jacqueline, his beautiful new boss—and his ultimate challenge. When Jacqueline turns the tables on this wolf, he becomes a lost and insecure pup.

MPAA Rating: R—For language and sexuality.

Trivia: Trekkies take note—while watching a *Star Trek* rerun on television with Angela (Halle Berry), Marcus describes himself as a Trekkie. He also describes Captain Kirk as the coolest white man alive.

Cast

Marcus	Eddie Murphy
Jacqueline	Robin Givens
Angela	Halle Berry
Gerard Jackson	David Alan Grier
Tyler	Martin Lawrence
Strange	Grace Jones
Nelson	Geoffrey Holder
Lady Eloise	Eartha Kitt
Yvonne	Tisha Campbell
Box office clerk	Irv Dotten
Lady Eloise's butler	Jonathan P. Hicks
Chemist	Leonard Jackson
Waitress	Rhonda Jensen
Salesman	Tom Mardirosian
Mrs. Jackson	Bebe Drake-Massey
Christie	Lela Rochon
Bony T	Chris Rock
Todd	John Canada Terrell
Editor	Melvin Van Peebles
Woman from Holland	Louise Vyent
Noreen	Alyce Webb
Mr. Jackson	John Witherspoon

Also with Raye Dowell, Reginald Hudlin, Warrington Hudlin, Angela Logan, Chuck Pfeifer and Frank Rivers.

Credits

Executive Producer	Mark Lipsky
Producers	Brian Grazer
	Warrington Hudlin
Co-Producers	Barry W. Blaustein
	David Sheffield
Associate Producer	Ray Murphy, Jr.
Director	Reginald Hudlin
Assistant Director	Joseph Ray
Director of Photography	Woody Omens
Additional Camera	Peter Deming
	Richard Quinlan
Sound	Russell Williams II
Editors	Earl Watson
	John Carter, Michael Jablow
Production Design	Jane Musky
Art Direction	William Barclay
Set Decoration	Alan Hicks
Costume Design	Francine Jamison-Tanchuck
Casting	Aleta Chappelle
Screenplay	Barry W. Blaustein
	David Sheffield
Story by	Eddie Murphy
Music	Marcus Miller
Stunt Coordinator	Jery Hewitt

Film Facts

Running Time	116 minutes
Soundtrack	LaFace Records
Film	Deluxe Color
Sound	Dolby Stereo
Location	New York

Brain Donors
(Paramount)

Critics Rating: Not Rated.

Genre: Comedy—Produced by the Zucker brothers (*Airplane, The Naked Gun*), *Brain Donors* is a sure-fire, zany, slapstick comedy for the entire family.

Tag Line: "In the tradition of Abbott and Costello, The Three Stooges, and the Reagan Administration."

Plot: John Turturro stars as Roland T. Flakfizer, a sleazy lawyer on the take. Taking from the rich and giving to himself, Flakfizer manages to get himself put in charge of running a ballet company for the wealthy widow, Mrs. Oglethorpe. His rival Lazlo (Savident), the family lawyer, is also after the position. The sight gags and slapstick humor are nonstop as the two men vie for position—each trying to ingratiate himself with the widow Oglethorpe. As Turturro says in one scene, "He's after your money and social standing, but I was here first."

MPAA Rating: PG

Cast

Roland T. Flakfizer	John Turturro
Jacques	Bob Nelson
Rocco Melonchek	Mel Smith
Volare	George De La Pena
Lisa	Juli Donald
Lillian Oglethorpe	Nancy Marchand
Lazlo	John Savident
Alan	Spike Alexander
Blonde	Teri Copley

Credits

Executive Producers	David Zucker
	Pat Proft
Producers	Gil Netter
	James D. Brubaker
Director	Dennis Dugan
Assistant Director	James S. Simons
Director of Photography	David M. Walsh
Sound	William B. Kaplan
Editor	Malcolm Campbell
Production Design	William J. Cassidy
Set Design	Gary A. Lee, Robert Maddy
	James J. Murakami, William J. Cassidy
Set Decoration	Jeannette M. Gunn
Costume Design	Robert Turturice
Casting	John Lyons
	Donna Isaacson
Screenplay	Pat Proft
Music	Ira Newborn
Choreographer	John Carrafa

Film Facts

Running Time	79 minutes
Film	Technicolor
Sound	Dolby Stereo
Location	Los Angeles
Other Working Titles	*Lame Ducks*

Bram Stoker's Dracula
(Columbia)

Critics Rating: ★★★

Genre: Horror—While faithfully following the 1897 novel, Coppolas epic version of the popular tale is a visual feast without a main course. Lacking is the emotion, the thrills, the horror, and a realistic setting. This is an intellectual exercise that will delight only the art-house audience. *The Hollywood Reporter* described it best, "Even Dracula...seems less a figure of destruction than a drag queen in geisha gear." Ultimately, we never care for anyone in this so-called love story.

Tag Line: "Love Never Dies."

Plot: Gary Oldman (*JFK*) plays the Romanian Count Dracula, a vampire who travels to London in the late 1800s in search of the love he lost 400 years earlier. Ryder plays Mina, the incarnation of Dracula's lost love. To win Mina, Dracula imprisons her fiancé, Jonathan (Reeves), leaving the young woman vulnerable to his supernatural powers. Once she is under his spell it is up to Jonathan and doctor-vampirologist Van Helsing (Hopkins) to capture and kill the evil monster. Ryder and Hopkins are the bright spots in this otherwise dark and deadly dull tale.

MPAA Rating: R—For horror violence and sexuality.

Trivia: *Dracula* sucked the blood out of the box-office becoming the biggest nonsummer movie opening in history. It also became Columbia's largest opening ever, earning over $30 million in its Friday the 13th opening weekend in November.

Cast

Dracula	Gary Oldman
Mina Murray/Elisabeta	Wynona Ryder
Prof. Abraham Van Helsing	Anthony Hopkins
Jonathan Harker	Keanu Reeves
Dr. Jack Seward	Richard E. Grant
Lord Arthur Holmwood	Cary Elwes
Quincey P. Morris	Bill Campbell
Lucy Westenra	Sadie Frost
R. M. Renfield	Tom Waits

Also with Monica Bellucci, Michaela Bercu, Florina Kendrick and Jay Robinson.

Credits

Executive Producers	Michael Apted
	Robert O'Connor
Producers	Francis Ford Coppola
	Fred Fuchs, Charles Mulvehill

Co-Producers....................................James V. Hart
....John Veitch
Associate Producer.............................Susie Landau
Director.................................Francis Ford Coppola
Assistant Director...............................Peter Giuliano
2nd Unit Director.............................Roman Coppola
Director of Photography.................Michael Ballhaus
2nd Unit Camera.............................Steve Yaconelli
Sound...Rober Janiger
Sound Design......................................Leslie Shatz
Editors..Nicholas C. Smith
....Glen Scantlebury
....Anne Goursaud
Production Design...........................Thomas Sanders
Art Direction....................................Andrew Precht
Set Decoration.....................................Garrett Lewis
Costume Design.................................Eiko Ishioka
Casting..Victoria Thomas
Screenplay..James V. Hart
Music..Wojciech Kilar
Visual Effects......................................Roman Coppola
Special Visual Effects............Fantasy II Film Effects
Makeup/Hair Design.......................Michele Burke
Special Makeup Effects.......................Greg Cannom

Film Facts

Running Time.......................................130 minutes
Soundtrack.....................................Columbia Records
Film..Technicolor
Sound...Dolby Stereo
Location...Los Angeles
Other Working Titles.......*Dracula: The Untold Story*

The Branches
Of The Tree

(Shakha Proshakha)

(Erato Films)

Critics Rating: Not Rated.

Genre: Drama—Indian director Satyajit Ray, who received an honorary Oscar in 1992, brings to the screen a heartfelt drama about the strained relationships between a family brought together under difficult circumstances.

Plot: In this simple story, Ananda Majunda is celebrating his 70th birthday. (This also happens to be the director's age at the time. He died shortly after the film was released.) Suffering a heart attack during the celebration, he survives, but is left in need of his family's assistance. As his sons come together to take care of their father, their many differences and past hostilities come to the surface. As their father heals, their lives begin to unravel in this intense look at the dynamics of one man's family.

MPAA Rating: Not Rated.

Cast

Ananda Majunda.................................Ajit Banerjee
Probodh..Maradan Banerjee
Uma..Lily Charraborty
Proshanto.....................................Soumitra Chatterjee
Probir..Deepankar De
Protap...Ranjit Mallik
Tapati..Mamata Shankar

Credits

Producers......................................Toscan du Plantier
....Gerard Depardieu
Director..Satyajit Ray
Director of Photography......................Barun Raha
Sound..Pierre Lenoir
....Denis Carquin
Editor...Dulal Dutt
Art Direction...Ashok Bose
Written by...Satyajit Ray
Music..Satyajit Ray

Film Facts

Country of Origin...............................India/France
Running Time.......................................120 minutes
Film..Color
Sound...Stereo
Location....................................Calcutta, India

Breaking The Rules

(Miramax)

Critics Rating: ★

Genre: Comedy—Roger Ebert of the Chicago *Sun Times* claimed, *"Breaking The Rules* is about a guy who finds he has a month to live and decides to spend it in the worst buddy movie ever made."

Tag Line: "Three best friends were searching for the meaning of life...Instead they found Mary."

Plot: Jason Bateman plays a young man dying of leukemia. As a last wish, he gets together with his two boyhood pals, and they set out on a cross-country trip to California, where he hopes to appear on *Jeopardy*. Before they reach their destination, however, they stop in a Nevada casino, where they meet a waitress, played by Annie Potts. Before long, she has changed all of their lives forever.

MPAA Rating: PG-13

Cast

Phil Stepler	Jason Bateman
Gene Michaels	C. Thomas Howell
Rob Konigsberg	Jonathan Silverman
Mary Klinglitch	Annie Potts
Rob's date	Krista Kesreau
Phil's dad	Kent Bateman

Credits

Executive Producers	Larry Thompson
	Deborah J. Simon
Producers	Jonathan D. Krane
	Kent Bateman
Line Producer	Elliot Rosenblatt
Director	Neal Israel
Assistant Director	Matthew Carlisle
2nd Unit Director	Chris Howell
Director of Photography	James Hayman
2nd Unit Camera	Bob New
Sound	Ed White
Editor	Tom Walls
Production Design	Donald Light-Harris
Costume Design	Giovanna Ottobe-Melton
Casting	Eliza Simons
	Pam Rack
Screenplay	Paul Shapiro
Music	David Kitay
Stunt Coordinator	Chris Howell

Film Facts

Running Time	100 minutes
Film	Technicolor
Sound	Dolby Stereo
Location	Sacramento, California
Other Titles	*Sketches*

Brenda Starr

(Triumph)

Critics Rating: ★

Genre: Comedy—Director Robert Ellis Miller has taken Dale Messick's comic-strip character Brenda Starr and turned her into a live-action comedy.

Plot: Brooke Shields stars as the fictional character Brenda come to life. As a reporter she is hot on the trail of the story's villain. Along the way she gets help from an admirer named Basil St. John (Timothy Dalton). Adding to the farce, the cartoon's animator also becomes involved in the chase. And, of course, they are both romantically interested in the comely Ms. Starr. In the end there are no surprises in store, just old fashioned, 1940s-style fun.

MPAA Rating: PG

Cast

Brenda Starr	Brooke Shields
Basil St. John	Timothy Dalton
Libby (Lips) Lipscomb	Diana Scarwid
Vladimir	Jeffrey Tambor
Luba	June Gable
Newspaper editor	Charles Durning
Mike Randall	Tony Peck
Police chief	Eddie Albert
Prof. Von Kreutzer	Henry Gibson
President Truman	Ed Nelson

Also with Tom Aldredge, Matthew Cowles, Avner Eisenberg, June Gable, Mary Lou Rosato, Nestor Serrano, John Short, Jeffrey Tambor and Kathleen Wilhoite.

Credits

Executive Producers	John D. Backe
	Alana H. Lambros
Producer	Myron A. Hyman
Associate Producers	Peggy Lamont
	Michael Tadross
Director	Robert Ellis Miller
Director of Photography	Freddie Francis
Sound	Sharon Smith Holley
Editor	Mark Melnick
Production Design	John J. Lloyd
Costume Design for Brooke Shields	Bob Mackie
Costume Design	Peggy Farrell
Casting	Pat McCorakle
Screenplay	Noreen Stone
	James David Buchanan, Jenny Wolkind
Story by	Noreen Stone
	James David Buchanan
Based on the Comic Strip by	Dale Messick
Music	Johnny Mandel
Executive Consultant	Teri Shields
Animation	Japhet Asher

Film Facts

Running Time	94 minutes
Film	Eastmancolor
Sound	Stereo

A Brief History Of Time
(Triton)

Critics Rating: ★★★★

Genre: Documentary—Based on the book by Stephen Hawking, this is an intelligent and absorbing film by Errol Morris (*Gates Of Heaven*, *The Thin Blue Line*). The book spent more than 100 weeks on the best seller list.

Plot: Focusing on the life and work of theoretical physicist Hawking, from the Big Bang theory of creation, to black holes to the destiny of the universe the filmmaker has further illuminated a fascinating subject. Making the topic even more accessible are comments by colleagues and family members.

MPAA Rating: Not Rated.

Cast

With Stephen Hawking, Isobel Hawking, Janet Humphrey, Mary Hawking, Basil King, Derek Powney, Norman Dix, Robert Berman, Gordon Berry, Roger Penrose, Dennis Sciama and John Wheeler.

Credits

Executive Producer	Gordon Freedman
Producer	David Hickman
Director	Errol Morris
Director of Photography	John Bailey
Additional Camera	Stefan Czapsky
Sound	Randy Thom
Editor	Brad Fuller
Production Design	Ted Bafaloukos
Art Direction	David Lee
Based on the book by	Stephen Hawking
Music Producer	Kurt Munkacsi
Original Music	Philip Glass
Motion control/Visual effects photography	Balsmeyer & Everett, Inc.
Computer animation	Rhythm & Hues

Film Facts

Country of Origin	Great Britain/United States
Running Time	84 minutes
Film	DuArt Color/Technicolor
Sound	Dolby Stereo

Brother's Keeper
(American Playhouse Theatrical Films/ Creative Thinking)

Critics Rating: ★★★★★

Genre: Documentary—Filmmakers Joe Berlinger and Bruce Sinofsky focus their cameras on the murder trial of Delbert Ward, who allegedly killed his older brother in 1990.

Plot: Ward was one of four brothers who had spent their entire lives living and working together as farmers in upstate New York. Following the death of one of the brothers by suffocation, the filmmakers captured the trial as it unfolded and the events that followed. The result is a moving portrait of a community brought to-gether by tragedy.

MPAA Rating: Not Rated.

Credits

Executive Producers	Lindsay Law
	Joe Berlinger
Producers/Directors/Editors	Joe Berlinger
	Bruce Sinofsky
Director of Photography	Douglas Cooper
Post Production Supervisor	Bruce Sinofsky
Music	Jay Unger
	Molly Mason

Film Facts

Running Time	80 minutes
Film	Color
Sound	Stereo

Buffy The Vampire Slayer
(20th Century Fox)

Critics Rating: ★★

Genre: Comedy—This is not your typical gory vampire movie. In this horror-comedy the director has turned the tables. The innocent blonde beauty is the aggressive attacker, instead of the usual submissive target. To confuse matters even more, this one's played for laughs. Unfortunately, the humor seldom rises to the campy occasion.

Tag Line: "Pert. Wholesome. Way Lethal."

Plot: Kristy Swanson (*Hot Shots!*, *Mannequin 2: On The Move*) plays Buffy, a ditzy cheerleader living in a Los Angeles suburb. However, she doesn't realize that she is the chosen one. That is, it's her destiny to slay vampires. It's up to her mentor, played by Donald Sutherland, to convince her and help her train. In the meantime, vampires are turning local teenagers and high school basketball players into the undead. A campy and scruffy-looking Paul Reubens, aka Pee Wee Herman, leads the vampires. After Buffy saves the life of a local high school drop out played by Luke Perry (TVs *Beverly Hills 90210*), she finds romance. However, romance has to wait until she slays a gang of teenage vampires who show up to crash the senior dance.

MPAA Rating: PG-13

Cast

Buffy	Kristy Swanson
Merrick	Donald Sutherland
Amilyn	Paul Reubens
Lothos	Rutger Hauer
Pike	Luke Perry
Jennifer	Michelle Abrams
Benny	David Arquette
Jeffrey	Randall Batinkoff
Buffy's mom	Candy Clark
Kimberly	Hilary Swank
Nicole	Paris Vaughan

Also with Mark DeCarlo, Sasha Jenson, Andrew Lowery, Stephen Root and Natasha Gregson Wagner.

Credits

Executive Producers	Sandy Gallin
	Carol Baum, Fran Rubel Kuzui
Producers	Kaz Kuzui, Howard Rosenman
Co-Producer	Dennis Stuart Murphy
Associate Producer	Alex Butler
Director	Fran Rubel Kuzui
Assistant Director	Josh King
2nd Unit Director	Terry J. Leonard
Director of Photography	James Hayman
Additional Camera	Tim Suhrstedt
Sound	Steve Aaron
Editors	Camilla Toniolo, Jill Savitt
Production Design	Lawrence Miller
Art Direction	James Barrows, Randy Moore
Set Decoration	Claire Bowin
Costume Design	Marie France
Casting	Johanna Ray
Written by	Joss Whedon
Executive Music Producer	Ralph Sall
Music Score by	Carter Burwell
Stunt Coordinator	Terry J. Leonard

Film Facts

Running Time	86 minutes
Soundtrack	Columbia Records
Film	Deluxe Color
Sound	Dolby Stereo
Location	Los Angeles

Cabeza De Vaca
(Concorde)

Critics Rating: Not Rated.
Genre: Drama—*Cabeza de Vaca,* which means "head of a cow," is a Spanish epic based on the true story of explorer Alvar Nunez de Vaca.
Plot: Juan Diego plays the role of the Spanish explorer who was shipwrecked in 1528 off the coast of Florida. Surviving the wreck, de Vaca and his expedition spend the next eight years journeying across North America.
MPAA Rating: R—For violence and language.
Cast

Alvar Nunez Cabeza de Vaca	Juan Diego
Dorantes	Daniel Gimenez Cacho
Cascabel/Araino	Roberto Sosa
Castillo	Carlos Castanon
Estebanico	Gerardo Villarreal
Lozoya	Roberto Cobo
Malacosa	Jose Flores
Hechicero	Eli Machuca (Chupadera)
Anciana Avavar	Josefina Echanove
Esquivel	Oscar Yoldi

Credits

Executive Producer	Bertha Navarro
Producers	Rafael Cruz
	Jorge Sanchez, Julio Solorzano Foppa
Director	Nicolas Echevarria
Assistant Director	Sabastian Silva
Director of Photography	Guillermo Navarro
Editor	Rafael Castanedo
Production Manager	Rosina Rivas
Production Design	Jose Luis Aguilar
Costume Design	Totita Figueroa
Written by	Guillermo Sheridan
	Nicolas Echevarria
Based on the Book *Shipwrecks* by	
	Alvar Nunez Cabeza de Vaca
Original Score	Mario Lavista
Special Effects	Laurencio (Chovi) Cordero
Special Effects Makeup	Guillermo del Toro
Choreography	Lidya Romero

Film Facts

Country of Origin	Spain/Mexico
Language	Spanish (subtitled)
Running Time	111 minutes
Film	Eastmancolor
Sound	Stereo

Candyman
(TriStar)

Critics Rating: ★★★
Genre: Horror—Based on the Clive Barker short story "The Forbidden."
Tag Line: "From the chilling imagination of Clive Barker."
Plot: Virginia Madsen (*Highlander II: The Quickening*) stars as Helen Lyle, a doctoral candidate at the University of Illinois. When a murder occurs in the Chicago projects it is attributed to the Candyman (Tony Todd, *Star Trek: The Next Generation*), a mythological hook-handed killer. Using the incident as a topic for her doctoral thesis Helen unintentionally opens the door to an unfathomable horror. The Candyman is looking to reclaim a romance denied him a century earlier and he has his eye set on Helen.
MPAA Rating: R—For violence and gore.
Trivia: In the scene where the Candyman's mouth is full of bees, a special mouth device was constructed that would hold up to 200 of the insects. Hired for his expertise on bees was Dr. Norman Gary, who also directed the bees in *My Girl* and *Fried Green Tomatoes.*
Cast

Helen Lyle	Virginia Madsen
Candyman	Tony Todd
Trevor Lyle	Xander Berkeley
Bernadette Walsh	Kasi Lemmons
Anne-Marie McCoy	Vanessa Williams

Jake..DeJuan Guy
Dr. Burke................................Stanley DeSantis
Det. Frank Delanto ....Gilbert Lewis
Clara..Marianna Eliott
Billy...Ted Raimi
Monica.......................................Ria Pavia
Diane......................................Lisa Ann Poggi
Danny....................................Adam Philipson
Harold...................................Eric Edwards
Stacey....................................Carolyn Lowery
Henrietta Mosely ....Barbara Alston
Kitty Culver...........................Sarina Grant
Baby Anthony..........Latesha Martin, Lanesha Martin
Purcell......................................Michael Culkin
Archie Walsh ....Bernard Rose
Crying mother............................Glenda Starr Kelly
Student ....Mark Daniels

Credits

Executive Producer ....Clive Barker
Producers.................................Steve Golin
.........................Sigurjon Sighvatsson, Alan Poul
Line Producer ....Gregory Goodman
Director ....Bernard Rose
1st Assistant Director..............Thomas Patrick Smith
2nd Assistant Directors................Suzanne L. Haasis
......................................Marcei A. Brubaker
Director of Photography ....Anthony B. Richmond
1st Assistant Camera ....Rory Knepp
2nd Assistant Camera ....David White
Sound ....Reinhard Stergar
Sound Design ....Nigel Holland
Editor...Dan Rae
Production Design ....Jane Ann Stewart
Art Direction ....David Lazan
Set Decoration............................Kathryn Peters
Costume Design ....Leonard Pollack
Casting ....Jason La Padura
Casting (Chicago)........................Jane Alderman
Written by ....Bernard Rose
Based on "The Forbidden" by ....Clive Barker
Music ....Philip Glass
Special Makeup Effects..........................Bob Keen
Special Effects..............................Martin Bresin
Visual Effects................................Cruse and Company
Stunt Coordinator ....Walter Scott

Film Facts

Running Time ....101 minutes
Film ....Deluxe Color
Sound ....Dolby Stereo
Location ....Chicago; Los Angeles

Captain Ron

(Buena Vista)

Critics Rating: ★★
Genre: Comedy—Light, good-natured, family entertainment.
Tag Line: "The only thing Martin wanted was a nice, quiet family vacation. Instead, he got … Captain Ron."
Plot: Martin Short plays Martin, a bumbling Chicago businessman who inherits a yacht. Martin, along with his wife (Place) and children hightail it to a Caribbean island, where the yacht is moored, with plans of sailing it back to the U.S. and selling it for a profit. After arriving, the family discovers the yacht to be more of a scrap heap, and the captain (Russell) hired to sail the vessel isn't in much better shape. Their cruise turns into a misadventure on the high seas, complete, of course with pirates, but is nevertheless an enjoyable trip.
MPAA Rating: PG-13—For elements of sensuality; some language.

Cast

Captain Ron ....Kurt Russell
Martin Harvey ....Martin Short
Katherine Harvey..........................Mary Kay Place
Benjamin Harvey ....Benjamin Salisbury
Caroline Harvey..........................Meadow Sisto

Credits

Executive Producer ....Ralph Winter
Producers ....David Permut
....Paige Simpson
Co-Producer..................................Ric Rondell
Associate Producers....................Susanne Goldstein
....Andy Cohen
Director.....................................Thom Eberhardt
Assistant Director......................Marty Eli Schwartz
Director of Photography ....Daryn Okada
Sound ....Mary H. Ellis
Editor..Tina Hirsch
Production Design ....William F. Matthews
Art Direction ....James F. Truesdale
Set Decoration ....Jeff Haley
.............................Irvin E. Jim Duffy, Jr.
Set Design ....Glenn Williams
Costume Design ....Jennifer Von Mayrhauser
Casting......................................Mary Gail Artz
....Barbara Cohen

Screenplay ....John Dwyer
....Thom Eberhardt
Story by ....John Dwyer
Music ....Nicholas Pike

Film Facts
Running Time ....100 minutes
Film ....Rank Film Laboratories Color
Sound ....Dolby Stereo

Center Of The Web
(Pyramid)

Critics Rating: Not Rated.
Genre: Thriller—*Center Of The Web* is a low-budget, action thriller that takes itself very seriously.
Plot: In a case of mistaken identity, Ted Prior plays John Phillips, a teacher abducted from his home. His kidnappers mistakenly believe he is a hit man. The authorities manage to kill the kidnappers but insist that Phillips go undercover for them. It seems that the whole episode is part of an intricate scheme to assassinate the governor. As the wrong man in the wrong place, Phillips is trapped.
MPAA Rating: R—For violence and language.

Cast
Stephen Moore.............................Tony Curtis
John Phillips...............................Ted Prior
Cathryn Lockwood......................Charlene Tilton
Richard Morgan ....Robert Davi
Frank Alessandro........................Bo Hopkins
Tony ....William Zipp
Also with Charles Napier.

Credits
Executive Producers......................David Winters
....Mark Winters
Producer ....Ruta K. Aras
Associate Producer ....Robert Willoughby
Director....................................David A. Prior
Director of Photography ....Andrew Parke
Editor ....Tony Malanowski
Art Direction..............................Linda Lewis
Screenplay ....David A. Prior
Music ....Greg Turner

Film Facts
Running Time ....88 minutes
Film ....Color
Sound ....Stereo
Location ....Mobile, Alabama

Chaplin
(TriStar)

Critics Rating: ★★★
Genre: Drama
Tag Line: "Everyone has a wild side, even a legend."
Plot: The film is told in flashback by Chaplin, as he discusses his autobiography with his editor (Hopkins). It chronicles the life of this comic genius from his troubled childhood in London to his triumphant return to Hollywood in 1972, and all the scandals inbetween. While the film is told in straightforward fashion, the performances are inspired. Downey seemed destined for this role, while Geraldine Chaplin was certainly born to play her real-life grandmother in a touching performance.
MPAA Rating: PG-13—For nudity and language.

Cast
Charlie Chaplin ....Robert Downey, Jr.
Mack Sennett ....Dan Aykroyd
Hannah Chaplin...........................Geraldine Chaplin
J. Edgar Hoover ....Kevin Dunn
George Hayden ....Anthony Hopkins
Mildred Harris ....Milla Jovovich
Hetty Kelly/Oona O'Neil.................Moira Kelly
Douglas Fairbanks........................Kevin Kline
Paulette Goddard.........................Diane Lane
Edna Purviance ....Penelope Ann Miller
Sydney Chaplin ....Paul Rhys
Fred Karno ....John Thaw
Mabel Normand ....Marisa Tomei
Joan Berry ....Nancy Travis
Lawyer Scott..............................James Woods
Charlie (age 5)............................Hugh Downer
Charlie (age 14) ....Tom Bradford
Stage manager............................Bill Paterson
Doctor ....Gerald Sim
Rollie Totheroh ....David Duchovny
Mary Pickford............................Maria Pitillo
David Raskin ....Michael Blevins
Stan Laurel................................Matthew Cottle
Frank Hooper ....Peter Crook
Lita Grey..................................Deborah Maria Moore
Lewis Seeley ....Sean O'Bryan
Sound engineer...........................Donnie Kehr
Master of Ceremonies ....Graham Sinclair
Butler ....John Standing

Ted the drunk ....Robert Stephens
German diplomat...............................Norbert Weisser
Credits
Producers ....Richard Attenborough, Mario Kassar
Co-Producer ....Terence Clegg
Associate Producer ....Diana Hawkins
Director......................................Richard Attenborough
Assistant Director.............................David Tomblin
2nd Unit Director (Los Angeles) ....Micky Moore
Director of Photography ....Sven Nykvist
2nd Unit Camera (Los Angeles)................Alex Witt
Sound...Edward Tise
Editor...Anne V. Coates
Production Design............................Stuart Craig
Art Direction Supervisor...................Norman Dorme
Art Direction (Los Angeles)...........Mark Mansbridge
Art Direction (London) ....John King
Set Design (Los Angeles).........................Stan Tropp
....Don Woodruff
Set Decoration (Los Angeles).............Chris A. Butler
Set Decoration (London) ....Stephenie McMillan
Costume Design............John Molla, Ellen Mirojnick
Casting..Mike Fenton
..........................Valorie Massalas, Susie Figgis
Screenplay..William Boyd
..........................Bryan Forbes, William Goldman
Story by..Diana Hawkins
Based on *My Autobiography* by ....Charles Chaplin
Based on *Chaplin: His Life
    and Art* by ....David Robinson
Music...John Barry
Chaplin prosthetic makeup
    created by.......................................John Gaglione, Jr.
Film Facts
Running Time ....144 minutes
Soundtrack ....Epic Soundtrax
Film..Technicolor
Sound...Dolby Stereo
Location....................Los Angeles; London, England
Other Working Titles......................................*Charlie*

Children Of Nature

(Born Natturunnar)
(Icelandic Film Corp.)

Critics Rating: Not Rated.
Genre: Drama—*Children Of Nature* is Iceland's first Academy Award entry. A story of an elderly man and woman who find romance, it is a nostalgic

drama laced with fantasy and humor.
Plot: Gisli Halldorsson stars as a 78-year-old man who has entered a nursing home against his will. There he meets a childhood sweetheart (Sigridur Hagalin), and together they decide to run away from the home. Their destination is the village where they grew up. Along the way they are aided by supernatural powers.
MPAA Rating: Not Rated.
Cast
Old man ....Gisli Halldorsson
Old woman....................................Sigridur Hagalin
Angel...Bruno Ganz
Also with Valgerdur Dan, Hallmar Sigurdsson, Rurik Haraldsson, Baldvin Halldorsson, Egill Olafsson, Tina Gunnlaugsdottir, Magnus Olafsson and Gudbrandur Gislason.
Credits
Producers ....Wolfgang Pfeiffer
............Fridrik Thor Fridriksson, Skule Hansen
Director.....................................Fridrik Thor Fridriksson
Assistant Director............................Kristin Palsdottir
Director of Photography ....Ari Kristinsson
Sound.......................................Kjartan Kjartansson
Editor...Skule Hansen
Art Direction ....Geir Ottar Geirsson
Costume Design ....Ragnheidur Olafsdottir
Written by ....Einar Mar Gudmundsson
....Fridrik Thor Fridriksson
Music ....Hilmar Orn Hilmarsson
Makeup.................................Margret Benediktsdottir
Film Facts
Country of Origin...Iceland
Running Time ....85 minutes
Film..Color
Sound...Dolby Stereo

Christopher Columbus - The Discovery

(Warner Bros.)

Critics Rating: Not Rated.
Genre: Adventure—A straightforward, historical drama. Audience and critics' reactions were considered disappointing. *The Hollywood Reporter* went so far as to call it a "colossal washout as a motion picture."

Tag Line: "Chosen by a queen. Driven by a dream. He dared to go to the edge, and kept going."

Plot: Newcomer George Corraface stars in the title role in this traditional, historical biography. While the film is not a true epic, the adventure follows Columbus from the beginning of his journey through his discovery of a new land.

MPAA Rating: PG-13

Cast

Torquemada	Marlon Brando
King Ferdinand	Tom Selleck
Christopher Columbus	George Corraface
Queen Isabella	Rachel Ward
Martin Pinzon	Robert Davi
Alvaro	Benicio Del Toro
Beatriz	Catherine Zeta Jones
Harana	Oliver Cotton
King John	Mathieu Carriere
Vicente Pinzon	Manuel de Blas
De La Cosa	Glyn Grain
Fra Perez	Peter Guinness
Roldan	Nigel Terry

Credits

Executive Producer	Jane Chaplin
Producer	Ilya Salkind
Co-Producer	Bob Simmonds
Director	John Glen
Assistant Director	Brian Cook
Ocean voyage unit director/camera	Arthur Wooster
Director of Photography	Alec Mills
Sound	Peter J. Devlin
Editor	Matthew Glen
Production Design	Gil Parrondo
Art Direction	Terry Pritchard
	Luis Koldo, Jose Maria Alarcon
Costume Design	John Bloomfield
Casting	Michelle Guish
Screenplay	John Briley
	Cary Bates, Mario Puzo
Story by	Mario Puzo
Music	Cliff Eidelman

Film Facts

Running Time	120 minutes
Soundtrack	Varese Sarabande
Film	Technicolor
Sound	Dolby Stereo
Location	Spain; Orlando, Florida; Caribbean; Malta
Other Working Titles	
	Christopher Columbus: The Film

City Of Joy
(TriStar)

Critics Rating: ★★★

Genre: Drama—Director Roland Joffe's (*The Killing Fields, The Mission*) epic drama contrasts the life of a privileged American doctor visiting Calcutta with a poor Indian man. The Indian has come to the city, bringing his family, in search of work. The fate of these men become bound when they are accidentally thrown together.

Plot: In his most challenging role to date, Patrick Swayze stars as Max Lowe, an American doctor who has left his profession and his life behind and gone in search of spiritual enlightenment. During his search, he is robbed and nearly killed on the streets. Rescued by Hasari Pal (Om Puri), a man living on the streets and in search of work, he ends up in a shantytown clinic. Run by an Irish nurse (Pauline Collins, *Shirley Valentine*), the clinic is known as "The City of Joy." Of course there is little joy in this poor city, but through their individual struggles the characters come to know a little more about themselves and one another.

MPAA Rating: PG-13

Cast

Max Lowe	Patrick Swayze
Joan Bethel	Pauline Collins
Hasari Pal	Om Puri
Kamla Pal	Shabana Azmi
Ashoka	Art Malik
Shambu Pal	Santu Chowdhury
Amrita Pal	Ayesha Dharker
Ram Chander	Debtosh Ghosh
Ghatak, the Godfather	Shyamanand Jalan
Manooj Pal	Imran Badsah Khan
Poomina	Suneeta Sengupta
Anouar	Nabil Shaban

Credits

Producers	Jake Eberts
	Roland Joffe
Co-Producer	Iain Smith
Director	Roland Joffe
Assistant Director	Bill Westley
Director of Photography	Peter Biziou
Sound	Daniel Brisseau
Editor	Gerry Hambling
Production Design	Roy Walker

Supervising Art Director..........................John Fenner
Art Direction...Asoke Bose
Set Decoration............................Rosalind Shingleton
Costume Design................................Judy Moorcroft
Casting...Priscilla John
Screenplay....................................Mark Medoff
Based on the Book by ....Dominique Lapierre
Music ....Ennio Morricone
Cultural Consultant....................Sunil Gangopadhyay

Film Facts
Country of Origin ....Great Britain/France
Running Time ....134 minutes
Soundtrack ....Epic Soundtrax
Film...................................Eclair Laboratories Color
Sound......................................Dolby Stereo
Location...Calcutta, India

Claire Of The Moon

(Demi-Monde Productions)

Critics Rating: Not Rated.
Genre: Drama—Critic Daniel M. Kimmel of *Variety* called this film, "A talky drama that plays like a lesbian version of *The Odd Couple*."
Plot: Todd and Trumbo play Claire and Noel, lesbian women who are forced into rooming together during a stay at a women writers' colony. Like Felix and Oscar, the women are opposites in every way. Taking an immediate dislike to one another, they eventually come around in the end, providing a warm and winning romance.
MPAA Rating: Not Rated.
Cast
Claire Jabrowski....................................Trisha Todd
Dr. Noel Benedict ....Karen Trumbo
Tara O'Hara..Caren Graham
BJ..Sheila Dickinson
Brian..Damon Craig

Credits
Executive Producer ....Nicole Conn
Co-Executive Producer..........Nannette M. Troutman
Producer..Pamela S. Kuri
Director..Nicole Conn
Director of Photography ....Randolph Sellars
Sound...Brian Crain
Editor......................................Michael Solinger
Written by ....Nicole Conn

Music ....Michael Allen Harrison
Film Facts
Running Time ....107 minutes
Film ....Foto-Kem Color
Sound ....Stereo
Location...Portland, Oregon

Class Act

(Warner Bros.)

Critics Rating: ★★★
Genre: Comedy—Rappers Kid 'N Play (Christopher Reid and Christopher Martin), who starred in the very successful *House Party* films, go back to high school in this comedy revolving around a case of mistaken identities.
Plot: When the high school records of honor student Duncan Pinderhughs (Reid) and delinquent Blade Brown (Martin) are accidentally switched, the scene is set for outrageous comic situations that often become slapstick. Energetic and original, the film's antidrug message is easy to take.
MPAA Rating: PG-13
Trivia: Director Randall Miller's big break came two years ago with a 30-minute AFI student film titled *Marilyn Hotchkiss' Ballroom Dancing and Charm School*.
Cast
Duncan Pinderhughes............Christopher "Kid" Reid
Blade Brown ....Christopher "Play" Martin
Popsickle...Doug E. Doug
Wedge ....Lamont Johnson
Ellen...Karyn Parsons
Damita...Alysia Rogers
John Pinderhughes (Duncan's dad) ..Meshach Taylor
Miss Simpson ....Rhea Perlman
Duncan's mom ....Mariann Aalda
Principal Kratz..Raye Birk
Jail guard.................................Andre Rosey Brown
Blade's mom................................Loretta Devine
Reichert ....Rick Ducommun
Julian Thomas..................................Pauly Shore
Credits
Executive Producers ....Joe Wizan
....Suzanne de Passe
Producers..Todd Black

...................................Maynell Thomas	
Co-Producer ....Jean Higgins	
Director...............................Randall Miller	
Assistant Director ....Barry K. Thomas	
Director of Photography ....Francis Kenny	
Sound.............................Will Yarbrough	
Editor................................John F. Burnett	
Production Design.............David L. Snyder	
Assistant Art Director ....Sarah Knowles	
Set Decoration...................Robin Peyton	
Costume Design..........Violette Jones-Faison	
Casting.....................................Jaki Brown	
Screenplay...........................John Semper	
...................................Cynthia Friedlob	
Story by ....Michael Swerdlick	
................Wayne Rice, Richard Brenne	
Music..............................Vassal Benford	

Film Facts

Running Time ....98 minutes
Soundtrack ....Giant Records
Film.................................Technicolor
Sound..............................Dolby Stereo
Location ....Los Angeles

Credits

Producers ....Stephen J. Roth
...................................Ian McDougall
Director ....Richard Bugajski
Assistant Director....................Bill Spahic
2nd Unit Director ....Ian McDougall
Director of Photography................Francois Protat
Sound.............................Clark McCarron
Editor ....Michael Rea
Production Design ....Perri Gorrara
Casting..............................Deirdre Bowen
Screenplay...........................Rob Forsyth
Based on the novel *A Dream Like Mine* by ....M. T. Kelly
Music...............................Shane Harvey
Post-Production Supervisor ....Catherine Hunt
Special Effects ....Ted Ross

Film Facts

Country of Origin.......................Canada
Running Time ....96 minutes
Film.................................Eastmancolor
Sound ....Stereo
Location ....Thunder Bay, Canada

Clearcut
(Northern Arts)

Critics Rating: ★★★
Genre: Drama—An ultra-violent ecological message film.
Plot: Graham Greene *(Dances With Wolves)* plays Arthur, a violent Canadian Indian with a score to settle even. Ron Lea plays Peter, a lawyer unsuccessfully battling loggers cutting trees on Indian land. Frustrated with Peter and the system's inability to end the destruction, Arthur takes the law into his own hands. Kidnapping the sawmill boss (Michael Hogan), as well as the lawyer, the trio sets out on a torturous and deadly journey.
MPAA Rating: R—For strong moments of torture and violence; and language.

Cast

Peter Maguire..............................Ron Lea
Arthur.............................Graham Greene
Bud Rickets.....................Michael Hogan
Wilf ....Floyd (Red Crow) Westerman
Louise.............................Rebecca Jenkins

Close To Eden
(Urga)
(Miramax)

Critics Rating: ★★★★
Genre: Drama—A warm, humorous and simple tale of the past and the future colliding, from the director of *Dark Eyes*. Winner of the Venice Film Festival Gold Lion Award.
Tag Line: "At the edge of the world, there's a place untouched by civilization. Things are about to change."
Plot: As if they were living in a time warp, the film revolves around a modern-day Mongolian nomad family. Father, mother and three children spend their days tending sheep and cattle, almost entirely oblivious to the world at large, until one day, when a stranger, Sergei (Gostukhin), gets lost and arrives at their tent. Gombo (Bayaertu), the father, joins Sergei on his trip back to the city. Once there, Gombo becomes involved in a series of humorous fish-out-of-water misadventures.
MPAA Rating: Not Rated.

Cast

Gombo	Bayaertu
Pagma	Badema
Sergei	Vladimir Gostukhin
Grandmother	Babushka

Also with Baoynhexige, Nikita Mikhalkov, Roustam Ibraguimbekov, Larissa Kuznetsova, Kinolai Vachtohiline, Wurinile, Bao Yongyan and Wang Zhiyong.

Credits

Executive Producer	Jean-Louis Piel
Supervising Producer	Michel Seydoux
Associate Producer	Rene Cleitman
Director/Original idea	Nikita Mikhalkov
Assistant Director	Anatoli Ermilov
Director of Photography	Vilenn Kaluta
Sound	Jean Umansky
Editor	Joelle Hache
Production Manager	Leonid Vereschchaguine
Production Design	Aleksei Levtchenko
Screenplay	Roustam Ibraguimbekov
Story by	Nikita Mikhalkov
	Roustam Ibraguimbekov
Music	Eduard Artemiev

Film Facts

Country of Origin	France/Russia
Language	Mongolian/Russian/Chinese
Running Time	106 minutes
Film	Color
Sound	Dolby Stereo

Cold Heaven

(Hemdale)

Critics Rating: ★★

Genre: Thriller—Director Nicolas Roeg brings to the screen a thriller involving retribution from the other side of the grave.

Plot: Theresa Russell stars as Marie, the wife of Dr. Alex Davenport, played by Mark Harmon. Marie, who is having an affair with another doctor, plans to inform her husband on a trip to Acapulco. Before she has the chance, however, he is killed in a boating accident. But in this film death is just a beginning. Rising from the dead, Marie's past comes back to haunt her.

MPAA Rating: R

Cast

Marie Davenport	Theresa Russell
Dr. Alex Davenport	Mark Harmon
Daniel	James Russo
Sister Martha	Talia Shire
Priest	Richard Bradford
Priest	Will Patton

Also with Julie Carmen.

Credits

Executive Producer	Jack Schwartzman
Producers	Allan Scott
	Jonathan D. Krane
Director	Nicolas Roeg
Assistant Director	Donald P. H. Eaton
Director of Photography	Francis Kenny
Sound	Jacob Goldstein
Editor	Tony Lawson
Production Design	Steven Legler
Art Direction	Nina Ruscio
Set Decoration	Cliff Cunningham
Costume Design	Del Adey-Jones
Casting	Joe D'Agosta
Screenplay	Allan Scott
Based on the novel by	Brian Moore
Music	Stanley Myers

Film Facts

Running Time	105 minutes
Film	Technicolor
Sound	Dolby Stereo

Cold Moon

(Lune Froide)

(Gaumont)

Critics Rating: Not Rated.

Genre: Drama—French actor-director Patrick Bouchitey has taken his Cesar award-winning short film *Mermaid* and expanded it into a feature debut drama.

Plot: Based on the work of author Charles Bukowski, the film is set in France and revolves around two deadbeat alcoholics, Simon (Jean-Francois Steverin) and Dede (Patrick Bouchitey), who spend their evenings drinking and picking up prostitutes. Their relationship goes back many years and includes an incident Simon cannot forget. Having had sex with the body of a dead girl, he is haunted by his past. This, it seems, was the only time he was able to find real love or meaning in life.

MPAA Rating: Not Rated.
Cast
Simon.............................Jean-Francois Stevenin
Dede ....Patrick Bouchitey
Gerard ....Jean-Pierre Bisson
Nadine..................................Laura Favali
Aunt Suzanne.........................Marie Mergey
Priest ....Jacky Berroyer
The whore ....Sylvana de Faria
The blonde ....Consuelo de Haviland
Denis ....Alain Le Floch
The mermaid ....Karin Nuris
Credits
Producers..................................Luc Besson
....Andree Martinez
Director ....Patrick Bouchitey
Assistant Director ....Vincent Canaple
Director of Photography ....Jean-Jacques Bouhon
Sound ....Guillaume Sciama
Editor ....Florence Bon
Production Manager ....Jerome Chalou
Production Design ....Frank Lagache
....Jean-Marc Pacaud
Costume Design ....Carine Sarfati
Screenplay....................Patrick Bouchitey
....Jacky Berroyer
Based on *Copulating Mermaid Of
Venice* and *Trouble With The
Battery* by ....Charles Bukowski
Music ....Didier Lockwood
Film Facts
Country of Origin.............................France
Running Time ....92 minutes
Film..................................Black & White
Sound ....Stereo

Color Adjustment
(California Newsreel)

Critics Rating: Not Rated.
Genre: Documentary—Documentary director Marlon Riggs (*Tongues Tied*) examines the roles and characters of African-Americans on TV from 1948 to 1988.
Plot: In a straightforward analysis, Riggs presents examples from the early days of television and contrasts them with more current depictions. While the former may be embarrassing, the latter, he

believes, are merely disguised images of racism that have been co-opted into the mainstream. Clips are used from such series as *Amos 'n' Andy, East Side West Side, I Spy, All in the Family, Good Times, Roots* and *The Cosby Show.*
MPAA Rating: Not Rated.
Credits
Executive Producer ....Marlon T. Riggs
Producer ....Vivian Kleiman
Director.............................Marlon T. Riggs
Directors of Photography ....Rick Butler
....Michael Anderson
Editor ....Deborah Hoffman
Written by..........................Marlon T. Riggs
Narrated by ....Ruby Dee
Film Facts
Running Time ....90 minutes
Film...Color
Sound ....Stereo

Complex World
(Hemdale)

Critics Rating: Not Rated.
Genre: Comedy—*Complex World* is a ridiculously silly, low-budget comedy.
Plot: Jeff Burgess (Dan Welch) is the owner of the Heartbreak Hotel, and he is also the son of Senator Robert Burgess (Bob Owczarek), a right-wing reactionary and former CIA director, who is running for President. The elder Burgess has conceived of a plan to rid himself of his oddball, embarrassing son and at the same time give a boost to his presidential campaign. Things don't go as planned but the climax is nevertheless explosive.
MPAA Rating: R
Trivia: Writer-director Jim Wolpaw received an Academy Award nomination in 1985 for his short *Keats and His Nightingale: A Blind Date.*
Cast
Morris Brock...............................Stanley Matis
Jeff Burgess ....Dan Welch
Senator Robert Burgess ....Bob Owczarek
Gilda..................................Margot Dionne
Boris Lee ....Captain Lou Albano
Malcolm...........................Daniel Von Bargen
Harpo ....Allen Oliver

Alex (the janitor) ....Joe Klimek
Klem..Jay Charbonneau
Hotel waiter ....Ernesto Luna
Miriam ....Dorothy Gallagher
Larry Newman............................David P. B. Stevens
The mayor...Rich Lupo
Also with Captain Lou Albano, Bree, Norm Buerklin, Lucinda Dohanan, Molly Fitch, Tilman Gandy, Jr., NRBQ, Roomful of Blues, and Russ.

Credits

Executive Producer....................................Rich Lupo
Producers..Geoff Adams
....Rich Lupo, Denis Maloney
Associate Producer ....Charlie Thompson
Director......................................James Wolpaw
1st Assistant Director............................Geoff Adams
2nd Assistant Director ....Mark Van Veen
Director of Photography ....Denis Maloney
Sound..Thomas Payne
Editor...Steven Gentile
Production Manager ....Donna Digiuseppe
Set Decoration................................Deb Davis
Written by....................................James Wolpaw
Music ....Steven Snyder

Film Facts

Running Time ....82 minutes
Soundtrack ("Helping Others") ....Heartbreak Hits
Film...DuArt Color
Sound ....Stereo
Location ....Providence, RI

Consenting Adults

(Buena Vista)

Critics Rating: ★★
Genre: Thriller—Audiences laughed on opening day during scenes that were clearly not intended to be comical. Despite its often improbable storyline the suspense begins to work and it becomes an involving and entertaining, if predictable, tale.
Tag Line: "Thou shalt not covet thy neighbor's wife."
Plot: Kline and Mastrantonio play Richard and Priscilla Parker, well-to-do yuppies living in a fashionable neighborhood. Kevin Spacey (*Glengarry Glen Ross*) and Rebecca Miller play Eddy and Kay Otis, the new neighbors from hell. It isn't long before the neighbors have become close friends. So close that Eddy suggests they swap partners. Richard reluctantly agrees with the idea, only to discover that it has been an elaborate setup and that he has been framed for the murder of Eddy's wife. There are many plot twists and turns as Kline races the clock to prove his innocence.

While this is not the most original psycho of the year to terrorize a family, Spacey's character is without a doubt the most deranged and disturbing of the lot. All of that makes the climax of the film that much more satisfying.
MPAA Rating: R—For language, violence and sexuality. Kevin Kline is seen from behind in a very brief and dark nude scene.

Cast

Richard Parker...............................Kevin Kline
Priscilla Parker ....Mary Elizabeth Mastrantonio
Eddy Otis...................................Kevin Spacey
Kay Otis.....................................Rebecca Miller
George Gordon..............................E. G. Marshall
David Duttonville ....Forest Whitaker
Lori Parker ....Kimberly McCullough

Credits

Executive Producer ....Pieter Jan Brugge
Producers ....Alan J. Pakula
....David Permut
Co-Producer...................................Katie Jacobs
Director......................................Alan J. Pakula
Assistant Director ....Alan B. Curtiss
Director of Photography ....Stephen Goldblatt
Sound ....James J. Sabat
Editor ....Sam O'Steen
Production Design ....Carol Spier
Art Direction................................Alicia Keywan
Set Decoration ....Gretchen Rau
Set Design ....Thomas Minton, Kathleen Sullivan
Costume Design ....Gary Jones, Ann Roth
Casting ....Alixe Gordin
Written by ....Matthew Chapman
Music ....Michael Small

Film Facts

Running Time ....100 minutes
Soundtrack ....Milan Records
Film..Technicolor
Sound ....Dolby Stereo
Location.................................Atlanta, Georgia
...............................Charleston, South Carolina

Cool World
(Paramount)

Critics Rating: ★

Genre: Fantasy-Animated—Director Ralph Bakshi, who created the X-rated cartoon-cult classic *Fritz The Cat* in 1972, is strictly PG-13 in this combination live-action and animation fantasy trip.

Plot: In order to endure his incarceration, animator Jack Beebs (Gabriel Byrne) creates an animated "Cool World" comic strip in which to escape. The star of his fantasy is Holli Would, played by Kim Basinger. Falling in love with his own creation, he enters his own animated world. The only trouble is, Holli is a toon who doesn't want to be one anymore and is doing everything she can to become a real live person. Adding to Beebs troubles, Frank Harris, played by Brad Pitt (*Johnny Suede, A River Runs Through It*), is a detective paid to keep "doodles" and real people apart.

MPAA Rating: PG-13

Cast

Holli Would	Kim Basinger
Jack Deebs	Gabriel Byrne
Frank Harris	Brad Pitt
Jennifer Malley	Michele Abrams
Isabelle Malley	Diedre O'Connell
Comic bookstore cashier	Carrie Hamilton
Frank Sinatra, Jr.	Frank Sinatra, Jr.

Voices:

Nails	Charles Adler
Slash/Holli's door	Joey Camen
Sparks	Michael David Lally
Doc Whiskers/Mash	Maurice LaMarche
Lonette/Bob	Candi Milo
Bash	Gregory Snegoff

Credits

Producer	Frank Mancuso, Jr.
Associate Producer	Vikki Williams
Director	Ralph Bakshi
Assistant Director	Marty Eli Schwartz
Director of Photography	John A. Alonzo
Sound	James Thornton
Editor	Steve Mirkovich
	Annamaria Szanto
Production Design	Michael Corenblith
Art Direction	David James Bomba
Set Decoration	Merideth Boswell
Set Design	Lori Rowbotham
	Mitchell Lee Simmons
Costume Design	Malissa Daniel
Casting	Carrie Frazier
	Shani Ginsberg
Written by	Michael Grais
	Mark Victor
Music Score by	Mark Isham
Cool World Conceptual Design	Barry Jackson
Animation Supervisor	Bruce Woodside
Character Layout/Design	Louise Zinagarelli
Design Layout/Animation	Greg Hill
	David Wasson
Animation Production Coordinator	Gina Shay
Cool World Background Characters	Milton Knight
	Mark S. O'Hare

Film Facts

Running Time	101 minutes
Soundtrack	Warner Bros.
Original Score	Varese Sarabande
Film	Technicolor
Sound	Dolby Stereo
Location	Las Vegas; Los Angeles

Cousin Bobby
(Cinevista)

Critics Rating: ★★★★

Genre: Documentary—Jonathan Demme (*The Silence Of The Lambs*) directs this very personal film, described as a nonfiction feature about the directors cousin.

Plot: Demme focuses his lens on his cousin, the Reverend Robert Castle. Castle is a minister at St. Mary's Episcopal Church in Harlem. He has devoted his life to civil rights and to helping people who are less fortunate. The film includes interviews with parishioners and family members, and revisits the neighborhood where Castle grew up. The film resembles a home movie and lacks the power of the directors features. However, *Bobby* is a touching portrait of a committed life that will appeal to a broad audience.

MPAA Rating: Not Rated.

Credits

Producer	Edward Saxon
Associate Producers	Valerie Thomas, Lucas Platt

Director ....Jonathan Demme
Directors of Photography.................Ernest Dickerson
.................................Craig Haagensen, Tony Jannelli
.................................Jacek Laskus, Declan Quinn
Sound...Judy Karp
.................................J. T. Takagi, Pam Yates
Editor ....David Greenwald
Music...Anton Sanko

Film Facts
Running Time ....70 minutes
Film ....Color
Sound ....Stereo
Location ....Harlem, New York

Criss Cross
(MGM)

Critics Rating: Not Rated.

Genre: Drama—*Criss Cross* is an emotionally charged, modern-day coming-of-age drama about a young boy's difficulties accepting his parent's divorce.

Plot: Newcomer David Arnott plays Chris Cross, a confused 12-year-old whose father has split, leaving him to be raised by his mother. Set in Key West, Florida, in 1969, mother, Tracy (Hawn), is shown working as a stripper to make ends meet. Needless to say, Chris isn't thrilled when he discovers what his mother does for a living. Stumbling upon a way to make money from drugs, he sees this as a way for his mom to be able to quit her job. Things come to a head, however, when Chris becomes the target of a drug bust.

MPAA Rating: R—Contains nudity, brief but strong sensuality; language and drug-related scenes. In one innocent scene Chris and his girlfriend strip naked (he is seen from behind) in her bedroom. Before they can decide what to do next, the girl's brother comes home.

Cast
Tracy Cross ....Goldie Hawn
Joe...Arliss Howard
Emmett..James Gammon
John Cross ....Keith Carradine
Chris Cross ....David Arnott
Louis...Steve Buscemi
Blacky ....Paul Calderon

Jetty...J. C. Quinn

Credits
Executive Producer ....Bill Finnegan
Producer..Anthea Sylbert
Co-Producer..Robin Forman
Director...Chris Menges
Assistant Director ....George Parra
Director of Photography.....................Ivan Strasburg
Sound ....Edward Tise
Editor ....Tony Lawson
Production Design ....Crispian Sallis
Art Direction.......................................Dayna Lee
Set Decoration.....................................Leslie Morales
Costume Design ....Lisa Jensen
Casting...David Rubin
Screenplay...Scott Sommer
Based on the novella by.......................Scott Sommer
Music...Trevor Jones

Film Facts
Running Time ....99 minutes
Soundtrack...Intrada Records
Film ....Continental Film Laboratories Color
Sound ....Dolby Stereo
Location ....Florida

Crossing The Bridge
(Buena Vista)

Critics Rating: ★★★

Genre: Drama—A coming-of-age tale of three friends and the paths they take following high school.

Tag Line: "Every day you make a million decisions. But it only takes one to change your life forever…"

Plot: Set in Detroit in the mid-1970s, Josh Charles plays Mort, a young writer whose main ambition in life is to write a television sitcom. His two best friends Tim (Gedrick, *Backdraft*) and Danny (Baldwin) are less ambitious. The three buddies wander aimlessly from one misadventure to the next. When they decide to cross the bridge over to Canada to buy hash from their supplier, their lives change unexpectedly forever. Their trip turns into something more than they expected and finds the friends in a crisis that ends in a tragedy and a new beginning.

61

MPAA Rating: R—For language and drug use.

Cast

Tim Reese	Jason Gedrick
Mort Golden	Josh Charles
Danny Morgan	Stephen Baldwin
Uncle Alby	Jeffrey Tambor
Carol Brockton	Cheryl Pollak
Kate Golden	Rita Taggart
Mitchell	Richard Edson
Manny Goldfarb	Hy Anzell

Also with Abraham Benrubi, Rana Haugen, Ken Jenkins, James Krag, Bob Nickman and David Schwimmer.

Credits

Producers	Jeffrey Silver
	Robert Newmyer
Co-Producers	Caroline Baron
	Jack Binder
Associate Producers	Judd Apatow
	Joel Madison
Director	Mike Binder
Director of Photography	Tom Sigel
Sound	Ed Novick
	Mark Goodermote
Editor	Adam Weiss
Production Design	Craig Stearns
Costume Design	Carol Ramsey
Casting	Richard Pagano
	Sharon Bialy, Debi Manwiller
Written by	Mike Binder
Music	Peter Himmelman

Film Facts

Running Time	103 minutes
Film	Deluxe Color
Sound	Dolby Stereo
Location	Minneapolis-St. Paul
Other Working Titles	*The Bridge*

The Crying Game
(Miramax)

Critics Rating: ★★★★★

Genre: Thriller—A compelling, unpredictable examination of the limits to which people will go for love, sex and political beliefs. The complex story and solid performances helped make it a top-10 favorite with American audiences.

Tag Line: "Sex. Murder. Betrayal. In Neil Jordan's new thriller, nothing is what it seems to be. Play at your own risk."

Plot: Set against the current political backdrop of Northern Ireland, Stephen Rea (*Life Is Sweet*) plays Fergus, an IRA conspirator who holds an English soldier named Jodi (Whitaker) hostage. Captor and captive become unlikely friends, and when things blow up in their faces, Fergus heads for London, to hide out from the authorities. There he looks up Jodi's girlfriend, Dil (Davidson), with whom he falls in love. He hides the fact that he was responsible for the death of Jodi. She hides an even bigger secret.

MPAA Rating: R—For strong violence, language and sexuality. Contains full-frontal male nudity.

Cast

Fergus	Stephen Rea
Jude	Miranda Richardson
Dil	Jaye Davidson
Jody	Forest Whitaker
Maguire	Adrian Dunbar
Tinker	Breffini McKenna
Eddie	Joe Savino
Tommy	Birdie Sweeney
Col	Jim Broadbent
Dave	Ralph Brown

Credits

Executive Producer	Nik Powell
Producer	Stephen Woolley
Co-Producer	Elizabeth Karlsen
Line Producer	Paul Cowan
Director	Neil Jordan
Assistant Director	Redmond Morris
Director of Photography	Ian Wilson
Sound	Colin Nicolson
Editor	Kant Pan
Production Design	Jim Clay
Art Direction	Chris Seagers
Set Decoration	Martin Childs
Costume Design	Sandy Powell
Casting	Susie Figgis
Screenplay	Neil Jordan
Music	Anne Dudley

Film Facts

Country of Origin	Great Britain
Running Time	112 minutes
Film	Metrocolor
Sound	Dolby Stereo

Cup Final

(G'mar Giviya)

(First Run Features)

Critics Rating: ★★★★

Genre: Drama—Often humorous, this morality tale is enjoyable and memorable.

Plot: Moshe Ivgi plays Cohen, an Israeli soldier who is captured by Palestinian guerrillas during the Lebanon War in 1982. An avid soccer fan, he soon discovers that his captors are also fans. Their hatred of one another soon dissolves as they share their joy for the sport. By the end of the film each side has gained a new understanding of the other.

MPAA Rating: Not Rated.

Cast

Cohen......................................Moshe Ivgi
Ziad...................................Muhammed Bakri
Omar.................................Suheil Haddad
With Gassan Abbass, Sharon Alexander, Salim Dau, Yussef Abu Warda and Bassam Zuamut.

Credits

Producer.........................Michael Sharfshtein
Director..................................Eran Riklis
Director of Photography.............Amnon Salomon
Editor...................................Anat Lubarsky
Screenplay ....Eyal Halfon
Based on an Idea by......................Eran Riklis
Music ....Raviv Gazit

Film Facts

Country of Origin...........................Israel
Running Time ....110 minutes
Film.......................................Color
Sound....................................Stereo
Location....Golan Heights; Abe Gosh; Tel Aviv-Jaffa

The Cutting Edge

(MGM)

Critics Rating: ★★

Genre: Drama

Tag Line: "The king of the rink is about to meet America's ice queen. The ultimate love/skate relationship."

Plot: The story is a simple and familiar one. When two equally independent ice skaters are forced to work together as a team, sparks fly—and romance ignites.

D.B. Sweeney (*Memphis Belle*) stars as Doug, a member of the USA hockey team whose career has been sidelined by an injury. Moira Kelly plays Kate, a self-centered figure skater who has lost her most recent partner. As fate would have it, her coach decides that Doug is the only one strong enough to stand up to Kate and to be a winning partner. And so the battle of the sexes begins.

MPAA Rating: PG

Cast

Doug...................................D. B. Sweeney
Kate ....Moira Kelly
Anton..................................Roy Dotrice
Jack...................................Terry O'Quinn
Walter.................................Chris Benson
Hale...................................Dwier Brown

Credits

Producers ....Ted Field
....Karen Murphy
.....................................Robert W. Cort
Co-Producers.........................Dean O'Brien
...................................Cynthia Sherman
Director............................Paul M. Glaser
Director of Photography..............Elliot Davis
Sound.....................................David Lee
Editor.............................Michael E. Polakow
Production Design ....David Gropman
Art Direction...........................Dan Davis
Set Decoration.....................Steve Shewchuk
Costume Design...................William Ivey Long
Casting..............................Marci Liroff
Written by ....Tony Gilroy
Music Supervisors......................Tim Sexton
...................................Becky Mancuso
Music ....Patrick Williams
Choreography.......................Robin Cousins

Film Facts

Running Time ....101 minutes
Film..............................Deluxe Color
Sound.............................Dolby Stereo
Location.....................Toronto, Ontario, Canada

D

Written by...Ilppo Pohjola
Music ....Elliot Sharp
Film Facts
Country of Origin ....Finland
Language.......................Finnish/English (subtitled)
Running Time ....60 minutes
Film ....Color (16mm)
Sound ....Stereo

Daddy And The Muscle Academy
(Zeitgeist)

Critics Rating: Not Rated.
Genre: Documentary—A tribute to the life and work of gay icon and artist Tom of Finland.
Plot: The film is a series of interviews with illustrator Touko Laaksonen, better known as Tom of Finland, just before his death in 1991 at age 71. In addition, there are testimonies by fans and admirers, including British director Isaac Julien (*Young Soul Rebels*), and images of the work itself.

Originally influenced by American body-building magazines, the young artist submitted his first male erotic images to *Physique Pictorial* in 1957 under the assumed name of Tom. The magazines editor Bob Mizer is credited with giving the artist the name Tom of Finland. Images of exaggerated, macho, muscle-bound men in leather in homosexual settings and situations make up the body of work that is explored explicitly and in depth in this fascinating and often humorous homage.
MPAA Rating: Not Rated—Contains full-frontal male nudity both actual and illustrated.
Cast
With Tom of Finland, Bob Mizer, Nayland Blake, Durk Dehner, Etienne and Isaac Julien.
Credits
Producers.................................Kari Paljakka
....Alvaro Pardo
Director.....................................Ilppo Pohjola
Director of Photography..................Kjell Lagerroos
Sound..Kauko Lindfors
....Pekka Karjalainen
Editor..Jorma Hori

Damage
(New Line Cinema)

Critics Rating: ★★★
Genre: Drama—Directed by Louis Malle, whose other credits include *Pretty Baby* and *Murmur Of The Heart*. *Damage* is a surprisingly cold and clinical exploration of the destructive power of raw, unbridled emotions.
Tag Line: "With love comes risk. With obsession comes damage."
Plot: Jeremy Irons plays Stephen Fleming, a middle-aged, conservative English politician who is happily married and has two grown children. His son Martyn (Rupert Graves) is a young journalist who is about to be married. When Stephen meets his son's fiancee, Anna (Juliette Binoche), there is an immediate attraction on both sides. Risking everything, the two become involved in a sexual relationship. Forced to lie to and deceive his family, his betrayal eventually catches up with him. In the end their affair leads to a devastating climax and damaged lives that can never be pieced together again.
MPAA Rating: R—For strong sexuality; and language. The film received a tremendous amount of attention for its original NC-17 rating. It was edited in order to gain the "R" rating.
Cast
Dr. Stephen Fleming ....Jeremy Irons
Anna Barton ....Juliette Binoche
Ingrid...Miranda Richardson
Martyn ....Rupert Graves
Edward Lloyd ....Ian Bannen
Elizabeth Prideaux ....Leslie Caron
Peter Wetzler....................................Peter Stormare
Sally...Gemma Clark

Donald Lyndsaymp ....Julian Fellowes
Prime Minister ....Tony Doyle
Credits
Producer/Director ....Louis Malle
Co-Producers ....Vincent Malle
....Simon Relph
Assistant Director ....Michel Ferry
Director of Photography ....Peter Biziou
Sound.....................................Jean-Claude Laureux
Editor ....John Bloom
Production Design....................................Brian Morris
Art Direction..Richard Earl
Set Decoration ....Jill Quertier
Costume Design............................Milena Canonero
Casting ....Patsy Pollock
Screenplay ....David Hare
Based on the Novel by.......................Josephine Hart
Music ....Zbigniew Preisner
Film Facts
Country of Origin ....Great Britain/France
Running Time ....112 minutes
Film...Technicolor
Sound...Dolby Stereo
Location..............................United Kingdom; France

Damned In The U.S.A.
(Diusa Releasing)

Critics Rating: ★★★★
Genre: Documentary—An international Emmy-Award-winning film released in theaters.
Plot: The debate between what is art and what is pornography is given a forum in this fascinating and often frightening documentary. As the spokesman for the Moral Majority, Rev. Donald Wildmon discusses censorship in America. As a counterbalance, the filmmakers give equal time to New York stand-up comic Jimmy Tingle, who offers another view. From Mapplethorpe to Madonna, images that straddle the line between offensive and creative are entertainingly debated.
MPAA Rating: Not Rated.
Trivia: In November 1992 after a two-year court battle with Wildmon, the New Orleans Federal Appeals Court ruled in favor of the producers allowing them to use interview footage with the minister.

Credits
Producer/Director......................................Paul Yule
Co-Producer...................................Jonathan Stack
Directors of Photography/Lighting ....Mark Benjamin
....Robert Achs
....Luke Sacher
Editor ....John Street
Film Facts
Running Time ....68 minutes
Film...Color
Sound...Stereo

Dandy
(Pandora/Peter Sempel)

Critics Rating: Not Rated.
Genre: Drama
Plot: This is a low-budget, underground experimental film. Essentially it is a collection of abstract images and thoughts set to equally abstract music. The film is a very dark and brooding piece for the adventuresome and curious.
MPAA Rating: Not Rated.
Cast
With Blixa Bargeld, Nick Cave, Nina Hagen, Imke Lagemann, Lene Lovich, Dieter Meier, Kazuo Ohno, Yoshito Ohno and Rattenjenny.
Credits
Producers..Niko Brucher
....Pandora-film
....Peter Sempel
Director...Peter Sempel
Directors of Photography...................Frank Blasberg
....Jonas Scholz
....Norimichi Kasamatsu
....Peter Sempel
Sound ....Drago Hari
....Takashi Endo
....Kai Wessel, Susanne Greuner
....Stefanie Hesse, Roxana Herbst
Editor ....Wolf Ingo Romer
Film Facts
Country of Origin...Germany
Running Time ....89 minutes
Film ....Color/Black & White
Sound ....Stereo
Location ....Berlin; Cairo; London;
....Marrakech; the Himalayas

Danzon

(Sony Pictures Classics)

Critics Rating: ★★★★

Genre: Drama—This film is a purposely slow but enjoyable tale of one woman's unexpected adventure.

Plot: Maria Rojo stars as Julia, a telephone operator by day and a ballroom dancer by night. When Carmello (Daniel Rergis), her dance partner of many years, suddenly disappears, she leaves her job and her daughter behind and goes in search of the man. Her journey turns into a soul-searching odyssey that finds this simple woman encountering a group of very lively and memorable characters who help her find herself, as well as her friend.

MPAA Rating: PG-13

Cast

Julia	Maria Rojo
Dona Ti	Carmen Salinas
La Colorada	Blanca Guerra
Susy	Tito Vasconcelos
Ruben	Victor Vascancelos
Silvia	Margarita Isabel

Credits

Executive Producer	Dulce Kuri
Producer	Jorge Sanchez
Director	Maria Novaro
Director of Photography	Rodrigo Garcia
Sound	Nerio Barberis
Editors	Nelson Rodriguez
	Maria Novaro
Art Direction	Marisa Pecanins
	Norberto Sanchez
Written by	Beatriz Novaro
	Maria Novaro

Film Facts

Country of Origin	Mexico
Language	Spanish (subtitled)
Running Time	103 minutes
Film	Color
Sound	Stereo

Dark Horse

(Republic Pictures/Live Entertainment)

Critics Rating: Not Rated.

Genre: Drama

Plot: Ari Meyers plays Allison, a 14-year-old girl who has just moved to a small town with her father following the death of her mother. Rebellious and troublesome, she soon finds herself packed off to a horse ranch to work out her problems. The owner of the ranch (Mimi Rogers) provides a positive role model for Allison, and a romantic interest for dad (Ed Begley, Jr.). Just when things begin to look up, an auto accident leaves Allison crippled.

MPAA Rating: PG

Cast

Jack Mills	Ed Begley, Jr.
Dr. Susan Hadley	Mimi Rogers
Curtis	Samantha Eggar
Allison Mills	Ari Meyers
Perkins	Tab Hunter

Also with Bojesse Christopher and Donovan Leitch.

Credits

Executive Producers	Larry Sugar
	Peter McIntosh
	Richard Gladstein
Producer	Alan Glaser
Co-Producer	Bonnie Sugar
Associate Producer	Michael Alden
Director	David Hemmings
Assistant Director	Tony Adler
Director of Photography	Steve Yaconelli
Sound	Mary Jo Devenney
Editor	Marjorie O'Connell
Art Direction	Prudence Hemmings
	Bernard Hyde
Costume Design	Dona Granata
Screenplay	J. E. Maslin
Story by	Tab Hunter
Music	Roger Bellon

Film Facts

Running Time	90 minutes
Film	Color
Sound	Ultra-Stereo

Daughters Of The Dust

(Kino International)

Critics Rating: ★★★

Genre: Drama—African-American producer,

director and screenwriter Julie Dash brings to the screen a sensitive and moving drama about the Gullah people living on one of the offshore islands of South Carolina at the turn of the century.

Plot: By focusing on the extended Peazant family, Dash explores the conflicts that occur when some of its members want to move north for jobs. Many of the family members, however, are intent on remaining true to their heritage.

MPAA Rating: Not Rated.

Trivia: This is the first feature to be directed by an African-American woman since Kathleen Collins Prettyman directed three features in 1979.

Cast

Nana Peazant	Cora Lee Day
Eula Peazant	Alva Rodgers
Eli Peazant	Adisa Anderson
Jaagar	Kaycee Moore
Mellow Mary	Barbara O
Myown	Eartha D. Robinson
Iona	Bahni Turpin
Viola	Cheryl Lynn Bruce
Mr. Snead	Tommy Hicks

Also with Umar Abdurrahman, Malik Farrakhan, Rev. Ervin Green, Vertamae Grosvenor, Sherry Jackson and Cornell (Kofi) Royal.

Credits

Executive Producer	Lindsay Law
Producer/Director	Julie Dash
Line Producer	Steven Jones
Assistant Directors	C. C. Barnes
	Nandi Bowe
Director of Photography	A. Jafa Fielder
Sound	Veda Campbell
Editors	Amy Carey
	Joseph Burton
Production Design	Kerry Marshall
Art Direction	Michael Kelly Williams
Costume Design	Arline Burks
Casting	Len Hunt
Written by	Julie Dash
Music	John Barnes

Film Facts

Running Time	114 minutes
Film	DuArt Color
Sound	Stereo
Location	South Carolina; Georgia

A Day In October
(En Dag I Oktober)
(Castle Hill)

Critics Rating: ★★

Genre: Drama—A stirring and memorable account of the 1943 Danish resistance movement and the rescue of Danish Jews from Denmark during the German occupation.

Plot: Sweeney stars as a resistance fighter who is wounded during a mission and taken in by a Jewish family. The father (Benzali) of the household is a bookkeeper who does not want to get involved. The family is soon left without a choice and reluctantly joins Sweeney in his fight, which eventually results in a successful evacuation of all Danish Jews to Sweden.

MPAA Rating: PG-13—For some violence.

Cast

Niels Jensen	D. B. Sweeney
Sara Kublitz	Kelly Wolf
Emma Kublitz	Tovah Feldshuh
Larsen	Ole Lemmeke
Arne	Kim Romer
Solomon Kublitz	Daniel Benzali
Kurt	Anders Peter Bro
Willy	Lars Oluf Larsen
Peter	Morten Suurballe
Paul	Jens Arentzen
Hansen	Arne Hansen

Credits

Executive Producer	Pernille Siesbye
Producers	Just Betzer
	Philippe Rivier
Associate Producer	Joan Borsten
Director	Kenneth Madsen
Assistant Director	Eric Heffron
Director of Photography	Henning Kristiansen
Sound	Stig Sparre-Ulrich
Editor	Nicolas Gaster
Production Design	Sven Wichmann
Set Decoration	Torben Baekmark Pedersen
Costume Design	Lotte Dandanell
Casting (Copenhagen)	Marie Louise Hedegaard
Screenplay	Damian F. Slattery
Music	Jens Lysdal
	Adam Gorgoni

Film Facts

Country of Origin	Denmark
Running Time	97 minutes
Film	Color
Sound	Stereo
Location	Denmark

Deadly Currents
(Alliance)

Critics Rating: ★★★
Genre: Documentary
Plot: Filmmaker Simcha Jacobovici takes a sobering and impartial up-close look at the Israeli-Palestinian conflict, which has raged for thousands of years. To understand the historical and current-day context, Jacobovici interviews the real people involved for a very personal glimpse into the logic and emotions held on both sides. While brutal, disturbing and often difficult to watch, the film is powerful and memorable.
MPAA Rating: Not Rated.

Credits

Executive Producers	David Green
	Jeff Sackman
	Robert Topol
Producers	Simcha Jacobovici
	Elliott Halpern
	Ric Esther Bienstock
Director	Simcha Jacobovici
Director of Photography	Mark Mackay
Sound	Chaim Gilud
Editor	Steve Weslak
Music	Stephen Price

Film Facts

Country of Origin	Canada
Language	Hebrew/Arabic
	(English subtitles/voiceover)
Running Time	115 minutes
Film	Color/Black & White
Sound	Stereo

Death Becomes Her
(Universal)

Critics Rating: ★★★

Genre: Comedy—Special-effects buffs will be the most impressed by this bizarre, dark comedy by director Robert Zemeckis (*Back To The Future*).
Tag Line: "In one small bottle...The fountain of youth. The secret of eternal life. The power of an ancient potion. Sometimes it works...sometimes it doesn't. Your basic black comedy."
Plot: Meryl Streep plays Madeline, a self-centered actress. Goldie Hawn plays Helen, an author. Both women are in competition for the same man. Ernest, a very eligible plastic surgeon, played by Bruce Willis, is the object of their desire. Madeline wins the prize, but the competition doesn't end there. Years later, the bitter rivals are again in competition, only this time they are in search of eternal youth. Isabella Rosellini helps here as Lisle, the sorceress with the magic potion.
MPAA Rating: PG-13
This is a dark and sophisticated film that pushes the limits of state-of-the-art special effects. Clever and witty, the characterizations and humor are meant for an equally sophisticated audience.
Trivia: The filmmakers cut the original happy ending. It had the Willis character escaping both Streep and Hawn by running off to Europe with Tracy Ullman. Also, film buffs may note that director Sydney Pollack makes an uncredited cameo appearance as a Beverly Hills doctor.

Cast

Madeline Ashton	Meryl Streep
Ernest Menville	Bruce Willis
Helen Sharp	Goldie Hawn
Lisle	Isabella Rossellini
Chagall	Ian Ogilvy
Dakota	Adam Storke

Also with Nancy Fish, William Frankfather, Alaina Reed Hall, John Ingle, Michelle Johnson and Mary Ellen Trainor.

Credits

Producers	Robert Zemeckis
	Steve Starkey
Co-Producer	Joan Bradshaw
Director	Robert Zemeckis
Assistant Director	Marty Ewing
2nd Unit Directors	Max Kleven
	Ken Ralston
Director of Photography	Dean Cundey

2nd Unit Camera ....Don Burgess
Sound...William B. Kaplan
Editor...Arthur Schmidt
Production Design.....................................Rick Carter
Art Direction ....Jim Teegarden
Set Design..Lauren Polizzi
....Elizabeth Lapp
....Masaka Masuda, John Berger
Set Decoration ....Jackie Carr
Costume Design ....Joanna Johnston
Casting ....Karen Rea
Written by..Martin Donovan
....David Koepp
Music ....Alan Silvestri
Special Visual Effects by ....Industrial Light & Magic
Visual Effects Supervisor ....Ken Ralston
Makeup Design ....Dick Smith
Prosthetics Makeup Supervisor..............Kevin Haney
Special Body Effects Design/Creation ......Alec Gillis
....Tom Woodruff, Jr.

Film Facts
Running Time ....103 minutes
Soundtrack ....Varese Sarabande
Film ....Deluxe Color
Sound ....Dolby Stereo
Location ....Los Angeles, CA

Deep Cover
(New Line Cinema)

Critics Rating: ★★★
Genre: Drama—An anti-drug drama, this is an emotionally wrenching film that follows an undercover agent who goes in so far that he nearly gets lost.
Tag Line: "He'd be the perfect criminal if he wasn't the perfect cop."
Plot: Larry Fishburne (*Boyz N The Hood*) stars as John Huff, a very straight Cincinnati police officer. Because of his reputation he is reassigned to an undercover operation in Los Angeles. His goal is to infiltrate the number-one drug dealer on the West Coast. As he descends into this underworld, he comes face-to-face with his own demons in this terrifying and realistic modern-day tale.
MPAA Rating: R—For violence, language, drug use and sensuality.

Cast
Russell Stevens, Jr./John Q. Hull ......Larry Fishburne
David Jason ....Jeff Goldblum
Felix Barbosa ....Gregory Sierra
Ken Taft..Clarence Williams III
Jerry Carver.............................Charles Martin Smith
Betty McCutcheon ....Victoria Dillard
Gopher ....Sydney Lassick
Hernandez ....Julio Oscar Mechoso
Eddie...Roger Guenveur Smith
Hector Guzman...Rene Assa
Molto ....Alex Colon
Also with Sandra Gould, Kamala Lopez, Arthur Mendoza, James T. Morris and Glynn Turman.

Credits
Executive Producer ....David Streit
Co-Executive Producer...................Michael De Luca
Producers.........................Pierre David, Henry Bean
Co-Producer ....Deborah Moore
Director...Bill Duke
Assistant Directors..Jerry Ziesmer
....Hope Goodwin
2nd Unit Director ....Conrad Palmisano
Director of Photography ....Bojan Bazelli
2nd Unit Camera................................Frank Holgate
Sound ....Tony Smyles
Editor ....John Carter
Production Design ....Pam Warner
Art Direction ....Daniel W. Bickel
Set Decoration ....Donald Elmblad
Costume Design.............................Arline Burks-Gant
Casting..Chemin Bernard
Screenplay ....Michael Tolkin, Henry Bean
Story by.......................................Michael Tolkin
Music Supervisors ....Sharon Boyle
....Jorge Hinojosa
Music...Michel Colombier

Film Facts
Running Time ....112 minutes
Soundtrack ....Solar/Epic Records
Film ....Deluxe Color
Sound ....Dolby Stereo

Delicatessen
(Miramax)

Critics Rating: ★★★★
Genre: Comedy—In an interview, codirectors Jean-

Pierre Jeunet and Marc Caro explained that their early influences were comic books rather than literature. That influence becomes obvious after viewing the comical and bizarre characters that make up this slapstick comedy about cannibalism.

Tag Line: "A futuristic comic feast."

Plot: The zany goings-on take place in an apartment building above a butcher's shop. The butcher is a resourceful man who substitutes people when he is short on farm animals. Adding to the ghoulish enjoyment of this film are the tenants living upstairs, who are so unusual that they make the butcher seem normal in this bizarre farce.

MPAA Rating: R—For violence.

Cast

Louison	Dominique Pinon
Julie Clapet	Marie-Laure Dougnac
Butcher	Jean-Claude Dreyfus
Robert	Rufus
Mr. Tapioca	Ticky Holgado
Mrs. Tapioca	Anne-Marie Pisani
Miss Plusse	Karin Viard

Also with Silvie Laguna, Chick Ortega, Jean-Francois Perrier and Dominique Zardi.

Credits

Producer	Claudie Ossard
Directors	Jean-Pierre Jeunet
	Marc Caro
Assistant Director	Jean-Marc Tostivint
Director of Photography	Darius Khondji
Sound	Jerome Thiault
Editor	Herve Schneid
Production Manager	Michele Arnould
Production Design	Jean-Philippe Carp
	Kreka Kjnakovic
Costume Design	Valerie Pozzo Di Borgo
Casting	Pierre-Jacques Benichon
Screenplay	Jean-Pierre Jeunet
	Marc Caro
	Gilles Adrien
Music	Carlos D'Alessio

Film Facts

Country of Origin	France
Running Time	96 minutes
Film	Color
Sound	Dolby Stereo

Desire & Hell At Sunset Motel
(Two Moon)

Critics Rating: Not Rated.

Genre: Thriller—Jealousy and betrayal are the guests at this hotel in a classy send-up of the period thriller genre.

Tag Line: "I want to be missed. I want to be mourned. I want to be wanted dead or alive. A sexy, comedy noir."

Plot: Set in Anaheim, California, in the late 1950s, Sherilyn Fenn stars as Bridey, the wife of a salesman, and her jealous husband, Chester DeSoto (Whip Hubley). Chester has hired an investigator to keep an eye on his wife who, as it turns out, happens to be sleeping with the man who is blackmailing her husband. These quirky characters coming together in one small but stylized hotel keep the twists and turns coming from start to finish.

MPAA Rating: PG-13

Cast

Bridey DeSoto	Sherilyn Fenn
Chester DeSoto	Whip Hubley
Deadpan Winchester	David Hewlett
Auggie March	David Johansen
Mr. Perry	Paul Bartel

Credits

Executive Producers	Pierre David
	Glenn Greene
	David Bixler
Producer	Donald P. Borchers
Associate Producer	Linda Francis
Director	Alien Castle
Assistant Director	Kris Krengel
Director of Photography	Jamie Thompson
Sound	Peter Devlin
Editor	James Gavin Bedford
Production Design	Michael Clausen
Set Decoration	Jacquelyn Lemmon
Costume Design	Betty Pecha Madden
Written by	Alien Castle
Music	Alien Castle
	Doug Walter

Film Facts

Running Time ....90 minutes
Film..CFI Color
Sound ....Stereo

Diary For My Loves

(Naplo Szerelmeimnek)

(Jasmine Tea Films, Inc.)

Critics Rating: Not Rated.
Genre: Drama—*Diary* is Hungarian director Marta Meszaros' semiautobiographical drama about a young woman's coming of age during Stalin's rule in Russia.
Plot: Zsuzsa Czinkoczi stars as Juli, a Hungarian girl who is unable to enter film school in her own country. Moving to Moscow, she finds acceptance in a program there. Interestingly enough, this makes it possible for her to eventually produce an anti-Soviet film.
MPAA Rating: Not Rated.

Cast

Juli ....Zsuzsa Czinkoczi
Magda ....Anna Polony
Janos/Father ....Jan Nowicki
Natasha..Adel Kovats
Anna Pavlovna............................Irina Kuberskaya
Erzsi ....Erzsi Kutvolgyi
Grandmother ....Mari Szemes
Grandfather.................................Pal Zolnay

Credits

Director ....Marta Meszaros
Director of Photography ....Miklos Jancso, Jr.
Sound...Istvan Sipos
Editor ....Eva Karmento
Production Design ....Eva Martin
Costume Design...............................Fanni Kemenes
Screenplay...................................Marta Meszaros
....Eva Pataki
Music...Zsolt Dome

Film Facts

Country of Origin ....Hungary
Language ....Hungarian (subtitled)
Running Time ....135 minutes
Film ....Eastmancolor/Black & White
Sound ....Stereo

Diary Of A Hitman

(Vision International)

Critics Rating: ★★★
Genre: Drama—Based on the play "Insider's Price" by Kenneth Pressman, Hitman is a fascinating psychological drama about a reluctant career killer.
Tag Line: "Nothing personal, purely business."
Plot: When hired hit man Dekker (Forest Whitaker, *Good Morning, Vietnam*) begins to have doubts about his career, he goes against his professional code by getting to know his next intended victim (Sherilyn Fenn, *Wild At Heart*). Hired by the intended victim's husband, Dekker discovers that the woman he is supposed to kill may just be his salvation.
MPAA Rating: R

Cast

Dekker...Forest Whitaker
Jain...Sherilyn Fenn
Kiki ....Sharon Stone
Shandy ....James Belushi
Sheila...Lois Chiles
Zidzyk..Lewis Smith
Koenig..Seymour Cassel
Also with John Bedford Lloyd.

Credits

Executive Producer ....Mark Damon
Producer..Amin Q. Chaudhri
Line Producer......................................Tim Healey
Associate Producers....................Karen Montgomery
....Robert Holof
Director..Roy London
Director of Photography ....Yuri Sokol
Sound ....Steve Rogers
Editor..Brian Smedley-Aston
Production Design....................Stephen Hendrickson
Art Direction ....Rusty Smith
Costume Design.........................Calista Hendrickson
Written by ....Kenneth Pressman
Based on the play "Insider's Price"
  by..Kenneth Pressman
Music...Michel Colombier

Film Facts

Running Time ....91 minutes

Film ....Color
Sound ....Dolby Stereo
Location ....Pittsburgh; Sharon, Pennsylvania;
...................................Youngstown, Ohio
Other Working Titles ....*Hit Man*

Diggstown
(MGM)

Critics Rating: ★★★
Genre: Action
Plot: James Woods stars as Gabriel Caine, a con and a hustler whose latest gig is in the slammer. On the day he is released, he heads for Diggstown to settle up on an old debt. It seems that a dirty dealing politico (Bruce Dern) has illegally and unfairly won most of the property in town, and Caine plans to win it back. With the help of Louis Gossett, Jr. and a few other friends, he stages a boxing match. However, the action doesn't stop there and neither do the surprises. All this leads up to the grand finale of surprises.
MPAA Rating: R—For language.
Cast
Gabriel Caine..................................James Woods
"Honey" Roy Palmer....................Louis Gossett, Jr.
John Gillon.....................................Bruce Dern
Fitz ....Oliver Platt
Emily Forrester ....Heather Graham
Robby Gillon.....................Thomas Wilson Brown
Wolf Forrester ....Randall (Tex) Cobb
Hambone Busby...............................Duane Davis
Hammerhead Hagan ....Willie Green
Victor Corsini..............................Orestes Matacena
Credits
Producer..Robert Schaffel
Co-Producer...........................Youssef Vahabzadeh
Line Producer ....Art Schaefer
Associate Producers ....Sharon Roesler
....Steven McKay
Director ....Michael Ritchie
Assistant Director..............................Tom Mack
Director of Photography.....................Gerry Fisher
Sound...................................Kim Harris Ornitz
Editor..Don Zimmerman
Production Design.......................Steve Hendrickson
Art Direction ....Okowita

Set Design.................................Gregory Van Horn
....Michael Devine
Set Decoration...............................Barbara Drake
Costume Design ....Wayne A. Finkelman
Casting..Rick Pagano
....Sharon Bialy
....Debi Manwiller
Screenplay...................................Steven McKay
Based on the Novel *The Diggstown
    Ringers* by ....Leonard Wise
Music......................................James Newton Howard
Fight Coordinators.......................James Nickerson
....Bobby Bass
Film Facts
Running Time ....97 minutes
Soundtrack ....Varese Sarabande
Film ....Deluxe Color
Sound ....Dolby Stereo
Location.............................Sacramento, California;
....Los Angeles; Montana
Other Working Titles..................*Diggstown Ringers*

The Distinguished Gentleman
(Buena Vista)

Critics Rating: ★★★
Genre: Comedy—Director Jonathan Lynn (*Clue, Nuns On The Run, My Cousin Vinny*) exposes both the cynicism and the satire of the congressional hucksters and hustlers of Washington, D.C., in light-hearted fashion. Murphy shines as he wise-cracks, impersonates and charms his way to the top.
Tag Line: "From con man to congressman."
Plot: Murphy stars as Thomas Jefferson Johnson, a small-time Florida con man who decides to go big-time. In a plausible scheme, he runs for Congress on name recognition alone and, in a surprise upset, wins the election. Arriving in Washington, Thomas is prepared to out hustle the hustlers. The money begins to pile up fast but, as luck would have it, a beautiful young woman (Rowell) with a social conscience comes along and spoils it all. Having to choose between love and money, Thomas turns the tables on Congress using his own sting and exposes the corruption in a very humorous and sentimental climax.

MPAA Rating: R—For language and a scene of sexuality.

Trivia: The screenplay was written by Walter Mondale's former speech writer Marty Kaplan. The film is also the first film ever to premiere worldwide in over 50 nations concurrently.

Cast

Thomas Jefferson Johnson	Eddie Murphy
Dick Dodge	Lane Smith
Miss Loretta	Sheryl Lee Ralph
Olaf Anderson	Joe Don Baker
Celia Kirby	Victoria Rowell
Arthur Reinhardt	Grant Shaud
Terry Corrigan	Kevin McCarthy
Elijah Hawkins	Charles S. Dutton
Jeff Johnson	James Garner
Armando	Victor Rivers
Homer	Chi
Van Dyke	Sonny Jim Gaines
Zeke Bridges	Noble Willingham
Iowa	Gary Frank

Credits

Executive Producer	Marty Kaplan
Producers	Leonard Goldberg
	Michael Peyser
Director	Jonathan Lynn
Assistant Director	Frank Capra III
Director of Photography	Gabriel Beristain
Sound	Russell Williams II
Editors	Tony Lombardo
	Barry B. Leirer
Production Design	Leslie Dilley
Art Direction	Ed Verreaux
Set Decoration	Doree Cooper
Costume Design	Francine Jamison-Tanchuck
Casting	Mary Goldberg
Screenplay	Marty Kaplan
Story by	Marty Kaplan
	Jonathan Reynolds
Music	Randy Edelman

Film Facts

Running Time	113 minutes
Soundtrack	Varese Sarabande
Film	Technicolor
Sound	Dolby Stereo
Location	Washington, D.C.; Los Angeles; Harrisburg, Pennsylvania; Baltimore

Dolly Dearest
(Trimark)

Critics Rating: Not Rated.

Genre: Horror—Like the devil doll, Chucky, in *Child's Play*, Dolly is a doll animated by supernatural spirits with evil intentions. This low-budget horror film received limited release in the Midwest in January before rushing to video.

Plot: In this familiar but nevertheless frightening tale, the Reed family has moved to Mexico to open a doll factory. An archeological team nearby has released an unfriendly spirit that makes its way into daughter Jessica's Dolly. The girl is also possessed by the spirit, and together they wreak havoc on all around, leading up to a horrific climax.

MPAA Rating: R—For horror violence.

Cast

Marilyn Reed	Denise Crosby
Eliot Reed	Sam Bottoms
Dr. Karl Resnick	Rip Torn
Jimmy Reed	Chris Demetral
Dolly double	Ed Gale
Luis	Will Gotay
Jessica Reed	Candy Hutson
Alva	Alma Martinez
Camilla	Lupe Ontiveros
Estrella	Enrique Renaldo

Credits

Executive Producer	Pierre David
Producer	Daniel Cady
Associate Producers	Channon Scott
	Rod Nave, Paul Aguilar
Director	Maria Lease
Assistant Director	Larry Litton
Director of Photography	Eric D. Andersen
Sound	Paul Coogan
Editor	Geoffrey Rowland
Production Design	W. Brooke Wheeler
Costume Design	Scott Tomlinson
Casting	Billy Da Mota
Screenplay	Maria Lease
Story by	Maria Lease
	Peter Sutcliffe
	Rod Nave
Music	Mark Snow
Dolly & Special Makeup Effects	Michael Burnett Prods.

Special Visual Effects Supv.	Alan G. Markowitz
Special Dolly Visual Effects	Prime Filmworks, Inc.
Stunt Coordinator	Cole McKay

Film Facts

Running Time	93 minutes
Film	CFI Color
Sound	Ultra-Stereo

Double Edge

(Castle Hill)

Critics Rating: ★★

Genre: Drama

Tag Line: "An American journalist confronts the issues facing Palestinians and Israelis."

Plot: Faye Dunaway stars as Faye Milano, a reporter for a New York newspaper, who gets a three-week assignment in Israel. A writer named David (director Amos Kollek) helps her gain access to top officials and insiders, to get revealing and realistic interviews. In the end, however, her pro-Palestinian slant gets her into trouble with both sides. The film ends with a dramatic and all too real confrontation between Faye and a group of angry Arabs.

MPAA Rating: PG-13—For a scene of violence.

Cast

Faye Milano	Faye Dunaway
David	Amos Kollek
Mustafa Shafik	Mohammad Bakri
Ahmed Shafik	Makram Khouri
Max	Michael Schneider
Moshe	Shmuel Shiloh
Censor	Anat Atzmon
Sarah	Ann Belkin

Also with Naomi Altaraz, Hanan Ashrawi, Abba Eban, Meir Kahane, Teddy Kolek and Ziad Abu Za'Yad.

Credits

Executive Producer	Michael Steinhardt
Producers	Amos Kollek
	Rafi Reifenbach
Director	Amos Kollek
Assistant Director	Udi Yerushalmi
Director of Photography	Amnon Salomon
Editors	David Tour
	Vicki Hiatt

Set Design	Zvika Aloni
Costume Design	Rakefet Levy
	Bernardine Morgan
Written by	Amos Kollek
Music	Mira J. Spektor

Film Facts

Country of Origin	United States/Israel
Running Time	86 minutes
Film	Color
Sound	Stereo

Double Threat

(Pyramid)

Critics Rating: Not Rated.

Genre: Thriller—A low-budget, melodramatic movie within a movie erotic thriller.

Plot: Sally Kirkland stars as Monica Martel, an aging actress on the come-back trail. Her producer and ex-husband (Franciosa) insists that she do a nude scene to generate publicity. When she refuses, a body double (Rose) is hired to do the sex scenes. But there's trouble on the set when Monica's lover and leading man (Stevens) falls for the body double. At this point the stage is set for behind-the-scenes humor, plot twists and an above-average finale. Performances and script are first-rate.

MPAA Rating: R

Cast

Monica Martel	Sally Kirkland
Eric Cline	Andrew Stevens
Lisa Shane	Sherri Rose
Crocker Scott	Anthony Franciosa
Stephen Ross	Chick Vennera
Coleman	Gary Swanson
Fenich	Richard Lynch
Tawny	Monique Detraz
Mugger	Ted Prior

Credits

Executive Producer	David Winters
Producer	Kimberley Casey
Associate Producer	Robert Willoughby
Director	David A. Prior
Assistant Director	Teddie Rae
Director of Photography	Gerald B. Wolfe
Sound	Sean Velour
Editor	Tony Malanowski

Production Manager ....Todd King
Art Direction ....Linda Lewis
Costume Design ....Valerie Finkel
Casting ....Jacov Bresler
Screenplay ....David A. Prior
Music ....Christopher Farrell
Stunt Coordinator ....Bob Ivy

Film Facts
Running Time ....96 minutes
Film ....Image Transform Color
Sound ....Stereo
Location....................Los Angeles; Mobile, Alabama

Double Trouble
(Motion Picture Corporation of America)

Critics Rating: Not Rated.
Genre: Comedy—Brothers David and Peter Paul (The Barbarians) star in this comic-action, buddy pic.
Plot: As dueling twins, David is a cop and Peter is a jewel thief. Teamed together to solve an international smuggling case, suffice it to say that they are no competition to Schwarzenegger and DeVito. While there are humorous moments in this film, the complicated plot is uneven and often difficult to follow. Fans of the Barbarian Brothers and audiences interested in the offbeat will provide an audience for this film.
MPAA Rating: R

Cast
Peter ....Peter Paul
David...David Paul
Mr. C ....David Carradine
Philip Chamberlain ....Roddy McDowall
Leonard Stewart ....Troy Donahue
O'Brien...James Doohan
Kent ....Steve Kanaly
Danitra ....A. J. Johnson
Bob ....Bill Mumy

Credits
Producers..Brad Krevoy
....Steve Stabler
Co-Producers ....Chad Oman
....Randy Pope
....David Tausik
Director..John Paragon

Assistant Director....................................Randy Pope
Director of Photography ....Richard Michalak
Sound...Jack Bornhoff
Editor ....Jonas Thaler
Production Design............................Johan Letenoux
....Gilbert Mercier
Set Decoration............................Marisol Jimenez
Casting ....Jan McGill
Written by...Jeffrey Kerns
....Kurt Wimmer
....Chuck Osborne
Story by ....Kurt Wimmer
....Chuck Osborne

Film Facts
Running Time ....90 minutes
Film ....Color
Sound ....Stereo

Dr. Giggles
(Universal)

Critics Rating: Not Rated.
Genre: Horror—A predictable, but entertaining bloodbath that goes for the laughs. The film arrived in theaters just before Halloween.
Tag Line: "If you're from Morrehigh and you get sick, fall on your knees and pray you die quick." "A new prescription for terror."
Plot: Larry Drake (*Darkman*) plays Evan Rendell, an escapee from an insane asylum who heads to his hometown, bent on revenge. It seems that as a young boy, he watched as his father was lynched by an angry mob of townspeople. His father was the town doctor who brutally murdered seven of his patients. Evan makes his father look like an amateur, however, as one by one he takes on most of the town, all leading up to a surprise ending.
MPAA Rating: R—For horror violence and gore, and language.
Cast
Dr. Evan Rendell....................................Larry Drake
Jennifer Campbell...................Holly Marie Combs
Tom Campbell ....Cliff De Young
Max Anderson....................................Glenn Quinn
Officer Joe Reitz ....Keith Diamond
Officer Hank Magruder...................Richard Bradford
Tamara..Michelle Johnson

Dr. Chamberlain ....John Vickery
Elaine Henderson ....Nancy Fish
Also with Denise Barnes, Doug E. Doug, Darin
Heames, Sara Melson, Zoe Trilling and Deborah
Tucker.

Credits
Executive Producer ....Jack Roe
Producer...Stuart M. Besser
Co-Producer ....Mike Richardson
Director..Manny Coto
Assistant Director ....Richard E. Espinoza
Director of Photography ....Robert Draper
Sound...Jim Stuebe
Editor...Debra Neil
Production Design ....Bill Malley
Art Direction ....Alan Locke
Costume Design...............................Sandy Culotta
Casting ....Karen Rea
Casting (Oregon) ....L & M Casting
Written by ....Manny Coto
....Graeme Whifler
Music ....Brian May
Special Makeup Effects ....
.................Kurtzman, Nicotero & Berger EFX Group
Special Effects ....Phil Cory Special EFX
Visual Effects............................Digital Fantasy, Inc.

Film Facts
Running Time ....95 minutes
Soundtrack...Victory Music
Film ....Deluxe Color
Sound ....Dolby Stereo

Dragon Inn
(Film Workshop)

Critics Rating: Not Rated.

Genre: Action—Martial-arts, historical epic about a
war between eunuchs and patriots during the Ming
dynasty.

Plot: Most of the action takes place at the Dragon
Inn, a place through which escapees from the
empire pass. Brigitte Lin plays Mo, a woman intent
on saving the children of a minister who was
murdered by the eunuchs. At the Inn, however, the
children are seized and sold by the proprietor, Jade
King (Maggie Cheung). When Mo's partner Chow
(Tony Leung) enters the picture, Jade feels

differently. In the end the three join forces to battle
the eunuchs.

MPAA Rating: Not Rated.

Cast
Jade King.......................................Maggie Cheung
Mo ....Brigitte Lin
Chow ....Tony Leung
Eunuch Tsao Yin...............................Donnie Yen
Also with Xiong Xin Xin, Lau Shun, Yem Yee
Kwan, Yuen Cheung Yan and Lawrence Ng Kai
Wah.

Credits
Producer...Tsui Hark
Line Producers...........................Cho King Man
....Ng Chi Ming
Director....................................Raymond Lee
Directors of Photography ....Lau Moon Tong
....Arthur Wong
Editor ....Poon Hung
Production Supervisor.......................Ching Siu Tung
Art Direction ....William Chang
....Mark Chiu
Set Design...............................Leung Chi Hing
....Chung Yee Fung
Screenplay.......................................Tsui Hark
....Carbon Cheung
....Xiao Wu
Music..Philip Chan
Martial-arts Directors ....Ching Siu tung
....Yuen Bun
Special Effects..........................Cinefex Workshop

Film Facts
Country of Origin................................Hong Kong
Language ....Cantonese (English/Chinese subtitles)
Running Time ....90 minutes
Film ....Color
Sound ....Stereo

Dream Deceivers
(First Run Features)

Critics Rating: Not Rated.

Genre: Documentary—Filmmaker David Van
Taylor's moving documentary takes a close look at
all involved in the deaths of two teenagers allegedly
resulting from the influence of heavy-metal band
"Judas Priest."

Plot: When two Reno, Nevada, teenagers attempt suicide after listening to the band's music, the parents sue the group. One of the boys dies immediately. The second boy survives, (only later to die in the hospital of an overdose of medication). The parents believe that subliminal messages caused the deaths of their sons. Interviews with the parents, members of the band, the surviving boy and others are a painful indictment of the lack of responsibility taken by all involved in this tragic situation.

MPAA Rating: Not Rated.

Credits

Producer/Director	David Van Taylor
Associate Director	Julie Gustafson
Editor	Mona Davis
Videographers	Julie Gustafson
	Darrell Manning

Film Facts

Running Time	60 minutes
Film	Color (16 mm)

Drive

(Megagiant Entertainment)

Critics Rating: Not Rated.

Genre: Drama—*Drive* is an independent and unusual black and white film that takes place while commuting to work.

Plot: David Warner and Steve Antin play two passengers in a car, who are on their way to work in Los Angeles. As they travel through the city, Warner does most of the talking, nonstop. Antin is suffering a recent breakup with a girlfriend and is mostly just along for the ride—like the audience.

MPAA Rating: Not Rated.

Cast

The driver	David Warner
The passenger	Steve Antin
The girl	Dedee Pfeiffer

Credits

Producers	Jefery Levy
	Gregory D. Levy
Director	Jefery Levy
Director of Photography	Steven Wacks
Sound	George Lockwood
Editor	Lauren Zuckerman
Production Design	Jefery Levy
Screenplay	Colin MacLeod
(in collaboration with)	Jefery Levy
Music	Charles H. Bisharat
	Dr. Lee

Film Facts

Running Time	86 minutes
Film	Black & White
Sound	Dolby Stereo/Mono
Location	Los Angeles

Echoes From A Somber Empire

(Echos Aus Einem Dusteren Reich)
(New Yorker)

Critics Rating: Not Rated.

Genre: Documentary

Plot: Director Werner Herzog investigates the rise and fall of Jean Bedel Bokassa, the former dictator of the Central African Republic. Seizing power in 1966 following a coup, Bokassa appoints himself president for life and later emperor. An egomaniac and an alleged cannibal, he is deposed in 1978. A death sentence is commuted to life in prison. His story is retold through interviews with family and friends.

MPAA Rating: Not Rated.

Cast

With Michael Goldsmith.

Credits

Executive Producer	Walter Saxer
Producers	Galeshka Moravioff
	Werner Herzog
Director	Werner Herzog
Directors of Photography	Jorg Schmidt-Reitwein
	Martin Manz
Sound	Harald Maury
Editors	Rainer Standke
	Thomas Balkenhohl

Film Facts

Country of Origin	Germany/France
Running Time	91 minutes
Film	Color
Sound	Stereo

Edward II

(Fine Line Features)

Critics Rating: ★★★

Genre: Drama—Director Derek Jarman brings to the screen a visually stylized and austere tale of a king brought down by his infatuation with a male lover. The story is based on Christopher Marlowe's Elizabethan tragedy and is staged in contemporary dress.

Plot: The plot centers around a revolt against England's openly homosexual monarch Edward II (Steven Waddington). Taking a male lover (Tiernan), the king rejects the affections of his queen (Swinton). Out of jealousy and revenge the queen enlists the aid of the palace guard Mortimer (Terry) in overthrowing the king and murdering his lover. The nobelmen and nobel women are equally outraged at the king's preferential treatment and love of a mere peasant and join the revolt, which turns into a civil war. The film climaxes with a humorous twist.

MPAA Rating: R—For strong violence and sexuality; and for some language. Includes full-frontal male nudity, simulated homosexual sex and gay kissing scenes.

Cast

King Edward II	Steven Waddington
Queen Isabella	Tilda Swinton
Mortimer	Nigel Terry
Gaveston	Andrew Tiernan
Lightborn	Kevin Collins
Kent	Jerome Flynn
Prince Edward	Jody Graber
Singer	Annie Lennox
Spencer	John Lynch
Bishop of Winchester	Dudley Sutton

Credits

Executive Producers	Sarah Radclyffe
	Simon Curtis
Producers	Steve Clark-Hall
	Antony Root
Director	Derek Jarman
Assistant Director	Cilla Ware
Director of Photography	Ian Wilson
Sound	George Richards
Editor	George Akers

Production Manager	Sarah Swords
Production Design	Christopher Hobbs
Screenplay	Derek Jarman
	Stephen McBride
	Ken Butler
Based on the play by	Christopher Marlowe
Music	Simon Fisher Turner

Film Facts

Country of Origin	Great Britain
Running Time	91 minutes
Film	Eastmancolor
Sound	Dolby Stereo

The Efficiency Expert

(Miramax)

Critics Rating: ★★★

Genre: Comedy—*The Efficiency Expert* is a warm-hearted and uplifting Australian comedy.

Tag Line: "He's about to teach big business that there's more to life than the bottom line."

Plot: Set in the mid-'60s, Anthony Hopkins stars as Errol, a consultant who earns his living putting people out of work in an effort to save large ailing businesses. When he takes on a job with a small family business located in the town of Spotswood, his old ways of doing business soon go out the window. For the first time, he sees the employees whose lives he affects as real people. And in the process of saving the company, he also finds romance.

MPAA Rating: PG

Cast

Errol Wallace	Anthony Hopkins
Carey	Ben Mendelsohn
Mr. Ball	Alwyn Kurts
Robert Spencer	Bruno Lawrence
Finn	John Walton
Wendy	Toni Collette
Kim Barrett	Russell Crowe
Gordon	John Flaus
Caroline Wallace	Angela Punch McGregor
Cheryl Ball	Rebecca Rigg
Ron	Jeff Truman
Frank Fletcher	Dan Wyllie

Credits

Producers	Richard Brennan, Timothy White
Director	Mark Joffe
Assistant Director	Euan Keddie
Director of Photography	Ellery Ryan
Sound	Lloyd Carrick
Editor	Nicholas Beauman
Production Manager	Bernadette O'Mahoney
Production Design	Chris Kennedy
Costume Design	Tess Schofield
Casting	Alison Barrett
Screenplay	Max Dann
	Andrew Knight
Music	Ricky Fataar

Film Facts

Country of Origin	Australia
Running Time	97 minutes
Film	Eastmancolor
Sound	Dolby Stereo
Other Titles	*Spotswood*

The Elementary School

(Obecna Skola)

(Filmexport Prague)

Critics Rating: Not Rated.

Genre: Comedy—Nominated for an Academy Award in 1991 for Best Foreign Language film, this is a nostalgic gem of a film.

Plot: Set in 1945, the action revolves around 10-year-old Eda (Vaclav Jakoubek), a rebellious young boy in a school for delinquents. When this group of boys drive their teacher out of the classroom, Igor Hnizdo (Jan Triska), an egotistical disciplinarian, takes her place. Despite his stern demeanor, the boys come to look up to and admire him.

MPAA Rating: Not Rated.

Cast

Eda	Vaclac Jakoubek
Tonda	Radoslav Budac
Igor Hnizdo	Jan Triska
Mr. Soucek	Zdenek Sverak
Mrs. Soucek	Lubuse Safrankova
Schoolmaster	Rudolf Hrusinsky
Miss Maxova	Daniela Kolarova
Tram driver's wife	Irena Pavlaskova
Tram driver	Oudrej Vetchy
Pliha	Boleslav Polivka
Fakir	Petr Cepek

Doctor ....Jiri Menzel
School inspector ....Karel Kachyna

Credits

Producer..Jaromir Lukas
Director..Jan Sverak
Director of Photography.......................F. A. Brabec
Sound ....Jiri Kriz
Editor ....Alois Fisarek
Production Design ....Vladimir Labsky
....Gabriela Kubenova
Costume Design................................Jan Kropacek
Written by ....Zdenek Sverak
Story by..Zdenek Sverak
Music ....Jiri Svoboda

Film Facts

Country of Origin............................Czechoslovakia
Running Time ....96 minutes
Film ....Color
Sound ....Stereo

Emma And Elvis

(Northern Arts Entertainment)

Critics Rating: Not Rated.

Genre: Drama—The title of this film refers to Emma Goldman and Elvis Costello, the heroes of the film's two lead characters The film itself is about the political activism of the 1960s in relationship to the activism of today.

Plot: Kathryn Walker plays Alice, a middle-aged documentary filmmaker in Dayton, Ohio, working on a film about the activism of the 1960s. Obsessed with her subject, she has been for years unable to complete this film. Enter Eddie (Jason Duchin), a 24-year-old video filmmaker and activist. Coming from different perspectives, they are at odds politically when they first meet but, before long, they bridge their own generation gap, and Alice is inspired to complete her film.

MPAA Rating: Not Rated.

Cast

Alice Winchek ....Kathryn Walker
Ben Winchek...Mark Blum
Croswell ....William Cain
Eddie..Jason Duchin
Findley ....Mike Hodge
Jenny..Margo Martindale

Harris ....Mark Mocahbee
Larry ....Jody O'Neil

Credits

Producers...Brenda Goodman
....Julia Reichert
Associate Producers ....Sallie Collins
...........................Steven Bognar, Stanley Plotnick
Director ....Julia Reichert
Assistant Director ....J. Miller Tobin
Director of Photography.....................Larry L. Banks
Sound ....Melanie Johnson
Editor ....Pamela Scott Arnold
Production Design...............................David Potts
Art Direction ....John McFarlane
Casting...Deborah Brown
Screenplay ....Steven Bognar
....Julia Reichert
....Martin M. Goldstein
Story by ....Steven Bognar
....Julia Reichert
Music ....Wendy Blackstone

Film Facts

Running Time ....105 minutes
Film ....Color
Sound ....Stereo

Enchanted April

(Miramax)

Critics Rating: ★★★★

Genre: Comedy—Similar in theme to this year's *Where Angels Fear To Tread, Enchanted April* is a comedy about four English women whose pent up emotions are released during a vacation in Italy.

Tag Line: "Imagine a month in paradise with nothing to do except everything you ever dreamed of."

Plot: When four very different English women (Richardson, Lawrence, Walker and Plowright) rent an Italian countryside estate for a vacation in 1922, they are each escaping their everyday lives and problems for different reasons. Before long, however, they get on each others' nerves. They also miss the men in their lives and invite them to visit. The men arrive, but things don't go quite as expected in this familiar but nonetheless entertaining comedy of manners.

MPAA Rating: PG
Cast
Rose Arbuthnot...........................Miranda Richardson
Lottie Wilkins ....Josie Lawrence
Lady Caroline Dester ....Polly Walker
Mrs. Fisher....................................Joan Plowright
Mellersh Wilkins ....Alfred Molina
George Briggs...............................Michael Kitchen
Frederick Arbuthnot ....Jim Broadbent
Credits
Executive Producers...........................Mark Shivas
....Simon Relph
Producer ....Ann Scott
Director ....Mike Newell
Director of Photography ....Rex Maidment
Sound ....John Pritchard
Editor ....Dick Allen
Production Design........................Malcolm Thornton
Costume Design ....Sheena Napier
Casting..Susie Figgis
Screenplay ....Peter Barnes
Based on the novel by ....Elizabeth von Arnim
Music.........................Richard Rodney Bennett
Film Facts
Country of Origin ....Great Britain
Running Time ....101 minutes
Film.......................................Color (16 mm)
Sound ....Dolby Stereo
Location................................London, England; Italy

The Enchantment
(Fuji TV)

Critics Rating: Not Rated.
Genre: Thriller—*The Enchantment* is a low-budget Japanese thriller that tells a familiar tale with drama and interest.
Plot: When a psychiatrist becomes involved with a psychotic and potentially homicidal patient, his life gets complicated. The psychiatrist, it seems, is also having an affair with his secretary. Out of jealousy, the secretary starts up a lesbian relationship with the psychiatrist's new patient. This is one love triangle that finds the women in control in the end.
MPAA Rating: Not Rated.
Cast
Miyako ....Kumiko Akiyoshi
Sotomura................................Masao Kusakari

Harumi ....Kiwako Harada
Credits
Producers ....Toshiro Kamata
....Kei Sasaki
Director ....Shunichi Nagasaki
Director of Photography...............Makato Watanabe
Screenplay...............................Goro Nakajima
Music.....................................Satosi Kadokura
Film Facts
Country of Origin ....Japan
Running Time ....109 minutes
Film..Color
Sound ....Stereo
Location.................................Tokyo, Japan

Encino Man
(Buena Vista)

Critics Rating: ★
Genre: Comedy—*Encino Man* is a predictably silly and lighthearted comedy that satirically depicts how easily a caveman fits in with today's teenagers.
Tag Line: "Where the Stone Age meets the Rock Age."
Plot: Sean Astin and MTV's Pauly Shore, star as modern-day high-school seniors, Dave and Stoney. While digging a swimming pool in the back yard, they uncover a caveman—uh, cave teen, whom they name Link (Brendan Fraser, *School Ties*). Once they've thawed him out and cleaned him up, they take him to school to show him off. The action is nonstop and so are the laughs, as Dave and Stoney contend with domesticating their new friend. It doesn't take long before Link becomes the most popular kid in school.
MPAA Rating: PG
Cast
Dave Morgan...........................Sean Astin
Link ....Brendan Fraser
Robyn Sweeney ....Megan Ward
Mrs. Morgan................................Mariette Hartley
Mr. Morgan..................................Richard Masur
Stoney Brown...............................Pauly Shore
Matt ....Michael DeLuise
Will..Dalton James
Ella ....Robin Tunney
Phil ....Patrick Van Horn

Credits

Executive Producer...............................Hilton Green
Co-Executive Producer.................Michael Rotenberg
Producer...George Zaloom
Director...Les Mayfield
Assistant Director.............................Jerry Ketcham
Director of Photography.............Robert Brinkmann
Sound..Robert Allan Wald
Editor ....Eric Sears
Additional Editing...........................Jonathan Siegel
Production Design..............................James Allen
Costume Design ....Marie France
Casting ....Kathleen Letterie
Screenplay ....Shawn Schepps
Story by..George Zaloom
....Shawn Schepps
Executive Music Producer.......................Ralph Sall
Original Score.................................J. Peter Robinson
Choreography ....Peggy Holmes

Film Facts

Running Time ....89 minutes
Soundtrack.............................Hollywood Records
Film..Technicolor
Sound...Dolby Stereo
Location ....Los Angeles

The End Of Old Times

(Konec Starych Casu)
(IFEX International)

Critics Rating: ★★★

Genre: Comedy—Director Jiri Menzel (winner of the 1966 Academy Award for Best Foreign Film, *Closely Watched Trains*), brings to the screen a nostalgic comedy that takes place in the post-World-War I era.

Plot: This is a simple story about a wealthy man named Josef Stoklasa, who is determined to obtain a country estate that belongs to the govern-ment. To gather support, he throws an elaborate party. When an unexpected guest arrives, however, the party turns into a comedy of errors, with Josef getting more than he bargained for.

MPAA Rating: Not Rated.

Cast

Prince Alexei Magalrogov ....Josef Abrham
Josef Stoklasa.......................................Marian Labuda
Bernard Spera ....Jaromir Hanzlik
Mr. Pustina ....Jan Hartl
Jan Lhota ....Jan Hrusinsky
Jakub Lhota ....Rudolf Hrusinsky
Michaela.......................................Barbara Leichnerova
Kotera...Jiri Adamira
Ellen...Alice Dvorakova
Suzanne ....Chantal Puollain-Polivkova

Credits

Producers..............................Barrandov Film Studios
....Czechoslovak Film
Director ....Jiri Menzel
Assistant Director ....Jan Prokop
Director of Photography ....Jaromir Sofr
Sound ....Karel Jaros
Editor ....Jiri Brozek
Art Direction ....Zybnek Hloch
Written by ....Jiri Menzel
....Jiri Blazek
Based on a novel by ....Ladislav Vancura
Music..Jiri Sust

Film Facts

Country of Origin ....Czechoslovakia
Language ....Czech (subtitled)
Running Time ....97 minutes
Film ....Color

Production Design.............................George Corsillo
Art Direction ....Todd Hatfield
Set Decoration..Sandi Cook
Costume Design.....................................Clark Foster
Written by..Larry McMurtry
Film Facts
Running Time ....100 minutes
Soundtrack ....Mercury Records
Film..Technicolor
Sound ....Dolby Stereo

Falling From Grace
(Columbia)

Critics Rating: ★★★

Genre: Drama—First time actor-director John Mellencamp makes an impressive debut in this drama that focuses on the big problems of a small town family.

Plot: Mellencamp stars as a country singer who returns with his wife (Mariel Hemingway) to his hometown. Rekindling a relationship with his former girlfriend (Kay Lenz), who is now his brother's wife, he adds fuel to the fire already smoldering in this small-town family, not to mention in his own marriage. True to life performances made this film one of the year's first big hits with the critics.

MPAA Rating: PG-13

Cast
Bud Parks ....John Mellencamp
Alice Parks ....Mariel Hemingway
Speck Parks..Claude Akins
Grandpa Parks ....Dub Taylor
P. J. Parks ....Kay Lenz
Ramey Parks..Larry Crane
Parker Parks...Brent Huff
Linda...Kate Noonan
Sally Cutler ....Deirdre O'Connell
Mitch Cutler..John Prine
Credits
Producer ....Harry Sandler
Associate Producer ....Richard Mellencamp
Director ....John Mellencamp
Assistant Director ....Michael Curtis
Director of Photography....................Victor Hammer
Sound ....Don Scales
Editor...Dennis Virkler

Far And Away
(Universal)

Critics Rating: ★★★

Genre: Adventure—Director Ron Howard's period epic is a stunningly beautiful old-fashioned, romantic adventure.

Plot: The film begins in Ireland in the 1890s. Tom Cruise stars as Joseph, a poor tenant farmer who dreams of one day farming his own land. Knowing that this will never happen in this class-locked society, he instead hooks up with a strong-willed and rich young woman (Nicole Kidman) and heads for America, where dreams can come true. Their very different personalities clash, but eventually they fall in love. Arriving in Boston, they discover that the streets aren't exactly paved with gold, but before long they earn enough to head for Oklahoma, toward the dream they now share together.

MPAA Rating: PG-13

Trivia: *Far And Away* is only the second such film since David Lean's *Ryan's Daughter* to be shot in super 70mm.

Cast
Joseph Donelly...Tom Cruise
Shannon Christie ....Nicole Kidman
Stephen ....Thomas Gibson
Daniel Christie ....Robert Prosky
Nora Christie ....Barbara Babcock
Danty Duff ....Cyril Cusack
Dermody ....Douglas Gillison
Grace...Michelle Johnson
Kelly..Colm Meaney
Molly Kay ....Eileen Pollock
Also with Wayne Grace, Clint Howard, Rance Howard, Barry McGovern and Niall Toibin.

Credits

Executive Producer	Todd Hallowell
Producers	Brian Grazer
	Ron Howard
Co-Producers	Larry DeWaay
	Bob Dolman
Associate Producer	Louisa Velis
Director	Ron Howard
Assistant Director	Aldric La'auli Porter
2nd Unit Director	Todd Hallowell
Director of Photography	Mikael Salomon
Sound	Ivan Sharrock
Editors	Michael Hill
	Daniel Hanley
Production Design (Montana)	Jack T. Collis
Production Design (Ireland)	Allan Cameron
Art Direction	Jack Senter
Art Direction (Ireland)	Steve Spence
	Tony Reading
Set Design	Joseph Hubbard
	Robert M. Beall
Set Decoration	Richard Goddard
Costume Design	Joanna Johnston
Casting	Karen Rea
	John Hubbard
	Ros Hubbard
Screenplay	Bob Dolman
Story by	Ron Howard
	Bob Dolman
Music	John Williams
"Book of Days" Performed by	Enya

Film Facts

Running Time	140 minutes
Soundtrack	MCA Records
Film	Deluxe Color
Sound	Dolby Stereo
Location	Billings, Montana; Ireland
Other Working Titles	*The Irish Story*

Father

(Northern Arts Entertainment)

Critics Rating: Not Rated.

Genre: Drama—This Australian film is similar in tone and story to the 1989 Costa-Gavras film *Music Box*.

Plot: Max von Sydow plays Joe Mueller, a German-born war survivor living in Melbourne. A widower, Mueller lives a quite life with his daughter, her husband and their two children. That is until one day they learn that Mueller is being accused of being a Nazi war criminal by a concentration-camp survivor (Julia Blake). All of their lives are turned upside down as Mueller must stand trial. After being acquitted, his guilt or innocence is left an uncertainty, and his life is changed forever.

MPAA Rating: Not Rated.

Cast

Joe Mueller	Max von Sydow
Anne Winton	Carol Drinkwater
Iya Zetnick	Julia Blake
Bobby Winton	Steve Jacobs
George Coleman	Tim Robertson

Credits

Executive Producer	Paul Douglas Barron
Producers	Damien Parer
	Tony Cavanaugh
	Graham Hartley
Director	John Power
Assistant Director	Stuart Wood
Director of Photography	Dan Burstall
Sound	Andrew Ramage
Editor	Kerry Regan
Production Manager	John Wild
Production Design	Phil Peters
Screenplay	Graham Hartley
	Tony Cavanaugh
Music	Peter Best

Film Facts

Country of Origin	Australia
Running Time	100 minutes
Film	Eastmancolor
Sound	Stereo

Fathers And Sons

(Pacific Pictures)

Critics Rating: ★★

Genre: Drama—About a troubled relationship between a father and son and their eventual reconciliation. Fine performances by all are the bright spot in this dark film.

Tag Line: "Worlds apart. A heartbeat away."

Plot: Jeff Goldblum plays Max Fish, a recovering alcoholic who is trying to put his life back together.

Leaving his fast-paced career, his Manhattan lifestyle and his troubles behind, he moves to a quiet New Jersey community and opens up a book store. His troubles are not so easily left behind, however. His wife dies shortly after the move and his teenage son Eddie (Cochrane) becomes more distant and troubled. Determined not to give up on himself or his son, Max stays the distance in this emotionally heavy family drama.

MPAA Rating: R—For sensuality, drug content, language and some violence.

Cast

Max Fish ....Jeff Goldblum
Eddie ....Rory Cochrane
Lisa ....Natasha Gregson Wagner
Smiley ....Mitchell Marchand
Doogy....................................Paul Hipp
Judy ....Ellen Greene
Kyle ....Franke Janssen
Also with Rocky Carroll and Rosanna Arquette.

Credits

Executive Producers ......Nick Wechsler, Keith Addis
Producer ....Jon Kilik
Associate Producer..........................David Pomier
Director ....Paul Mones
Director of Photography....................Ron Fortunato
Editor ....Janice Keuhnelian
Production Design............................Eve Cauley
Casting...............................Marcia Shulman
Screenplay....................................Paul Mones
Music ....Mason Daring

Film Facts

Running Time ....99 minutes
Soundtrack ....Columbia Records
Film ....Color
Sound...............................Dolby Stereo
Location ....New York City; Belmar, New Jersey;
..............................Asbury Park, New Jersey

The Favor, The Watch And The Very Big Fish
(Trimark)

Critics Rating: ★★★
Genre: Comedy—Quirky and comical, *Favor* is an unpredictable farce about a group of unlikely characters who cross paths at just the right moment.

Plot: Bob Hoskins (*Passed Away*) stars as Louis, a modern-day Parisian photographer who receives little respect from those around him. While doing a favor for a friend, he meets and falls for Sybil (Natasha Richardson). Sybil introduces him to her former boyfriend (Jeff Goldblum) who in turn does a favor for him. The loony antics continue from here, all adding up to a low-key but satisfying romp.

MPAA Rating: R

Cast

Louis Aubinard ....Bob Hoskins
Pianist ....Jeff Goldblum
Sybil.................................Natasha Richardson
Norbert ....Michel Blanc
Charles....................................Jacques Villeret
Elizabeth ....Angela Pleasance
Zalman....................................Jean-Pierre Cassel
Grandfather ....Samuel Chaimovitch

Credits

Executive Producer..Antoine de Cleremont-Tonnerre
Producer ....Michelle de Broca
Co-Producer....................................Simon Perry
Director....................................Ben Lewin
Assistant Director ....Eric Sliman
Director of Photography ....Bernard Zitzermann
Sound ....Edward Tise
Editor....................................John Grover
Production Design...................Carlos Conti
Costume Design ....Elizabeth Tavernier
Casting....................................Margot Capelier
Screenplay ....Ben Lewin
Adapted from the short story
  "Rue Saint-Sulpice" by ......Marcel Ayme
Music ....Vladimir Cosma
Special Effects ....Pierre Foury

Film Fact

Country of Origin ....France/Great Britain
Running Time ....89 minutes
Film ....Kodak Eastman Color
Sound...............................Dolby Stereo
Location...Paris

Feed
(Original Cinema)

Critics Rating: ★★★
Genre: Documentary—By the filmmakers of *Blood*

In The Face, Kevin Rafferty and James Ridgeway.

Plot: Focusing on the 1992 presidential campaign from a different perspective, the filmmakers have compiled off-air video of the candidates as they wait patiently and not-so-patiently to go on the air. With delays and technical problems to deal with, the candidates reactions are often humorous and revealing as they are caught unaware. Many of the supporters and detractors, from Hillary Clinton to Arnold Schwarzenegger, are also caught in the act.

MPAA Rating: Not Rated.

Credits

Producers/Directors ....Kevin Rafferty
....James Ridgeway
Directors of Photography ....James Ridgeway
....Jenny Darrow
Sound ....Charles Arnot, Wolfgang Held
Editors ....Sarah Durham, Kevin Rafferty
Satellite "backhaul" material
  provided by...Brian Springer

Film Facts

Running Time ....76 minutes
Film...DuArt Color
Sound ....Stereo

FernGully...The Last Rainforest

(20th Century Fox)

Critics Rating: ★★★

Genre: Animated—One of the many politically correct films of 1992, *FernGully* imaginatively combines animation and social consciousness in a humorous and entertaining film.

Plot: In this simple story a fairy named Crysta, living in the fictional rain forest of FernGully, discovers one day that humans are destroying her habitat. To teach them a lesson she shrinks one of the young men down to her size. Before long, he joins Crysta in her fight, and together, with an assortment of other forest creatures, they battle the humans to save the forest.

MPAA Rating: G

Cast

Voices:
Hexxus ....Tim Curry
Crysta ....Samantha Mathis
Pip ....Christian Slater
Batty Koda...Robin Williams
Magi Lune...Grace Zabriskie
Ralph ....Geoffrey Blake
Root ....Tommy Chong
Stump ....Cheech Marin
Tony ....Robert Pastorelli
The Goanna..Tone-Loc
Zak ....Jonathan Ward

Credits

Executive Producers..........Ted Field, Robert W. Cort
Co-Executive Producers ....Jeff Dowd
....William F. Willett
Producers.......................Wayne Young, Peter Faiman
Co-Producers ....Brian Rosen
....Jim Cox, Richard Harper
Line Producer ....Tom Klein
Director..Bill Kroyer
Editor..Gillian Hutshing
Animation Production ....Kroyer Films, Inc.
Coordinating Art Director ....Susan Kroyer
Art Direction (color stylist)..............Ralph Eggleston
Art Direction (layout design) ....Victoria Jenson
Casting ....Marci Liroff
Screenplay ....Jim Cox
Based on the stories of *FernGully*
  by ....Diana Young
Music Supervisors ....Tim Sexton, Becky Mancuso
Music ....Alan Silvestri
Creative Consultant ....Matthew Perry
Animation Production
  Consultant ....Charles Leland Richardson
Animation Director ....Tony Fucile
Special Effects Animation Director..........Sari Gennis

Film Facts

Running Time ....76 minutes
Soundtrack......................................MCA Records
Film ....Deluxe Color
Sound ....Dolby Stereo
Location................Los Angeles (principal animation)

A Few Good Men

(Columbia)

Critics Rating: ★★★★

Genre: Drama—Courtroom drama adapted by

playwright Aaron Sorkin from his 1989 Broadway play about a military murder and cover-up. Although briskly paced, entertaining and captivating, the film is most noteworthy for its spectacular performances by an all-star cast. Kevin Bacon deserves special mention for his strongest performance to date, as prosecuting attorney Capt. Jack Ross.

Plot: Tom Cruise stars as the cavalier, hot-shot Navy lawyer Lt. Kaffee, a young man living in the shadow of his father's reputation. Authorities counting on him to settle or lose the case have him assigned to defend the two young Marines (Marshall and Bodison) charged with the murder of a fellow Marine. Lt. Cdr. Joanne Galloway (Moore), provokes Kaffee to investigate and take the case seriously. When he discovers that the Marines are innocent, he is faced with a personal and moral dilemma of heroic proportions. In the end, like the biblical David, Kaffee takes on menacing Col. Jessep (Nicholson), the military's Goliath, and the climactic courtroom battle alone is worth the price of admission.

MPAA Rating: R—For language.

Cast

Lt. J. G. Daniel Kaffee	Tom Cruise
Col. Jessep	Jack Nicholson
Lt. Commander Joanne Galloway	Demi Moore
Lt. Sam Weinberg	Kevin Pollak
Lt. Jonathan James Kendrick	Kiefer Sutherland
Capt. Jack Ross	Kevin Bacon
Pfc. Louden Downey	James Marshall
Lt. Col. Markinson	J. T. Walsh
Lance Corp. Dawson	Wolfgang Bodison
Dr. Stone	Christopher Guest
Judge Randolph	J. A. Preston
Lt. Spradling	Matt Craven

Credits

Executive Producers	William S. Gilmore
	Rachel Pfeffer
Producers	Rob Reiner
	David Brown
	Andrew Scheinman
Co-Producers	Steve Nicolaides
	Jeffrey Stott
Director	Rob Reiner
Assistant Director	Frank Capra III
Director of Photography	Robert Richardson
2nd Unit Camera	Gary Kibbe
Sound	Bob Eber
Editor	Robert Leighton
Production Design	J. Michael Riva
Art Direction	Dave Klassen
Set Design	Virginia Randolph
	Rob Woodruff
Set Decoration	Michael Taylor
Costume Design	Gloria Gresham
Casting	Jane Jenkins
	Janet Hirshenson
Screenplay	Aaron Sorkin
Based on the play by	Aaron Sorkin
Music	Marc Shaiman

Film Facts

Running Time	138 minutes
Soundtrack	Columbia Records
Film	Color
Sound	Dolby Stereo
Location	Washington, D.C.; Los Angeles

Final Analysis
(Warner Bros.)

Critics Rating: ★★

Genre: Thriller—Hitchcock is alive and well in this suspenseful psychological thriller about a psychologist who becomes entangled in the deadly web of two equally psychotic sisters.

Plot: When San Francisco psychologist (Richard Gere) becomes involved with a patient's sister (Kim Basinger), he unwittingly becomes a pawn in their game of murder and deception. It isn't long before Basinger's gangster husband turns up dead and Gere finds that he is about to be framed for the murder. From this point on, the game begins to unravel at a rapid pace that will keep audiences on the edge of their seats, even as the film goes over the top a bit on its way to a melodramatic, but nonetheless satisfying climax.

MPAA Rating: R—For language, violence and a scene of strong sensuality.

Cast

Isaac Barr	Richard Gere
Heather Evans	Kim Basinger
Diana Baylor	Uma Thurman
Jimmy Evans	Eric Roberts

Det. Huggins ....Keith David
Mike O'Brien ....Paul Guilfoyle
Alan Lowenthal ....Robert Harper
Pepe Carrero...............................Agustin Rodriguez
D. A. Brakhage ....Harris Yulin
Credits
Executive Producers............................Richard Gere
....Maggie Wilde
Producers.......................................Charles Roven
....Paul Junger Witt
....Tony Thomas
Co-Producers ....John Solomon
....Ted Kurdyla
Associate Producer ....Kelley Smith
Director ....Phil Joanou
Assistant Director...........................Pat Kehoe
Director of Photography...............Jordan Cronenweth
Sound ....Lee Orloff
Editor ....Thom Noble
Production Design.........................Dean Tavoularis
Art Direction ....Angelo Graham
Set Decoration ....Bob Nelson
Costume Design....................Aude Bronson-Howard
Casting..David Rubin
Screenplay ....Wesley Strick
Story by ....Robert Berger
....Wesley Strick
Music...George Fenton
Special Visual Effects...............Dream Quest Images
Visual Effects Supervisor ....Hoyt Yeatman
Film Facts
Running Time ....124 minutes
Soundtrack ....Varese Sarabande
Film...Technicolor
Sound ....Dolby Stereo
Location ....Los Angeles; San Francisco

Final Impact
(PM Entertainment)

Critics Rating: Not Rated.
Genre: Action—*Final Impact* is a kickfighting film with frequent fights and a predictable story line.
Plot: Lorenzo Lamas stars as Nick, an ex-champion who now manages up-and-coming fighters. Out for revenge against the current champ, he agrees to manage Danny (Michael Worth) and use him to get his revenge.

MPAA Rating: R
Cast
Nick Taylor.....................................Lorenzo Lamas
Maggie ....Kathleen Kinmont
Jake ....Jeff Langton
Girl in bar ....Kathrin Lautner
Roxy ....Mimi Lesseos
Joe...Mike Toney
Danny ....Michael Worth
Credits
Producers...Richard Pepin
....Joseph Merhi
Directors..Joseph Merhi
....Stephen Smoke
Assistant Director ....Charla Driver
Director of Photography ....Richard Pepin
Sound ....Mike Hall
Editors ....Geraint Bell
....John Weidner
Production Manager ....Jean Levine
Production Design ....Richard Dearborn
Screenplay.......................................Stephen Smoke
Music...John Gonzalez
Fight Choreography ....Eric Lee
Film Facts
Running Time ....102 minutes
Film...Foto-Kem Color
Sound ....Stereo

The Final Incident
(Scoplin Pictures)

Critics Rating: Not Rated.
Genre: Horror—*The Final Incident* is an all-too-familiar, low-budget horror flick.
Plot: When a group of Iranian immigrant students from a Southern California college ventures off into the woods on a camping trip, the excursion is plagued by problems. But not until the "final incident" and bloody climax do these campers learn what real problems are.
MPAA Rating: Not Rated.
Cast
Mr. Nori...Bahman Mofid
Mrs. Nori..Soraya Mofid
Ahmad ....Babak Habibifar
Mohummad ....Andy Bagheri
Laila ....Roya Shagagi

Ali ....Ramin Lebaschi
Mondona...................................Sohaila Rahmaney
Afsone ....Sepideh Mashiah
Bijan ....Mohummad Derakhshanian
Credits
Producer ....Jack Kaprielian
Associate Producer.........................Sana Al-Qumlas
Director ....Kayvon Derakhshanian
Director of Photography ....Del Chouis
Editors ....Kayvon Derakhshanian
....Jack Kaprielian
Casting ....New Concept Casting
Screenplay ....Ali Emami
Story by ....Kayvon Derakhshanian
Film Facts
Running Time ....90 minutes
Film ....Color
Sound ....Stereo

A Fine Romance
(Tchin-Tchin)
(Castle Hill)

Critics Rating: ★★
Genre: Comedy—A straightforward, light, romantic comedy.
Tag Line: "The only thing they have in common is that his wife is sleeping with her husband."
Plot: Andrews plays Pamela, a stiff English woman who is abandoned by her husband in Paris. Her husband has run off with the wife of Cesareo (Mastroianni), an Italian construction engineer. The only thing left to do is for Pamela and Cesareo to win their spouses back. In the process, however, this odd couple discovers that they have more in common than they thought and begin their own romance.
MPAA Rating: PG-13—For nudity.
Cast
Pamela Piquet ....Julie Andrews
Cesareo Gramaldi ....Marcello Mastroianni
Bobby ....Ian Fitzgibbon
Marcel ....Jean-Pierre Castaldi
Dr. Noiret ....Jean-Jacques Dulon
Miss Knudson ....Maria Machado
Madame Legris ....Denise Grey
Dr. Picquet ....Jean-Michel Cannone

Marguerite ....Catherine Jarret
Madeleine................................Francoise Michaud
Credits
Producers...................................Arturo La Pegna
....Massimiliano La Pegna
Director ....Gene Saks
Director of Photography ....Franco di Giacomo
Editors ....Richard Nord
....Anna Poscetti
Production Manager........................Serge Touboul
Sets ....Jean Michel Hugon
....Michel Albournac
Costume Design...........................Gianni Versace
Screenplay ....Ronald Harwood
Music ....Pino Donaggio
Film Facts
Country of Origin ....Italy
Running Time ....82 minutes
Film ....Color
Sound ....Dolby Stereo

Finzan
(California Newsreel)

Critics Rating: Not Rated.
Genre: Drama—Writer-director Cheick Oumar Sissoko brings to the screen a moving drama about the women of an African tribe called Bambara, who are oppressed by the men of their village.
Plot: Surprisingly humorous and touching, this is overall a horrific tale of women who are treated no better than slaves by their husbands, who are blindly bound by tradition. Nanyuma plays a woman whose husband has died. Having endured a torturous eight year marriage the only thing she feels is relief. When the chief decides that her former husband's brother shall become her new husband, she refuses and runs away from the village and her home.
MPAA Rating: Not Rated.
Cast
Nanyuma................................Diarrah Sanogo
Bala............................Oumar Namory Keita
Village Chief...............................Balla Moussa Keita
Also with Helene Diarra and Saidou Toure.
Credits
Producer...Kora-Films

Director	Cheick Oumar Sissoko
Director of Photography	Cheick Hamala Keita
Sound	Ibrahim Khalil Thera
Editor	Ouoba Motandi
Written by	Cheick Oumar Sissoko

Film Facts

Country of Origin	Malia
Language	Bambara (subtitled)
Running Time	107 minutes
Film	Color
Sound	Stereo

Flaming Ears

(Rote Ohren Setzen Durch Afche)
(Women Make Films)

Critics Rating: Not Rated.

Genre: Science Fiction—This futuristic, and somewhat experimental, sci-fi lesbian film opened the New York International Festival of Gay and Lesbian Films.

Plot: The film is set in the year 2700 in a city inhabited primarily by women. Susanna Heilmayr plays Spy, a woman in search of the women who burned down her establishment and put her out of business. She tracks down the two women responsible but gets more than she bargained for.

MPAA Rating: Not Rated.

Cast

Spy	Susanna Heilmayr
Volley	Ursula Puerrer
Nun	Angela Hans Scheirl
Man with cactus	Anthony Escott
Little girl	Luise Kubelka
M (chauffeur)	Margarete Neumann
Undertaker	Dietmar Schipek
Blood	Gabriele Szekatsch

Credits

Producers/Directors	Angela Hans Scheirl
	Dietmar Schipek
	Ursula Puerrer
Associate Producer	Ulrike Zimmerman
Directors of Photography	Margarete Neumann
	Curd Duca
	Hermann Lewetz
	Manfred Neuwirth
Written by	Angela Hans Scheirl
	Dietmar Schipek

	Ursula Puerrer
Music	Dietmar Schipek
Models/Special Effects	Anthony Escott
	Andrea Witzmann

Film Facts

Country of Origin	Austria
Running Time	83 minutes
Film	Color (16 mm)
Sound	Stereo

Flirting

(Samuel Goldwyn)

Critics Rating: ★★★★★

Genre: Drama—A sequel (in a planned trilogy) to the popular 1987 film *The Year My Voice Broke*, it won the 1990 Australian Best Picture Film Award.

Plot: Noah Taylor returns to his role of Danny, an intelligent 14-year-old boy who shies away from sports and stays to himself in the all-boys boarding school that he attends. When Danny meets Thandiwe (Newton), an African student from the all-girls school across the lake, they are immediately attracted to one another. Theirs is an innocent relationship that is soon filled with conflict. When it comes time for Thandiwe to return home to Africa, the two consummate their relationship as a way of holding onto one another. Unlike American teen films, this is a sensitive, charming and thoughtful coming-of-age tale that will appeal to a much broader and older audience.

MPAA Rating: Not Rated.

Cast

Danny Embling	Noah Taylor
Thandiwe Adjewa	Thandie Newton
Nicola Radcliffe	Nicole Kidman
Gilby Fryer	Bartholomew Rose
Slag Green	Kiri Paramore
Melissa Miles	Kym Wilson
Morris Cutts	Jeff Truman
Rupert Elliott	Marshall Napier

Credits

Producers	George Miller
	Doug Mitchell
	Terry Hayes
Associate Producer	Barbara Gibbs
Director	John Duigan

Assistant Director ....Charles Rotherham
Director of Photography.......................Geoff Burton
Sound...Ross Linton
Editor ....Robert Gibson
Production Manager ....Barbara Gibbs
Production Design ....Roger Ford
Postproduction...............................Marcus D'Arcy
Casting ....Liz Mullinar
Written by...John Duigan
Film Facts
Country of Origin...............................Australia
Running Time ....100 minutes
Film ....Color
Sound ....Dolby Stereo

Folks!
(20th Century Fox)

Critics Rating: Not Rated.
Genre: Comedy—Nutty is the best way to describe this black comedy.
Tag Line: "When you shake the family tree all the nuts fall out."
Plot: Tom Selleck plays all-around good guy Jon Aldrich, a Chicago stockbroker with a few skeletons in his closet, so to speak. When his elderly parents begin to need looking after, he goes to their rescue. Before long, however, they have made a shambles of his life. Not wanting to be any more of a burden, his parents ask Jon to kill them and put an end to all of their miseries. He reluctantly agrees, but in his various attempts the only one he manages to harm is himself.
MPAA Rating: PG-13
Cast
Jon Aldrich ....Tom Selleck
Harry Aldrich...Don Ameche
Mildred Aldrich ....Anne Jackson
Arlene Aldrich ....Christine Ebersole
Audrey Aldrich ....Wendy Crewson
Ed ....Michael Murphy
Fred ....Robert Pastorelli
Credits
Executive Producers.....................Mario Cecchi Gori
....Vittorio Cecchi Gori
Co-Executive Producer.....................Gianni Nunnari
Producers ....Victor Drai

....Malcolm R. Harding
Associate Producer ....Burton Elias
Director...Ted Kotcheff
Assistant Director ....Howard Ellis
2nd Unit Director......................Conrad E. Palmisano
Director of Photography ....Larry Pizer
Sound...Scott D. Smith
Editor ....Joan E. Chapman
Production Design.....................William J. Creber
Costume Design ....Jay Hurley
Casting...Lynn Stalmaster
Casting (Chicago).........................Jane Alderman
....Susan Wielder
Written by.......................................Robert Klane
Music..................................Michel Colombier
Stunt Coordinator ....Conrad E. Palmisano
Film Facts
Running Time ....108 minutes
Film ....Technicolor
Sound ....Dolby Stereo
Location ....Florida; Chicago

The Footman
(Il Portaborse)
(Titanus)

Critics Rating: Not Rated.
Genre: Comedy—A political satire that lampoons a corrupt Italian politician as well as the entire political system. Although controversial, the film was a hit with audiences and critics alike in Italy.
Plot: Silvio Orlando plays Luciano, a high school literature teacher of high moral standards. To supplement his income he takes a job as a ghost-writer for a political columnist. This in turn leads to a job with the corrupt minister of government investment (Moretti). The innocent and unsuspecting Luciano unwittingly helps the minister in his deceitful attempt to win the election. When he finally realizes that he has been duped, his attempts to turn the tables lead to a lively and humorous conclusion in this fast-paced satire.
MPAA Rating: Not Rated.
Cast
Luciano Sandulli ....Silvio Orlando
Cesare Botero.....................................Nanni Moretti
Francesco Sanna ....Giulio Brogi

Juliette...Anne Roussel
Irene...Angela Finocchiaro
Sebastiano Tramonti ....Graziano Giusti
Also with Guido Alberti, Lucio Allocca, Dario Cantarelli, Renato Carpintieri, Silvia Cohen, Antonio Petrocelli and Gianna Paola Scaffidi.

Credits
Producers.......................................Nanni Moretti
....Angelo Barbagallo
Director ....Daniele Luchetti
Director of Photography ....Alessandro Pesci
Editor...Mirco Garrone
Art Direction.................................Giancarlo Basili
....Leonardo Scarpa
Screenplay ....Sandro Petraglia
....Stefano Rulli
Screenplay Collaborator ....Daniele Luchetti
Story...Franco Bernini
....Angelo Pasquini
Music ....Dario Lucantoni

Film Facts
Country of Origin ....Italy/France
Language.......................................Italian (subtitled)
Running Time ....93 minutes
Film...Technicolor
Sound ....Stereo

For Sasha
(Pour Sacha)
(MK2)

Critics Rating: ★★
Genre: Drama—A dramatic romance with subtitles set against the backdrop of war.
Plot: The year is 1967. Richard Berry plays Sasha, a young man living with his girlfriend, Laura (Sophie Marceau), on a kibbutz in Isreal. When three old friends come to visit the couple, the lives of all involved become complicated. As the war nears, the group's interpersonal relationships and past histories together are strained to the breaking point.
MPAA Rating: Not Rated.
Cast
Laura...Sophie Marceau
Sasha ....Richard Berry
Dan Chemtov ....Jean-Claude De Goros

Simon ....Niels Dubost
Paul ....Fabien Orcier
Michel ....Frederic Quiring
David...Gerard Darman
Myriam's mother ....Emmannuelle Riva

Credits
Producers.......................................Alexandre Arcady
....Diane Kurys
Director..Alexandre Arcady
Assistant Director ....Adi Shoval
Director of Photography ....Robert Alazraki
Sound...Jean-Louis Ughetto
Editor ....Martine Barraque
Production Manager.......................Bernard Grenet
Production Design ....Tony Egry
Written by......................................Alexandre Arcady
....Daniel Saint-Hamont
Music ....Philippe Sarde

Film Facts
Country of Origin...........................France
Language ....French (subtitled)
Running Time ....110 minutes
Film...Agfacolor
Sound ....Stereo

Forever Young
(Warner Bros.)

Critics Rating: ★★
Genre: Drama—A sentimental, humorous and heartwarming Rip Van Winkle-like tale. It is similar in theme to last years *Late For Dinner*.
Tag Line: "Fifty years ago he volunteered for a dangerous experiment. All in the name of love. Time waits for no man, but true love waits forever."
Plot: Opening in 1939, Mel Gibson plays Daniel, a test pilot head-over-heels in love with his girlfriend Helen (Glasser). Before he can get up the nerve to propose, she steps in front of a speeding truck and is left in a coma. Being devastated by the accident, Daniel volunteers for an Army cryogenics experiment. In the bureaucracy of the military, he gets lost in the system, only to be accidentally discovered in 1992, more than 50 years later, by two ten-year-old boys. It isn't long before Daniel moves in with Nat (Wood), one of the boys who thawed him out, and his mom (Curtis). While not

the most original of tales, Gibson's strong performance lifts this delightful and enjoyable stranger-in-a-strange-land story to new heights.

MPAA Rating: PG—For some language and domestic conflict. The film contains brief nudity.

Cast

Daniel	Mel Gibson
Claire	Jamie Lee Curtis
Nat	Elijah Wood
Helen	Isabel Glasser
Harry	George Wendt
Cameron	Joe Morton
John	Nicolas Surovy
Wilcox	David Marshall Grant
Felix	Robert Hy Gorman
Susan Finley	Millie Slavin

Credits

Executive Producers	Jeffrey Abrams
	Edward S. Feldman
Producer	Bruce Davey
Director	Steve Miner
Assistant Director	Matt Earl Beesley
Director of Photography	Russell Boyd
Sound	Jim Tanenbaum
Editor	Jon Poll
Production Design	Gregg Fonseca
Art Direction	Bruce A. Miller
Set Decoration	Jay R. Hart
Set Design	Jann K. Engel
	Richard Yanez, Steve Jeffrey Wolff
Costume Design	Aggie Guerard Rodgers
Casting	Marion Dougherty
Screenplay	Jeffrey Abrams
Music	Jerry Goldsmith
Creative Makeup Design	Dick Smith
Special Makeup Created/Applied by	Greg Cannom

Film Facts

Running Time	105 minutes
Soundtrack	Big Screen Records
Film	Color
Sound	Stereo
Location	Los Angeles; Northern California
Other Working Titles	*The Rest Of Daniel*

1492: Conquest Of Paradise

(Paramount)

Critics Rating: ★★

Genre: Drama—Historical epic of the voyage and discovery of the new world by Columbus. Visually grand and stunning in every way, the drama itself was considered by most to be run of the mill.

Tag Line: "Centuries before the exploration of space, there was another voyage into the unknown."

Plot: Hailed as visually stunning and spectacularly boring, the story is linear and straightforward in depicting Columbus' life and his determination to discover a new world. Columbus is portrayed as a sensitive and religious man who is forced by others to wreak havoc on the Americas by conquering and nearly annihilating the inhabitants of this so-called paradise all in the name of greed.

MPAA Rating: PG-13—For historical violence and brutality.

Cast

Columbus	Gerard Depardieu
Sanchez	Armand Assante
Queen Isabel	Sigourney Weaver
Older Fernando	Loren Dean
Beatrix	Angela Molina
Marchena	Fernando Rey
Moxica	Michael Wincott
Pinzon	Tcheky Karyo
Captain Mendez	Kevin Dunn
Giacomo	Fernando G. Cuervo
Alonso	Jose Luis Ferrer
Brother Buyl	John Heffernan
Santangel	Frank Langella
Bobadilla	Mark Margolis
Utapan	Bercelio Moya
Arojaz	Kario Salem
Fernando (age 10)	Billy Sullivan
Guevara	Arnold Vosloo
Bartolome	Steven Waddington

Credits

Executive Producers	Mimi Polk Sotela
	Iain Smith
Producers	Ridley Scott
	Alain Goldman
Co-Producers	Marc Boyman
	Roselyne Bosch
	Pere Fages
Associate Producer	Garth Thomas
Director	Ridley Scott
Assistant Director	Terry Needham
2nd Unit Director	Hugh Johnson
Director of Photography	Adrian Biddle

Sound ....Pierre Gamet
Editors ....William Anderson
....Francoise Bonnot
Production Design ....Norris Spencer
Supervising Art Directors ....Benjamin Fernandez
....Leslie Tomkins
Art Direction........Raul Antonio Paton, Kevin Phipps
..........................Martin Hitchcock, Luke Scott
Set Decoration....................................Ann Mollo
Costume Design.........Charles Knode, Barbara Rutter
Casting ....Louis Digiaimo
Written by ....Roselyne Bosch
Music ....Vangelis
Special Effects Supervisor ....Kit West

Film Facts
Country of Origin.............Great Britain/France/Spain
Running Time ....152 minutes
Soundtrack........................East West Records
Film.....................................Rank Color
Sound ....Dolby Stereo
Location ....Costa Rica; Spain
Other Working Titles.............................*Columbus*
....*Christopher Columbus*

Freddie As F.R.O.7
(Miramax)

Critics Rating: Not Rated.
Genre: Animated—Predictable, energetic and lighthearted tale.
Tag Line: "He's a secret agent with super powers...A leaping green fighting machine...Defending the world against forces of evil..."
Plot: We learn at the outset that super-agent Freddie the frog was once upon a time a human prince whose evil aunt turned him into a frog. Freddie grew up among other frogs until he matured and became a human-sized frog. As a full-sized frog he moved to Paris and again was forced to battle his aunt and an assortment of other evildoers.
MPAA Rating: PG—For some menacing moments.
Cast
Voices:
Freddie ....Ben Kingsley
El Supremo ....Brian Blessed

Trilby ....Jonathan Pryce
Daffers ....Jenny Agutter
Brigadier G....................................Nigel Hawthorne
King...Michael Hordern
Nessie..Phyllis Logan
Young Freddie ....Edmund Kingsley
Old Gentleman Raven.....................Victor Maddern
Queen...Prunella Scales
Scotty...John Sessions
Messina..Billie Whitelaw

Credits
Producers...Norman Priggen
....Jon Acevski
Director..Jon Acevski
Storyboard Director ....Denis Rich
Animation Director ....Tony Guy
Director of Photography ....Rex Neville
Sequence Directors...........................Dave Unwin
....Bill Hajee
....Richard Fawdry
....Stephen Weston
....Roberto Casale
....Alain Maindron
Sound ....Gerry Humphreys
....Dean Humphreys
....John Bateman
Editors...Alex Rayment
....Mick Manning
Art Direction ....Paul Shardlow
Character Designer ....Richard Fawdry
Visual Effects Supervisor ....Peter Chiang
Casting ....Marilyn Johnson
Screenplay.......................................Jon Acevski
....David Ashton
Music ....David Dundas
....Rick Wentworth
Lyrics by ....Don Black
....Jon Acevski
....David Ashton
Sung by ....George Benson, Patti Austin, Adrian De la Touche, Grace Jones, Barbara Dickson, Asia, Boy George and Holly Johnson.

Film Facts
Country of Origin ....Great Britain
Running Time ....90 minutes
Soundtrack.......................JRS/Great Pyramid Records
Film...Fujicolor
Sound ....Dolby Stereo
Location ....London (principal animation)

Freejack

(Warner Bros.)

Critics Rating: Not Rated.
Genre: Science Fiction—Entertaining futuristic science-fiction action adventure.
Tag Line: "Alex Furlong died today. Eighteen years from now he'll be running for his life."
Plot: Emilio Estevez stars as Alex Furlong, a race car driver who is apparently killed in an auto accident and explosion. In reality, the crash and his faked death have been masterminded by a dead man who wants his body. Furlong has been transported to the year 2009 and finds himself in a harsh new world. He manages to escape, however, only to be pursued by Mick Jagger who plays an evil bounty hunter working for the dead man. The film is one long and lively chase leading to a spectacular special-effects climax.
MPAA Rating: R

Cast

Alex Furlong	Emilio Estevez
Vacendak	Mick Jagger
Julie Redlund	Rene Russo
McCandless	Anthony Hopkins
Michelette	Jonathan Banks
Brad	David Johansen
Nun	Amanda Plummer
Boone	Grand L. Bush
Eagle Man	Frankie Faison
Ripper	Esai Morales
Morgan	John Shea

Credits

Executive Producers	James G. Robinson
	Gary Barber
	David Nicksay
Producers	Ronald Shusett
	Stuart Oken
Associate Producers	Joe Alves
	Linda Shusett
	Anthony Jon Ridio
Director	Geoff Murphy
Assistant Directors	Jerry Ballew
	Michael Haley
2nd Unit Director	Mickey Gilbert
Director of Photography	Amir Mokri
Sound	Glenn E. Berkovitz
Editor	Dennis Virkler
Production Design	Joe Alves
Costume Design	Lisa Jensen
Casting	Pam Dixon
Screenplay	Steven Pressfield
	Ronald Shusett
	Dan Gilroy
Screen Story by	Steven Pressfield
	Ronald Shusett
Based on the novel *Immortality, Inc.* by	
	Robert Sheckley
Music	Trevor Jones
Visual Effects Supervisor	Richard Hoover
Stunt Coordinator	Mickey Gilbert

Film Facts

Running Time	110 minutes
Soundtrack	Morgan Creek Records
Film	Technicolor
Sound	Dolby Stereo
Location	Atlanta; New York
Other Working Titles	*Free-jack*

Frozen Assets

(RKO)

Critics Rating: Not Rated.
Genre: Comedy
Tag Line: "At First Family Sperm Bank, she banks on babies, he banks on bucks."
Plot: Corbin Bernsen (TV's *L.A. Law*) plays an executive who accepts a job in a small town in Oregon, only to discover too late that he has made a big mistake. Expecting to become president of a bank, he is shocked to discover that it is a sperm bank. After deciding to make a go of it, he begins to market the company aggressively with humorous results. Adding to his problems (and the laughs) he becomes involved with Dr. Grace Murdock (Long), the former owner of the sperm bank. There aren't many surprises here, except that it is predictably good fun.
MPAA Rating: PG-13—For sex-related elements.

Cast

Dr. Grace Murdock	Shelley Long
Zach Shepard	Corbin Bernsen
Newton Patterson	Larry Miller
Mrs. Patterson	Dody Goodman
J. F. Hughes	Matt Clark

Zach's mother ....Jeanne Cooper
McTaggert...Paul Sand
Gloria..Gloria Camden
Peaches ....Teri Copley
Also with Gerrit Graham.

Credits
Executive Producer...................Harvey A. Bookstein
Producer ....Don Klein
Associate Producers ....Lee Imperial
....Howard Lam
Director ....George Miller
Assistant Director ....George Parra
Directors of Photography ....Ron Lautore
....Geza Sinkovics
Sound ....Reinhard Sterger

Editor ....Larry Bock
Production Design........................Dorian Vernacchio
....Deborah Raymond
Costume Design.................................Sandi Culotta
Casting ....Meryl O'Loughlin
Screenplay..Don Klein
....Tom Kartozian
Music ....Michael Tavera

Film Facts
Running Time ....93 minutes
Soundtrack ....Colossal Records
Film ....Eastmancolor
Sound ....Dolby Stereo
Location..Portland, Oregon

Gas, Food, Lodging
(I.R.S. Releasing)

Critics Rating: ★★★★
Genre: Drama—*Variety* described the film this way: "Fresh and unfettered pic emerges distinctively as an example of a new cinema made by women and expressive of their lives."
Plot: Fairuza Balik plays Shade, a sensitive teenage girl living with her mother and sister in a very small trailer home in Laramie, Wyoming. Mom (Brooke Adams) is a truck-stop waitress who has kept men at a distance ever since her husband walked out on her. Promiscuous older sister, Trudi (Ione Skye), is unwed and pregnant. The tension among the three runs high, and emotions run deep.
MPAA Rating: R—For language and sensuality.

Cast

Nora	Brooke Adams
Trudi	Ione Skye
Shade	Fairuza Balik
Dank	Robert Knepper
Darius	Donovan Leitch
Hamlet	David Lansbury
Raymond	Chris Mulkey
John Evans	James Brolin
Javier	Jacob Vargas
Thelma	Laurie O'Brien
Tanya	Julie Condra
Brett	Adam Biesk

Credits

Executive Producers	Carl-Jan Colpaert
	Christoph Henkel
Producers	Daniel Hassid
	Seth M. Willenson
	William Ewart
Line Producer	Albert T. Dickerson III
Director	Allison Anders
Assistant Director	Matthew J. Clark
Director of Photography	Dean Lent
Sound	Clifford Gynn
Editor	Tracy S. Granger
Production Design	Jane Stewart
Art Direction	Lisa Denker, Carla Weber
Set Decoration	Mary Meeks
Casting	Pagano/Bialy/Manwiller
Screenplay	Allison Anders
Based on the novel *Don't Look And It Won't Hurt* by	Richard Peck
Music	J Mascis
Additional Orchestrations	Barry Adamson

Film Facts

Running Time	100 minutes
Soundtrack	Mute Records
Film	Color
Sound	Dolby Stereo
Location	New Mexico

Gate II
(Triumph)

Critics Rating: Not Rated.
Genre: Horror—Following up on the successful 1987 original, the sequel follows its unsuspecting lead character as he summons up the spirits of the dead in this supernatural horror film.
Plot: Louis Tripp stars as Terry, a young man with good intentions, who only wants to help his alcoholic father. Instead he unleashes a terror from the gates of hell, bent on ruling the Earth. As Terry battles the evil one there are a few frightening and memorable moments, otherwise this is little more than a run-of-the-mill genre film.
MPAA Rating: R

Cast

Terry	Louis Tripp
Liz	Pamela Segall
Art	Neil Munro
Moe	Simon Reynolds
John	James Villemaire
Mr. Coleson	James Kidnie
Minion	Andrea Ladanyi

Credits

Executive Producer	John Kemeny

Producer	Andras Hamori
Associate Producer	Gordon Woodside
Line Producer	Peter Gray
Director	Tibor Takacs
Assistant Director	Michael Zenon
2nd Unit Director	Randall William Cook
Director of Photography	Bryan England
Sound	Steve Joles
Editor	Ronald Sanders
Production Manager	Patti Meade
Production Design	William Beeton
Costume Design	Beth Pasternak
Casting	John Buchan
Written by	Michael Nankin
Based on Characters Created by	Michael Nankin
Music	George Blondheim
Special Makeup	Craig Reardon
Special Effects Designed/ Created by	Randall William Cook
Stunt Coordinator	Ron Van Hart

Film Facts

Running Time	93 minutes
Film	Film House Color
Sound	Ultra-Stereo

The Giant Of Thunder Mountain

(Castle Hill)

Critics Rating: Not Rated.

Genre: Adventure—*The Giant Of Thunder Mountain* is an entertaining and wholesome wilderness adventure.

Plot: Seven-foot tall Richard Kiel plays Eli, a hermet living in the wild. When Eli befriends children from town he gets more than he bargained for. The children decide to introduce him to their widowed mom. Coming to town, however, turns out to be more dangerous than being on his own, as he is unjustly accussed of wrongdoing. But fortunately for Eli, this is a family film, and a happy ending is just around the corner for this loveable giant.

MPAA Rating: PG

Trivia: Kiel is best known for his role as "Jaws" in the James Bond films.

Cast

Eli	Richard Kiel

Hezekiah Crow	Jack Elam
Alicia Wilson	Marianne Rogers
Amy Wilson	Noley Thornton
Bear	Bart the Bear
Tommy	Chance Michael Corbitt
Agnes	Ellen Crawford
Ben	Ryan Todd

Also with Foster Brooks, George (Buck) Flower and William Sanderson.

Credits

Executive Producers	John Herklotz
	Richard Kiel
Producer	Joseph Raffill
Line Producers	Joan Weidman
	Von Bernuth
Director	James Roberson
Director of Photography	Stephen G. Shank
Sound	Trevor Black
Editor	Richard E. Rabjohn
Production Design	Phillip Thomas
Art Direction	Beau Petersen
Casting	Ruth Conforte
Screenplay	Richard Kiel
	Tony Lozito
Music	Al Kasha
	Joel Hirschhorn
Stunt Coordinator	Burt Marshall

Film Facts

Running Time	101 minutes
Film	Foto-Kem Color
Sound	Ultra-Stereo
Location	Austin, Texas

The Giving

(Northern Arts)

Critics Rating: ★★

Genre: Drama—29-year-old video and documentary filmmaker Eames Demetrios makes his feature debut in this uneven, highly stylized, low-budget, black-and-white film. It is the story of one man's attempt to help the homeless and, in the process, help himself.

Tag Line: "A house divided against itself will not stand. Welcome to L.A."

Plot: Kevin Kildow plays Jeremiah Pollock, a wealthy young L.A. bank executive who donates

$10,000 to the homeless during a benefit. When he discovers that throwing money at the problem will do little to change the plight of the homeless, he becomes more deeply involved. Going on a hunger strike and living as a homeless person on the streets, he loses his job and continues in a downward spiral leading up to a poignant climax.

MPAA Rating: Not Rated.

Cast

Jeremiah Pollock	Kevin Kildow
Gregor	Lee Hampton
Stefan	James Asher Salt
Carl Lepus	Russell Smith
Tiffany	Satyla Cyprian
Ruth	Gail L. Green
Ashley	Kellie A. McKuen
Cortez	Joel "Wolf" Parker

Also with Eleanor Alpert, Paul Boesing, Stephen Hornyak, Michael McGee, Oliver Patterson, Southern Comfort, Lionel Stoneham and Lois Yaroshefsky.

Credits

Executive Producer	Tim Disney
Producers	Cevin Cathell
	Tim Disney
	Eames Demetrios
Director	Eames Demetrios
Assistant Director	Donald L. Sparks
Director of Photography	Antonio Soriano
2nd Unit Camera	Dino Parks, Kate Butler
Sound	Jerry Wolfe
Editors	Bruce Barrow, Nancy Richardson
Production Design	Diane Romine Clark
	Lee Shane
Casting	Laurel Smith
Screenplay	Eames Demetrios
Music	Stephen James Taylor

Film Facts

Running Time	100 minutes
Film	Black & White
Sound	Dolby Stereo
Location	Los Angeles

Gladiator

(Columbia)

Critics Rating: ★★★

Genre: Action—Using boxing as a vehicle out of Chicago's poor South Side, boys from the neighborhood are lured into an underworld of ruthless boxing matches, in this high-energy action drama.

Plot: In this straightforward story, James Marshall stars as Tommy Riley, a tough high school student with aspirations of going to college. His dad, however, is in debt to a loan shark and forces Tommy into the ring to earn enough money to pay off the loan. The weekly undercover rings are run by a vicious and evil promoter named Horn (Brian Dennehy). Horn uses Tommy for his own revenge but in the end the tables are turned in a satisfying, if predictable, climax.

MPAA Rating: R—For violence and language.

Cast

Tommy Riley	James Marshall
Lincoln	Cuba Gooding, Jr.
Horn	Brian Dennehy
Pappy Jack	Robert Loggia
Noah	Ossie Davis
John Rile	John Heard
Dawn	Cara Buono
Romano	Jon Seda
Miss Higgins	Francesca P. Roberts
Leroy (Spits)	T. E. Russell
Charlene	Debra Sandlund
Shortcut	Lance Slaughter

Credits

Producers	Frank Price
	Steve Roth
Director	Rowdy Herrington
Assistant Director	Christine Larson
Director of Photography	Tak Fujimoto
Sound	Glenn Williams
Editors	Peter Zinner
	Harry B. Miller III
Production Manager	Kenneth Utt
Production Design	Gregg Fonseca
Costume Design	Donfeld
Casting	Amanda Mackey
	Cathy Sandrich
Screenplay	Lyle Kessler
	Robert Mark Kamen
Story by	Djordje Milicevic
	Robert Mark Kamen
Executive Music Producer	Budd Carr
Music	Brad Fiedel

Boxing Coordinator ....Jim Nickerson

Film Facts

Running Time ....99 minutes
Soundtrack ....Columbia Records
Film...Technicolor
Sound ....Dolby Stereo
Location...Chicago
Other Working Titles ....*Gladiators*

Glengarry Glen Ross

(New Line Cinema)

Critics Rating: ★★★★

Genre: Drama—Based on David Mamet's popular Pulitzer Prize-winning play that opened on Broadway in 1984. This powerful, intense, humorous and visually stunning actors' showcase is a dark character study of desperate men in desperate times in a desperate situation.

Plot: Set in a New York City boiler room, a group of slimeball, huckster salesmen peddle worthless real estate developments to unsuspecting victims over the phone. The problem is that the company is feeding them worthless leads that no one could sell. On top of this, the company has decided to degrade and humiliate them into selling more. Out of desperation, one of the men breaks into the office at night and steals the prime Glengarry leads. The remainder of the film is a fascinating whodunit with a surprising twist ending.

Every one of the performances is award-winning caliber and reason enough to see the film. Mike Clark in *USA Today* went so far as to say, "Baldwin's cameo runs just 10 minutes, but they're the best 10 he's yet had on screen."

MPAA Rating: R—For language.

Cast

Ricky Roma ....Al Pacino
Shelley Levene.....................................Jack Lemmon
Blake ....Alec Baldwin
Dave Moss...Ed Harris
George Aaronow ....Alan Arkin
James Link.......................................Jonathan Pryce
John Williamson...............................Kevin Spacey
Mr. Spannel ....Bruce Altman
Policeman...Paul Butler
Detective...Jude Ciccolella

Credits

Executive Producer.................Joseph Caracciola, Jr.
Producers ....Jerry Tokofsky
....Stanley R. Zupnik
Co-Producers ....Morris Ruskin
....Nava Levin
Associate Producer......................Karen L. Oliver
Director ....James Foley
Assistant Director..........................Thomas A. Reilly
Director of Photography ....Juan Ruiz Anchia
Sound ....Danny Michael
Editor ....Howard Smith
Production Design ....Jane Musky
Set Decoration..................................Robert J. Franco
Costume Design.............................Jane Greenwood
Casting..Bonnie Timmermann
Screenplay ....David Mamet
Based on the play by ....David Mamet
Music.................................James Newton Howard
Saxophone solos ....Wayne Shorter

Film Facts

Running Time ....100 minutes
Soundtrack ....Elektra Records
Film..DuArt Color
Sound ....Dolby Stereo
Location..New York

Guilty As Charged

(I.R.S. Releasing)

Critics Rating: ★★

Genre: Horror—A campy, low-budget send-up, of the classic gothic horror film.

Plot: Rod Steiger plays Ben Kallin, a meat packer who uses his refrigerated warehouse as a dungeon and execution chamber. His victims are murderers who have managed to escape justice through the legal system. Unfortunate for them as they face the horrors of this vigilante prison. The horrors, however, are played for laughs making this a highly unusual and unusually enjoyable tale.

MPAA Rating: R—For violence and language.

Cast

Ben Kallin ....Rod Steiger
Deek ....Irwin Keyes
Rev. Aloysius.....................................Isaac Hayes
Kimberly ....Heather Graham
Mark Stanford.....................................Lyman Ward

Liz Stanford..Lauren Hutton
James Hamilton ....Michael Beach
Edna...Zelda Rubinstein

Credits

Executives in Charge of Production.........Steve Reich
....Toni Phillips
Executive Producers.................Miles A. Copeland III
....Paul Colichman
Producer..Randolph Gale
Co-Producer...AdamMoos
Director ....Sam Irvin
Assistant Director ....James B. Rogers
Director of Photography ....Richard Michalak
Sound ....Cameron Hamza
Editor..Kevin Tent
Production Design ....Byrnadette DiSanto
Art Direction..Ian Hardy
Set Decoration...............................Pascale Vaquette
Costume Design................Madeline Ann Kozlowski
Costume Design (Lauren Hutton) ....Bob Mackie
Casting...Debra Rubinstein
Screenplay..Charles Gale
Music ....Steve Bartek

Film Facts

Running Time ....95 minutes
Film ....Foto-Kem Color
Sound..Dolby Stereo
Location...............................Hollywood, California

The Gun In Betty Lou's Handbag

(Buena Vista)

Critics Rating: ★

Genre: Comedy—Predictable light screwball comedy has its moments.

Tag Line: "In the tradition of the most notorious criminals of all time…Bugsy. Capone. Clyde. Betty Lou Perkins? She was a nobody, until someone found…The Gun In Betty Lou's Handbag."

Plot: Penelope Ann Miller (*Year Of The Comet*) stars as Betty Lou, a part-time librarian, desperate for attention. Her husband (Eric Thal), a local cop, is too preoccupied with his work to take much notice of her. When Betty Lou stumbles upon a gun used in a murder, she gets herself arrested. This not only gets her husband's attention, but the real killer's attention as well.

MPAA Rating: PG-13

Cast

Betty Lou.....................................Penelope Ann Miller
Beaudeen ....William Forsythe
Reba...Cathy Moriarty
Ann ....Alfre Woodard
Alex..Eric Thral
Elinor...Julianne Moore
Herrick..Andy Romano
Frank..Ray McKinnon
Marchat..Xander Berkeley
Jergens ....Michael O'Neill
Brown ....Christopher John Fields

Credits

Executive Producers.................................Ted Field
....Robert W. Cort
Producer ....Scott Kroopf
Co-Producers ....Ira Halberstadt
....Cynthia Sherman
Associate Producer............................Sarah Bowman
Director..Allan Moyle
Assistant Director................................Tom Davies
Director of Photography ....Charles Minsky
Sound...Douglas Axtell
Editors ....Janice Hampton
....Erica Huggins
Production Design ....Michael Corenblith
Art Direction ....David J. Bomba
Set Design ....Lori Rowbotham
Set Decoration............Merideth Boswell Charbonnet
Costume Design ....Lisa Jensen
Casting...Billy Hopkins
....Suzanne Smith
Screenplay..Grace Cary Bickley
Music ....Richard Gibbs

Film Facts

Running Time ....95 minutes
Film...Astro Color Labs Color
Sound..Dolby Stereo
Location..................................Mississippi

The Hairdresser's Husband
(Le Mari De La Coiffeuse)
(Triton)

Critics Rating: ★★★★
Genre: Comedy—An endearing and insightful romantic comedy by the director of *Monsieur Hire*.
Plot: Jean Rochefort stars as Antoine, a man obsessed with an erotic fantasy that began at an early age. When he meets Mathilde (Anna Galiena), a female barber, he finds a partner to act out his fantasy. Obsessed, they act out this sexual fantasy until they have both had too much of a good thing, and things go bad.
MPAA Rating: Not Rated.

Cast
Antoine	Jean Rochefort
Mathilde	Anna Galiena

Also with Roland Bertin, Maurice Cehvit, Philippe Clevenot, Henri Hocking and Ticky Holgado.

Credits
Executive Producer	Monique Guerrier
Producer	Thierry De Ganay
Director	Patrice Leconte
Director of Photography	Eduardo Serra
Sound	Pierre Lenoir
Editor	Joelle Hache
Art Direction	Ivan Maussion
Screenplay	Claude Klotz, Patrice Leconte
Story by	Patrice Leconte
Music	Michael Nyman

Film Facts
Country of Origin	France
Running Time	82 minutes
Film	Color
Sound	Stereo

The Hand That Rocks The Cradle
(Buena Vista)

Critics Rating: ★★★
Genre: Thriller—In this chilling psychological thriller, a woman whose life has been ruined is out for the ultimate revenge.
Tag Line: "Trust is her weapon. Innocence her opportunity. Revenge her only desire."
Plot: The film takes place in the ideal setting of Tacoma, Washington. When a doctor is justifiably accused of sexual molestation he takes his own life. His wife, played by Rebecca De Mornay is left penniless (due to lawsuits) and pregnant. The final blow is when she miscarries. Seeking revenge on the woman (Annabella Sciorra) responsible for turning her husband in to the authorities, she assumes a new identity and accepts a job in the woman's home as a nanny. De Mornay's deranged character believes that if she can just get rid of the wife she will have the husband and child that were taken away from her.
MPAA Rating: R—For terror, violence, language and a scene of molestation.
Trivia: De Mornay won the MTV Film Award in 1992 for the Best Villain of the year.

Cast
Peyton Flanders	Rebecca DeMornay
Claire Bartel	Annabella Sciorra
Michael Bartel	Matt McCoy
Solomon	Ernie Hudson
Dr. Mott	John de Lancie
Marlene	Julianne Moore
Marty	Kevin Skousen
Emma Bartel	Madeline Zima

Credits
Executive Producers	Ted Field
	Rick Jaffa
	Robert W. Cort
Producer	David Madden
Co-Producer	Ira Halberstadt
Director	Curtis Hanson
Assistant Directors	Michael Daves
	Ray Greenfield
Director of Photography	Robert Elswit
Sound	James Pilcher

Editor ....John F. Link
Production Design...........................Edward Pisoni
Art Direction ....Mark Zuelzke
Set Design.................................Gilbert Wong
Set Decoration ....Sandy Reynolds Wasco
Visual Consultant..........................Carol Fenelon
Costume Design ....Jennifer von Mayrhauser
Casting ....Junie Lowry-Johnson
Written by ....Amanda Silver
Music ....Graeme Revell

Film Facts
Running Time ....105 minutes
Soundtrack............................Hollywood Records
Film ....Alpha Cine Color
Sound ....Dolby Stereo
Location ....Tacoma; Seattle

Hard Promises

(Columbia)

Critics Rating: ★★
Genre: Comedy—Sissy Spacek and William Petersen star as Chris and Joey, a recently divorced couple with one big problem—they're still deeply in love with each other.
Plot: This romantic comedy breaks the mold and traverses a mine field of mixed emotions, conflicts and ultimately self-control, as Chris decides to take charge of her own life. Because Joey, has left their home in Lockhart, Texas, once too often. When he returns this time, he finds his former wife a few hours away from the altar.
MPAA Rating: PG
Cast
Christine Coalter ....Sissy Spacek
Joey Coalter...........................William Petersen
Walter Humphrey ....Brian Kerwin
Dawn ....Mare Winningham
Pinky...Jeff Perry
Beth Coalter ....Olivia Burnette
Stuart Haggart......................Peter MacNichol
Chris' mom ....Ann Wedgeworth
Also with Lois Smith and Amy Wright.
Credits
Executive Producers ....Rick Bieber
....Peter McAlevey
Producers ....Cindy Chvatal, William Petersen
Co-Producer...............................Paul Kurta

Director.................................Martin Davidson
Assistant Director ....Joel Tuber
Director of Photography ....Andrzej Bartkowiak
Editor ....Bonnie Koehler
Production Design ....Dan Leigh
Costume Design ....Susan Gammie
Casting...............................Mary Colquhoun
Written by.................................Jule Selbo
Music Supervisor ....Dick Rudolph
Music ....George S. Clinton

Film Facts
Running Time ....95 minutes
Film ....Deluxe Color
Sound ....Dolby Stereo
Location ....Austin, Texas

Hellraiser III - Hell On Earth

(Dimension)

Critics Rating: Not Rated.
Genre: Horror—A slick, quirky, imaginative and spellbinding tale for hard-core horror fans, by Clive Barker, the author of *Candyman*.
Plot: Again the setting is New York City. This time Terry Farrell stars as Joey, a woman who is contacted by an otherworldly figure through her nightmares. The figure, or ghost, is that of Capt. Elliott Spencer (Bradley), a man who previously has unleashed supernatural spirits upon the world creating a hell on earth. The spirits are led by the evil Pinhead, the ultimate hellraiser. The gore and grotesque special effects are a series of spectacular setups leading up to an ultra-violent confrontation between Joey and Pinhead.
MPAA Rating: R—For strong violence and sexuality; and language.
Trivia: While Barker created the character Pinhead in the original *Hellraiser*, he later sold the rights for $1 million and in turn was given the opportunity to direct the original film. He has acted as a consultant on the sequels.
Cast
Joey Summerskill ....Terry Farrell
Terri ....Paula Marshall
J. P. Monroe ....Kevin Berhardt
Joey's father...............................Peter Boynton

Pinhead/Elliott Spencer.........................Doug Bradley
Doc/Camerahead.................................Ken Carpenter
Sandy...Aimee Leigh
Bum..Lawrence Mortorff

Credits

Executive Producer ....Clive Barker
Producer....................................Lawrence Mortorff
Co-Producer..............................Christopher Figg
Associate Producer ....Olive McQueen
Director ....Anthony Hickox
Assistant Director ....Paul Martin
2nd Unit Director...................................Bob Keen
Director of Photography ....Gerry Lively
Sound...Kim Ornitz
Supervising Editor ....Christopher Cibelli
Editor ....James D. R. Hickox
Production Design...............................Steve Hardie
Costume Design ....Leonard Pollack
Casting (Los Angeles) ....Geno Havens
Casting (New York)..........................Leonard Finger
Casting (North Carolina) ....Clayton D. Hill
Written by ....Peter Atkins
Based on a Story by ....Peter Atkins
....Tony Randel
Based on Characters Created by ....Clive Barker
Music Supervisors..............................Carol Sue Baker
....Xavier Du Bois
Music ....Randy Miller
Additional Music ....Christopher Young
Special Effects Coordinator.........................Bob Keen
Mechanical Special Effects
   Coordinator ....Bob Stephens

Film Facts

Running Time ....93 minutes
Soundtrack...........................Victory Music/PLG
Orchestral Soundtrack ....GRP Crescendo
Film ....Foto-Kem Color
Sound...Ultra-Stereo
Location ....North Carolina

Hero
(Columbia)

Critics Rating: ★★★

Genre: Comedy—An enjoyable, light-hearted
fantasy sporting a fine cast and supporting cast,
including an uncredited Chevy Chase.

Plot: Dustin Hoffman stars as Bernie Laplante, a
small-time thief who one day stumbles upon a plane
crash. In the heat of the moment, he reluctantly and
matter-of-factly rescues three passengers, before
going on his way. One of the people he saves is
Gale Gayley (Davis), a television reporter. Gayley
makes it her mission, through a television
campaign, to uncover the identity of the man who
saved her. Incarcerated, Bernie is unable to step
forward. In Bernie's absence an opportunist he met
named, John Bubber (Garcia) steps forward in his
place and becomes a hero. Once released, Bernie
tries in vain to set things right. Eventually he
triumphs and brings to this warm-hearted tale a
very happy ending.

MPAA Rating: PG-13—For uses of strong
language.

Trivia: At the time of the film's release
(September), screenwriter David Webb Peoples
could boast two other films in concurrent release:
Unforgiven and a re-released version of *Blade
Runner*.

Cast

Bernie Laplante ....Dustin Hoffman
Gale Gayley..Geena Davis
John Bubber ....Andy Garcia
Pete ....Chevy Chase
Evelyn ....Joan Cusack
Joey...James Madio
Chucky ....Kevin J. O'Connor
Winston..Maury Chaykin
Wallace ....Stephen Tobolowsky
Conklin...Christian Clemenson
Chick ....Tom Arnold
Also with Fisher Stevens.

Credits

Executive Producer...................Joseph M. Caracciolo
Producer...Laura Ziskin
Associate Producer ....Sandy Isaac
Director ....Stephen Frears
Assistant Director ....Louis D'Esposito
Director of Photography...................Oliver Stapleton
Sound...Jerry Ross
Editor ....Mick Audsley
Production Design ....Dennis Gassner
Art Direction.....................................Leslie McDonald
Set Decoration ....Nancy Haigh
Costume Design...............................Richard Hornung
Casting........................Juliet Taylor, Howard Feuer

Screenplay.................................David Webb Peoples
Story by ....Laura Ziskin
....Alvin Sargent
....David Webb Peoples
Music..George Fenton
"Heart of a Hero" Performed by.......Luther Vandross
Film Facts
Running Time ....112 minutes
Soundtrack ....Epic Soundtrax
Film ....Technicolor
Sound ....Dolby Stereo
Location ....Chicago; Los Angeles
Other Working Titles ....*Hero And A Half*

Highway 61
(Skouras)

Critics Rating: ★★★
Genre: Drama—Not just another offbeat road picture, *Highway 61* is a bizarre joyride from Canada to New Orleans in search of the Blues—sort of.
Plot: Don McKellar stars as Pokey Jones, a small-town barber looking for an excuse to hit the road. One day he finds the body of a young man in his yard. Claiming to be the man's sister, Jackie Bangs (Valerie Buhagiar) convinces Pokey to transport the body to New Orleans. Being a jazz lover, he agrees. Along the way they meet up with an odd assortment of characters along this road to nowhere.
MPAA Rating: R—For language and and a scene of sensuality.
Cast
Pokey Jones ....Don McKellar
Jackie Bangs..................................Valerie Buhagiar
Otto ....Art Bergmann
Customs Agent No. 1 ....Jello Biafra
Mr. Watson....................................Peter Breck
Customs Agent No. 2 ....Hadley Obodiac
Mr. Skin (aka Satan).....................Earl Pastko
Credits
Executive Producer.........................Daniel Salerno
Producers.......................................Bruce McDonald
....Colin Brunton
Director ....Bruce McDonald
Director of Photography ....Miroslaw Baszak
Editor ....Michael Pacek

Written by ....Don McKellar
Story by...Don McKellar
....Bruce McDonald
....Allan Magee
Music...Nash the Slash
Film Facts
Country of Origin ....Canada/Great Britain
Running Time ....102 minutes
Film ....Color
Sound ....Dolby Stereo

Highway To Hell
(Hemdale)

Critics Rating: Not Rated.
Genre: Horror—A stylish and humorous, modern-day horror film a cut above the standard genre fare.
Tag Line: "Highway To Hell: Where the toll is your soul."
Plot: Chad Lowe stars as Charlie Sykes, a teenager about to elope with his girlfriend, Rachel (Kristy Swanson). On the way to their destination, they are pulled over by a cop from hell (C.J. Graham). When the cop abducts Rachel, Charlie goes after him. His pursuit finds him face to face with the devi,l and in the end he is pitted in a race with the Hellcop for the right to leave with his fiancee.
MPAA Rating: R
Cast
Beezle/Devil ....Patrick Bergin
Royce ....Adam Storke
Charlie Sykes ....Chad Lowe
Rachel Clarke................................Kristy Swanson
Sam ....Richard Farnsworth
Hitchhiker ....Lita Ford
Clara ....Pamela Gidley
Hitler ....Gilbert Gottfried
Sgt. Bedlam (Hellcop).....................C. J. Graham
Charon...Kevin Peter Hall
Adam..Jarrett Lennon
Also with Anne Meara, Amy Stiller, Ben Stiller and Jerry Stiller.
Credits
Producers ....Mary Anne Page
....John Byers
Co-Producers ....Brian Helgeland
....Daniel Rogosin

Line Producer ....Barry Rosen
Director ....Ate De Jong
Assistant Director...........................Michael Waxman
2nd Unit Director......................................Jack Gill
Director of Photography ....Robin Vidgeon
2nd Unit Camera.......................Philip Alan Waters
Sound...Douglas Axtell
Editors...Todd Ramsay
....Randy Thornton
Production Design....................Philip Dean Foreman
Costume Design............................Florence Kemper
Casting...Diane Dimeo
Casting (Arizona) ....Darlene Wyatt
Written by..Brian Helgeland
Music..Hidden Faces
Additional Music........................Tangerine Dream
Special Makeup Effects.......................Steve Johnson
Special Visual Effects ....Randall William Cook
....Cinema Research Corp.
Stunt Coordinators ....Christine Baur
....Jack Gill

Film Facts
Running Time ....95 minutes
Film...CFI Color
Sound ....Dolby Stereo

Hoffa
(20th Century Fox)

Critics Rating: ★★★

Genre: Drama—Opening on Christmas day opposite *Chaplin*, *Hoffa* became the last in a long line of epic biopics in 1992.

Tag Line: "He did what he had to do."

Plot: Jack Nicholson turns in another tour-de-force performance, this time as controversial labor leader Jimmy Hoffa. Director Danny DeVito plays Bobby Cairo, Hoffa's personal aide and confidant. The film explores his early days as a single-minded union leader; his dealings with the mob; his confrontations with Robert Kennedy; the time spent in jail; his rise to the Teamsters presidency; and the speculation following his unsolved disappearance. Hoffa's public life is told in a straightforward fashion. Told in flashback, beginning with his 1975 disappearance, the film portrays this man as an icon, a hero of the people who battled the darker forces and won or lost, depending on your perspective.

MPAA Rating: R

Cast

James R. Hoffa..............................Jack Nicholson
Bobby Ciaro ....Danny DeVito
Carol D'Allesandro.......................Armand Assante
Frank Fitzsimmons ....J. T. Walsh
Billy Flynn ....Robert Prosky
Pete Connelly ....John C. Reilly
Young Kid ....Frank Whaley
Robert Kennedy ....Kevin Anderson
Red Bennett ....John P. Ryan
Jo Hoffa ....Natalija Nogulich
Hoffa's attorney...............................Nicholas Pryor
Ted Harmon.......................................Paul Guilfoyle
Young woman at RTA.........................Karen Young
Solly Stein ....Cliff Gorman

Credits

Executive Producer...............................Joseph Isgro
Producers..............................Edward R. Pressman
....Danny DeVito
....Caldecot Chubb
Co-Producer...............................Harold Schneider
Associate Producers ....David Mamet
....William Barclay Malcolm
Director..Danny DeVito
Assistant Director ....Ned Dowd
Director of Photography ....Stephen H. Burum
Sound..Thomas D. Causey
Editors ....Lynzee Klingman
....Ronald Roose
Production Design.................................Ida Random
Art Direction......................................Gary Wissner
Set Design ....Charles Daboub, Jr.
....Robert Fechtman
Costume Design ....Deborah L. Scott
Casting....................................David Rubin, Debra Zane
Screenplay ....David Mamet
Music ....David Newman
Visual Consultant ....Harold Michelson

Film Facts

Running Time ....140 minutes
Soundtrack.........Twentieth Century Fox Film Scores
Film..Color
Sound ....Dolby Stereo
Location ....Pittsburgh; Detroit;
....Los Angeles; Chicago

Home Alone 2: Lost In New York

(20th Century Fox)

Critics Rating: ★★
Genre: Comedy—Predictably cute. Predictably familiar. Predictably a box-office mega-hit.
Tag Line: "He's up past his bedtime in the city that never sleeps."
Plot: In this childhood fantasy come true, Macaulay Culkin plays the precocious adolescent Kevin McCallister, who outwits all the adults, while single-handedly defeating the bad guys. This Christmas the clan is planning to spend the holiday in Florida, but surprise—Kevin boards the wrong plane with the wrong handbag and ends up in New York City with his dad's credit cards. Coincidentally, the villainous bandits (Stern and Pesci) have escaped prison and have also just arrived in the Big Apple. Not to worry, though; Kevin has been watching television long enough to know how to foil these cartoon characters, but not before an endless series of humorous, wacky, audience-pleasing, slapstick capers.
MPAA Rating: PG—For comic action and mild language.

Cast

Kevin	Macaulay Culkin
Harry	Joe Pesci
Marv	Daniel Stern
Peter	John Heard
Concierge	Tim Curry
Pigeon Lady	Brenda Fricker
Kate	Catherine O'Hara
Buzz	Devin Ratray
Megan	Hilary Wolf
Linnie	Maureen Elisabeth Shay
Jeff	Michael C. Maronna
Uncle Frank	Gerry Bamman
Aunt Leslie	Terrie Snell
Mr. Duncan	Eddie Bracken

Credits

Executive Producers	Mark Radcliffe
	Duncan Henderson
	Richard Vane
Producer	John Hughes
Director	Chris Columbus
Assistant Director	James Giovanetti, Jr.
2nd Unit Director	Freddie Hice
Director of Photography	Julio Macat
Sound	Jim Alexander
Editor	Raja Gosnell
Production Design	Sandy Veneziano
Art Direction	Gary Lee
Set Decoration	Marvin March
Set Design	Stephen Berger
Costume Design	Jay Hurley
Casting	Janet Hirshenson
	Jane Jenkins
Screenplay	John Hughes
Based on Characters Created by	John Hughes
Music	John Williams
Stunt Coordinator	Freddie Hice
Visual Effects Supervisor	Craig Barron

Film Facts

Running Time	120 minutes
Soundtrack	Fox Records
Film	Deluxe Color
Sound	Dolby Stereo
Location	New York City
Other Working Titles	*Home Alone, Again*

Honey, I Blew Up The Kid

(Buena Vista)

Critics Rating: ★★★
Genre: Comedy—A sequel to the 1989 Disney hit *Honey, I Shrunk The Kids*, this takeoff on the sci-fi pics of the 1950s retains all the warmth and good-natured comedy that made the first film so popular. Topnotch special effects add credibility to this otherwise goofy tale.
Plot: Rick Moranis again plays Wayne Szalinski the nerdy, bumbling scientist, whose latest invention accidentally turns his 2-year-old into a seven-foot menace. To make matters worse, the toddler grows in size whenever he is near an electrical field. It just so happens that the Szalinski family lives in a Las Vegas suburb—Las Vegas, of course, being the electricity capital of the world. The humor comes easily as baby Adam grows to a wopping 112 feet in height. From here, mom and dad spend most of their time frantically trying to rescue their toddler and keep him from terrorizing the neighborhood.

MPAA Rating: PG

Trivia: Character actor Kenneth Tobey, who played in numerous 1950's science-fiction films (such as the 1955 *It Came From Beneath The Sea* about a giant octopus that invades San Francisco), makes an appearance here as a guard at Shea's Lab.

Cast

Wayne Szalinski	Rick Moranis
Diane Szalinski	Marcia Strassman
Clifford Sterling	Lloyd Bridges
Nick Szalinski	Robert Oliveri
Charles Hendrickson	John Shea
Adam Szalinski	Daniel Shalikar, Joshua Shalikar
Marshall Brooks	Ron Canada
Capt. Ed Meyerson	Michael Milhoan
Amy Szalinski	Amy O'Neill
Mandy Park	Keri Russell
Smitty	Ken Tobey

Credits

Executive Producers	Albert Band
	Stuart Gordon
Co-Executive Producer	Deborah Brock
Producers	Dawn Steel
	Edward S. Feldman
Co-Producer	Dennis E. Jones
Director	Randal Kleiser
Assistant Directors	Frank Capra III
	Douglas C. Metzger
2nd Unit Assistant Director	Jeffrey Wetzel
Director of Photography	John Hora
2nd Unit Camera	Allen Easton
Sound	Roger Pietschmann
Editors	Michael A. Stevenson
	Harry Hitner
Additional Editing	Tina Hirsch
Production Design	Leslie Dilley
Art Direction	Ed Verreaux
Lead Set Design	Antoinette J. Gordon
Set Design	John Berger
	Gina B. Cranham
Set Decoration	Dorree Cooper
Costume Design	Tom Bronson
Casting	Renee Rousselot
Screenplay	Thom Eberhardt
	Peter Elbling
	Garry Goodrow
Story by	Garry Goodrow
Based on Characters Created by	Stuart Gordon
	Brian Yuzna

	Ed Naha
Music	Bruce Broughton
Stunt Coordinator	Bobby J. Foxworth
Visual Effects Producer/Unit Director	
	Thomas G. Smith
Visual Effects Coordinator	Michael Muscal
Visual Effects Camera	John V. Fante
Visual Effects Unit Assistant Director	Benita Allen
Buena Vista Visual Effects Producer	Carolyn Soper
BV Visual Effects Supervisor	Harrison Ellenshaw
BV Visual Effects Co-Supervisors	Mark Dornfeld
	Kevin Koneval
Mechanical Effects Designer/Coordinator	
	Peter M. Chesney
Baby Adam's Special Makeup Effects	Kevin Yagher

Film Facts

Running Time	89 minutes
Soundtrack	Intrada
Film	Technicolor
Sound	Dolby Stereo
Location	Las Vegas; Los Angeles
Other Working Titles	*Honey, I Blew Up The Baby*

Honeymoon In Vegas
(Columbia)

Critics Rating: ★★★

Genre: Comedy—Light slapstick, romantic comedy.

Tag Line: "A comedy about one bride, two grooms, and 34 flying Elvises."

Plot: Nicholas Cage plays Jack, a private eye who has a difficult time committing to his girlfriend. Sarah Jessica Parker plays his girlfriend, Betsy-Donna, a second grade teacher. When Jack finally decides to tie the knot, the two run off to Las Vegas. However, before the wedding he loses Betsy for the weekend in a card game to James Caan. From here on out Jack spends most of his time trying to win his fiancee back and goes to some zany extremes to do it.

MPAA Rating: PG-13

Cast

Jack Singer	Nicholas Cage
Betsy-Donna	Sarah Jessica Parker
Tommy	James Caan
Mahi Mahi	Pat Morita

Bea Singer	Anne Bancroft
Chief Orman	Peter Boyle
Johnny Sandwich	Johnny Williams
Sally Molars	John Capodice
Sidney Tomashefsky	Robert Costanzo
Sid Feder	Jerry Tarkanian
Roy	Burton Gilliam

Credits

Executive Producer	Neil Machlis
Producer	Mike Lobell
Associate Producer	Adam Merims
Director	Andrew Bergman
Assistant Director	Yudi Bennett
2nd Unit Director	Mark Parry
Director of Photography	William A. Fraker
Sound	David MacMillan
	Tom Fleischman
	Steve Maslow
	Robert Beemer
Editor	Barry Malkin
Production Design	William A. Elliott
Art Direction	John Warnke
Set Decoration	Linda De Scenna
Costume Design	Julie Weiss
Casting	Michael Fenton
	Valorie Massalas
Written by	Andrew Bergman
Music	David Newman
Stunt Coordinator	Rick Barker

Film Facts

Running Time	95 minutes
Soundtrack	Epic Soundtrax
Film	CFI Color
Sound	Dolby Stereo
Location	New York; Las Vegas;
	Los Angeles; Kauai, Hawaii

The Hours And Times
(Antarctic)

Critics Rating: ★★★★★
Genre: Drama—Shot in black and white over four days in Barcelona, *Hours And Times* is a fictionalized account of what might have happened between Beatle John Lennon and manager Brian Epstien on a vacation together in 1963.
Plot: The filmmaker speculates that Lennon, played by Ian Hart, may have reluctantly become involved sexually with Epstien (David Angus), who was known to be gay and quite taken with the young Lennon. In addition to their sexuality, the film is equally fascinating as it explores other aspects of their personality and relationship. This controversial interpretation and speculation about a real-life event is sure either to shock or to fascinate Beatles' fans and a handful of other curious filmgoers as well.
MPAA Rating: Not Rated.

Cast

Brian Epstein	David Angus
John Lennon	Ian Hart
Quinones	Robin McDonald
Marianne	Stephanie Pack

Credits

Producer/Director/Editor	Christopher Munch
Directors of Photography	Christopher Munch
	Juan Carlos Valls
Sound	Christopher Munch
Written by	Christopher Munch

Film Facts

Running Time	60 minutes
Film	Black & White
Sound	Stereo

Housesitter
(Universal)

Critics Rating: ★★★
Genre: Comedy—In the tradition of the 1930s screwball romantic comedy, Steve Martin and Goldie Hawn star as opposites that attract—with serious and humorous repercussions. This is a silly, lighthearted, romantic comedy with broad appeal.
Plot: Martin plays Newton Davis, a Boston architect, who builds a dream house for his girlfriend Becky (Delaney) as an engagement present. Becky has other plans, however, and turns down his proposal.

Hawn plays Gwen, a chronic liar and woman on the run from herself. On the rebound, Gwen and Newt become briefly involved. One thing leads to another and before he knows what has happened Gwen has moved into home, convinced the town that they are married and turned his life upside down. In return for room and board she concocts a plan to help him win back Becky, the woman he still loves. There's only one hitch, they fall for each other and their plan backfires.

MPAA Rating: PG

Cast

Newton Davis	Steve Martin
Gwen	Goldie Hawn
Becky	Dana Delany
Edna Davis	Julie Harris
George Davis	Donald Moffat
Marty	Peter MacNicol
Moseby	Roy Cooper
Ralph	Richard B. Shull
Mary	Laurel Cronin
Reverend Lipton	Christopher Durang
Travis	Heywood Hale Broun
Harv	Ken Cheeseman
Hazel	Alice Duffy
Patty	Cherry Jones
Lorraine	Mary Klug
Karol	Vasek Simek
Moseby's secretary	Suzanne Whang

Credits

Executive Producer	Bernie Williams
Producer	Brian Grazer
Associate Producers	Karen Kehela
	Michelle Wright
Director	Frank Oz
Assistant Director	James W. Skotchdopole
Director of Photography	John A. Alonzo
Sound	Martin Raymond Bolger
	Lee Dichter
Editor	John Jympson
Production Design	Ida Random
Art Direction	Jack Blackman, Jeff Sage
Set Design	Philip Messina
Set Decoration	Tracey A. Doyle
Costume Design	Betsy Cox
Casting	John Lyons
Screenplay	Mark Stein
Story by	Mark Stein, Brian Grazer
Music	Miles Goodman
House Design	Trumbull Architects

Film Facts

Running Time	102 minutes
Film	Deluxe Color
Sound	Dolby Stereo
Location	Boston

How U Like Me Now!

(Lange and Associates)

Critics Rating: Not Rated.

Genre: Comedy—A low-budget ($500,000) original film by 30-year-old director Darryl Roberts.

Plot: Set in Chicago, the story revolves around a middle-class African-American couple and the ups and downs they experience with relationships, money, careers, sex, friends and other social pressures that threaten to pull them apart.

Darnell Williams (*Sidewalk Stories*) plays Thomas, a less-than-ambitious young man with few plans in life. His girlfriend is Valerie (Richardson), a woman who knows what she wants out of life and is determined to have it, with or without his help. Their fragile relationship is like an accident waiting to happen.

MPAA Rating: R—For sexuality and strong language.

Trivia: Fans of the daytime drama *All My Children* will recognize Williams from his two-time Emmy Award winning role as Jesse Hubbard.

Cast

Thomas	Darnell Williams
Valerie	Salli Richardson
Spoony	Daniel Gardner
Alex	Raymond Whitfield
Michelle	Debra Crable
B. J.	Darryl Roberts
Pierre	Byron Stewart
Brandon	Scott Goodrich
Sharon	Jonelle Kennedy
Jack T. Jackson	D. J. Howard
Paula	Charnele Brown
Irma	Zelda Pulliam
Carl	Gerald McQuirter
Beverly	Julie Welborne
Andre	Darion Best
Helen	Jenna Ward
Barb	Kim Jones Clark
C. C.	Patrick R. Huey
Leroy	El Feigo N. Goodum

Credits

Executive Producer	Bob Woolf
Producer	Darryl Roberts

Associate Producer	Sharese Locke
Director	Darryl Roberts
Assistant Director	Neil Kinsella
Director of Photography	Michael Goi
Sound Mixer	Mike Terry
Editor	Tom Miller
Art Direction	Kathy Domokos
Screenplay	Darryl Roberts
Music	Kahil El Zabar, Chuck Webb

Film Facts

Movie	Color
Sound	Stereo
Location	Chicago

Howards End
(Sony PicturesClassics)

Critics Rating: ★★★★★
Genre: Drama—E.M. Forster's period drama set in England at the turn of the century is essentially a story about coincidence and fate. On a more personal level it is about three families from different classes and how their lives become ironically and tragically entwined. Director James Ivory and producer Ismail Merchant have created a compelling and multilayered character study that will appeal to a sophisticated audience. Performances and technical achievements are first-rate all around.
Plot: Emma Thompson stars as Margaret Schlegel, a warm and free-spirited middle-class woman living in London with her sister Helen (Bonham Carter) and brother Tibby (Magenty). By sheer coincidence, Margaret meets and eventually marries Henry Wilcox, a wealthy aristocrat. Simultaneously, her sister Helen meets and forever becomes involved with Leonard Bast (West), a lower-class young married man struggling to get by financially. As both relationships develop, they take opposite paths, and the sisters become estranged. As Margaret stands by her heartless husband, she must repress her true nature. Unable to repress her feelings, Helen is considered mad, insane and abnormal for having normal feelings of compassion and love. When Helen becomes pregnant with Leonard's baby, what follows is a series of tragic consequences that lead to a poignantly ironic end.

MPAA Rating: PG
Cast

Margaret Schlegel	Emma Thompson
Helen Schlegel	Helena Bonham Carter
Henry Wilcox	Anthony Hopkins
Ruth Wilcox	Vanessa Redgrave
Jacky Bast	Nicola Duffet
Tibby Schlegel	Adrian Ross Magenty
Leonard Bast	Sam West
Charles Wilcox	James Wilby
Miss Avery	Barbara Hicks
Dolly Wilcox	Susan Lindeman
Evie Wilcox	Jemma Redgrave
Aunt Juley	Prunella Scales

Also with Joseph Bennett, Simon Callow, Jo Kendall and Mark Payton.

Credits

Executive Producer	Paul Bradley
Producer	Ismail Merchant
Co-Producer	Ann Wingate
Director	James Ivory
Assistant Director	Chris Newman
Director of Photography	Tony Pierce-Roberts
Sound	Mike Shoring
Editor	Andrew Marcus
Production Managers	John Downes, Caroline Hill
Production Design	Luciana Arrighi
Art Direction	John Ralph
Set Decoration	Ian Whittaker
Costume Design	Jenny Beavan, John Bright
Casting	Celestia Fox
Written by	Ruth Prawer Jhabvala
Based on the novel by	E. M. Forster
Music	Richard Robbins

Film Facts

Country of Origin	Great Britain
Running Time	140 minutes
Soundtrack	Nimbos Records
Film	Technicolor
Sound	Dolby Stereo
Location	England

Hugh Hefner: Once Upon A Time
(I.R.S. Releasing)

Critics Rating: ★★★
Genre: Documentary—In black and white and color.

111

Plot: Narrated by James Coburn, the filmmakers follow the life and career of Playboy founder Hugh Hefner, in a straightforward manner. The film traces his puritanical, repressed, Methodist upbringing in the Midwest to the creation of a Playboy empire that has changed the world. The film also captures and contrasts the social, sexual and political history of the times. Equal time is also given to the low points in Hefner's life. The murder of Playmate Dorothy Stratten, the suicide of personal assistant Bobbie Arnstein and the demise of the Playboy clubs are all documented. More than anything, this is a story about a man who has succeeded like few others in living out the American Dream.

MPAA Rating: Not Rated.

Cast
Narrator ....James Coburn

Credits
Executive Producer....................................Mark Frost
Producers ....Gary H. Grossman
....Robert Heath
Coordinating Producers ....Denise Contis
....Marijane Miller
Executive in Charge of Production ....Ken Scherer
Director...Robert Heath
Directors of Photography ....Van Carlson
.................................Dustin Teel, Tony Zapata
Editor ....Michael Gross
Written by ....Gary H. Grossman
...............................Michael Gross, Robert Heath
Music...Charlotte Lansberg
Additional Music ....Reeves Gabrels
....Tom Dube
Research...Jerilynn Goodman

Film Facts
Running Time ....90 minutes
Film ....Color/Black & White
Sound ....Stereo

Plot: In this case, Michael Dudikoff plays good guy Doug Matthews, a former U.S. military man. Seeking revenge for an event in the past, bad guy Ali (Steve Inwood), an Iraqi military man, kidnaps Matthews' younger brother Ben (Tommy Hinkley). Holding his brother hostage in Baghdad, Matthews is forced into a rescue attempt. Of course, like any good action hero Matthews single-handedly takes on the Iraqi army and comes out on top with little more than a bruise.

MPAA Rating: R—For war violence.

Cast
Doug Matthews..............................Michael Dudikoff
Ben Matthews ....Tommy Hinkley
Ali Dallal ....Steve Inwood
Lila Haddilh.........................Hana Azoulay-Hasfari
Also with Gil Dagon, Uri Gavriel, Avi Keidar, Geula Levy and Michael Shillo.

Credits
Producers ....Christopher Pearce, Elie Cohn
Director ....Ted Post
Assistant Director ....Eli Cohn
Director of Photography ....Yossi Wein
2nd Unit Camera...............................Danny Schneor
Sound...Eli Yarkoni
Editors ....Daniel Cahn, Matthew Booth
Production Design ....Itzik Albalak
Art Direction..Yehuda Ako
Costume Design ....Rakefet Levy
Casting ....Dalia Hovers
Screenplay...Mann Rubin
Story by ....Mike Webb, Mann Rubin
Music...Stephen Barber
Special Effects ....Yoram Pollack
Stunt Coordinator ....Guy Norris

Film Facts
Running Time ....90 minutes
Film ....Deluxe Color
Sound...Ultra-Stereo

The Human Shield
(Cannon)

Critics Rating: Not Rated.
Genre: Action—Like most action-genre films, *The Human Shield* is the story of an evil bad guy seeking revenge on a reluctant good guy.

Hunting
(Skouras)

Critics Rating: Not Rated.
Genre: Drama
Plot: John Savage plays Michael Bergman, a wealthy drug dealer who gets involved in money

laundering and other sordid activities. Kerry Armstrong plays Michelle Harris, a secretary whose marriage is on the rocks. She enters into an affair with Bergman but her husband soon finds out. Following a confrontation with Bergman, Michelle's husband is found dead. It would seem that all obstacles are now out of the way but in fact the problems are just beginning to surface and the violent finale is just around the corner.

MPAA Rating: R—For strong sensuality, language, violence and drug use.

Cast
Michael Bergman	John Savage
Michelle Harris	Kerry Armstrong
Larry Harris	Jeffrey Thomas
Sharp	Guy Pearce
Debbie McCormick	Rebecca Rigg
Bill Stockton	Rhys McConnochie
Piggott	Nicholas Bell
Holmes	Ian Scott
Roberts	Stephen Whittaker

Credits
Executive Producer	Peter Boyle
Producer/Director	Frank Howson
Co-Producer	James Michael Vernon
Line Producer	Barbi Taylor
Assistant Director	John Powditch
Directors of Photography	David Connell
	Dan Burstall
Sound	John Rowley
Editor	Philip Reid
Production Manager	Lesley Parker
Production Design	Jon Dowding
Costume Design	Aphrodite Kondos
Casting	Greg Apps
Written by	Frank Howson
Music	John French, David Herzog

Film Facts
Country of Origin	Australia
Running Time	97 minutes
Film	Color
Sound	Stereo

Husbands And Wives
(TriStar)

Critics Rating: ★★★★

Genre: Comedy—Released September 18th, a few weeks after the very public separation of Allen and Farrow became national headline news. The film went on to be a huge critical success. Near the beginning of the film Farrow's character, Judy, upon learning of her friend's separation says, I feel sick. Audiences will feel the same after a few minutes of Carlo Di Palma's jerky and annoying hand-held camerawork. Despite this constant irritation, the film is a comic gem about relationships falling apart.

Plot: This is a modern-day tale of loneliness, desperation and dead-end relationships set in Manhattan. The plot isn't exactly new territory for Allen, but it is by far the most engaging and most realized of his films. Allen plays Gabe Roth, a university professor who leaves his marriage to pursue Rain (Juliette Lewis), a 21-year-old student. His wife leaves to marry the man (Neeson) her best friend Sally (Davis) rejected. Sally has gone back to her husband Jack (Pollack), who earlier dumped her for a young aerobics instructor (Lysette Anthony). As their loves and lives intersect paths, humor and sadness are revealed in equal measure.

MPAA Rating: R—For language and a scene of sexuality.

Trivia: In its debut weekend the film earned approximately $3.5 million, becoming the director's best opening at the box-office. In comparison, *Shadows And Fog*, which opened at the beginning of the year had earned a reported $2.5 million to date.

Cast
Gabe Roth	Woody Allen
Judy Roth	Mia Farrow
Jack	Sydney Pollack
Sally	Judy Davis
Michael	Liam Neeson
Rain	Juliette Lewis
Harriet	Galaxy Craze
Sam	Lysette Anthony
Rain's mother	Blythe Danner
Shawn Grainger	Cristi Conaway
Peter Styles	Bruce Jay Friedman
Paul	Timothy Jerome
Interviewer/narrator	Jeffrey Kurland
Rain's analyst	Ron Rifkin
Judy's ex-husband	Benno Schmidt
Dinner party guest	Jerry Zaks

Credits

Executive Producers.............................Jack Rollins
....Charles H. Joffe
Producer ....Robert Greenhut
Co-Producers ....Helen Robin
....Joseph Hartwick
Associate Producer ....Thomas Reilly
Director ....Woody Allen
Assistant Director................................Thomas Reilly
Director of Photography ....Carlo Di Palma
Sound...James Sabat
Editor ....Susan E. Morse

Production Design ....Santo Loquasto
Art Direction..Speed Hopkins
Set Decoration ....Susan Bode
Costume Design ....Jeffrey Kurland
Casting...Juliet Taylor
Screenplay...Woody Allen

Film Facts

Running Time ....107 minutes
Film...DuArt Color
Sound ....Dolby Stereo
Location..New York City

I Don't Buy Kisses Anymore
(Skouras)

Critics Rating: Not Rated.

Genre: Comedy—This modestly-budgeted comedy-romance is about an overweight man who falls for a woman who has other than romantic intentions.

Plot: Jason Alexander stars as Bernie Fishbine, a shoe-store owner who still lives at home with his Jewish mother (Lainie Kazan). During a chance encounter he meets and falls for a young woman. She eventually falls for him as well but before any happy endings are in order, he discovers that she was simply using him as a case study for a college thesis.

MPAA Rating: PG

Cast

Bernie Fishbine	Jason Alexander
Theresa Garabaldi	Nia Peeples
Sarah	Lainie Kazan
Gramps (Irving Fein)	Lou Jacobi
Frieda	Eileen Brennan
Norman Fishbine	David Bowe
Connie Klinger	Michele Scarabelli
Ada Fishbine	Hilary Shepard

Also with Marlena Giovi, Lela Ivey, Ralph Monaco, Al Ruscio, Arleen Sorkin, Larry Storch and Cassie Yates.

Credits

Executive Producer	Charles Weber
Producer	Mitchell Matovich
Line Producer	Gary M. Bettman
Director	Robert Marcarelli
Assistant Directors	Gregory Everage
	Lynn D'Angona
Director of Photography	Michael Ferris
Sound	David Waelder
Editor	Joanne D'Antonio
Production Design	Byrnadette di Santo
Set Decoration	Katherine Orrison
Costume Design	Patte Dee
Casting	Cathy Henderson
Written by	Jonnie Lindsell
Additional Dialogue	Ross McKerras
Music	Cobb Bussinger

Film Facts

Running Time	112 minutes
Film	Color
Sound	Ultra-Stereo
Location	Los Angeles; Philadelphia

The Importance Of Being Earnest
(Eclectic Concepts/Paco Global)

Critics Rating: Not Rated.

Genre: Comedy—This rendition of the Oscar Wilde classic comedy of manners boasts an all-black cast.

Plot: Set in present-day England, the plot revolves around two women who believe that they can only love a man named Earnest. Two men eager for their affections set out to oblige but then the best laid plans often go astray. The charm, wit and high jinks that follow, of course, all lead up to a happy ending.

MPAA Rating: Not Rated.

Cast

Algernon	Wren T. Brown
Jack	Daryl Roach
Gwendolyn	Chris Calloway
Cecily	Lanei Chapman
Lady Bracknell	Ann Weldon
Dr. Chausible	Brock Peters
Miss Prism	C. C. H. Pounder
Lane	Obba Babatunde
Merriman	Barbara Isaacs

Credits

Executive Producer	Peter Andrews
Producer	Nancy Carter Crow
Associate Producers	Deani Wood
	Jimmy Richardson
Director	Kurt Baker

Directors of Photography ....Mark Angell
.................................Joseph Wilmond Calloway
Sound...Romeo Williams
Editor...Tracey Alexander
Art Design...Lennie Barin
Set Design ....Toni Singman
Screenplay...Peter Andrews
....Kurt Baker
Based on the stageplay by ....Oscar Wilde
Music ....Roger Hamilton Spotts

Film Facts
Running Time ....123 minutes
Film ....Color
Sound ....Stereo

Production Manager........................Jonathan Winfrey
Production Design ....Hector Velez
Costume Design ....Meta Marie Jardine
Casting..Steve Rabiner
Written by ....Rodman Flender
Music ....Art Wood
....Ken Rarick

Film Facts
Running Time ....82 minutes
Film ....Foto-Kem Color
Sound..Ultra-Stereo
Location ....Los Angeles

In The Heat Of Passion
(Concorde)

Critics Rating: Not Rated.
Genre: Thriller—This low-budget thriller follows a struggling actor who meets and falls for a rich woman. Igniting his passion, she sets the stage for the suspense and surprise to follow.
Plot: Nick Corri plays a mostly unemployed actor named Charlie Bronson. When he meets and becomes involved with a rich and beautiful married woman, their passions lead to disaster and intrigue.
MPAA Rating: R

Cast
Lee ....Sally Kirkland
Charlie Bronson...Nick Corri
Stan ....Jack Carter
Sanford Adams ....Michael Greene
Perez...Carlos Carrasco
Det. Rooker ....Carl Franklin
Betty..Gloria Le Roy

Credits
Executive Producer ....Roger Corman
Producer/Director ....Rodman Flender
Co-Producer....................................Mike Elliott
Assistant Director ....Juan A. Mas
2nd Unit Director ....Charles Philip Moore
Director of Photography.......................Wally Pfister
2nd Unit Camera ....William Molina
Sound..Chris Taylor
....Cameron Hamza
Editor...Patrick Rand

In The Soup
(Triton)

Critics Rating: ★★★★
Genre: Comedy—Winner of the 1992 Sundance Film Festival Grand Jury Prize. A low-budget, independent, black-and-white comedy-drama about the hidden side of filmmaking.
Plot: Steve Buscemi (*Barton Fink*, *Billy Bathgate*) plays Adolpho, a naive would-be filmmaker just barely staying afloat on New York's Lower East Side. To pay his rent, he places his 500-page script for sale in a classified ad. Answering the ad is Joe (Cassel), a fast-talking con-artist and would-be film producer. The unlikely pair embark on a series of humorous fund-raising vignettes that unfortunately lead to a dead end. Much fun is had along the way including memorable cameos by Carol Kane and Jim Jarmusch as producers of a nude talk show on cable access.
MPAA Rating: Not Rated.

Cast
Adolpho Rollo ....Steve Buscemi
Joe ....Seymour Cassel
Angelica ....Jennifer Beals
Dang...Pat Moya
Skippy ....Will Patton
Monty ....Jim Jarmusch
Barbara..Carol Kane
Old man ....Sully Boyer
Louis Bafardi ....Steven Randazzo
Frank Bafardi ....Francesco Messina
Also with Elizabeth Bracco, Debi Mazar, Rockets Redgrave and Stanley Tucci.

Credits

Executive Producer	Ryuichi Suzuki
Co-Executive Producers	Chosei Funahara
	Junichi Suzuki
Producers	Jim Stark
	Hank Blumenthal
Director	Alexandre Rockwell
Assistant Director	Mary Beth Hagner
Director of Photography	Phil Parmet
Sound	Pavel Wdowczak
Editor	Dana Congdon
Production Design	Mark Friedberg
Art Direction	Ginger Tougas
Costume Design	Elizabeth Bracco
Casting	Walken & Jaffe
Screenplay	Alexandre Rockwell
	Tim Kissell
Music	Mader

Film Facts

Running Time	93 minutes
Film	DuArt Black & White
Sound	Stereo
Location	New York

Incident At Oglala
(Miramax)

Critics Rating: ★★★★

Genre: Documentary—Directed by Michael Apted (*35 Up*) and narrated by Robert Redford, *Incident At Oglala* is a powerful and provocative film that probes the case of Native American Leonard Peltier. Peltier was jailed for the murder of two FBI agents in 1975.

Plot: The FBI agents were murdered while investigating the American Indian Movement on the Pine Ridge reservation in South Dakota. The film, however, focuses on the injustice done to Peltier. Based solely on circumstantial evidence the trial resulted in two consecutive life sentences for the murders. The documentary makes a case, at the very least, for a new trial.

MPAA Rating: PG

Credits

Executive Producer	Robert Redford
Producer	Arthur Chobanian
Associate Producer	Chip Selby
Director	Michael Apted
Director of Photography	Maryse Alberti
Editor	Susanne Rostock
Musical Score Producers	John Trudell
	Jackson Browne
Narration	Robert Redford

Film Facts

Running Time	90 minutes
Film	Color
Sound	Stereo

Indochine
(Sony Pictures Classics)

Critics Rating: ★★★★

Genre: Drama—Set in Vietnam in the 1930s, *Indochine* is a romantic saga about a woman, her daughter and the man who comes between them. Strong performances and a powerfully told story have won the film praise with critics and audiences alike.

Tag Line: "Before Vietnam there was a land called Indochine."

Plot: Catherine Deneuve stars as Eliane, a Frenchwoman and plantation owner. Newcomer Linh Dan Pham plays her adopted Indochinese daughter, Camille. When both women unexpectedly fall for the same man, their lives are profoundly changed and take tragic and ironically different directions as a result. When the man they both love, French Navy officer Jean-Baptiste (Perez) is transferred away, Camille follows. They have a child, but before they can settle down together their lives are disrupted by an incident that forces them to go undercover to escape the authorities. Eliane is left to raise the child, who learns of his parents' story when he reaches adulthood, the point from which the story is told.

MPAA Rating: PG-13—For some violence, sensuality and drug-related scenes.

Cast

Eliane	Catherine Deneuve
Jean-Baptiste	Vincent Perez
Camille	Linh Dan Pham
Guy	Jean Yanne
Yvette	Dominique Blanc
Emile	Henri Marteau
Shen	Mai Chau

Mrs. Minh Tam ....Thi Hoe Tranh Huu Treiu
Also with Carlo Brandt, Alain Fromager, Chu
Hung, Gerard Lartigau, Hubert Saint-Macary and
Andrzej Seweryn.

Credits

Producer	Eric Heumann
Director	Regis Wargnier
Director of Photography	Francois Catonne
Sound	Guillaume Sciama
Editor	Genevieve Winding
Sets	Jacques Buenior
Costume Design	Gabriella Pescucci
Casting	Pierre Amzallag
Screenplay	Erik Orsenna
	Louis Gardeal
	Catherine Cohen
	Regis Wargnier
Music	Patrick Doyle

Film Facts

Country of Origin	France
Running Time	158 minutes
Movie	Color
Sound	Dolby Stereo

The Inland Sea
(Films, Inc./Voyager)

Critics Rating: Not Rated.
Genre: Documentary—Filmmakers Lucille Carra and Brian Cotnoir have retraced the course of historian Donald Richie's 30-year-old travelogue, "The Inland Sea."
Plot: Contrasting the old with the new, the filmmakers depict a way of life in the Japanese Aegean Sea that is quickly being overrun by progress. Narrated by Richie, the film is a personal look at a changing time and place.
MPAA Rating: Not Rated.

Credits

Executive Producer	Gerald Carrus
Producers	Brian Cotnoir
	Lucille Carra
Associate Producers	Larry Massett
	Art Silverman
Director	Lucille Carra
Director of Photography	Hiro Narita
Sound	Tom Hartig
Editor	Brian Cotnoir

Written by	Donald Richie
Based on the Book by	Donald Richie
Music	Toru Taketa
Narrated by	Donald Richie

Film Facts

Running Time	57 minutes
Film	DuArt Color
Sound	Stereo
Location	Japan

Innocent Blood
(Warner Bros.)

Critics Rating: ★★
Genre: Horror—A horror-comedy from the director of *An American Werewolf In London*.
Tag Line: "For generations, the Mafia preyed on the innocent. Tonight, someone's feasting on them."
Plot: Anne Parillaud (*La Femme Nikita*) plays Marie, a sexy, red-eyed, foul-mouthed vampire living in modern-day Pittsburgh. Setting her sights on the town's bad guys, she sinks her teeth into Mob kingpin Sal (Robert Loggia). Unfortunately, he comes back from the dead stronger than ever. This puts a new kink in undercover cop Joe Gennaro's (Anthony LaPaglia) sting operation. Before long, Joe and Marie join forces to stop this out-of-control, bloodthirsty gangster. All of this, of course, is merely a setup for the played-for-laughs blood bath and mayhem.
MPAA Rating: R—For vampire violence, sexuality and language.

Cast

Marie	Anne Parillaud
Sal "The Shark" Macelli	Robert Loggia
Joe Gennaro	Anthony LaPaglia
Emmanuel Bergman	Don Rickles
Frannie Bergman	Elaine Kagan
Lenny	David Proval
Tony	Chazz Palminteri

Also with Kim Coates and Rocco Sisto.

Credits

Executive Producer	Jonathan Sheinberg
Producers	Lee Rich
	Leslie Belzberg
Associate Producer	Michael Wolk

Director	John Landis
Assistant Director	Nicholas Mastandrea
Director of Photography	Mac Ahlberg
Sound	Joseph Geisinger
Editor	Dale Beldin
Production Design	Richard Sawyer
Set Design	Carl Stensel
Set Decoration	Peg Cummings
Costume Design	Deborah Nadoolman
Casting	Sharon Howard-Field
Written by	Michael Wolk
Music	Ira Newborn
Special Visual Effects	Syd Dutton, Bill Taylor
Special Makeup Effects	Steve Johnson
Stunt Coordinator	Rick Avery

Film Facts

Running Time	112 minutes
Film	Technicolor
Sound	Dolby Stereo
Location	Pittsburgh

Innocents Abroad
(Dox Deluxe)

Critics Rating: Not Rated.

Genre: Documentary—Documentary director Les Blank has chosen an unusually lighthearted topic on which to focus his lens. The subjects examined are American tourists on a two-week European bus tour. While the film is often humorous, it is also a bit disturbing. At times it seems that all of Europe is just an endless museum and that tourism is the continent's biggest industry.

MPAA Rating: Not Rated.

Credits

Producer	Vikram Jayanti
Director	Les Blank
2nd Unit Director	Miel Van Hoogenbemt
Director of Photography	Les Blank
2nd Unit Camera	Louis Phillipe Capelle
Sound/Editor	Chris Simon
2nd Unit Sound	Phillipe Selier

Film Facts

Running Time	84 minutes
Film	Technicolor (16mm)
Sound	Stereo
Location	England; Germany; Switzerland; The Netherlands; Italy; France

Inspecteur Lavardin
(MK2)

Critics Rating: Not Rated.

Genre: Drama—*Inspecteur Lavardin* is a 1986 murder mystery by director Claude Chabrol.

Plot: Jean Poiret, who died March 14, 1992, (see Obituaries), stars as police detective Lavardin, a man obsessed with investigating the murder of a friend. The suspects are numerous, from members of the under-world to a number of family members. Lavardin himself was personally involved with many of the suspects, which only adds to the humor and chaos.

MPAA Rating: Not Rated.

Cast

Inspecteur Lavardin	Jean Poiret
Claude Alvarez	Jean-Claude Brialy
Helene Mons	Bernadette Lafont
Max Charnet	Jean-Luc Bideau
Raoul Mons	Jacques Dacqmine
Veronique Manguin	Hermine Claire
Marcel Vigouroux	Pierre-Francois Dumeniaud
Francis	Florent Gibassier
Buci	Guy Louret
Volga	Jean Depusse

Credits

Producer	Martin Karmitz
Director	Claude Chabrol
Director of Photography	Jean Rabier
Editors	Monique Fardoulis
	Angela Braga-Mermet
Production Manager	Catherine Lapoujade
Art Direction	Francois Benoit-Fresco
Screenplay	Dominique Roulet, Claude Chabrol
Music	Matthieu Chabrol

Film Facts

Country of Origin	France
Running Time	100 minutes
Film	Eastmancolor
Sound	Stereo

Intergirl
(Interdevotchka)
(University of Minnesota Film Center)

Critics Rating: Not Rated.

Genre: Drama—This Soviet drama looks at a familiar topic from a new and original point of view.

Plot: Elena Yakovleva plays Tatyana, a nurse living in Leningrad who must supplement her income by working as a call girl. When one of her clients, a Swedish businessman, falls in love with her, she sees this as her big opportunity. After marrying the man and moving to Sweden, she finds she has everything she wants. Despite her newfound wealth, she is lonely and homesick, longing for her family and homeland. She is a woman caught between two worlds.

MPAA Rating: Not Rated.

Cast

Tatyana	Elena Yakovleva
Edvard	Tomas Laustiola
Alla Sergeevna	Larisa Malevannaya
Lyalka	Anastasiya Nemolaeva

Credits

Director	Pyotr Todorovski
Director of Photography	Valery Shuvalov
Production Design	Valentin Konovalov
Screenplay	Vladimir Kunin
Music	Pyotr Todorovski

Film Facts

Country of Origin	Soviet Union/Sweden
Running Time	155 minutes
Film	Color
Sound	Stereo

Intervista

(Castle Hill)

Critics Rating: ★★★★

Genre: Drama—Originally filmed in 1987, it is only now being released in the U.S., with Martin Scorsese's help. Art-house audiences will appreciate that the filmmaker has not lost his humor, warmth nor style.

Plot: In this film within a film within a film, Fellini plays himself and is preparing to film Kafka's *America*. During the filming, a Japanese TV crew arrives to film the filmmaker. In a flashback, we witness the director's introduction to the film business. In another scene, he is joined by Marcello Mastroianni and Anita Ekberg, who play themselves. Together they watch a clip from *La Dolce Vita*, the Fellini masterpiece in which they starred. It is a touching moment in a charming and delightful film.

MPAA Rating: Not Rated.

Cast

The reporter	Sergio Rubini
The assistant director	Maurizio Mein
The star	Paola Liguori
The vestal virgin	Nadia Ottaviani
The wife	Lara Wendel
The girl	Antonella Ponziani

Also with Anita Ekberg and Marcello Mastroianni.

Credits

Line Producer	Pietro Notarianni
Director	Federico Fellini
Director of Photography	Tonino Delli Colli
Editor	Nino Baragli
Production Design	Danilo Donati
Screenplay	Federico Fellini
Screenplay Collaborator	Gianfranco Angelucci
Music	Nicola Piovani

Film Facts

Country of Origin	Italy
Language	Italian (subtitled)
Running Time	108 minutes
Movie	Color
Sound	Stereo

Intimate Stranger

Critics Rating: Not Rated.

Genre: Documentary—Filmmaker Alan Berliner tells the story of his grandfather, Joseph Cassuto. Cassuto was, in many ways, a mystery man. Although his family lived in New York, he spent much of his professional life living in Japan as a trader.

Plot: Through the use of vintage photos, home films and commentary by his family and business associates, a fascinating life story is told. In the telling, a larger story of a historical time and place is also revealed.

MPAA Rating: Not Rated.

Credits

Producer/Director/Editor	Alan Berliner

Written by ....Alan Berliner
Film Facts
Genre......................................Documentary
Running Time ....60 minutes
Movie............................DuArt Color/Black & White
Sound ....Stereo

Into The Sun

(Trimark)

Critics Rating: ★

Genre: Action—This knockoff of last year's *The Hard Way,* starring Michael J. Fox, is an action comedy about a Hollywood actor who gets himself assigned to work with a resentful Air Force pilot to research an upcoming role.

Tag Line: "At Mach 2 you have two choices—win or die."

Plot: Anthony Michael Hall plays the cocky actor, Tom Slade. Michael Pare plays pilot Paul Watkins, a man serious about his work and put off by Slade. Things come easily to Slade, including Watkins's girl. But when the two men accidentally get caught in the middle of some real action and are shot down, they eventually discover that they need one another to survive.

MPAA Rating: R—For language.

Cast
Tom Slade................................Anthony Michael Hall
Capt. Paul Watkins.............................Michael Pare
Mitchell Burton ....Terry Kiser
Major Goode............................Deborah Maria Moore
Lt. Wolf.............................Michael St. Gerard
Lt. DeCarlo..................................Brian Haley
Dragon.......................................Linden Ashby

Credits
Executive in Charge of Production...........................
....Joseph Akerman
Executive Producer ....Mark Amin
Producers ....Kevin M. Kallberg
....Oliver G. Hess
Supervising Producer ....Jim Begg
Director ....Fritz Kiersch
Assistant Director ....George Parra
2nd Unit Director ....Ernie F. Orsatti
Director of Photography ....Steve Grass
Insert Camera/Aerial Camera ....Lee Redmond
Sound ....Ed White
Editor ....Barry Zetlin
Editor (Additional)....................Marc Grossman
Production Manager ....Cristen M. Carr
Production Design ....Gary T. New
Art Direction..................................Dana Torrey
Set Decoration....................A. Rosalind Crew
Casting ....Jack Jones
Screenplay and story by ....Michael Ferris
....John Brancato
Music ....Randy Miller
Visual Effects Supervisor ....Richard Kerrigan
Stunt Coordinator..........................Ernie F. Orsatti
Additional Flying Sequences.......David Stipes Prods.

Film Facts
Running Time ....100 minutes
Film ....Foto-Kem Color
Sound ....Dolby Stereo

Jennifer 8

(Paramount)

Critics Rating: ★★★
Genre: Thriller—A straightforward serial-killer plot with a few very suspenseful cinematic turns.
Tag Line: "On the trail of a serial killer, detective John Berlin has no clues, no suspects and no alibi."
Plot: Andy Garcia *(Hero)* stars as Sgt. John Berlin, a former Los Angeles detective with a new job investigating serial killings in a small Northern California town. During the investigation he becomes romantically involved with Helena (Thurman), a blind witness who resembles his ex-wife. He believes she is the killer's next intended victim. An FBI agent (Malkovich), however, believes that Berlin may be responsible for the murders.
MPAA Rating: R—For sexuality, nudity, violence and language.

Cast

John Berlin	Andy Garcia
Helena Robertson	Uma Thurman
Freddy Ross	Lance Henriksen
Margie Ross	Kathy Baker
John Taylor	Graham Beckel
Citrine	Kevin Conway
St. Anne	John Malkovich
Travis	Perry Lang
Bisley	Nicholas Love
Serato	Michael O'Neill
Venables	Paul Bates
Blattis	Lenny Von Dohlen

Credits

Executive Producer	Scott Rudin
Producers	Gary Lucchesi
	David Wimbury
Associate Producers	Grace Gilroy
	Steve Lim
Director	Bruce Robinson
Assistant Directors	David B. Householter
	Newton D. Arnold
Director of Photography	Conrad L. Hall
Sound	Arthur Rochester
Editor	Conrad Buff
Production Design	Richard MacDonald
Art Direction	William Durrell, Jr.
	John Willett
Set Design	Jim Bayliss
	Louis M. Mann, Cosmos A. Demetriou
Set Decoration	Casey C. Hallenbeck
	Elizabeth Wilcox
Costume Design	Judy Ruskin
Casting	Billy Hopkins
	Suzanne Smith
Written by	Bruce Robinson
Music	Christopher Young
Technical Adviser	T. J. Hageboeck

Film Facts

Running Time	127 minutes
Soundtrack	RCA Records
Film	Deluxe Color
Sound	Dolby Stereo
Location	Vancouver, British Columbia;
	Los Angeles

The JFK Assassination: The Garrison Tapes

(Blue Ridge/Filmtrust)

Critics Rating: Not Rated.
Genre: Documentary
Plot: Using archive film clips, reports from eyewitnesses and testimony from New Orleans District Attorney Jim Garrison, this straightforward documentary takes another stab at investigating the JFK assassination. TV journalist John Barbour follows the investigation and conspiracy theory without the glitz and glamour portrayed in Oliver Stone's 1991 film.
MPAA Rating: Not Rated.
Trivia: Jim Garrison, who appeared in Oliver Stone's film *JFK* died October 21, 1992, in New Orleans of heart disease.

Credits

Executive Producer ....Tom Kuhn
Co-Executive Producer ....Lamar Card
Associate Producer ....Christopher Barbour
Co-Producer ....Sarita Barbour
Director...John Barbour
Directors of Photography.......................Greg Bader
....Dennis P. Boni
....Steve Elkins, Robert Perrin
Sound..Michael Weatherwax
Written by...John Barbour
Music ....David Wheatly

Film Facts

Running Time ....92 minutes
Film ....Color/Black & White
Sound ....Stereo

Johanna D'Arc
Of Mongolia
(Women Make Films)

Critics Rating: Not Rated.
Genre: Drama—In this odd tale, modern-day women go on a retreat each year to reenact the traditions of their past.
Plot: When a group of travelling Western women is abducted from the Trans-Mongolian Express by a group of female Mongolians, the stage is set for a reenactment of past traditions. The women spend a month in this female camp exploring their traditions.
MPAA Rating: Not Rated.

Cast

Lady Windermere.............................Delphine Seyrig
Ulun Iga..Xu Re Huar
Frau Muller-Vohwinkel ....Irm Hermann
Fanny Ziegfield....................................Gillian Scalici
Giovanna..Ines Sastre
Mickey Katz ....Peter Kern
Colonel Muravjev ....Nougzar Sharia
Alyosha...Christoph Eichhorn
The Kalinka Sisters...Jacinta
....Else Nabu
....Sevembike Elibay
Also with Badema, Lydia Billiet, Alfredo Cocozza, Jan Deckers, Amadeus Flossner, Tu Hai, Xu Ren Hu, Kunio Sato, Marek Szmelkin, Yi Tuo Ya and Dong Zihao.

Credits

Producer/Director/Editor....................Ulrike Ottinger
Director of Photography ....Ulrike Ottinger
Sound ....Margit Eschenbach
Production Managers ....Renne Gundelach
....Hanna Rogge
....Harald Muchametow
....Erica Marcus
Production Managers (China) ....Ren Da Hui
....Weng Dao Cai
....Lian Zhen Hua
....China Central TV
....CITV Beijing
Production Design............................Ulrike Ottinger
....Peter Bausch
Costume Design ....Gisela Storch
Written by..Ulrike Ottinger
Music Arrangements.............Wilhelm Dieter Siebert

Film Facts

Country of Origin.................................Germany
Running Time ....165 minutes
Film ....Color
Sound ....Stereo

John Lurie And
The Lounge Lizards
Live In Berlin
(Telecom Japan)

Critics Rating: Not Rated.
Genre: Documentary—Garret Linn makes his feature directorial debut.
Plot: The film is a straightforward concert film focusing on actor-saxophonist John Lurie. Spotlighting his jazz-fusion style, the action takes place in the Quartier Latin nightclub in Berlin. Lurie is known primarily for his roles in Jim Jarmusch films.
MPAA Rating: Not Rated.

Cast

With John Lurie, Michael Blake, Steven Bernstein, Jane Scarpantoni, Bryan Carrot, Michele Navazio, Billy Martin, Oren Bloedow, and Grant Calvin Weston.

Credits

Executive Producer ....Kenji Okabe
Producers...Valerie Goodman
....Taku Nishimae

Director ....Garret Linn
Directors of Photography ....Uta Badura
....Andre Harris
....Garret Linn
Sound ....Tom Lazarus
Editor..Caleb Oglesby
Music ....John Lurie
Concept ....Robert Burden

Film Facts
Country of Origin.....................Japan/United States
Running Time ....101 minutes
Film ....Color
Sound ....Stereo
Location ....Berlin

Johnny Stecchino
(New Line Cinema)

Critics Rating: ★★★

Genre: Comedy—Italian writer, director and actor Roberto Benigni (*Night On Earth*) brings to the American screen a high-energy, slapstick, mistaken-identity tale that has become one of the most popular films in Italian history.

Plot: Benigni stars as Dante, a simple school-bus driver. His life is fairly uneventful until the day he is mistaken for mobster Johnny Stecchino, who is in hiding. After Johnny's wife, Maria (Braschi), discovers that Dante is a dead ringer for her husband, she decides to set him up and get her husband off the hook. Her plans quickly change, however, when she falls for Dante, finding him much more appealing than her husband.

MPAA Rating: R—For language and drug-related humor.

Cast
Dante ....Roberto Benigni
Maria..Nicoletta Braschi
D'Agata..Paolo Bonacelli
Cozzamara ....Ignazio Pappalardo
Minister..Franco Volpi

Credits
Producers ....Mario Cecchi Gori
....Vittorio Cecchi Gori
Director..Roberto Benigni
Director of Photography.....................Giuseppe Lanci
Editor ....Nino Baragli

Art Direction ....Paolo Biagetti
Written by ....Vincenzo Cerami
....Roberto Benigni
Music..Evan Lurie

Film Facts
Country of Origin ....Italy
Language ....Italian (subtitled)
Running Time ....105 minutes
Film ....Color
Sound ....Stereo

Johnny Suede
(Miramax)

Critics Rating: ★★★

Genre: Comedy—In this unusual romantic comedy, a young man from New York's Lower East Side dreams of making it big as a rock 'n' roll star.

Tag Line: "He's a heartbreaker...lover...loner... Keeping up an image can be a full time job."

Plot: Brad Pitt (*Cool World, A River Runs Through It*) plays Johnny Suede, a no-talent singer and songwriter who idolizes Ricky Nelson. He naively dreams of achieving musical greatness like his idol. The fun begins and ends as he tries to make his dream come true.

MPAA Rating: R—For language and elements of sexuality.

Cast
Johnny ....Brad Pitt
Yvonne......................................Catherine Keener
Deak..Calvin Levels
Freak Storm...Nick Cave
Mrs. Fontaine..Tina Louise

Credits
Executive Producers ....Ruth Waldburger
....Steven Starr
Producers ....Yoram Mandel
....Ruth Waldburger
Co-Producers ....Alain Klarer
....Bruno Pesery
....Janet Jacobsen
Director...Tom DiCillo
Director of Photography ....Joe DeSalvo
Sound ....Dominick Tavella
Editor ....Geraldine Peroni
Production Design ....Patricia Woodbridge

Costume Design ....Jessica Haston
Casting..Marcia Shulman
Screenplay ....Tom DiCillo
Music ....Jim Farmer
Additional Music......................................Link Wray

Film Facts
Running Time ....97 minutes
Film ....Color
Sound ....Stereo

Juice
(Paramount)

Critics Rating: ★★★

Genre: Drama—*Juice* is a sensitive film with an antiviolence message. Unfortunately, it was the first film of the year to bring real-life violence to the theaters in what seems to be a growing trend.

Tag Line: "Power, respect, juice. How far will you go to get it?"

Plot: Focusing on the lives of four New York City teenage blacks, Bishop, Q, Raheem and Steel, the story moves from petty crimes to big-time crime. Following what was intended to be a routine robbery of a local store, the friends' lives and ambitions are shattered when Bishop accidentally kills the store owner. As their lives deteriorate, Bishop eventually turns on his friends as well in a homicidal rage.

MPAA Rating: R—For strong language and some violence.

Cast
Q..Omar Epps
Steel ....Jermaine Hopkins
Raheem..Khalil Kain
Bishop...Tupac Shakur
Yolanda...Cindy Herron
Trip ....Samuel L. Jackson
Radames.......................................Vincent Laresca

Credits
Producers ....David Heyman
....Neal H. Moritz
....Peter Frankfurt
Co-Producer ....Preston Holmes
Associate Producers ....James Bigwood
....Gerard Brown
Director...Ernest R. Dickerson

Assistant Director.....................................H.H. Cooper
Director of Photography ....Larry Banks
Sound ....Franklin D. Stettner
Editors ....Sam Pollard
....Brunilda Torres
Production Manager ....Brent Owens
Production Design.................................Lester Cohen
Set Decoration ....Alyssa Winter
Costume Design ....Donna Berwick
Casting...Jaki Brown
Screenplay...Gerard Brown
....Ernest R. Dickerson
Story by ....Ernest R. Dickerson
Music Supervisor......................................Kathy Nelson
Music...............Hank Shocklee and The Bomb Squad

Film Facts
Running Time ....92 minutes
Soundtrack ...............................S.O.U. L. Records
Film ....TVC- Precision Color
Sound ....Dolby Stereo
Location..New York

Jumpin' At The Boneyard
(20th Century Fox)

Critics Rating: ★★★

Genre: Drama—Harsh, downbeat tale of the ravaging effects of drug addiction and the bonds shared between two brothers. High marks are given for its memorable performances.

Tag Line: "Brothers don't always love each other, but sometimes they have to."

Plot: Tim Roth and Alexis Arquette star as Manny and Dan, two brothers headed down different paths. When their paths collide, Manny is forced to open his eyes to Dan's cocaine addiction and the depths to which he has sunk. From this point on Manny makes it his mission to help his brother overcome his situation. Then just as he is getting his life on track again, tragedy strikes and he is derailed.

MPAA Rating: R—For language.

Cast
Manny...Tim Roth
Dan ....Alexis Arquette
Jeanette ....Danitra Vance
Mom...Kathleen Chalfant
Mr. Simpson ....Samuel L. Jackson

Taxi driver...Luis Guzman
Cathy ....Elizabeth Bracco

Credits

Executive Producer........................Lawrence Kasdan
Producers ....Nina R. Sadowsky
....Lloyd Goldfine
Director ....Jeff Stanzler
Director of Photography ....Lloyd Goldfine
Sound...Catherine Benedek
Editor...Christopher Tellefsen
Production Design...........................Caroline Wallner
Costume Design...............................Natasha Landau
Makeup ....Roosevelt Madison
Written by ....Jeff Stanzler
Music ....Steve Postel

Film Facts

Running Time ....107 minutes
Film ....Color
Sound..Dolby Stereo

Just Like In The Movies
(Cabriolet)

Critics Rating: Not Rated.

Genre: Comedy—Cowriters and -directors, Bram Towbin and Mark Halliday have produced an original, low-budget, oddball comedy-drama about the life of a private investigator.

Plot: Jay O. Sanders (*JFK, V.I. Warshawski*) stars as Ryan Legrand, an uptight, New York private investigator. His partner, Dean (Ruck) is easy-going and full of life. Together they follow spouses in matrimonial cases. As Ryan watches marriages and families fall apart, he tries desperately to put his own life and family back together.

MPAA Rating: Not Rated.

Cast

Ryan Legrand.......................................Jay O. Sanders
Dean...Alan Ruck
Tura ....Katherine Borowitz
Vernon..Michael Jeter
Carter ....Alex Vincent

Credits

Producer..Alon Kasha
Directors ....Bram Towbin
....Mark Halliday
Director of Photography ....Peter Fernberger
Editor..Jay Keuper
Production Design......................Marek Dobrowolski
Costume Design ....Linda Fisher
Casting ....Brian Chavanne
Written by...Bram Towbin
....Mark Halliday
Music...John Hill

Film Facts

Running Time ....90 minutes
Film ....Color
Sound ....Stereo

K2: The Ultimate High

(Paramount)

Critics Rating: ★★★

Genre: Action—*K2* is a peak experience. It's also the adventure story of two buddies who scale the second highest peak in the Himalayas.

Tag Line: "The Ultimate High, 28,000 feet. You're hanging on by your fingernails. The adrenaline alone could kill you."

Plot: Michael Biehn (*Terminator, Rampage*) stars as Seattle lawyer and mountain climber, Taylor. After convincing his good friend, Harold, to leave his family behind for the ultimate adventure, he takes his friend along to join the U. S. Climbing Team for the trek. One by one the others fall by the wayside, leaving the two friends to make it on their own.

MPAA Rating: R—For language.

Cast

Taylor Brooks	Michael Biehn
Harold Jamison	Matt Craven
Phillip Claiborne	Raymond J. Barry
Takane Shimuzu	Hiroshi Fujioka
Jacki Metcalfe	Patricia Charbonneau
Dallas Woolf	Luca Bercovici
Cindy Jamison	Julia Nickson-Soul

Also with Annie Grindlay, Jamal Shah and Elena Stiteler.

Credits

Executive Producers	Melvyn J. Estrin
	Hal Weiner
Producers	Jonathan Taplin
	Marilyn Weiner
	Tim Van Rellim
Associate Producer	Masa Mikage
Director	Franc Roddam
Assistant Director	John Watson
Director of Photography	Gabriel Beristain
2nd Unit Camera	Peter Pilafian
Sound	David Stephenson
	Martin Evans
	Robin O'Donoghue
Editor	Sean Barton
Production Design	Andrew Sanders
Art Direction	Richard Hudolin
Set Decoration	Ted Kuchera
Costume Design	Kathryn Morrison
Casting (London)	Victoria Thomas
Casting (Vancouver)	Michelle Allen
Screenplay	Patrick Meyers
	Scott Roberts
Based on the play by	Patrick Meyers
Music	Chaz Jankel

Film Facts

Country of Origin	Great Britain
Running Time	104 minutes
Film	Fujicolor
Sound	Dolby Stereo

Kickboxer III: The Art Of War

(Kings Road/Vision International)

Critics Rating: Not Rated.

Genre: Action—Number three in the martial-arts series that started with Jean-Claude Van Damme.

Plot: Sasha Mitchell (*Death Before Dishonor*, *Spike Of Bensonhurst*) once again plays American kickboxing champion David Sloan. In this outing he is in Rio de Janeiro for a charity tournament. While there, he befriends Costa (Verduzco) and his sister Lora (Miranda), two street urchins and fans. When Lane (Comar), the fight promoter, meets Lora, he is taken with the young girl and has her kidnapped for his secret prostitute service. When David learns that Lane is responsible for the kidnapping, the scene is set for nonstop violence and martial-arts stunts, all leading to a predictable happy ending.

MPAA Rating: R—For some strong violence.

Cast

David	Sasha Mitchell
Xian	Dennis Chan

Lane	Richard Comar
Marcos	Noah Verduzco
Sargeant	Milton Goncalves
Isabella	Alethea Miranda
Marcelo	Miguel Orniga
Alberto	Ricardo Petraglia
Pete	Gracindo Junior
Branco	Renato Coutinho
Martine	Ian Jacklin
Machado	Manitu Felipe
Reinaldo	Shuki Ron
Father Bozano	Bernardo Jablownsky

Credits

Executive Producer	Luciana Boal Marinho
Producer	Michael Pariser
Associate Producer	Kinga Kozdron
Director	Rick King
Assistant Director	Vincente Amorim
Director of Photography	Edgar Moura
Sound Mixer	Lee Orloff
Editor	Dan Lowenthal
Production Design	Clovis Bueno
Art Direction	Toni Vanzolini
Costume Design	Isabela Braga
Casting	Mary Jo Slater
Casting (Brazil)	Isabel Diegues
Screenplay	Dennis Pratt
Music	Harry Manfredini
Stunt Coordinator/Fight Choreographer	Webster Whinery

Film Facts

Running Time	92 minutes
Film	Deluxe Color
Sound	Ultra-Stereo
Location	Los Angeles; Brazil

Killer Image

(Groundstar Entertainment)

Critics Rating: Not Rated.

Genre: Thriller—Canadian film released on video during the summer and re-released in theaters in December for Oscar consideration.

Plot: M. Emmet Walsh plays Sam Kane, a corrupt senator. When Kane is confronted by Ric Oliver (Austin), a photographer with incriminating photos of the senator and a prostitute, the photographer turns up dead. His brother Max (Pyper-Ferguson) is determined to avenge his brother's death but is foiled by the senator's equally corrupt brother, Luther (Ironside). Things get a bit complicated but Max is eventually able to turn the two Kane brothers against one another and even the score.

MPAA Rating: R

Cast

Sam Kane	M. Emmet Walsh
Max Oliver	John Pyper-Ferguson
Shelly	Krista Errickson
Luther	Michael Ironside
Stacey	Barbra Gajewskia
Ric Oliver	Paul Austin
Lori	Chantelle Jenkins
Carrie	Kristie Baker

Credits

Executive Producer	Jim Murphy
Producers	David Winning
	Rudy Barichello
	Bruce Harvey
Line Producer	Les Kimber
Associate Producer	Andre Lauzon
Director	David Winning
Assistant Director	David MacLeod
Director of Photography	Dean Bennett
Sound	George Tarrant
Editor	Alan Collins
Art Direction	Bruce Sinski
Casting	Leslie Swan
Screenplay	David Winning
	Stan Edmonds
	Jaron Summers
Music	Stephen Foster

Film Facts

Country of Origin	Canada
Running Time	96 minutes
Film	Fuji Color
Sound	Stereo

The Killing Floor

(Made in USA)

Critics Rating: Not Rated.

Genre: Drama—Originally airing on PBS eight years ago, *The Killing Floor*, a painful and powerful drama about the struggle to establish labor unions in the World War I era, is only now being released theatrically.

Plot: Damien Leake stars as Frank Custer, a poor black man living in Chicago who played a major role in the early union movement. When Frank moves to Chicago looking for work, he quickly finds a job in a meat-packing plant. Not surprisingly, he also finds prejudice. After joining the union, he eventually battles not only the company but the prejudice of co-workers as well.

MPAA Rating: PG

Cast

Mattie Custer	Alfre Woodard
Harry	Dennis Farina
Heavy Williams	Moses Gunn
Frank Custer	Damien Leake
Bill Bremer	Clarence Felder
Thomas Joshua	Ernest Rayford

Credits

Executive Producer	Elsa Rassbach
Director	Bill Duke
Director of Photography	Bill Birch
Editor	John Carter
Screenplay	Leslie Lee
Story by	Elsa Rassbach
Adapted by	Ron Milner
Music	Elizabeth Swados

Film Facts

Running Time	118 minutes
Film	Color
Sound	Stereo

Kuffs

(Universal)

Critics Rating: ★

Genre: Comedy—Full of charm and good-natured fun, this comedy about the difficulties of growing up tackles a familiar topic with a fresh new attitude.

Plot: Christian Slater stars as George Kuffs, a high-school dropout with a pregnant girlfriend and no intention of assuming responsibility for his future. That is, until the day his brother (Bruce Boxleitner), the owner of a private San Francisco police patrol, is murdered by a local gang. George inherits his brother's business and sets out to avenge his death. In the process he grows up in spite of himself.

MPAA Rating: PG-13

Cast

George Kuffs	Christian Slater
Ted Sukovsky	Tony Goldwyn
Brad Kuffs	Bruce Boxleitner
Maya Carlton	Milla Jovovich
Sam Jones	George De La Pena
Captain Morino	Troy Evans
Harriet	Lu Leonard
Kane	Leon Rippy

Also with Aki Aleong, Joshua Cadman, Stephen Park, Kim Robillard, Henry G. Sanders, Mary Ellen Trainor and Scott Williamson.

Credits

Producer	Raynold Gideon
Associate Producer	Lisa Fitzgerald
Line Producer/Production Manager	Mel Dellar
Director	Bruce A. Evans
Assistant Director	Dennis Maguire
2nd Unit Director	David Ellis
Director of Photography	Thomas Del Ruth
2nd Unit Camera	Paul Edwards
Sound	David Brownlow
Sound (San Francisco)	Agamemnon Andrianos
Editor	Stephen Semel
Production Design	Victoria Paul
	Armin Ganz
Costume Design	Mary E. Vogt
Casting	Sally Dennison
	Julie Selzer
Written by	Bruce A. Evans
	Raynold Gideon
Music	Harold Faltermeyer
Stunt Coordinator	David Ellis
Special Effects Coordinator	Dale Martin

Film Facts

Running Time	101 minutes
Film	Technicolor
Sound	Dolby Stereo
Location	Los Angeles; San Francisco
Other Working Titles	*Hero Wanted*; *Gun For Hire*

L' Elegant Criminel

(RKO Pictures)

Critics Rating: ★★★
Genre: Drama—This stylish drama is based on the real life of one of France's most infamous murderers, Pierre-Francois Lacenaire.
Tag Line: "Poet. Thief. Hero. Killer. Truly a man of many convictions."
Plot: The film begins in 1836 with the final days of Lacenaire's life. At age 36, facing charges of murder, this charming, homosexual, roguish sociopath argues his own case and pleads for a guilty verdict and a death sentence. While awaiting his trial he writes a best-selling autobiography. All of this to ensure his immortality.
MPAA Rating: Not Rated.

Cast
Pierre Lacenaire	Daniel Auteuil
Allard	Jean Poiret
Avril	Patrick Pineau
Arago	Jacques Weber
Hermine	Maiwenn Le Besco
Princess Ida	Marie-Armelle Deguy
Lusignan	Samuel Labarthe
Lacenaire's father	Francois Perier
Lacenaire's mother	Genevieve Casile

Credits
Producer	Ariel Zeitoun
Director	Francis Girod
Assistant Directors	Olivier Horlait
	Jerome Navarro
Director of Photography	Bruno de Keyzer
Sound	Andre Hervee
Costume Design	Yvone Sassinot De Nesle
Written by	Francis Girod
	George Conchon
Music	Lauren Petitgirard

Film Facts
Country of Origin	France
Language	French (subtitled)
Running Time	120 minutes
Film	Color
Sound	Stereo
Other Titles	*Lacenaire*

La Discrete
(The Discreet)
(MK2)

Critics Rating: ★★★
Genre: Drama—Making his directorial debut, Christian Vincent brings to the screen a French tale of romantic deception that backfires. The film's plot is similar to last year's *Dogfight*.
Plot: Fabrice Luchini plays Antoine, an egotistical writer whose girlfriend has jilted him. His editor, Jean (Maurice Garrel), suggests a way for him to get even, not only with his former girlfriend but with all women. His scheme is to place an ad for a typist, seduce her, make her fall for him and then dump her. Antoine likes the plan. However, he accidentally falls in love with the woman, Catherine (Judith Henry), who is not even his type. To make matters worse, she discovers his original plan and leaves him. This is a witty, charming and insightful tale about romance and game playing.
MPAA Rating: Not Rated.

Cast
Antoine	Fabrice Luchini
Catherine	Judith Henry
Jean	Maurice Garrel
Solange	Marie Bunel
Manu	Francois Toumarkine

Credits
Producer	Alain Rocca
Associate Producer	Adeline Lescallier
Director	Christian Vincent
Director of Photography	Romain Winding
Editor	Francois Ceppi
Screenplay	Christian Vincent
	Jean-Pierre Ronssin
Music	Jay Gottlieb

Film Facts
Country of Origin	France

Language ....French (subtitled)
Running Time ....95 minutes
Film ....Color
Sound ....Stereo

Ladybugs
(Paramount)

Critics Rating: Not Rated.
Genre: Comedy—A typical Rodney Dangerfield comedy, *Ladybugs* goes to just about any length to provide the laughs and entertaining family fun— and manages to succeed.
Plot: Dangerfield stars as Chester Lee, a salesman out to do whatever it takes to impress his boss and get a raise. The boss, of course, is looking for a coach for the company's all-girl soccer team. Chester takes the job, but finds himself on a losing team. His only chance of winning it seems is to enlist the help of his fiancee's son, Matthew (Jonathan Brandis, *The Never Ending Story*). The only way Matthew can join the team is by dressing in drag. This of course sets the stage for the real fun as the two, do whatever it takes to play out the charade.
MPAA Rating: PG-13
Cast
Chester Lee ....Rodney Dangerfield
Julia Benson ....Jackee
Matthew/Martha............................Jonathan Brandis
Bess ....Ilene Graff
Dave Mullen ....Tom Parks
Kimberly Mullen................................Vinessa Shaw
Glynnis Mullen.............................Jeanetta Arnett
Coach Bull ....Blake Clark
Coach Cannoli......................Tommy Lasorda
Coach Annie ....Nancy Parsons
Credits
Executive Producer.....................Gray Frederickson
Co-Executive Producer ....Lloyd Bloom
Producers ....Albert S. Ruddy
....Andre E. Morgan
Associate Producer.......................Harry Basil
Director ....Sidney J. Furie
Assistant Directors............................James Freitag
....Newton Arnold
Director of Photography......................Dan Burstall

Sound ....Jim Emerson
Editors..John W. Wheeler
....Timothy N. Board
Production Design......................Robb Wilson King
Set Decoration......................................Penny Stames
Costume Design............................Isis Mussenden
Casting...Mike Fenton
....Valorie Massalas
Written by...Curtis Burch
Music ....Richard Gibbs
Soccer Technical Advisor ....Garry Moore
Film Facts
Running Time ....89 minutes
Film ....Deluxe Color
Sound ....Dolby Stereo
Location...Denver

The Last Act
(Pardehe Akhar)

Critics Rating: Not Rated.
Genre: Drama—A first-rate Iranian murder mystery with a surprise ending.
Plot: Plotting to murder their widowed sister-in-law for her inheritance, a brother and sister come up with an elaborate scheme. The two hire a band of gypsies to frighten the woman to death. Following each failed attempt an investigator is called in. The investigator finally suspects that there is foul play among the gypsies and gathers them together in the final scene. As it turns out, the attempted murder was not foul play, but a staged play, and the investigator becomes a part of it in the last act.
MPAA Rating: Not Rated.
Cast
With Farimah Farjami, Dariush Arjomand, Jamshid Hashempoor, Saeed Poorsamimi, Niku Kheradmand and Mohaya Petrosian.
Credits
Producers..Majid Modaresi
....M. M. Dadgoo
Director/Editor ....Varuzh Karim-Masihi
Director of Photography......................Asghar Fafi'ie
Sound ....Parviz Abnar
Executive Project Manager......................
....Mohammed Mehdi Dadgu
Set Design ....Hassan Farsi

Music ....Babak Bayat
Makeup ....Masud Valadbeigi
....Mozhdeh Shamsai

Film Facts
Country of Origin ....Iran
Running Time ....105 minutes
Film ....Color
Sound ....Stereo

The Last Of
The Mohicans
(20th Century Fox)

Critics Rating: ★★★

Genre: Adventure—Based on the James Fenimore Cooper classic tale of war, revenge, heroism, romance, adventure and sacrifice. The film premiered in Paris before its fall American release.

Plot: Daniel Day-Lewis stars as Hawkeye, an orphaned child raised by Indians. The setting is the British colonies in America in 1757. A bloody war is raging between the French and the British. While en route to be with their father, sisters Alice (Jodhi May) and Cora (Madeleine Stowe) are ambushed in hostile territory. Hawkeye comes to their aid and a relationship soon develops between Hawkeye and Cora, set against an action-packed backdrop. In the film's most memorable line, Hawkeye pleads to Cora, "Stay alive, no matter the cost. I will find you."

It's difficult to imagine a time when survival was an everyday concern. The film's strength lies in the fact that it manages to capture a brutal and hostile time and place, and contrast it with the spectacle and majestic beauty of the land.

MPAA Rating: R—For violence.

Cast
Hawkeye ....Daniel Day-Lewis
Cora ....Madeleine Stowe
Chingachgook ....Russell Means
Uncas ....Eric Schweig
Alice ....Jodhi May
Gen. Montcalm ....Patrice Chereau
Col. Munro ....Maurice Roeves
Magua ....Wes Studi
Heyward ....Steven Waddington

Credits
Executive Producer ....James G. Robinson
Supervising Producer ....Ned Dowd
Producers ....Michael Mann
....Hunt Lowry
Director ....Michael Mann
Assistant Director ....Michael Waxman
2nd Unit Directors ....Mickey Gilbert
....Gusmano Cesaretti
Director of Photography ....Dante Spinotti
Additional Camera ....Doug Milsome
2nd Unit Camera ....Jerry G. Callaway
Sound ....Simon Kaye
....................................Paul Massey, Doug Hemphill
....................................Mark Smith, Chris Jenkins
Editors ....Dov Hoenig
....Arthur Schmidt
Production Design ....Wolf Kroeger
Art Direction ....Richard Holland, Robert Guerra
Set Design ....Karl Martin, Masako Masuda
Set Decoration ....Jim Erickson, James V. Kent
Casting ....Bonnie Timmerman
Casting (London) ....Susie Figgis
Screenplay ....Michael Mann
....Christopher Crowe
Based on the novel by ....James Fenimore Cooper
Based on the screenplay for 1936
    United Artists version by ....Philip Dunne
With adaptation by ....John L. Balderston
....................................Paul Perez, Daniel Moore
Music ....Trevor Jones
....Randy Edelman
Additional Music ....Daniel Lanois
Stunt Coordinator ....Mickey Gilbert

Film Facts
Running Time ....122 minutes
Soundtrack ....Morgan Creek Records
Film ....Deluxe Color
Sound ....Dolby Stereo
Location ....North Carolina

The Lawnmower Man
(New Line Cinema)

Critics Rating: ★★★

Genre: Horror—The star of this Stephen King sci-fi horror fantasy is without a doubt the stunning computer animation and visual effects.

Plot: The story revolves around Dr. Lawrence Angelo, played by Pierce Brosnan. Having quit his top-secret job on a project involving intelligence enhancing, he tries his experiment on his simple-minded gardener, Jobe (Jeff Fahey). His experiment works and Jobe becomes a genius. When the chemicals used in the experiment are switched without the doctor's knowledge, Jobe becomes a psychotic monster with visions of ruling the world. All of this takes place in a Virtual Reality system that becomes all too real.

MPAA Rating: R—For language, sensuality and a scene of violence.

Cast

Jobe Smith	Jeff Fahey
Dr. Lawrence Angelo	Pierce Brosnan
Marnie Burke	Jenny Wright
Terry McKeen	Geoffrey Lewis
Sebastian Timms	Mark Bringleson
Director	Dean Norris
Father McKeen	Jeremy Slate

Credits

Executive Producers	Edward Simons, Steve Lane
	Clive Turner, Robert Pringle
Producer	Gimel Everett
Co-Producer	Milton Subotsky
Associate Producers	Peter McRae
	Masao Takiyama
Director	Brett Leonard
Assistant Director	Ian McVey
Director of Photography	Russell Carpenter
Sound	Russell Fager
Editor	Alan Baumgarten
Production Design	Alex McDowell
Art Direction	Chris Farmer
Costume Design	Mary Jane Fort
Screenplay	Brett Leonard, Gimel Everett
Based on a short story by	Stephen King
Music	Dan Wyman
Computer Animation and Design	Xaos, Inc.
Computer Animation and Visual Effects	Angel Studios
Special Effects	Western Images

Film Facts

Running Time	105 minutes
Film	Deluxe Color
Sound	Dolby Stereo
Location	Los Angeles

Laws Of Gravity
(RKO)

Critics Rating: ★★★★

Genre: Drama—Low-budget realistic tale of a group of young white hoods from Brooklyn.

Plot: Peter Greene and Adam Trese star as Jimmy and Jon, two buddies from boyhood. Jon is a loose cannon who likes to beat up his girlfriend, that is, when he's not committing petty crimes. Jimmy is the more level-headed of the two and spends much of his time looking after his friend. When Jon gets involved with a gun runner, it puts their friendship on the line and brings tragedy into their lives.

MPAA Rating: Not Rated.

Cast

Jimmy	Peter Greene
Denise	Edie Falco
Jon	Adam Trese
Celia	Arabella Field
Tommy	Tony Fernandez
Frankie	Paul Schulzie
Sal	Saul Stien

Also with James McCauley and Anibal Lierras.

Credits

Executive Producer	Larry Meistrich
Producers	Bob Gosse
	Larry Meistrich
Associate Producer	Danny Silverman
Director	Nick Gomez
Director of Photography	Jean de Segonzac
Sound	Jeff Pullman
	Jean Gilliland
Editor	Tom McArdle
Production Design	Monica Bretherton
Written by	Nick Gomez

Film Facts

Running Time	100 minutes
Film	Color
Sound	Stereo

Le Ciel De Paris
(Sara Films)

Critics Rating: Not Rated.

Genre: Drama—This French drama with subtitles is about the tragedy of unrequited love.

Plot: The simple story revolves around Suzanne (Sandrine Bonnaire) and Marc (Marc Fourastier), two best friends who live together platonically. Their life together is pleasant until one day a young man named Lucien (Paul Blain) enters the picture and turns their world upside down. Lucien falls in love with Suzanne. In turn, Marc falls in love with Lucien. This is a sad tale in which no one gets what they want.

MPAA Rating: Not Rated.

Cast

Suzanne	Sandrine Bonnaire
Marc	Marc Fourastier
Lucien	Paul Blain
Clothilde	Evelyn Bouix
Lucien's father	Armand Lecampe
Florist	Tanya Lopert

Credits

Executive Producer	Christine Gozlan
Producer	Alain Sarde
Director	Michael Bena
Assistant Director	Hubert Engammare
Director of Photography	Jean-Marc Fabre
Sound	Jean-Pierre Duret
Editor	Catherine Schwartz
Production Design	Sylvia Laquerbe
Costume Design	Francoise Clavel
Casting	Anne Isabelle Estrada
Written by	Isabelle Coudrier-Kleist
	Cecil Vargaftig
	Michael Bena
Music	Jorge Arriagada

Film Facts

Country of Origin	France
Language	French (subtitled)
Running Time	90 minutes
Film	Color
Sound	Stereo

A League Of Their Own

(Columbia)

Critics Rating: ★★★

Genre: Comedy—Director Penny Marshall's warm and winning comedy was inspired by a little-remembered time in American history when women played the only baseball game in town.

Plot: In the 1940s, most professional baseball players were shipped off to war. To fill the void and to make a buck, wealthy Chicago candy magnate Walter Harvey (Garry Marshall) formed the All-American Girl's Professional Baseball League in the Midwest. Although the league lasted for 11 years, the story here focuses on the first year start-up and most poignantly on the rivalry between sisters Dottie Hinson (Geena Davis) and Kit Keller (Lori Petty), who both play for the Rockford Peaches. As the women struggle to make the team and then to make it succeed, Kit is struggling to find her way out of her big sister's shadow. As the star player, Dottie casts a long one. But in the end they are both victorious in their own ways.

MPAA Rating: PG

Cast

Jimmy Dugan	Tom Hanks
Dottie Hinson	Geena Davis
Mae Mordabito	Madonna
Kit Keller	Lori Petty
Ernie Capadino	Jon Lovitz
Ira Lowenstein	David Strathairn
Walter Harvey	Garry Marshall
Doris Murphy	Rosie O'Donnell
Marla Hooch	Megan Cavanagh
Betty Horn	Tracy Reiner
Evelyn Gardner	Bitty Schram
Alice Gaspers	Renee Coleman
Shirley Baker	Ann Cusack
Helen Haley	Anne Elizabeth Ramsay
Ellen Sue Gotlander	Freddie Simpson

Also with Pauline Brailsford, Lynn Cartwright, Eddie Jones, Bill Pullman and Justin Scheller.

Credits

Executive Producer/Director	Penny Marshall
Producers	Robert Greenhut
	Elliot Abbott
Co-Producers	William Pace
	Ronnie Clemmer
	Joseph Hartwick
Associate Producer	Amy Lemisch
Assistant Director	Michael Haley
Director of Photography	Miroslav Ondricek
Additional Camera	Thomas Priestley
Sound	Les Lazarowitz
Editor	George Bowers
Film Editor	Adam Bernardi

Production Design	Bill Groom
Art Direction	Tim Galvin
Set Decoration	George DeTitta, Jr.
Costume Design	Cynthia Flynt
Casting	Ellen Lewis
	Amanda Mackey
Screenplay	Lowell Ganz
	Babaloo Mandel
Based on a story by	Kim Wilson
	Kelly Candaele
Music	Hans Zimmer

Film Facts

Running Time	124 minutes
Soundtrack	Columbia Records
Film	Technicolor
Sound	Dolby Stereo
Location	Chicago; Evansville, Indiana

Leap Of Faith
(Paramount)

Critics Rating: ★★★

Genre: Drama—An entertaining and moving look at the high-tech marketing of religion.

Tag Line: "Are you ready for a miracle?"

Plot: Steve Martin stars as Jonas Nightingale, a sequined, state-of-the-art faith healer and con man. Debra Winger plays Jane, his behind-the-scenes partner in evangelical crime. Their hugely successful traveling road show through the South has brought them fame and fortune but left them morally and spiritually bankrupt. Before long, the tables are turned, and they are transformed by the power of love and a real-life miracle of faith. Jane falls for the local Sheriff (Neeson), while Jonas succumbs to the powers of a local waitress (Davidovich) and her son. Although the happy Hollywood ending is predictably sentimental, it is nonetheless moving.

MPAA Rating: PG-13—For some language.

Cast

Jonas	Steve Martin
Jane	Debra Winger
Marva	Lolita Davidovich
Will	Liam Neeson
Boyd	Lukas Haas
Hoover	Meat Loaf

Matt	Philip Seymour Hoffman
Tiny	M.C. Gainey

Credits

Executive Producer	Ralph S. Singleton
Producers	Michael Manheim
	David V. Picker
Associate Producers	Janus Cercone
	Burt Bluestein
	Roger Joseph Pugliese
Director	Richard Pearce
Assistant Directors	Doug Metzger
	Anthony Brand
Director of Photography	Matthew F. Leonetti
Sound	Petur Hiddal
Editors	Don Zimmerman
	Mark Warner
	John F. Burnett
Production Design	Patrizia von Brandenstein
Art Direction	Dennis Bradford
Set Decoration	Gretchen Rau
Costume Design	Theodora Van Runkle
Casting	Gretchen Rennell
Screenplay	Janus Cercone
Music	Cliff Eidelman

Film Facts

Running Time	110 minutes
Soundtrack	MCA Records
Film	Deluxe Color
Sound	Dolby Stereo
Location	Amarillo and Dallas, Texas

Leaving Normal
(Universal)

Critics Rating: ★★

Genre: Drama—Directed by Edward Zwick (*Glory*), *Normal* is a sweet, on-the-road female buddy picture.

Tag Line: "Sometimes the only way to find where you're going is to lose your way."

Plot: Christine Lahti (*Gross Anatomy*) plays Darly, a cocktail waitress disgusted with her life. Meg Tilly (*The Two Jakes*) plays Marianne, a woman trying to find a life. Together these two women set out on the road for Alaska in search of themselves. What they discover, however, is how different they are from one another. Despite their differences they have more in common than first meets the eye. This, of course, leads to many volatile, humorous and ultimately touching conflicts along the way toward finding friendship, love and a home.

MPAA Rating: R—For language.

Cast

Marianne	Meg Tilly
Darly	Christine Lahti
Leon	Maury Chaykin
Kurt	Brett Cullen
66	Patrika Darbo
Walt	James Gammon
Harrison	Lenny Von Dohlen
Emily	Eve Gordon

Also with Rutanya Alda and James Eckhouse.

Credits

Executive Producer	Sydney Pollack
Producer	Lindsay Doran
Co-Producer	Sarah Caplan
Line Producer	Fitch Cady
Associate Producer	Edward Solomon
Director	Edward Zwick
Assistant Director	Skip Cosper
Director of Photography	Ralf Bode
Sound	Rob Young
Editor	Victor Du Bois
Production Design	Patricia Norris
Art Direction	Sandy Cochrane
Costume Design	Patricia Norris
Casting	Mary Colquhoun
Screenplay	Edward Solomon
Music	W. G. Snuffy Walden
Special Visual Effects	Visual Concepts Engineering

Film Facts

Running Time	110 minutes
Film	Deluxe Color
Sound	Dolby Stereo
Location	Vancouver, British Columbia

Legend Of Wolf Mountain

(Hemdale)

Critics Rating: Not Rated.

Genre: Adventure—Based on popular folklore and Indian legend, *Wolf Mountain* is a family adventure set in Northern Utah.

Plot: When three small-town friends are kidnapped by escaped convicts, the action begins. Planning to shoot the children, who just happened to be in a stolen getaway car, the convicts take them to an isolated area of Wolf Mountain. The children manage to escape with the stolen money but are faced with surviving the wilderness and the pursuing killers. Lost on the mountain, one of the children has a dream that a wolf is transformed into an Indian warrior or guardian (Don Shanks). The guardian manages to help them survive the elements and protect them from the criminals long enough for the search party to arrive.

MPAA Rating: PG

Cast

Ranger Haynes	Bo Hopkins
Jocko Painter	Robert Z'Dar
Maggie Haynes	Natalie Lund
Kerrie Haynes	Nicole Lund
Jensen	Mickey Rooney
Dewayne Bixby	David Shark
Kathy Haynes	Vivian Schilling
Simcoe	Don Shanks
John Page	Jonathan Best
Casey James	Matthew Lewis
Sheriff Page	Frank Magner
Deputy	Frank Garrish
Principal	Barta Heiner
Scotty	Peadair S. Addie
Henry	Curt Jackson
Mrs. James	Star Roman
Helen	Saxon Trainor

Also with Lance August, Brett Clark, Kasey Clyde, Jan Fillmore, Sandra Gee, Marea Pond and Andreas Tessi.

Credits

Executive Producers	Charles A. Lund
	Eric Parkinson
Producer	Bryce Fillmore
Associate Producers	Ray Tremblay
	Marc Zavat
	Jeff Rice
	Tony Chopelas
Director	Craig Clyde
1st Assistant Director	Troy Rohovit
2nd Assistant Director	Mari Raymer
Director of Photography	Gary Eckert
Sound	Michael McDonough
Editor	Michael Amundsen
Art Direction	Michael Klint

Costume Design	Kip Lane Wilson
Casting	Billy DaMota
Written by	Craig Clyde
	James Hennessy
Music	Jon McCallum
Special Effects	Illusion Tech
Stunt Coordinator	Don Shanks

Film Facts
Running Time	91 minutes
Film	Color
Sound	Dolby Stereo
Location	Salt Lake City; Los Angeles

Legends
(Tara)

Critics Rating: Not Rated.
Genre: Documentary
Plot: Filmmaker Ilana Bar-Din focuses her lens on the popular Las Vegas stage show "Legends." The act features impersonators of Elvis Presley, Marilyn Monroe and Judy Garland. What makes this film involving is experiencing the backstage, underside of this business. During the filming, Jonathan Von Brana and Susan Griffiths, who play Elvis and Marilyn are fired by the volatile producer, John Stuart, when they ask for top billing. Maris, who appears emotionally unstable during the filming, later dies of lung cancer. This is a revealing and uncomfortable look behind the scenes at the lives and relationships of performers caught in the act of real life.
MPAA Rating: Not Rated.
Cast
With Susan Griffiths, Monica Maris, John Stuart and Jonathon Von Brana.
Credits
Producers	Ilana Bar-Din
	Claes Thulin
	Sarah Jackson
Director	Ilana Bar-Din
Director of Photography	Claes Thulin
Editor	Kate Amend

Film Facts
Running Time	55 minutes
Film	Color
Sound	Stereo

Lethal Weapon 3
(Warner Bros.)

Critics Rating: ★★★
Genre: Action—This take-your-breath-away action sequel is a nonstop thrill ride equal to and in many ways superior to its two predecessors. Turning violence into humor has become an art form in film today, and only Schwarzenegger does it as well as Gibson, Glover and the hilariously quirky Joe Pesci.
Plot: "I'm getting too old for this shit," moans Murtaugh (Danny Glover) once again. But this time he's just eight days away from retirement and knows that gonzo partner Riggs (Mel Gibson) is going to make these the longest days of his life. When Gibson says, "Trust me," he's certain of it.

This time around the two partners stumble upon a ring of illegal-weapons dealers led by a ruthless ex-LAPD cop. Tracking down this cop-gone-wrong, Riggs and Murtaugh come up against numerous tough characters, but none as tough as sexy internal investigator Lorna (Rene Russo, *Major League, One Good Cop*). Joining forces with the boys, and a very hyper Leo (Pesci), the foursome manage to destroy a good part of Los Angeles and light up the night in a spectacular climax.
MPAA Rating: R—For violence and language.
Trivia: Earning nearly $34 million, the film became the biggest non-summer, 3-day opener in film history.
Cast
Martin Riggs	Mel Gibson
Roger Murtaugh	Danny Glover
Leo Getz	Joe Pesci
Lorna Cole	Rene Russo
Jack Travis	Stuart Wilson
Nick Murtaugh	Damon Hines
Captain Murphy	Steve Kahan
Trish Murtaugh	Darlene Love
Carrie Murtaugh	Ebonie Smith
Rianne Murtaugh	Traci Wolfe

Credits
Producers	Joel Silver
	Richard Donner
Co-Producers	Steve Perry
	Jennie Lew Tugend

Associate Producers	Alexander B. Collett
	Michael E. Klastorin
Director	Richard Donner
Assistant Director	Michael Alan Kahn
Director of Photography	Jan De Bont
Sound	Thomas Causey
Editors	Robert Brown
	Battle Davis
Production Design	James Spencer
Art Direction	Greg Papalia
Set Decoration	Richard Goddard
Costume Supervisor	Nick Scarano
Casting	Marion Dougherty
Screenplay	Jeffrey Boam
	Robert Mark Kamen
Story by	Jeffrey Boam
Based on characters created by	Shane Black
Music	Michael Kamen
	Eric Clapton
	David Sanborn
Stunt Coordinators	Charlie Picerni
	Mic Rogers
Special Effects Supervisor	Matt Sweeney

Film Facts

Running Time	125 minutes
Soundtrack	Warner Bros. Records
Film	Technicolor
Sound	Dolby Stereo
Location	Los Angeles; Orlando, Florida

Life On A String

(Bian Zou Bian Chang)

(Kino)

Critics Rating: ★★★★

Genre: Drama—Director Chen Kaige (*Yellow Earth, King Of The Children*) again brings to life a mythical and legendary tale within a magnificently realized and beautifully photographed setting.

Plot: The story follows a blind boy who has been given a secret cure for his blindness. Before he can use it, however, he must play his banjo until 1,000 strings have been broken. He spends his life wandering from town to town playing his instrument for food, accompanied by a young blind disciple. Over the years he comes to be regarded as a saint. As an old man he finally breaks the 1,000th string, but the result is not what he expected, but

magical nonetheless.

MPAA Rating: Not Rated

Cast

The saint	Liu Zhongyuan
Shitou	Huang Lei
Lanxiu	Xu Qing
Noodle shop owner's wife	Ma Ling

Also with Yao Jingou and Zhang Zhenguan.

Credits

Executive Co-Producers	Cai Rubin
	Karl Baumgartner
Producer	Don Ranvaud
Associate Producers	Hong Huang
	Masato Hara
Director	Chen Kaige
Assistant Director	Zhang Jinzhan
Director of Photography	Gu Changwei
Sound	Tao Jing
Editor	Pei Xiaonan
Production Managers	Yang Kebing
	Xu Xiaoqing
Production Design	Shao Ruigang
Screenplay	Chen Kaige
Based on a Short Story by	Shi Tiesheng
Music	Qu Xiaosong
Berlin Supervisors	Michael Bohme
	Klaus Zimmermann
Hong Kong Supervisor	Shu Kei

Film Facts

Country of Origin	Germany/Great Britain/Japan/China
Language	Mandarin
Running Time	120 minutes
Film	Color
Sound	Dolby Stereo
Location	China

Life On The Edge

(Festival Entertainment)

Critics Rating: Not Rated.

Genre: Comedy—The shooting title of this comedy was *The Big One* and referred to the earthquake that gets the humorous situation rolling.

Plot: Set on the trendy West Coast, Jeff Perry plays Ray, a man in debt to a loan shark. He has invested the money in a bad real estate deal. Trying to escape his problems, he attends a neighbor's party.

As his luck would have it, an earthquake occurs, trapping all the party guests in the home. From here on, the film turns to sexual high jinks as the guests play musical bedrooms—and then there's the search for gold.

MPAA Rating: Not Rated.

Cast

Ray Nelson	Jeff Perry
Karen Nelson	Jennifer Holmes
Roger Hardy	Andrew Prine
Joanie Hardy	Greta Blackburn
Shelli Summers	Denny Dillon
Suzi Hughes	Jennifer Edwards
Elliot Goldman	Tom Henschel

Also with Martin Beswicke, Ralph Bruneau, Susan Powell, Thalmus Rasulala, Liz Sagal, Kat Sawyer-Young, Jessie Scott, Ken Stoddard and Michael Tulin.

Credits

Executive Producer	Bill Yates
Producers	Eric Lewald
	Andrew Yates
Co-Producer	Miriam Preissel
Associate Producer	Jesse Long
Director	Andrew Yates
Assistant Directors	Randy Pope
	Keith Carpenter
Directors of Photography	Tom Fraser
	Nicholas von Sternberg
Sound	Clifford (Kip) Gynn
Editor	Armen Minasian
Production Design	Amy Van Tries
Art Direction	Greg P. Oehler
Casting	Jean Sarah Frost
Written by	Mark Edens
Music	Mike Garson
Special Visual Effects Supervisor	Barry A. Nolan

Film Facts

Running Time	75 minutes
Film	Foto-Kem Color
Sound	Ultra-Stereo
Other Working Titles	*The Big One*

Light Sleeper

(New Line Cinema)

Critics Rating: ★★★
Genre: Drama—Director Paul Schrader brings his familiar trademark style to this follow-up to *Taxi Driver* and *American Gigolo*.

Plot: Willem Dafoe stars as John LeTour, a 40-something drug delivery man in the middle of a mid-life crisis. His long-time boss, Ann (Susan Sarandon), is planning to go legit and get out of her dwindling drug business. This forces John to confront his wasted past and a more frightening future. He feels trapped, and his transition ultimately leads to a violent and bloody climax.

MPAA Rating: R—For language.

Cast

John LeTour	Willem Dafoe
Ann	Susan Sarandon
Marianne	Dana Delany
Robert	David Clennon
Teresa	Mary Beth Hurt
Tis	Victor Garber
Randy	Jane Adams

Credits

Executive Producer	Mario Kassar
Co-Executive Producer	Ronna Wallace
Producer	Linda Reisman
Co-Producer	G. Mac Brown
Director	Paul Schrader
Assistant Director	Glen Trotiner
Director of Photography	Ed Lachman
Sound	Doug Michael
Editor	Kristina Bowden
Production Design	Richard Hornung
Art Direction	Jim Feng
Set Design	Jessica Lanier
Casting	Ellen Chenowith
Written by	Paul Schrader
Music	Michael Been

Film Facts

Running Time	103 minutes
Film	DuArt Color
Sound	Stereo
Location	New York

The Linguini Incident

(Academy Entertainment)

Critics Rating: ★★
Genre: Comedy—Bizarre and very offbeat comedy.

Tag Line: "He wants to be tied down. She wants to be tied up. It's not what you think."

Plot: David Bowie plays Monte, an Englishman on the run and desperately seeking a wife and a green card. In no time at all, he hits on Lucy (Rosanna Arquette), a waitress in the trendy Manhattan restaurant where he works. Her dream is to follow in the footsteps of Harry Houdini. Joining forces they decide to make both of their dreams come true by robbing the restaurant. What follows is an enjoyable series of pitfalls and pratfalls.

MPAA Rating: R

Cast

Lucy	Rosanna Arquette
Monte	David Bowie
Vivian	Eszter Balint
Dante	Andre Gregory
Cecil	Buck Henry
Miracle	Viveca Lindfors
Jeanette	Marlee Matlin

Also with Lewis Arquette, Michael Bonnabel, Eloy Casados, Iman, Julian Lennon and Maura Tierney.

Credits

Executive Producer	Richard Gagnon
Producer	Arnold Orgolini
Co-Producer	Sarah Jackson
Line Producer	Patricia Foulkrod
Associate Producer	Susan Hopper
Director	Richard Shepard
Assistant Director	Phillip Christon
Director of Photography	Robert Yeoman
Additional Camera	David Sperling
Sound	Vic Carpenter
	David Chornow
Editor	Sonya Polonsky
Additional Editing	Susan R. Crutcher
Production Design	Marcia Hinds-Johnson
Art Direction	Bo Johnson
Costume Design	Richard von Ernst
Casting	Danielle Eskanazi
Screenplay	Tamar Brott
	Richard Shepard
Music Supervisor	Diane DeLouise Wessel
Music	Thomas Newman
Additional Music	Mark Lundquist

Film Facts

Running Time	99 minutes
Film	CFI Color
Sound	Ultra-Stereo

Liquid Dreams

(Northern Arts Entertainment)

Critics Rating: Not Rated.

Genre: Thriller—A low-budget, science-fiction thriller that's light on the thrills.

Plot: Candice Daly stars as Eve, a woman whose sister has been murdered. Receiving little help from the authorities in this future world, she decides to investigate the crime herself. She eventually learns that her sister's death has been caused by a company by the name of Neurovid that is using mind-altering videos as a way to take control of the population. Having uncovered the mystery, she is determined to stop the organization in its tracks.

MPAA Rating: R—For sexuality, violence, drug content and language.

Cast

Eve Black	Candice Daly
Cecil	Tracey Walter
Rodino	Richard Steinmetz
The Major	Barry Dennen
Juno	Juan Fernandez
Maurice	James Oseland
Paula	Frankie Thorn
Cab driver	John Doe
Felix	Mink Stole
Violet	Marilyn Tokuda

Credits

Executive Producers	Ted Fox
	Cassian Elwes
Producers	Zane W. Levitt
	Diane Firestone
Associate Producer	Zack Davis
Director	Mark Manos
Director of Photography	Sven Kirsten
Editor	Karen Joseph
Production Design	Pam Moffatt
Costume Design	Merrie Lawson
Written by	Zack Davis
	Mark Manos
Music	Ed Tomney
Choreographer	Lexandre Magno

Film Facts

Running Time	92 minutes
Film	Color
Sound	Stereo

Little Nemo - Adventures In Slumberland
(Hemdale)

Critics Rating: ★★
Genre: Animated
Tag Line: "Take off on a wondrous adventure."
Plot: The film is based on the comic strip by Winsor McCay. The story follows little Nemo and his nighttime adventures into an enchanted and magical world called Slumberland. Nemo's flying pet squirre, Icarus, accompanies him. In Slumberland Nemo meets a king who gives him a key that can unlock all the evil in the world.

MPAA Rating: G

Cast
Voices:
Flip	Mickey Rooney
Professor Genius	Rene Auberjonois
Nemo	Gabriel Damon
Icarus	Danny Mann
Princess Camille	Laura Mooney
King Morpheus	Bernard Erhard
Nightmare King	William E. Martin

Credits
Producer	Yutaka Fujioka
Co-Producers	Barry Glasser
	Shunzo Kato
	Eiji Katayama
Associate Producer	Koji Takeuchi
Directors	Masami Hata
	William Hurtz
Assistant Directors	Hiroaki Sato
	Keiko Oyamada
Animation Directors	Kazuhide Tomonaga
	Nobuo Tomizawa
Directors of Photography	Kenichi Kobayashi
	Moriyuki Terashita, Takahisa Ogawa,
	Kazushige Ichinozuka, Atsuko Ito, Koji Asai
	Takashi Nomura, Jin Nishiyama
	Kiyoshi Kobayashi, Atsushi Yoshino
	Kyoko Oosaki, Akio Saitoh
	Hiroshi Kanai, Hitoshi Shirao
	Hironori Yoshino, Mika Sakai
	Rie Takeuchi, Kazushi Torigoe
Sound	Kunio Ando
	Shizuo Kurahashi
Editor	Takeshi Seyama
Screenplay	Chris Columbus, Richard Outten

Story by	Jean Mobius Giraud
	Yutaka Fujioka
Story Consultants	Frank Thomas
	Oliver Johnston, David Hilberman
	Koji Shimizu, Robert Towne
Based on the comic strip by	Winsor McCay
Concept for the screen	Ray Bradbury
Music	Thomas Chase, Steve Rucker
Songs by	Richard M. Sherman
	Robert B. Sherman
Title Song Sung by	Melissa Manchester
Background Music	London Symphony Orchestra

Film Facts
Country of Origin	Japan
Running Time	85 minutes
Film	Tokyo Laboratories Color
Sound	Dolby Stereo

Little Noises
(Monument)

Critics Rating: ★★★
Genre: Comedy—Occasionally humorous and quirky little film about a few very odd characters.
Plot: Crispin Glover (*River's Edge*) plays Joey, an aspiring New York writer who hasn't written a word and whose life is a mess. Meeting a young poet named Marty (Matthew Hutton), whose life is even more of a mess, he takes advantage of the boy. Desperate for money, Joey sells Marty's poems to an agent as his own. His mistreatment of Marty comes back to haunt Joey, however, and he makes amends.

MPAA Rating: Not Rated.

Cast
Joey	Crispin Glover
Stella	Tatum O'Neal
Elliott	Tate Donovan
Marty	Matthew Hutton
Mathias	Rik Mayall
Stu	John McGinley
Timmy	Steven Schub
Dolores	Nina Siemaszko

Credits
Producers	Michael Spielberg
	Brad Gilbert
Director	Jane Spencer

Director of Photography ....Makoto Watanabe
Sound...Mathew Price
Editor ....Ernie Fritz
Production Design ....Charles Lagola
Screenplay...Jane Spencer
....Jon Zeiderman
Music...Kurt Hoffman
....Fritz van Orden

Film Facts
Running Time ....110 minutes
Film ....Color
Sound ....Stereo

The Living End

(Strand)

Critics Rating: ★★★
Genre: Drama—Underground director, writer, photographer and editor, Gregg Araki, brings to the screen a quirky, campy, low-budget tragi-comic buddy picture whose lead characters are two HIV-positive, angry gay men.
Tag Line: "An irresponsible film by Gregg Araki."
Plot: Craig Gilmore plays Jon, a film critic who has just learned that he is HIV-positive. Mike Dytri plays Luke, a drifter who has just blown away three would-be gay bashers. And that was after he escaped from two would-be killer lesbians, taking their gun.

Jon and Luke meet by chance and discover that they are both members of the HIV club. With nothing to lose, Luke continues his murderous rage and soon the two are running from the law. Somewhere along the way this love story turns sour, and they reach the end of their road and quirky romance.
MPAA Rating: Not Rated. The gay sex scenes are strictly above the belt. Also contains violence and profanity.

Cast
Luke...Mike Dytri
Jon...Craig Gilmore
Peter...Scot Goetz
Darcy ....Darcy Marta
Daisy ....Mary Woronov
Fern ....Johanna Went

Credits
Executive Producers ....Evelyn Hu
....Jon Jost
....Henry Rosenthal
....Mike Thomas
Producers...Marcus Hu
....Jon Gerrans
Co-Producer..Jim Stark
Associate Producer....................Andrea Sperling
Director/Editor..Gregg Araki
Director of Photography ....Gregg Araki
Lighting...Chris Munch
Sound ....George Lockwood
Written by ....Gregg Araki
Music...Cole Coonce

Film Facts
Running Time ....92 minutes
Film ....Color
Sound ....Stereo

Locked-Up Time

(Verriegelte Zeit)
(Zeitgeist)

Critics Rating: Not Rated.
Genre: Documentary—Shot in black and white by filmmaker Sibylle Schonemann.
Plot: After attempting to leave East Germany in 1984 Schonemann is imprisoned for a year, along with her husband. Returning following the fall of the Berlin Wall, she confronts those responsible for her unjust incarceration. Simply and powerfully Schonemann conveys her anger and frustration as she searches for answers in this memorable film.
MPAA Rating: Not Rated.

Credits
Producers ....Bernd Burkhardt
....Alfred Hurmer
Director...................................Sibylle Schonemann
Director of Photography....................Thomas Plenert
(with) ....Michael Lowenberg
Sound..Ronald Gohlke
Mix ....Ulrich Fengler
Lighting ....Wolfgang Hirschke
Editor...Gudrun Steinbruck
Production Director.....................Herbert Kruschke
Music ....Thomas Kahane

Film Facts
Country of Origin.....................................Germany
Language ....German (subtitled)
Running Time ....90 minutes
Film ....Black & White
Sound ....Stereo

London Kills Me
(Fine Line)

Critics Rating: ★★
Genre: Drama—Scriptwriter Hanif Kureishi (*My Beautiful Laundrette, Sammy And Rose Get Laid*) makes his directorial debut with this drama about the contemporary drug scene in London.
Plot: Justin Chadwick stars as Clint, one of a gang of small-time drug dealers, who decides he's ready to go straight. But getting out of his present situation is not as easy as it might seem. The leader of the group and boyhood friend, Muffdiver (Steven Mackintosh), isn't supportive. Then there's Sylvie (Emer McCourt), a very bad influence. But the biggest obstacle in this quirky tale is Clint's lack of a descent pair of shoes to wear for a restaurant job.
MPAA Rating: R—For drug use, language and some nudity.

Cast
Clint...Justin Chadwick
Muffdiver ....Steven Mackintosh
Sylvie...Emer McCourt
Dr. Bubba...Roshan Seth
Headley ....Fiona Shaw
Hemingway ....Brad Dourif
Stone...Alun Armstrong
Lily..Eleanor David
Burns..Tony Haygarth
Tom Tom...Stevan Rimkus
Also with Naveen Andrews, Garry Cooper and Nick Dunning.

Credits
Executive Producer ....Graham Bradstreet
Producer ....Tim Bevan
Co-Producer ....Judy Hunt
Associate Producer ....David Gothard
Director ....Hanif Kureishi
Assistant Director..............................Benita Allen
Director of Photography....................Ed Lachman
Sound...........................Albert Bailey, Sue Baker

Editor..Jon Gregory
Production Design..............................Stuart Walker
Costume Design ....Amy Roberts
Casting...Joyce Nettles
Written by ....Hanif Kureishi
Music Coordinator ....Charlie Gillett
Music ....Mark Springer
....Sarah Sarhandi

Film Facts
Country of Origin ....Great Britain
Running Time ....107 minutes
Film ....Color
Sound ....Dolby Stereo
Location ....London, England

Lonely Hearts
(Gibraltar Entertainment)

Critics Rating: Not Rated.
Genre: Thriller—Psychological thriller about an emotionally needy woman and her dangerous obsessions.
Plot: Beverly D'Angelo stars as Alma, a woman with low self-esteem, who used to be obsessed with food and overweight. Having recently lost weight she places a personal ad. When she meets Frank (Eric Roberts), she believes she has met Mr. Right. Before long, however, she discovers that he is a ruthless sociopath who preys on lonely women.
MPAA Rating: R—For sensuality, language and violence.

Cast
Frank...Eric Roberts
Alma..Beverly D'Angelo
Erin Randall ....Joanna Cassidy
Maria ....Bibi Besch
Gran (Annie) ....Herta Ware

Credits
Executive Producers.............................Joel Levine
....Richard N. Gladstein
Producers...Andrew Lane
....R. E. Daniels
Associate Producer ....Gregory Small
Director ....Andrew Lane
Assistant Director................................Greg Jacobs
Director of Photography ....Paul Ryan
Sound...George Alch
Editor..Julian Semilian

143

Production Design ....Pamela Woodbridge
Art Direction ....Carlos Barbosa
Set Decoration ....Marty Huyette
Costume Design ....Libbie Aroff Lane
....Peggy Schnitzer
Casting ....Michelle Guillermin
Screenplay..Andrew Lane
....R. E. Daniels
Story by...R. E. Daniels
Music ....David McHugh

Film Facts
Running Time ....109 minutes
Film ....Color
Sound ....Stereo
Location..................................Los Angeles; Phoenix

Lorenzo's Oil
(Universal)

Critics Rating: ★★★★

Genre: Drama—An intense, heartfelt true-life drama about devoted parents who refuse to let their son die without doing everything humanly possible to save him from a rare disease.

Plot: Taking place in 1984, Nick Nolte and Susan Sarandon play Augusto and Michaela Odone, the parents of 5-year-old son Lorenzo (Greenburg) who is diagnosed with a rare disease. The disease, adrenoleukodystrophy (ALD), the parents discover, afflicts only young boys between 5 and 10 years of age and is terminal within two years. The parents refuse to accept their son's fate and devote themselves to finding a cure for the disease. What they discover is an oil that halts the progression of the disease until a cure can be found. This is an intense, exhausting and uplifting story for sophisticated audiences.

MPAA Rating: PG-13—For a child's life threatening ordeal.

Cast
Augusto Odone ....Nick Nolte
Michaela Odone...............................Susan Sarandon
Lorenzo Odone ....Zack O'Malley Greenburg,
....Billy Amman, Noah Banks,
....E. G. Daily, Michael Haider
....and Cristin Woodworth
Professor Nikolais.................................Peter Ustinov
Deirdre Murphy.............................Kathleen Wilhoite
Doctor Judalon...............................Gerry Bamman
Wendy Gimble ....Margo Martindale
Ellard Muscatine ....James Rebhorn
Loretta Muscatine ....Ann Hearn
Omuouri...Maduka Steady
Comorian teacher ....Mary Wakio
Don Suddaby ....Don Suddaby

Credits
Executive Producer ....Arnold Burk
Producers...Doug Mitchell
....George Miller
Associate Producers ....Johnny Friedkin
....Daphne Paris, Lynn O'Hare
Director ....George Miller
Assistant Director ....Steven E. Andrews
Director of Photography.........................John Seale
Sound ....Ben Osmo
Sound Design ....Lee Smith
Editors ....Richard Francis-Bruce
....Marcus D'Arcy
....Lee Smith
Production Design ....Kristi Zea
Art Direction ....Dennis Bradford
Set Decoration...............................Karen A. O'Hara
Costume Design ....Colleen Atwood
Casting...John Lyons
Screenplay..George Miller
....Nick Enright
Music Supervisor ....Christine Woodruff

Film Facts
Running Time ....135 minutes
Film ....Atlab Australia
Sound ....Dolby Stereo
Location..Pittsburgh

Lost Prophet
(Rockville Pictures)

Critics Rating: Not Rated.

Genre: Drama

Plot: Shot in black and white, this experimental film follows Jim (James Burton) as he aimlessly wanders from scene to scene. During his travels, he meets an unusual woman, who introduces him to a book titled "Mick Prophet." He later appears to become the prophet himself in this obscure and uneven film.

MPAA Rating: Not Rated.
Cast

Jim	James Burton
Kym	Zandra Huston
Real estate agent/Mick Prophet	Drew Morone
Kid	James Tucker

Also with Shannon Goldman, Larry O'Neil, Sophia Ramos, Steven Tucker and Christian Urich.

Credits

Executive Producers	Ann de Avila
	Rolando de Avila
	Rose Stewart
	Diana Neeley
	Anne Maria Cronin
	Pilar Pinsley
	Howard Pinsley
Producer/Director	Michael de Avila
Assistant Director	Shannon Goldman
Director of Photography/Editor	Michael de Avila
Sound	Chris Cliadakis
	Marissa Bennideto
Screenplay	Michael de Avila
	Drew Morone
	Larry O'Neil
	Shannon Goldman
Music	TRF Music Libraries

Film Facts

Running Time	72 minutes
Film	DuArt Black & White
Sound	Stereo

Love Crimes
(Millimeter)

Critics Rating: Not Rated.
Genre: Thriller—The story of prosecutor Dana Greenway, played by Sean Young, a woman out to entrap a man. The man in question is obsessed with sexually humiliating female victims in this by-the-numbers thriller.
Plot: Posing as a famous photographer, Patrick Bergin plays the sexually obsessed man who lures his victims into photo sessions that turn into sexual and psychological abuse. Dana eventually tracks him down, but he escapes, only to turn the tables on her in a predictable climax.
MPAA Rating: R—For language and sensuality.

Cast

David Hanover	Patrick Bergin
Dana Greenway	Sean Young
Det. Maria Johnson	Arnetia Walker
Stanton Gray	James Read
Det. Tully	Ron Orbach

Also with Donna Biscoe, Fern Dorsey and Tina Hightower.

Credits

Executive Producer	Forrest Murray
Producers	Rudy Langlais
	Lizzie Borden
Director	Lizzie Borden
Assistant Director (Dallas)	Mike Dempsey
Assistant Director (Atlanta)	Lisa Zimble
Director of Photography	Jack N. Green
Additional Camera	Ben Butin
Additional Camera (Atlanta)	Phedon Papamichael
Sound	Brit Warner
Sound (Dallas)	Michael Haines
Editors	Nicholas C. Smith
	Mike Jackson
Additional Editing	Christy Richmond
Production Manager (Dallas)	Mike Dempsey
Production Manager (Atlanta)	Victoria Westhead
Production Design	Armin Ganz
Costume Design	Irene Albright, Ira Lewis
Casting	Pat Golden, John McCabe
Casting (Dallas)	Carla Posey
Screenplay	Allan Moyle
	Laurie Frank
Story by	Allan Moyle
Music	Graeme Revell
	Roger Mason
Stunt Coordinator	Lonnie R. Smith, Jr.

Film Facts

Running Time	91 minutes
Film	Deluxe Color
Sound	Ultra-Stereo

Love Field
(Orion)

Critics Rating: ★★★
Genre: Drama—A character study about a woman's journey to find herself.
Tag Line: "Her life began when her world fell apart."

Plot: The title, which refers to a famous Dallas airport, may be a bit misleading. Set in 1963, Michelle Pfeiffer plays Laurene, a hairdresser and not-so-happily married woman who one day leaves her boring husband and boring life behind. Hopping a Greyhound bus out of town, her destination is the state funeral service for President Kennedy. On the bus she meets a man who is also running from his past—only their reasons for running are very different. Her new travel companion Paul (Haysbert) is a black man running with his daughter Jonell (McFadden) from prejudice and hate. Together, they help each other find themselves and a new direction in life.

MPAA Rating: PG-13

Cast

Lurene Hallett	Michelle Pfeiffer
Paul Cater	Dennis Haysbert
Ray Hallett	Brian Kerwin
Jonell	Stephanie McFadden
Mrs. Enright	Louise Latham
Mrs. Heisenbuttal	Peggy Rea
Hazel	Beth Grant

Credits

Executive Producers	Kate Guinzburg
	George Goodman
Producers	Sarah Pillsbury, Midge Sanford
Co-Producer	Don Roos
Associate Producer	Sulla Hamer
Director	Jonathan Kaplan
Assistant Director	Tom Davies
2nd Unit Director	Ralf Bode
Director of Photography	Ralf Bode
Sound	Glen Anderson
Editor	Jane Kurson
Production Design	Mark Freeborn
Art Direction	David Wilson, Lance King
Set Decoration	Jim Erickson
Costume Design	Peter Mitchell
Michelle Pfeiffer's costumes	Colleen Atwood
Casting	Julie Selzer, Sally Dennison
Screenplay	Don Roos
Music	Jerry Goldsmith

Film Facts

Running Time	104 minutes
Soundtrack	Varese Sarabande
Film	Technicolor
Sound	Dolby Stereo

Love Potion No. 9
(20th Century Fox)

Critics Rating: ★

Genre: Comedy—Screenwriter Dale Launer (*Ruthless People*, *My Cousin Vinny*) makes his directorial debut. The film, inspired by the 1959 hit song, is a one-joke comedy with a few very appealing and original moments.

Tag Line: "Imagine if sex appeal came in a bottle."

Plot: Donovan and Bullock play Paul and Diane, two equally shy and nerdy scientists. Both are miserable failures with the opposite sex until Paul visits Madam Ruth (Bancroft)—you know, the gypsy with the gold-capped tooth. Ruth provides him with a potion that does the trick with the women, but not without a few complications along the way. Eventually the potion leads them to a mutually happy ending.

MPAA Rating: PG-13

Cast

Paul Matthews	Tate Donovan
Diane Farrow	Sandra Bullock
Gary	Dale Midkiff
Marisa	Mary Mara
Prince Geoffrey	Dylan Baker
Enrico Pazzoli	Adrian Paul
Sally	Hillary Bailey Smith
Motorcycle cop	Blake Clark
Madame Ruth	Anne Bancroft

Credits

Executive Producer	Thomas M. Hammel
Producer/Director	Dale Launer
Associate Producer	Jeffrey Downer
Assistant Director	James Sbardellati
Director of Photography	William Wages
Sound	Jim Hawkins
Editor	Suzanne Pettit
Production Design	Linda Pearl
Art Direction	Thomas Minton
Set Decoration	Sally Nicolaou
Costume Design	Timothy D'Arcy
Casting	Wendy Kurtzman
Written by	Dale Launer
Inspired by the song by	Jerry Leiber, Mike Stoller
Music	Jed Leiber

Film Facts

Running Time	96 minutes

Film ....CFI Color
Sound ....Dolby Stereo

The Lover
(L'Amant)
(MGM)

Critics Rating: ★★★
Genre: Drama—Erotic tale of an interracial love affair adapted from the best-selling memoir by Marguerite Duras. *Time* film critic Richard Corliss wrote, "*The Lover*, on page and screen, is not about fornication; it is about fidelity, when an obsession becomes a religion."
Plot: Set in Vietnam during the late 1920s, Jane March plays a poor, 15-year-old French girl who enters into an affair with a 32-year-old Chinese businessman (Leung). The two are from different worlds culturally and socially, which forces them to hide their relationship. Because their relationship is forbidden, she is reluctant to give herself completely, but is at the same time compelled. It isn't until she is returning to France that she realizes the depths of her feelings for the man. Beautifully atmospheric and evocative of the time, the film also contains numerous scenes of explicit sexuality that border on soft porn.
MPAA Rating: R—For graphic and explicit sexuality. Originally rated NC-17.
Cast
The young girl ....Jane March
The Chinese man..............................Tony Leung
The mother..........................Frederique Meininger
Narrator..Jeanne Moreau
Also with Lisa Faulkner, Arnaud Giovaninetti and Melvil Poupaud.
Credits
Producer...Claude Berri
Associate Producers ....Jacques Tronel
....Josee Benabent-Loiseau
Director ....Jean-Jacques Annaud
Director of Photography......................Robert Friasse
Sound..Laurent Quaglio
Editor ....Noelle Boisson
Production Design ....Thanh At Hoang
Costume Design................Yvonne Sassinet de Nesle
Screenplay ....Gerard Brach

....Jean-Jacques Annaud
Based on the novel by ....Marguerite Duras
Music..Gabriel Yared
Film Facts
Country of Origin ....France/Great Britain
Running Time ....103 minutes
Soundtrack ....Varese Sarabande
Film ....Color
Sound ....Dolby Stereo
Location..................................Vietnam; France; Italy

Lovers
(Amantes)
(Aries)

Critics Rating: ★★★
Genre: Thriller—Set in Spain in the 1950s, this thriller, based on a true story, is the tale of a love triangle that turns deadly.
Plot: Jorge Sanz plays Paco, a young man about to be married and in search of a job to support his wife-to-be, Trini (Maribel Verdu). When the unsuspecting Paco is seduced by Luisa (Victoria Abril), his plans change. She turns out to be a con artist, and she persuades him to join her. Together they conspire to rob Trini of her life savings, then murder her.
MPAA Rating: Not Rated.
Cast
Luisa ....Victoria Abril
Paco ....Jorge Sanz
Trini...Maribel Verdu
Credits
Producer ....Pedro Costa-Muste
Director.......................................Vicente Aranda
Director of Photography ....Jose Luis Alcaine
Sound ....Miguel Angel Polo
Editor..Teresa Font
Production Manager..................Carlos Ramon Lluch
Production Design ....Josep Rosell
Costume Design ....Nereida Bonmati
Screenplay.......................................Alvaro Del Amo
..................Carlos Perez Merinero, Vicente Aranda
Music ....Jose Nieto
Film Facts
Country of Origin ....Spain
Running Time ....103 minutes
Film ....Color

Sound ....Stereo
Location ....Madrid, Spain

The Lunatic
(Triton)

Critics Rating: Not Rated.
Genre: Comedy—Uplifting fantasy.
Tag Line: "Come to Jamaica where the sun is warm, the water is cool, the breeze is soft, and the people are sometimes a little extreme."
Plot: Paul Campbell stars as Aloysius, the lovable lunatic of a small Jamaican village. Aloysius talks to the trees and the cows and they talk back—often offering sage and humorous advice. When a strange woman arrives in the village, Aloysius is quickly smitten. Before long she has persuaded him to help her in a robbery that leads to his arrest. The point of this film seems to be that not all madmen or women are as easily recognizable as a simple lunatic.
MPAA Rating: R

Cast

Inga ....Julie T. Wallace
Aloysius..Paul Cambell
Busha/Voice of Strongheart Tree..........Reggie Carter
Service...Carl Bradshaw
Sarah..Linda Gambrill
Widow Dawkins............................Rosemary Murray
The judge..Lloyd Reckford
Lindstrom ....Winston Stona

Credits

Executive Producers ....Chris Blackwell
....Dan Genetti
Producers ....Paul M. Heller, John Pringle
Co-Producer ....Matthew Binns
Associate Producers........................Kathy Zebrowski
....Marnee K. Bie
Director...Lol Creme
Assistant Director.................................Laura Groppe
Director of Photography ....Richard Greatrex
Sound ....Kim Ornitz
Editor..Michael Connell
Art Direction......................................Giorgio Ferrari
Costume Design............................Patricia Griffiths
Screenplay...............................Anthony C. Winkler
Based on the novel *The Lunatic*
   by...Anthony C. Winkler

Music ....Wally Badarou

Film Facts

Running Time ....93 minutes
Soundtrack..................................Mango Records
Film...CFI Color
Sound ....Dolby Stereo

Lunatics: A Love Story
(Renaissance Pictures)

Critics Rating: ★★★
Genre: Comedy—This low-budget, black comedy is about two downbeat losers who accidentally find one another and fall in love—sort of.
Plot: Theodore Raimi stars as Hank, a poet who is agoraphobic and unable to leave his home. To make contact with the outside world he calls 976 numbers. One day he misdials and finds himself talking to a woman (Deborah Foreman) who has just been dumped by her boyfriend, leaving her without a place to stay. Before long she is staying with Hank. The two have much in common for such an unusual alliance.
MPAA Rating: PG-13

Cast

Nancy ....Deborah Foreman
Hank...Theodore Raimi
Ray ....Bruce Campbell
Comet..George Aguilar
Presto...Brian McCree

Credits

Executive Producers..........Robert Tapert, Sam Raimi
Co-Executive Producers ....Brian C. Manoogian
....James A. Courtney
Producer..Bruce Campbell
Co-Producer ....David Goodman
Director..Josh Becker
Assistant Director ....John Cameron
Director of Photography ....Jeff Dougherty
Editor..Kaye Davis
Production Design ....Peter Gurski
Written by...Josh Becker
Music ....Joe Lo Duca

Film Facts

Running Time ....87 minutes
Film..Color
Sound ....Stereo

The Magical World Of Chuck Jones
(Warner Bros.)

Critics Rating: Not Rated.
Genre: Documentary
Tag Line: "The What's Up Doc-umentary."
Plot: Filmed in celebration of the legendary animator's 80th birthday, the documentary includes clips from his work over the past 50 years, as well as comments and interviews by friends, associates and family. Many well-known performers and directors discuss how Jones's work influenced their own work. The film is told in a straightforward manner.
MPAA Rating: PG—For some mild language.

Cast
With Steven Spielberg, Whoopi Goldberg, Ron Howard, Matt Groening, Leonard Maltin, Joe Dante, George Lucas, Steve Guttenberg, Chris Connelly, Danny Elfman, Gary Rydstrom, Friz Freleng, Roddy McDowall, June Foray, Kathleen Helppie-Shipley, Maurice Noble, Roger Mayer, Linda Jones Clough, Marian Jones, Valerie Kausen and Chuck Jones.

Credits
Executive Producer .... Valerie Kausen
Producers .... David Ka Lik Wong
.... George Daugherty
Director .... George Daugherty
Director of Photography .... Peter Bonilla
Sound .... Robb Wenner
Editor .... Peter E. Berger
Music .... Cameron Patrick

Film Facts
Running Time .... 93 minutes
Film .... Color
Sound .... Dolby Stereo

Malcolm X
(Warner Bros.)

Critics Rating: ★★★★
Genre: Drama—Only occasionally is Lee's stylistic trademark filmmaking visible in this well-received historical epic.
Tag Line: "Scholar. Convict. Leader. Disciple. Hipster. Father. Hustler. Minister. Black Man. Every Man."
Plot: Denzel Washington plays Malcolm Little, the African-American leader who transcends his early beginnings as a hustler and con to become the charismatic spokesman for Elijah Muhammad and the Islamic faith. There are many powerful, memorable moments in this film, but it is the performances by Washington, Al Freeman, Jr., Delroy Lindo and many others that take this film to a higher level and sustain it.
MPAA Rating: PG-13—For a scene of violence, drugs and profanity.
Trivia: On its opening day the film earned $2.4 million. By comparison, last year's *JFK* earned $1.45 million on its opening day.

Cast
Malcolm X .... Denzel Washington
Betty Shabazz .... Angela Bassett
Baines .... Albert Hall
Elijah Muhammad .... Al Freeman, Jr.
West Indian Archie .... Delroy Lindo
Shorty .... Spike Lee
Laura .... Theresa Randle
Sophia .... Kate Vernon
Louise Little .... Lonette McKee
Earl Little .... Tommy Hollis
Also with Karen Allen, Peter Boyle, Ossie Davis, William Kunstler, Christopher Plummer, Bobby Seale and Al Sharpton.

Credits
Producers .... Marvin Worth, Spike Lee
Co-Producers .... Monty Ross
.... Jon Kilik, Preston Holmes
Associate Producer .... Fernando Sulichin
Director .... Spike Lee
Assistant Director .... Randy Fletcher
Director of Photography .... Ernest Dickerson
Sound .... Rolf Pardula
Editor .... Barry Alexander Brown

Production Design.............................Wynn Thomas
Art Direction ....Tom Warren
Costume Design.................................Ruth Carter
Casting ....Robi Reed
Screenplay.......................................Arnold Perl
....Spike Lee
Based on the book *The Autobiography
of Malcolm X* as told to ....Alex Haley
Original Music Score ....Terence Blanchard
Choreographer ....Otis Sallid

Film Facts
Running Time ....201 minutes
Soundtrack..................................Qwest Records
Original Score ....40 Acres/Columbia Records
Film...DuArt Color
Sound ....Dolby Stereo
Location..................New York; New Jersey; Boston;
....Egypt; Mecca; South Africa

The Mambo Kings

(Warner Bros.)

Critics Rating: ★★★
Genre: Drama—About two Cuban brothers who come to New York in 1952 with big "American Dreams." The story is adapted from Oscar Hijuelos' Pulitzer-Prize-winning novel.
Plot: Armand Assante stars as Cesar, a Havana singer who, along with his brother, Nestor (Antonio Banderas, *Tie Me Up! Tie Me Down!*), works in a meat-packing plant by day and plays the clubs by night. The brothers have very different dreams, however, which eventually lead to a tragic end.

Desi Arnaz, Jr. makes a rare and memorable cameo performance, playing his father. In one of the most memorable scenes, the two brothers meet Desi and are invited on the *I Love Lucy* show, which is imaginatively recreated for the film.
MPAA Rating: R—For sensuality. Contains violence, profanity and brief male and female nudity.

Cast
Cesar Castillo............................Armand Assante
Nestor Castillo ....Antonio Banderas
Lanna Lake.................................Cathy Moriarty
Dolores Fuentes.....................Maruschka Detmers
Desi Arnaz ....Desi Arnaz, Jr.

Evalina Montoya ....Celia Cruz
Fernando Perez ....Roscoe Lee Brown
Tito Puente ....Tito Puente
Blanca ....Theodora Castellanos
Miguel Montoya ....Vondie Curtis-Hall
Ismelda Perez ....Anh Duong
Anna Maria ....Cordelia Gonzales
Pablo...Lazara Perez
Carlo Ricci...................................Joe Petruzzi
Maria Rivera ....Talisa Soto
Mambo Kings Band........................Pablo Calogero,
Scott Cohen, Mario Grillo, Ralph Irizarry, Pete Macnamara, Jimmy Medina, Marcos Quintanilla, J. T. Taylor, William Thomas, Jr. and Yul Vazquez.

Credits
Executive Producer ....Steven Reuther
Producers..Arnon Milchan
....Arne Glimcher
Co-Producer.............................Jack B. Bernstein
Associate Producer........................Anna Reinhardt
Director...Arne Glimcher
Assistant Director ....Benjamin Rosenberg
Director of Photography.................Michael Ballhaus
Sound.......................................Susumu Tokunow
Editor...Claire Simpson
Production Design............................Stuart Wurtzel
Art Direction ....Steve Saklad
Set Decoration.............................Kara Lindstrom
Costume Design ....Ann Roth
....Gary Jones
....Bridget Kelly
Casting ....Billy Hopkins, Suzanne Smith
Screenplay.......................................Cynthia Cidre
Based on the novel *The Mambo
Kings Play Songs Of Love* by ....Oscar Hijuelos
Executive Music Producer ....Robert Kraft
Original Score................................Robert Kraft
....Carlos Franzetti
Theme Song..................................Robert Kraft
....Arne Glimcher
Mambo Arrangements..........................Ray Santos
Choreographer ....Michael Peters

Film Facts
Running Time ....101 minutes
Soundtrack ....Elektra Records
Film...Deluxe Color
Sound ....Dolby Stereo
Location ....Los Angeles
Other Working Titles ....
....*Mambo Kings Play Songs Of Love*

Man Trouble
(20th Century Fox)

Critics Rating: ★

Genre: Comedy—This much-anticipated film turned out to be a by-the-numbers romantic comedy-thriller and something of a disappointment, according to most critics.

Plot: Ellen Barkin plays Joan, an opera singer who has been the victim of a break-in and other threats. Joan hires Harry Bliss (Jack Nicholson), a con man and the owner of a guard-dog service, to protect her. This is more than a case of whodunit, it's a case of opposites' attracting.

MPAA Rating: PG-13

Trivia: In 1970 the film *Five Easy Pieces*, also directed by Bob Rafelson and written by Carole Eastman, put Nicholson on the Hollywood map.

Cast
Harry Bliss	Jack Nicholson
Joan Spruance	Ellen Barkin
Redmond Layls	Harry Dean Stanton
Andy Ellerman	Beverly D'Angelo
Eddy Revere	Michael McKean
Laurence Moncrief	Saul Rubinek
Helen Dextra	Veronica Cartwright
Hospital administrator	Rebecca Broussard
Socorro	Betty Carvalho
Lewie Duart	David Clennon
June Huff	Viveka Davis
Butch Gable	Gary Graham
Det. Melvenos	John Kapelos
Lee MacGreevy	Paul Mazursky
Nurse Sonya	Mary-Robin Redd
Adele Bliss	Lauren Tom

Credits
Executive Producer	Vittorio Cecchi Gori
Co-Executive Producer	Gianni Nunnari
Producers	Bruce Gilbert
	Carole Eastman
Assistant Producer	Michael Silverblatt
Director	Bob Rafelson
Assistant Director	Marty Ewing
Director of Photography	Stephen H. Burum
Sound	David Ronne
Editor	William Steinkamp
Production Design	Mel Bourne
Set Decoration	Samara Schaffer
Costume Design	Judy Ruskin
Casting	Terry Liebling
Written by	Carole Eastman
Music	Georges Delerue
Stunt Coordinator	Loren Janes

Film Facts
Running Time	100 minutes
Soundtrack	Varese Sarabande
Film	Technicolor
Sound	Dolby Stereo
Location	Los Angeles

The Man Without A World
(Milestone Film & Video)

Critics Rating: Not Rated.

Genre: Drama—A black-and-white tribute to the silent era by avant-garde director Eleanor Antin.

Plot: Passing itself off as a long-lost Russian silent film that has just been discovered, the story centers on a Polish village before the 1939 Nazi invasion. Pier Marton plays Zevi, a Yiddish poet who falls in love with Rukheleh (Christine Berry). Her parents are opposed to her relationship with Zevi and she is forced to leave the family.

MPAA Rating: Not Rated.

Cast
Zevi	Pier Marton
Rukheleh	Christine Berry
Sooreleh	Anna Henriques
The ballerina	Eleanor Antin
The butcher	John Borba
Rukheleh's mother	Marcia Goodman
Rukheleh's father	Sergun A. Tont
Zevi's mother	Luyba Talpalatsky
Yisoel	George Leonard
Gedaliah	Don Sommese

Also with Bennet Berger, Sabato Fiorella, James Scott Kerwin, Nicolai Lennox, Lisa Welti and Ellen Zweig.

Credits
Producer/Director	Eleanor Antin
Associate Producer	Lynn Burnstan
Assistant Directors	Marcia Goodman
	David Antin
Director of Photography	Rich Wargo
Editor	Lynn Burnstan
Art Direction	Sabato Fiorella

151

Costume Design................................Judy Ryerson
Written by.......................................Eleanor Antin
Music...Charlie Morrow
....Lee Erwin
Choreography ....Melissa Cottle

Film Facts
Running Time ....98 minutes
Film...Black & White

The Match Factory Girl
(Tulitikkutehtaan Tytto)
(Kino)

Critics Rating: ★★★★
Genre: Comedy—By Finnish director Aki Kaurismaki (*Shadows In Paradise, Ariel*).
Plot: Kati Outinen plays Iris, a poor, shy, non-descript match-factory assembly-line worker. Taken for granted, used and abused by everyone in her life, Iris quietly submits to the abuse, until one day when she becomes pregnant and her parents kick her out of the house. Having taken all the abuse and insults she can take, she gathers her strength and methodically plans her revenge—which is shocking but sweet.
MPAA Rating: Not Rated.

Cast
Iris...Kati Outinen
Her mother......................................Elina Salo
Her stepfather ....Esko Nikkari
Man in dancehall ....Vesa Vierikko
Also with Klaus Heydemann, Outi Maenpaa, Marja Packalen, Silu Seppala and Reijo Taipale.

Credits
Executive Producers ....Klas Olofsson
....Katinka Farago
Producer ....Aki Kaurismaki
Director ....Aki Kaurismaki
Assistant Director............................Pauli Pennti
Director of Photography ....Timo Salminen
Sound...Jouko Lumme
Editor...Aki Kaurismaki
Production Design.............................Rista Karhula
Production Managers.........................Klaus Heydemann
....Jaakko Talaskivi
Screenplay......................................Aki Kaurismaki

Film Facts
Country of Origin ....Finland

Running Time ....70 minutes
Film...Eastmancolor
Sound ....Stereo

Meatballs 4
(Filmstore)

Critics Rating: Not Rated.
Genre: Comedy—Director Ivan Reitman helped launch Bill Murray's theatrical career in 1979 with the original *Meatballs*. Thirteen years later, the fourth in this series has almost no relationship to the first, other than its appropriately corny, screwball antics and sophomoric humor.
Plot: Corey Feldman ("I was in *Goonies*!" he exclaims at one point in the film) stars as Ricky, a water skier hired by the Lakeside Water Ski Camp. A nearby rival camp is intent on putting Lakeside out of business, in order to buy the land for—what else—real-estate development. The camps compete in a winner-take-all ski meet, and suffice it to say, the ending is less than a mystery.
MPAA Rating: R—For nudity and a scene of sensuality.

Cast
Ricky Wade.......................................Corey Feldman
Neil Peterson ....Jack Nance
Monica..Sarah Douglas
Wes..Bojesse Christopher
Victor...Johnny Cocktails
Howie...J. Trevor Edmond
Jennifer..Paige French
Dick ....John Mendoza
Kyle...Bentley Mitchum
Hillary..Christy Thom
Kelly ....Deborah Tucker

Credits
Executive Producer ....Ken Halloway
Producer ....Donald P. Borchers
Associate Producer ....Kris Krengel
Director ....Bob Logan
Assistant Director............................Kris Krengel
Director of Photography ....Vance Burberry
Sound...Beau Franklin
Editor ....Peter H. Verity
Production Design...........................Dorian Vernacchio
....Deborah Raymond

Costume Design ....Angela Calin
Screenplay..Bob Logan
Music...Steve Hunter
Water Ski Coordinator.............................P. J. Marks
Stunt Coordinator ....Kurt Bryant

Film Facts
Running Time ....87 minutes
Film ....Film House Color
Sound...Ultra-Stereo

Medicine Man
(Buena Vista)

Critics Rating: ★★

Genre: Drama—This ecology-minded drama set in the rain forests of Venezuela follows a man in search of a cure for cancer. Along the way he must overcome a few minor obstacles. One is a developer intent on bulldozing the forest; the other is a woman.

Plot: Sean Connery stars as Dr. Robert Campbell, a man hiding out in the jungle after a failed life and broken marriage. He discovers a possible cure for cancer in the rain forests, but needs assistance and equipment to continue his work. When assistance arrives, it is in the form of an antagonistic female. The two spend the remainder of the film battling one another in this predictable and tired plot that sidetracks the film's more engaging message.

MPAA Rating: PG-13

Cast
Dr. Robert Campbell ....Sean Connery
Dr. Rae Crane ....Lorraine Bracco
Tanaki.....................................Rodolfo De Alexandre
Dr. Miguel Ornega.....................................Jose Wilker
Medicine Man ....Angelo Barra Moreira
Jahausa.....................Francisco Tsirene Tsere Rereme
Palala.......................................Elias Monteiro Da Silva
Kalana.......................Edinei Maria Serrio Dos Santos
Imana ....Bec-Kana-Re Dos Santos Kaiapo

Credits
Executive Producer ....Sean Connery
Producers..Andrew G. Vajna
....Donna Dubrow
Line Producer ....Beau Marks
Director....................................John McTiernan
2nd Unit Director.....................................Fred Waugh

Assistant Director..................................Tom Mack
Assistant Director (Mexico)................Sebastian Silva
Director of Photography ....Donald McAlpine
Sound..Douglas B. Arnold
Editor...................................Michael R. Miller
Production Design ....John Krenz Reinhart, Jr.
Art Direction ....Don Diers
....Jesus Buenrostro
(Brazilian Indian crew).....................Marlisi Storchi
Set Decoration ....Enrique Estevez
Costume Design ....Marilyn Vance-Straker
(Brazilian Indian crew)......................Rita Murtimho
Casting..Bonnie Timmermann
Screenplay ....Tom Schulman
....Sally Robinson
Story by ....Tom Schulman
Original Music ....Jerry Goldsmith
Brazilian Indian Choreographer ....
....Maria Fatima Toledo
Special Effects Supervisors...................John Thomas
....Laurencio Cordero

Film Facts
Running Time ....106 minutes
Soundtrack ....Varese Sarabande
Film...Technicolor
Sound..Dolby Stereo
Location ....Mexico; Brazil
Other Working Titles...............................*The Stand*;
....*The Last Days of Eden*

Mediterraneo
(Mediterranean)
(Miramax)

Critics Rating: ★★★★

Genre: Comedy—The 1991 Academy Award winning Best Foreign Language picture is an old-fashioned Italian comedy about a group of soldiers marooned on a Greek Island.

Plot: When a platoon is stationed on an Aegean island in the early 1940s, they are somehow forgotten by their superiors. The island is inhabited solely by women and the elderly, much to the delight of the men. Life is sweet for a number of years until the military discovers its error and puts an end to this simple and idyllic life on the island.

MPAA Rating: Not Rated.

Cast

Lt. Montini	Claudio Bigagli
Sgt. Lo Russo	Diego Abatantuono
Vasilissa	Vanna Barba
Shepherdess	Irene Grazoli
Strazzabosco	Gigio Alberti
Novente	Claudio Bisio
Colasanti	Ugo Conti
Garina	Giuseppe Cederna

Also with Memo Dini, Irene Grazioli, Vasco Mirandola and Luigi Montini.

Credits

Producers	Mario Cecchi Gori
	Vittorio Cecchi Gori
	Gianni Minervini
Director	Gabriele Salvatores
Director of Photography	Italo Pettriccione
Editor	Nino Baragli
Art Direction	Thalia Istikopoulos
Costume Design	Francesco Panni
Screenplay	Vincenzo Monteleone
Music	Giancarlo Bigazzi
	Mario Falagiani

Film Facts

Country of Origin	Italy
Language	Italian (subtitled)
Running Time	92 minutes
Film	Telecolor
Sound	Stereo

Commissar Vay	Janos Acs
Karoly Eotvos	Tamas Fodor
Amsel Vogel	Franciszek Pieczka
Matej	Andras Stohl
Smilovics	Tamas Eross
Jozsef Scharf	Robert Koltay
Salamon Schwarcz	Andor Lukats
Moric Scharf	Istvan Meszaros
Jacob	Zoltan Mucsi
Sara Hersko	Gyorgyi Tarjan
Rebecca Weiss	Bertha Dominguez

Credits

Producers	Gabor Hanak
	Hubert Niogret
Director	Judit Elek
Director of Photography	Gabor Halasz
Sound	Gyorgy Kovacs
Editor	Katalin Kabdebo
Art Direction	Tamas Banovich
Costume Design	Erzsebet Miaklovszky
Screenplay	Judit Elek
Music	Peter Eotvos

Film Facts

Country of Origin	Hungary/France
Language	Hungarian (subtitled)
Running Time	147 minutes
Film	Eastmancolor
Sound	Stereo

Memoirs Of A River

(Tutajosok)
(Castle Hill)

Critics Rating: ★★★★
Genre: Drama—Based on a true story, this Hungarian drama with subtitles focuses on the events surrounding a murder and the resulting historic trial.
Plot: This tale of anti-Semitism and hate focuses on a simple Jewish farmer who witnesses the murder of his son and the burning of his home. Running for his life, his desperation takes him on a tragic journey.
MPAA Rating: Not Rated.

Cast

David Hersko	Sandor Gaspar
Csepkanics	Pal Hetenyi

Memoirs Of An Invisible Man

(Warner Bros.)

Critics Rating: ★★★
Genre: Comedy—With the exception of a few state-of-the-art special effects, this romantic-comedy-thriller is for the most part a by-the-numbers remake of a much classier classic.
Plot: Chevy Chase stars as Nick Halloway, a stock-market analyst who happens to be at the wrong place at the wrong time. When he is accidentally "cycolotroned" by a lab running experiments for the CIA, the scene is set for the fun to follow. The CIA decides it must eliminate Halloway before the world learns of its experiment, and so begins an endless madcap chase to capture an invisible man.
MPAA Rating: PG-13

Cast

Nick Halloway	Chevy Chase
Alice Monroe	Darryl Hannah
David Jenkins	Sam Neill
George Talbot	Michael McKean
Warren Singleton	Stephen Tobolowsky
Dr. Bernard Wachs	Jim Norton

Credits

Executive Producer	Arnon Milchan
Producers	Bruce Bodner
	Dan Kolsrud
Director	John Carpenter
Assistant Director	William M. Elvin
Director of Photography	William A. Fraker
Sound	Jim Alexander
Editor	Marion Rothman
Production Design	Lawrence G. Paull
Art Direction	Bruce Crone
Set Design	Elizabeth Lapp
Set Decoration	Rick Simpson
Casting	Sharon Howard-Field
Screenplay	Robert Collector
	Dana Olsen
	William Goldman
Based on the book by	H. F. Saint
Music	Shirley Walker
Special Visual Effects	Industrial Light & Magic
Visual Effects Supervisor	Bruce Nicholson
Visual Effects Producer	Ned Gorman
Digital Effects Supervisor	Stuart Robertson
Computer Graphics Supervisor	Doug Smythe

Film Facts

Running Time	99 minutes
Soundtrack	Varese Sarabande
Film	Technicolor
Sound	Dolby Stereo
Location	San Francisco; Los Angeles

A Midnight Clear
(Interstar)

Critics Rating: ★★★★
Genre: Drama—Set in 1944, this war drama focuses on the futility and absurdity of war.
Plot: Ethan Hawke (*Mystery Date*) stars as Will, the squad leader and narrator of the film. Put in an impossible situation by his commander, he is sent on a pointless mission with his troop. When the senior soldier goes berserk, his actions prove fatal. Will manages to escape the Germans with his men, only to be sent back into combat in this futile game of war.
MPAA Rating: R—For language, war violence and a scene of sensuality.

Cast

Will Knott	Ethan Hawke
Bud Miller	Peter Berg
Mel Avakian	Kevin Dillon
Stan Shutzer	Arye Gross
Vince (Mother) Wilkins	Gary Sinise
Paul (Father) Mundy	Frank Whaley
Major Griffin	John C. McGinley

Also with Rachel Griffin, David Jensen, Larry Joshua and Curt Lowens.

Credits

Executive Producers	Armyan Bernstein
	Tom Rosenberg
	Marc Abraham
Producers	Dale Pollock
	Bill Borden
Associate Producer	Margaret Hilliard
Director	Keith Gordon
Assistant Director	Scott Javine
Director of Photography	Tom Richmond
Sound	John (Earl) Stein
Editor	Don Brochu
Production Manager	Margaret Hilliard
Production Design	David Nichols
Art Direction	David Lubin
Costume Design	Barbara Tfank
Casting	Gary Zuckerbrod
Screenplay	Keith Gordon
Based on the Novel by	William Wharton
Music	Mark Isham
Stunt Coordinator	Steve Davison

Film Facts

Running Time	107 minutes
Film	Alpha Cine Color
Sound	Dolby Stereo
Location	Park City, Utah

The Mighty Ducks
(Buena Vista)

Critics Rating: ★★★
Genre: Comedy—In the tradition of *The Bad News*

Bears, an underdog ice-hockey team takes on the championship team.

Plot: Emilio Estevez stars as Gordon Bombay, an arrogant attorney charged with driving under the influence. He is sentenced to perform community service work as coach to a team of losers. To make matters worse, they are in competition with the champion Hawks. Harboring a grudge against the coach of the Hawks, having once been a player for the team, Gordon sees this as his opportunity for revenge. In the end, however, it is an opportunity for Gordon and his team to learn the true meaning of sportsmanship and winning.

MPAA Rating: PG—For mild language.

Cast

Gordon Bombay	Emilio Estevez
Hans	Joss Ackland
Coach Reilly	Lane Smith
Casey	Heidi Kling
Gerald Ducksworth	Josef Sommer
Charlie Conroy	Joshua Jackson
Fulton Reed	Elden Ratliff
Goldberg	Shaun Weiss
Connie	Marguerite Moreau

Credits

Producers	Jordan Kerner
	Jon Avnet
Co-Producers	Lynn Morgan
	Martin Huberty
Director	Stephen Herek
Assistant Director	Douglas E. Wise
Director of Photography	Thomas Del Ruth
Sound	Ed Novick
Editors	Larry Bock
	John F. Link
Production Design	Randy Ser
Art Direction	Tony Fanning
Set Design	Jack Ballance
Set Decoration	Julie Kay Fanton
Costume Design	Grania Preston
Casting	Renee Rousselot
Written by	Steven Brill
Music	David Newman
Special Effects Supervisor	Paul Murphy

Film Facts

Running Time	100 minutes
Film	Technicolor
Sound	Dolby Stereo
Location	Minnesota

Other Working Titles .... *Bombay*

The Mission Of Raoul Wallenberg
(Missija Raulja Wallenberga)
(Innova-Film)

Critics Rating: Not Rated.

Genre: Documentary

Plot: Raoul Wallenberg was a Swedish diplomat imprisoned by the Soviets in 1947 after the Red Army occupied Budapest. His crime was saving approximately 100,000 Jews from the death camps by issuing them diplomatic protection. The film is an investigation of his alleged death. The official version has long been held that he died at the hands of the KGB during an interrogation. To flesh out the truth, the film uses archival footage, stills, interviews and Soviet records.

MPAA Rating: Not Rated.

Credits

Director	Alexander Rodnyansky
Directors of Photography	Wladimir Gujiewski
	Igor Iwanow
Written by	Leonid Gurewitsch
	Alexander Rodnyansky

Film Facts

Country of Origin	Soviet Union
Running Time	70 minutes
Film	Color/Black & White
Sound	Stereo

Mississippi Masala
(Samuel Goldwyn Co.)

Critics Rating: ★★★★

Genre: Drama—Like Spike Lee's *Jungle Fever*, this modern-day love story between two people from different ethnic groups is emotionally charged and irreverently funny.

Plot: The story takes place in the melting pot of the Deep South. Mina (Sarita Choudhury) is a 24-year-old Hindu woman who has recently immigrated with her family to America. Cleaning bathrooms to make a living, one day she crashes her car into Demetrius (Denzel Washington, *Malcolm X*), a prominent young man with his own business. Though Mina's parents are desperate for her to marry, they are horrified when the two fall in love. Thus, the scene is set for conflict and comedy between families and ethnic groups in this very natural film.

MPAA Rating: R—For sensuality and language.

Cast

Demetrius	Denzel Washington
Jay	Roshan Seth
Mina	Sarita Choudhury
Tyrone	Charles S. Dutton
Williben	Joe Seneca
Dexter	Tico Wells
Kinnu	Sharmila Tagore
Okelo	Konga Moandu
Anil	Ranjit Chowdhry
Pontiac	Mohan Gokhale
Kanti Napkin	Mohan Agashe
Aunt Rose	Yvette Hawkins
Jammubhai	Anjan Srivastava
Chanda	Dipti Suthar

Credits

Executive Producer	Cherie Rodgers
Producers	Michael Nozik
	Mira Nair
Co-Producer	Mitch Epstein
Associate Producer	Lydia Dean Pilcher
Director	Mira Nair
Director of Photography	Ed Lachman
Editor	Roberto Silvi
Production Design	Mitch Epstein
Art Direction	Jefferson Sage
Set Decoration	Jeanette Scott
Costume Design (Mississippi)	Ellen Lutter
Costume Design (Uganda)	Susan Lyall
Costume Design (Indian)	Kinnari Panikar
Casting (Mississippi)	Judy Claman
Casting (New York)	Simon/Kumin Casting
Casting (Uganda)	Dinaz Stafford
Casting (London)	Susie Figgis
Written by	Sooni Taraporevala
Music	L. Subramaniam

Film Facts

Running Time	118 minutes
Soundtrack	JRS Records
Film	Color
Sound	Dolby Stereo
Location	Mississippi; Africa

Mistress
(Rainbow/Tribeca)

Critics Rating: ★★★

Genre: Drama—Not without its humorous side, *Mistress* directed and cowritten by Barry Primus is a darker look at the business of filmmaking than *The Player.*

Tag Line: "Everybody has a passion...Every passion has a price."

Plot: Robert Wuhl plays Marvin Landisman, a former director eager to make a comeback in the film business. When an independent producer (Martin Landau) shows an interest in his script, the stage is set and Marvin begins his education in Hollywood deal making. In order to raise money for the film, Marvin is forced to deal with a series of money men, who see the film as a perfect vehicle for their mistresses. However, things only get worse from here. Mr. Wright (Robert De Niro) thinks this sensitive story of a suicide needs more sex. All of this adds up to an entertaining if dark look at this fickle business.

MPAA Rating: R—For strong sensuality and violence; and language

Cast

Marvin Landisman	Robert Wuhl
Jack Roth	Martin Landau
Evan M. Wright	Robert De Niro
Stuart Stratland, Jr.	Jace Alexander
Rachel Landisman	Laurie Metcalf
Carmine Rasso	Danny Aiello
Warren Zell	Christopher Walken
George Lieberhoff	Eli Wallach
Peggy	Tuesday Knight
Beverly	Sheryl Lee Ralph
Ernest Borgnine	Ernest Borgnine

Also with Jean Smart.

Credits

Executive Producer	Ruth Charny
Producers	Meir Teper
	Robert De Niro
Co-Producer	Bertil Ohlsson
Director	Barry Primus
Assistant Director	Bruce Franklin
Director of Photography	Sven Kirsten
Sound	Jacob Goldstein
Editor	Steven Weisberg

Production Design	Phil Peters
Costume Design	Susan Nininger
Casting	Gail Levin
Screenplay	Barry Primus
	J. F. Lawton
Based on a story by	Barry Primus
Music	Galt MacDermot
Musical Sequences Staged by	Julie Arenal

Film Facts

Running Time	109 minutes
Film	CFI Color
Sound	Stereo
Location	Los Angeles

Mo' Money
(Columbia)

Critics Rating: ★★

Genre: Comedy—Executive producer, writer, comedian and star Damon Wayans (*The Last Boy Scout*) brings to the screen an irreverent action-comedy about a pair of hustling scam artists.

Plot: Wayans plays Johnny, a street-wise con artist. He's raising his younger brother Seymour, played by Damon's real-life younger brother Marlon Wayans. Johnny becomes smitten with a beautiful young woman (Stacey Dash), and finds that he needs more money to impress her. He takes a job with her credit card company in the mailroom. This, of course, is a bit like putting the fox in charge of the hen house. Before long, Johnny and Seymour are running a credit card scam. This leads them into an even larger scam perpetrated by a ruthless company executive. Only this time Johnny joins forces with the law and foils the evil executive in an action-packed Hollywood-style finale.

MPAA Rating: R—For violence and language.

Trivia: Reports had Marlon Wayans cast as the character who becomes Robin in *Batman Returns*. Unfortunately, the filmmakers cut the character from the film.

Cast

Johnny Stewart	Damon Wayans
Amber Evans	Stacey Dash
Lt. Raymond Walsh	Joe Santos
Keith Heading	John Diehl
Seymour Stewart	Marlon Wayans

Charlotte	Almayvonne
Chris Fields	Mark Beltzman
Tom Dilton	Harry J. Lennix

Credits

Executive Producers	Damon Wayans
	Eric L. Gold
Producer	Michael Rachmil
Co-Producer	Carl Craig
Director	Peter Macdonald
Assistant Director	Tyrone L. Mason
Director of Photography	Don Burgess
Sound	Russell Williams II
Editor	Hubert C. De la Bouillerie
Production Design	William Arnold
Costume Design	Michelle Cole
Casting	Aleta Chappelle
Written by	Damon Wayans
Music Underscore	Jay Gruska
Songs by	Jimmy Jam
	Terry Lewis

Film Facts

Running Time	89 minutes
Soundtrack	Perspective Records
Film	Color
Sound	Dolby Stereo
Location	Chicago

Mom And Dad Save The World
(Warner Bros.)

Critics Rating: Not Rated.

Tag Line: Boldly borrowing from another sci-fi film series, the promotional tag line read, "Boldly going where no parents have gone before."

Genre: Comedy—*Mom And Dad* is a goofy, late-summer family sci-fi comedy about an egomaniacal ruler of a not-too-distant planet who is intent on destroying the Earth. Chris Matheson and Ed Solomon (*Bill & Teds Bogus Journey*) wrote the script.

Plot: Jon Lovitz stars as Tod Spengo, the emperor of a planet of idiots, appropriately named Spengo. As he is about to blow up the Earth, he spots Marge Nelson (Teri Garr), a suburban housewife, and falls in love. With an electromagnetic beam, he transports Marge and her husband back to his planet. From here on, husband Dick (Jeffrey Jones) spends his time battling Spengo for his wife and his life.

MPAA Rating: PG

Cast

Marge Nelson	Teri Garr
Dick Nelson	Jeffrey Jones
Emperor Tod Spengo	Jon Lovitz
King Raff	Eric Idle
Sirk	Dwier Brown
Semage	Kathy Ireland
Afir	Thalmus Rasulala
Sibor	Wallace Shawn

Credits

Producer	Michael Phillips
Co-Producers	Michael Irwin
	Max Kirishima
Line Producer	Daryl Kass
Associate Producer	Deirdre Kelly Sullivan
Director	Greg Beeman
Assistant Director	Richard W. Abramitis
Director of Photography	Jacques Haitkin
Sound	James Thornton
Editor	W. O. Garret
Additional Editing	Michael Jablow
Production Design	Craig Stearns
Art Direction	Randy Moore
Set Design	Bill Rea
Set Decoration	Dorree Cooper
Costume Design	Robyn Reichek
Casting	Lisa Beach
Written by	Chris Matheson
	Ed Solomon
Music	Jerry Goldsmith
Creature Effects	Alterian Studios
Special Visual Effects	Perpetual Motion Pictures
Visual Effects Coordinator	Michael Muscal
Stunt Coordinator	Dennis (Danger) Madalone

Film Facts

Running Time	88 minutes
Soundtrack	Varese Sarabande
Film	Foto-Kem Color
Sound	Dolby Stereo

The Money Tree
(Black Sheep Films)

Critics Rating: Not Rated.

Genre: Drama—In this low-budget and often humorous indy film, money *does* grow on trees.

Plot: Christopher Dienstag plays David, a young marijuana grower looking to make it big with the proceeds from his cash crop. What better way to make a living—unless, of course, your fiancee doesn't approve. Then there's the competition and the law to deal with. Those, however, are only petty annoyances to this determined entrepreneur.

MPAA Rating: Not Rated.

Cast

David	Christopher Dienstag
Erica	Monica T. Caldwell
Chad	Nik Martin
Girlfriend	Kathrine Schutzman
Vincent	Malcolm Cohen
Pasquel	Carlos Deloche
Charly	Richard Roughgarden
Rusty	Gregory Wilker

Credits

Producer	Christopher Dienstag
Director	Alan Dienstag
Director of Photography	Don Bonato
Editor	Susan Crutcher
Dialog improvised from a story by	Alan Dienstag
	Christopher Dienstag
Music	Lorin Rowan

Film Facts

Running Time	94 minutes
Film	Color
Sound	Stereo

Monster In A Box
(Fine Line Features)

Critics Rating: ★★★★

Genre: Comedy—Continuing where *Swimming To Cambodia* ended, writer-performer Spalding Gray again fills the stage with wise and witty monologue that will keep you riveted to your seat.

Plot: The "Monster in a Box" is an autobiographical novel Gray is writing titled "Impossible Vacation." Gray's adventures spring from the many welcome interruptions in life that keep him from completing his book. These interruptions take him from country to country, adventure to adventure and from one humorous situation to another.

MPAA Rating: PG-13

Trivia: The film was shot at London's Riverside Studios in 1991 before a live audience. It originally opened as a one-act play at Lincoln Center in 1990.

Credits

Producer	Jon Blair
Co-Producer	Renee Shafransky
Associate Producer	Norman I. Cohen
Director	Nick Broomfield
Director of Photography	Michael Coulter
Sound	Sandy Macrae
Editor	Graham Hutchings
Production Design	Ray Oxley
Written and Performed by	Spalding Gray
Music	Laurie Anderson

Film Facts

Running Time	88 minutes
Soundtrack	Gang of Seven Records
Film	Eastmancolor
Sound	Stereo

Montana Run

(Greycat)

Critics Rating: Not Rated.

Genre: Comedy—A winning, low-budget comedy about the not-so-glamorous side of the entertainment business.

Plot: Randy Thompson plays Andy Miller, an up-and-coming comic who winds up, by accident, playing the Montana nightclub/bar circuit. Together with two fellow comics and a manager, the foursome hit the road and discover some important things about themselves and each other along the way.

MPAA Rating: Not Rated.

Cast

Andy Miller	Randy Thompson
Brock Mason	Dan Lishner
Doug Atkins	Ron Reid
Charli McKnight	Mayne Paul-Thompson

Credits

Producer/Director	Randy Thompson
Director of Photography	William Brooks Baum
Editors	Randy Thompson, Tim Maffia
Written by	Randy Thompson
	Ron Reid, Dan Lishner
Music	Randy Thompson

Film Facts

Running Time	97 minutes
Film	Color
Sound	Stereo

Mr. Baseball

(Universal)

Critics Rating: ★★★

Genre: Comedy—A humorous, by-the-numbers, fish-out-of-water tale.

Tag Line: "He's the biggest thing to hit Japan since Godzilla."

Plot: Tom Selleck stars as Jack Elliot, an American baseball player at the end of his career. Put on waivers by his team he is picked up by the Japanese Chuchini Dragons. It doesn't take long, however, before Jack has offended the manager of the team (Ken Takakura) as well as the players. He also has a difficult time fitting in in other ways as well. However, before the final inning he manages to hit a home run in this light, entertaining and energetic tale.

MPAA Rating: PG-13—For sensuality and language.

Cast

Jack Elliott	Tom Selleck
Max "Hammer" Dubois	Dennis Haysbert
Uchiyama	Ken Takakura
Hiroko Uchiyama	Aya Takanashi
Yoji Nishimura	Toshi Shioya
Ryoh Mukai	Toshizo Fujiwara
Toshi Yamashita	Kohsuke Toyohara
Shinji Igarashi	Mak Takano
Hiroshi Kurosawa	Kenji Morinaga
Tomohiko Ohmae	Joh Nishimura

Credits

Executive Producers	John Kao
	Jeffrey Silver
Executive Producer (Japan)	Susumu Kondoh
Producers	Fred Schepisi
	Doug Claybourne
	Robert Newmyer
Line Producer (Japan)	Tomoo Ito
Director	Fred Schepisi
Assistant Director	Bruce Moriarty
Assistant Director (Japan)	Kazuto Kunishige
Director of Photography	Ian Baker

Sound ....David Kelson
Editor...Peter Honess
Production Design ....Ted Haworth
Art Direction ....Katsumi Nakazawa
Set Decoration ....Yuuki Sato
....Hirohide Shibata
Costume Design ....Bruce Finlayson
Casting.................................Dianne Crittenden
Casting (Japan) ....Kenji Saitoh
Screenplay...Gary Ross
...............................Kevin Wade, Monte Merrick
Story by ....Theo Pelletier
....John Junkerman
Music...Jerry Goldsmith

Film Facts
Running Time ....113 minutes
Soundtrack ....Varese Sarabande
Film ....Deluxe Color
Sound ....Dolby Stereo
Location...............................Japan; Los Angeles
Other Working Titles......................*Tokyo Diamond*;
....*Mr. Besuboru*

Mr. Saturday Night
(Columbia)

Critics Rating: ★★★
Genre: Comedy—Billy Crystal makes his directorial debut with this bittersweet, sentimental and consistently funny story about a fictional veteran comedian. The story follows his career ups and downs from childhood to old age.
Plot: Crystal stars as Buddy Young, Jr., an aging New York stand-up comic who looks back over his life and work. Never quite making it to the top, he has been his own worst enemy. In nostalgic flashbacks he also looks at his rivalry and close bond with his brother and manager Stan, a doormat to Buddy's abuse. Stan was the only thing that meant as much to Buddy as his career. Now at the end of his career he is reduced to performing in retirement homes and his brother is finally ready to end their partnership.
MPAA Rating: R—For language.
Cast
Buddy Young, Jr. ....Billy Crystal
Stan Yankelman..................................David Paymer

Elaine..Julie Warner
Annie ....Helen Hunt
Susan ....Mary Mara
Phil Gussman ....Jerry Orbach
Larry Meyerson ....Ron Silver
Mom ....Sage Allen
Freddie...Carl Ballantine
Gene...Jackie Gayle
Jerry Lewis...Jerry Lewis
Abie (age 15) ....Jason Marsden
Stan (age 18) ....Michael Weiner
Joey ....Slappy White

Credits
Executive Producers ....Lowell Ganz
....Babaloo Mandel
Producer/Director ....Billy Crystal
Co-Producer ....Peter Schindler
Assistant Director.................................Jim Chory
2nd Unit Director ....Peter Schindler
Director of Photography ....Don Peterman
2nd Unit Camera.................................Gabor Kover
Sound...Jeff Wexler
Editor..Kent Beyda
Production Design ....Albert Brenner
Art Direction.............................Carol Winstead Wool
Set Design ....Harold Fuhrman
Set Decoration...................................Kathe Klopp
Costume Design ....Ruth Myers
Makeup/Hair Design ....Peter Montagna
...............................Bill Farley, Steve LaPorte
Casting ....Pam Dixon
Written by..Billy Crystal
........................Lowell Ganz, Babaloo Mandel
Music ....Marc Shaiman
Choreography....................................Lester Wilson

Film Facts
Running Time ....119 minutes
Soundtrack ....Big Screen Records
Film...Technicolor
Sound ....Dolby Stereo
Location..............................Los Angeles; New York

Munchie
(Concorde)

Critics Rating: Not Rated.
Genre: Comedy—An entertaining family film and sequel to the 1987 Bettina Hirsch film, *Munchies*.

Plot: The story revolves around an oversized puppet-come-to-life named Munchie, voiced by Dom DeLuise. Jamie McEnnan plays Gage Dobson, a lonely young boy. When he finds the puppet, he not only finds a friend, but gets a few wishes granted at the same time.

MPAA Rating: PG

Cast

Cathy	Loni Anderson
Voice of Munchie	Dom DeLuise
Elliott	Andrew Stevens
Prof. Cruikshank	Arte Johnson
Gage Dobson	Jamine McEnnan
Ashton	Scott Ferguson
Miss Laurel	Monique Gabrielle
Andrea	Love Hewitt
Principal Thornton	Ace Mask
Mrs. Blaylok	Toni Naples
Mr. Kurtz	Jay Richardson
Leon	Mike Simmrin

Also with Chuck Cirino, George (Buck) Flower, Paul Hertzberg, Becky LeBeau, Fred Olen Ray, R. J. Robinson, Angus Scrimm, Linda Shayne and Brinke Stevens.

Credits

Executive Producer	Roger Corman
Producer	Mike Elliott
Co-Producer	Michele Weisler
Director	Jim Wynorski
Assistant Director	Larry Kent Linton
2nd Unit Director	Steve Mitchell
Director of Photography	Don E. Fauntleroy
Sound	Christopher Taylor
Editor	Rick Gentner
Production Design	Stuart Blatt
Art Direction	Carey Meyer
Costume Design	Lisa Cacavas
Casting	Andrew Hertz
Screenplay	R. J. Robertson
	Jim Wynorski
Additional Muchie Dialogue	Vin DiStefano
Music	Chuck Cirino
Muchie Creators	Gabe Bartalos
	Dave Kindlon
Stunt Coordinator	Patrick Statham

Film Facts

Running Time	80 minutes
Film	Foto-Kem Color
Sound	Ultra-Stereo

The Muppet Christmas Carol
(Buena Vista)

Critics Rating: ★★★

Genre: Drama—Directed by Brian Henson, son of the late Jim Henson.

Plot: Michael Caine plays Scrooge in this latest adaptation of the Charles Dickens classic. The Great Gonzo narrates the story as Dickens himself. The story of course centers on Scrooge's encounters with the Ghosts of Christmas Past, Present and Yet to Come. While not as light as past Muppet outings, the film is nevertheless enjoyable holiday fare. It would be difficult not to appreciate the humor in casting Kermit the Frog as Bob Cratchit or Miss Piggy as his wife Emily.

MPAA Rating: G

Cast

Bob Cratchit	Kermit the Frog
Emily Cratchit	Miss Piggy
Charles Dickens	The Great Gonzo
Scrooge	Michael Caine

Also with Rizzo the Rat and Fozzie Bear.

Voices:

The Great Gonzo/Robert Marley/ Bunsen Moneydew/Betina Cratchit	Dave Goelz
Rizzo the Rat/Bean Bunny/Kermit the Frog/Beaker/Belinda Cratchit	Steve Whitmire
Tiny Tim Cratchit/Jacob Marley/ Ma Bear	Jerry Nelson
Miss Piggy/Fozzie Bear/Sam Eagle/ Animal	Frank Oz
Peter Cratchit/Old Joe/ Swedish Chef	David Rudman
Ghost of Christmas Present	Donald Austen
	Jerry Nelson
Ghost of Christman Yet To Come	Donald Austen
	Rob Tygner
Ghost of Christmas Past	Karen Prell/Rob Tygner/
	William Todd Jones/Jessica Fox

Credits

Executive Producer	Frank Oz
Producers	Brian Henson
	Martin G. Baker
Co-Producer	Jerry Juhl
Line Producer	David Barron
Director	Brian Henson

Assistant Director ....Crispin Reece
2nd Unit Director ....Nick Willing
Director of Photography ....John Fenner
2nd Unit Camera ....Ivan Bartos
Sound ....Bobby Mackston
Editor ....Michael Jablow
Production Design ....Val Strazovec
Art Direction Supervisor ....Alan Cassie
Art Direction ....Dennis Bosher
Set Decoration ....Michael Ford
Costume Design ....Polly Smith
Casting ....Suzanne Crowley
....Gilly Poole, Mike Fenton
Screenplay ....Jerry Juhl
Based on the novella by ....Charles Dickens
Original Score ....Miles Goodman
Songs ....Paul Williams
Choreography ....Pat Garrett
Electro/Mechanical Effects Supervisor ....
....Larry Jameson
Miniatures Unit Director ....Paul Gentry
Miniatures Unit Camera.........................Paul Wilson
Muppet Performers ....Dave Goelz, Steve Whitmire
....Jerry Nelson, Frank Oz

Film Facts
Running Time ....85 minutes
Soundtrack ....Jim Henson Records
Film ....Technicolor
Sound ....Dolby Stereo
Location ....London

The Music Tells You
(Pennebaker Associates)

Critics Rating: Not Rated.
Genre: Documentary—The focus of this lively documentary is jazz saxophonist Branford Marsalis, the new musical director of *The Tonight Show* with Jay Leno.
Plot: Whether performing in front of a crowd or in between performances on a tour bus, the filmmakers let the performer tell his own story and paint his own portrait.
MPAA Rating: Not Rated.
Cast
With Prof. David Baker, Jerry Garcia, Bruce Hornsby, Robert Hurst, Branford Marsalis, Sting and Jeff (Tain) Watts.

Credits
Executive Producers ....Steve Bekowitz
....Ann Marie Wilkins
Producer ....Frazer Pennebaker
Directors ....Chris Hegedus
....D. A. Pennebaker
Directors of Photography ....Nick Doob
....Ronald Gray
....Crystal Griffiths
....Chris Hegedus
....D. A. Pennebaker
Sound ....Patrick Smith
Editors ....Chris Hegedus
....D. A. Pennebaker, Erez Laufer
Music ....Branford Marsalis

Film Facts
Running Time ....60 minutes
Film ....Color
Sound ....Dolby Stereo

My Cousin Vinny
(20th Century Fox)

Critics Rating: ★★★★
Genre: Comedy—When recent Brooklyn law-school graduate Vinny travels to Alabama to defend his distant cousin—who has been wrongly accused of murder—the fun begins, in this high-energy comedy. Vinnie soon finds himself in the kind of situation that law school never prepared him for.
Plot: Joe Pesci stars as cousin Vinny, a newly graduated lawyer, out to rescue his cousin Bill (Ralph Macchio). Accompanied by his girlfriend Mona Lisa Vito (Marisa Tomei), Vinny could use a little rescuing of his own. But before long, out-of-towner Vinny has even bigger problems to deal with and situations that keep the laughs coming.
MPAA Rating: R—For language.
Cast
Vinny Gambini...Joe Pesci
Bill Gambini....................................Ralph Macchio
Mona Lisa Vito ....Marisa Tomei
Stan Rothenstein ....Mitchell Whitfield
Judge Chamberlain Haller ....Fred Gwynne
Sheriff Farley ....Bruce McGill
John Gibbons ....Austin Pendleton
Jim Trotter III ....Lane Smith

Credits

Producers................................Dale Launer
....Paul Schiff
Director ....Jonathan Lynn
Assistant Director ....Frank Capra III
Director of Photography......................Peter Deming
Sound....................................Robert Anderson, Jr.
Editor ....Tony Lombardo
Production Design ....Victoria Paul
Art Direction ....Randall Schmook
Set Decoration........................Michael Seirton
Costume Design ....Carol Wood
Casting....................................David Rubin
Screenplay..............................Dale Launer
Music......................................Randy Edelman

Film Facts

Running Time ....119 minutes
Soundtrack ....Varese Sarabande
Film ....Color
Sound ....Dolby Stereo
Location..................................Georgia

My General
(Mi General)
(M. D. Wax/Courier Films)

Critics Rating: Not Rated.

Genre: Comedy—About a group of military old-timers who must go back to school to learn about modern-day warfare.

Plot: The fun begins when these older men realize they are to be taught by men less than half their age and rank. The instructors, it turns out, have their hands full as they try to teach these old Generals new tricks.

MPAA Rating: Not Rated.

Cast

With Fernando Rey, Fernando Fernan-Gomez, Hector Alterio, Jose Luis Lopez Vazquez, Monica Randall Rafael Alonso, Amparo Baro, Alvara de Luna, Alfredo Luchetti, Joaquin Kremel and Juanjo Puigcorbe.

Credits

Executive Producer...............Antoni Maria C. Baquer
Director...................................Jaime de Arminan
Director of Photography...................Teo Escamilla
Sound......................................Joan Quilis
Editor ....Jose Luis Matesanz

Production Design................................Felix Murcia
Screenplay ....Jaime de Arminan
.....................................Fernando Fernan-Gomez
....Manuel Pilares
Music ....Vainica Doble

Film Facts

Country of Origin ....Spain
Running Time ....107 minutes
Film ....Agfa Color
Sound ....Stereo

My New Gun
(I. R. S. Releasing)

Critics Rating: ★★★

Genre: Comedy—Writer-director Stacy Cochran makes her feature film debut with an off-beat, dark comedy about a unlikely chain of events set off by a gun.

Tag Line: "A comedy about the American Dream."

Plot: Diane Lane and Stephen Collins star as Debbie and Gerry Bender, a New Jersey couple whose lives are turned upside down by a gun. When the couple's close friends buy a gun, Gerry decides they need a gun as well. After their neighbor Skippy (LeGros) steals the gun, Gerry is forced to take it back. In the process he shoots himself and winds up in the hospital. During the time Gerry is recovering, Skippy and Debbie are falling in love. This is just the start of a very unusual tale.

MPAA Rating: R—For language.

Cast

Debbie Bender................................Diane Lane
Gerald Bender ....Stephen Collins
Skippy ....James LeGros
Kimmy Hayes..............................Tess Harper
Andrew.....................................Bill Raymond
Irwin Bloom ....Bruce Altman
Myra..Maddie Corman
Chris Hoffman ....Phillip Seymour
Janice Phee................................Patti Chambers
Al Schlyen ....Stephen Pearlman
Kelly Jane ....La Chanze
Ray Benson.................................Matt Malloy

Credits

Executive Producers...............Miles A. Copeland III
.....................................Paul Colichman, Harold Welb

Executives in Charge of Production......Melissa Cobb
....Steven Reich
....Kevin Reidy
Producer...Michael Flynn
Co-Producer................................Lydia Dean Pilcher
Director..Stacy Cochran
Assistant Director ....Eric Heffron
Director of Photography.......................Ed Lachman
Editor ....Camilla Toniolo
Production Design..............................Tony Corbett

Set Decoration....................................Catherine Davis
Costume Design ....Eugenie Bafaloukos
Casting..Todd M. Thaler
Written by ....Stacy Cochran
Music ....Pat Irwin

Film Facts

Running Time ....99 minutes
Film...DuArt Color
Sound ....Dolby Stereo
Location ....New Jersey; New York

Nervous Ticks
(I.R.S. Releasing)

Critics Rating: Not Rated.

Genre: Comedy—A zany slapstick comedy-romance, *Nervous Ticks* is fast-paced, good fun.

Plot: Bill Pullman (*Liebestraum, Bright Angel*) stars as York Daley, an airline employee about to leave for Rio with his girlfriend (Julie Brown) to get married. The trouble is, she's still married. But that seems the least of their problems, because their trip seems doomed when one obstacle after another gets in their way. Last minute foul-ups make it impossible for York to get away from his job. He stumbles upon a suitcase full of money, wins a radio contest and his fiancee insists that he kill her husband.

MPAA Rating: R—For language.

Cast

York Daley	Bill Pullman
Nancy Rudman	Julie Brown
Ron Rudman	Peter Boyle
Cole	Brent Jennings
Rusty	James Le Gros
Cheshire	Paxton Whitehead

Credits

Executive Producer	Harold Welb
Producer	Arthur Goldblatt
Co-Producer	John E. Jacobsen
Associate Producer	John Robert Zaring
Director	Rocky Lang
Assistant Director	Gary Sales
Director of Photography	Bill Dill
Sound	Tony Smyles
Editor	Carrie Coughlin
Production Design	Naomi Shohan
Art Direction	Dan Whifler
Set Decoration	Amy Wells

Screenplay	David Frankel
Music	Jay Ferguson

Film Facts

Running Time	90 minutes
Film	Color
Sound	Stereo
Location	Los Angeles; Arizona

Newsies
(Buena Vista)

Critics Rating: ★★

Genre: Musical—Choreographer Kenny Ortega (*Dirty Dancing*) makes his directorial debut with this first true musical since the 1986 film *Little Shop Of Horrors*. Taking a gamble, the Disney Studio has put together a likable and entertaining old-fashioned musical that, for the most part, hits the right notes.

Plot: The story is set in New York at the turn of the century and is based on a real-life strike by newspaper boys—"Newsies." Christian Bale (*Empire Of The Sun*) stars as Jack "Cowboy" Kelly, an orphan who becomes the leader of the striking boys. David Moscow (*Big*) and Max Casella (TV's *Doogie Howser, M.D.*) are his sidekicks. The villain of this film is *New York World* publisher Joseph Pulitzer, played by Robert Duvall.

MPAA Rating: PG

Cast

Jack Kelly/Francis Sullivan	Christian Bale
Bryan Denton	Bill Pullman
Medda Larkson	Ann-Margret
Joseph Pulitzer	Robert Duvall
David Jacobs	David Moscow
Les Jacobs	Luke Edwards
Racetrack	Max Casella
Gov. Theodore Roosevelt	David James Alexander
Crutchy	Marty Belafsky
William Randolph Hearst	Ken Belsky
Seitz	Charles Cioffi
Sarah Jacobs	Ele Keats
Weasel	Michael Lerner
Mush	Aaron Lohr
Boots	Arvie Lowe
Snyder	Kevin Tighe

Credits

Producer...Michael Finnell
Associate Producers ....Ira Shuman
....Marianne Sweeny
Director..Kenny Ortega
Assistant Director ....Dennis M. White
Director of Photography ....Andrew Laszlo
Sound ....David Kelson
Editor ....William Reynolds
Production Design ....William Sandel
Art Direction ....Nancy Patton
Set Design...Brad Ricker
....Carl J. Stensel
Set Decoration....................................Robert Gould
Costume Design.......................................May Routh
Casting ....Elizabeth Leustig
Written by ....Bob Tzudiker
....Noni White
Songs Orchestrated/Conducted by.........Danny Troob
Original Songs: Music ....Alan Menken
Original Songs: Lyrics.........................Jack Feldman
Original Underscore ....J. A. C. Redford
Choreography ....Kenny Ortega
....Peggy Holmes
Stunt Coordinators ....Michael M. Vendrell
....Ceci Vendrell
Special Visual Effects ....Syd Dutton
....Bill Taylor
....Illusion Arts, Inc.

Film Facts

Running Time ....124 minutes
Soundtrack...........................Walt Disney Records
Film...Technicolor
Sound ....Dolby Stereo
Location ....Los Angeles

Nickel & Dime
(Hometown)

Critics Rating: Not Rated.
Genre: Drama
Plot: C. Thomas Howell stars as Jack Stone, a cynical, down-on-his-luck private investigator. Wallace Shawn plays Everett Willits, an IRS accountant investigating Stone for unpaid back taxes. This odd couple becomes involved in a search for the lost daughter of a businessman. The daughter turns out to be Stone's former fiancee (Lise Cutter). Adding to the confusion, Stone must contend with a rival investigator and a group of thugs who also have an interest in the woman. While the story is straightforward, the performances keep this by-the-numbers mystery upbeat and entertaining.
MPAA Rating: PG

Cast

Jack Stone...................................C. Thomas Howell
Everett Willits.................................Wallace Shawn
Cathleen Markson ....Lise Cutter
Sammy Thornton...........................Roy Brocksmith

Credits

Executive Producer ....Paul Mason
Producers..Ben Moses
....Lynn Danielson
Associate Producer ....Fred Wardell
Director ....Ben Moses
Director of Photography ....Henry E. Lebo
Sound ....Trevor Black
Editor ....Joan E. Chapman
Casting ....Karen Rea
....Doreen Lane
Written by..Seth Front
....Eddy Polon
Music ....Stephen Bedell

Film Facts

Running Time ....96 minutes
Film ....Color
Sound ....Stereo

Night And Day
(Nuit Et Jour)
(International Film Circuit, Inc.)

Critics Rating: Not Rated.
Genre: Drama—A simple yet complex tale of young love between a woman and the two men in her life.
Plot: Set in Paris, most of the film takes place in an apartment. Guilaine Londez plays Julie, a young woman in love with Jack (Langmann), a taxi driver. The newly in love couple are so enamored with one another that they spend all of their time in bed and little of it sleeping. If only they did not have to leave the confines of their apartment walls, love would be bliss. Before long, however, the real

world creeps in. Jack introduces Julie to his co-worker Joseph and the two hit it off. They are physically attracted to each other and decide to act on it. Julie idealistically believes that she can share herself equally with the two men. The two men unfortunately are not as idealistic.

MPAA Rating: Not Rated. Contains nudity and scenes of sexuality.

Cast

Julie	Guilaine Londez
Jack	Thomas Langmann
Joseph	Francois Negret

Credits

Executive Producer	Rosalie Lecan
Producers	Martine Marignac, Maurice Tinchant
Director	Chantal Akerman
Directors of Photography	
	Jean-Claude Neckelbrouck
	Pierre Gordower
	Bernard Delville, Olivier Dessalles
Sound	Alix Comte, Pierre Tucat
Editors	Francine Sandberg
	Camille Bordes Resnais
Production Manager (France)	Pierre Wallon
Production Manager (Belgium)	Marilyn Watelet
Set Design	Michel Vandestien
	Dominique Douret
Costume Design	Brigitte Nierhaus
	Michele Blondeel
Screenplay	Chantal Akerman, Pascal Bonitzer
Based on an idea by	Michel Vandestien
Original Music	Marc Herouet
Musical Conception	Sonia Wieder-Atherton
Makeup	Nicole Mora

Film Facts

Country of Origin	France/Belgium/Switzerland
Language	French (subtitled)
Running Time	90 minutes
Film	Color
Sound	Stereo

Night And The City

(20th Century Fox)

Critics Rating: ★★★

Genre: Drama—A remake of the 1950 film-noire classic of the same name, the film is also dedicated to the original director Jules Dassin.

Tag Line: "When you're down to your last dream, you either live it or lose it."

Plot: De Niro stars as Harry Fabian, an aging, ne'er-do-well, small-time lawyer who comes up with a last-chance scheme to make something of himself. Lange plays Helen, the wife of a bar owner and financial backer in the venture-who is lured away by Harry. Harry persuades a few key players to back him as a boxing promoter but his scamming, dirty dealing and desperation are his eventual undoing.

MPAA Rating: R—For strong language.

Cast

Harry Fabian	Robert De Niro
Helen Nasseros	Jessica Lange
Phil Nasseros	Cliff Gorman
Al Grossman	Jack Warden
Boom Boom Grossman	Alan King
Peck	Eli Wallach
Tommy Tessler	Barry Primus
Resnick	Gene Kirkwood
Cuda Sanchez	Pedro Sanchez

Credits

Executive Producers	Harry J. Ufland
	Mary Jane Ufland
Producers	Jane Rosenthal, Irwin Winkler
Co-Producer	Rob Cowan
Associate Producer	Nelson McCormick
Director	Irwin Winkler
Assistant Director	Joseph Reidy
Director of Photography	Tak Fujimoto
Sound	Tod Maitland
Editor	David Brenner
Production Design	Peter Larkin
Art Direction	Charley Beale
Set Decoration	Robert J. Franco
Costume Design	Richard Bruno
Casting	Todd Thaler
Screenplay	Richard Price
Based on the novel by	Gerald Kersh
Music	James Newton Howard
Original 1950 film directed by	Jules Dassin
Original 1950 screenplay by	Jo Eisinger

Film Facts

Running Time	120 minutes
Soundtrack	Hollywood Records
Film	Technicolor
Sound	Dolby Stereo
Location	New York

Night On Earth
(Fine Line Features)

Critics Rating: ★★★

Genre: Drama—Jim Jarmusch has brought to the screen another offbeat road-trip film that follows five different cab drivers and the relationships that develop between them and their passengers.

Plot: During the first ride, Winona Ryder plays a Los Angeles cabby transporting an upscale Beverly Hills casting agent, played by Gena Rowlands. Other drivers and passengers reach their destinations in Rome, New York, Paris and Helsinki. Each fare is a unique story. Often humorous, these odd vignettes are also occasionally downbeat. This is perhaps the ultimate road trip and perhaps the most entertaining film yet offered by Jarmusch.

MPAA Rating: R—For language and sensuality.

Cast

Corky	Winona Ryder
Victoria Snelling	Gena Rowlands
Yo Yo	Giancarlo Esposito
Helmut	Armin Mueller-Stahl
Angela	Rosie Perez
Rome cab driver	Roberto Benigni
Priest	Paolo Bonacelli
Blind woman	Beatrice Dalle
Paris cab driver	Isaach De Bankole
Mika (Helsinki cab driver)	Matti Pellonpaa
Passenger No. 1	Kari Vaananen

Credits

Co-Executive Producers	Masahiro Inbe
	Noboru Takayama
Executive Producer	Jim Stark
Producer/Director	Jim Jarmusch
Co-Producer	Demetra J. MacBride
Line Producer	Rudd Simmons
Assistant Director (Los Angeles)	Terence Edwards
Assistant Director (New York)	Howard McMaster
Assistant Director (Paris)	Jeanne Marie de la Fontaine
Assistant Director (Rome)	Joseph Rochlitz
Assistant Director (Helsinki)	Pauli Pentti
Director of Photography	Frederick Elmes
Sound	Drew Kunin
Editor	Jay Rabinowitz
Production Manager (Los Angeles)	Susan Shapiro
Production Manager (New York)	Kathie Hersh
Production Manager (Paris)	Gilles Sacuto
Production Managaer (Rome)	Manuela Pineski-Berger
Written by	Jim Jarmusch
Music	Tom Waits
Songs by	Tom Waits, Kathleen Brennan

Film Facts

Running Time	130 minutes
Soundtrack	Island Records
Film	DuArt Color
Sound	Dolby Stereo

1991: The Year Punk Broke
(Tara)

Critics Rating: Not Rated.

Genre: Documentary—Filmmaker Dave Markey, who parodied punk in his previous films, *Desperate Teenage Lovedolls* and *Lovedoll Superstar*, attempts here to document the music's crossover into the mainstream.

Plot: Markey follows successful alternative bands Sonic Youth and Nirvana on tour and on stage, in a series of hand-held glimpses of the music and the musicians. Uneven and unfocused, this is little more than a very rough concert film for fans of the groups.

MPAA Rating: Not Rated.

Cast

With Babes in Toyland, Dinosaur Jr., Gumball, Nirvana, The Ramones and Sonic Youth.

Credits

Director/Editor	Dave Markey
Director of Photography	Dave Markey
Sound (Sonic Youth live)	Terry Parson
Sound (Nirvana live)	Craig Montgomery

Film Facts

Running Time	99 minutes
Film	Color/Black-and-White (16mm)
Sound	Stereo

No Fear, No Die
(S'en Fout La Mort)
(Art Logic Laboratories)

Critics Rating: Not Rated.

169

Genre: Drama—French-German drama by the acclaimed director of *Chocolat*.

Plot: Isaach de Bankole and Alex Descas play Dah and Jocelyn, two close friends of African descent who train cocks for illegal fighting games. "No Fear, No Die" is the name of their best cock. In this gritty and brutal underworld, the bond these two men share is all they have. When a woman comes between them, she disrupts their lives and leads to an eventual tragic end.

MPAA Rating: Not Rated.

Cast

Dah	Isaach de Bankole
Jocelyn	Alex Descas
Pierre Ardennes	Jean-Claude Brialy
Toni	Soveig Dommartin
Michel	Christopher Buchholz
Ti Emile	Gilbert Felmar
Henri	Daniel Bellus
Francois	Francois Oloa Biloa
Toni's mother	Christa Lang

Credits

Producers	Francis Boespflug, Philippe Carcassonne
Director	Claire Denis
Assistant Director	Gabriel Julien Laferriere
Directors of Photography	Pascal Marti, Damien Morisot, Agnes Godard
Sound	Jean-Paul Mugel
Editor	Dominique Auvray
Production Managers	Nicolas Daguet, Brigitte Faure
Production Design	Jean-Jacques Caziot
Written by	Jean-Pol Fargeau, Claire Denis
Music	Abdullah Ibrahim

Film Facts

Country of Origin	France
Language	French (subtitled)
Running Time	97 minutes
Film	Color
Sound	Stereo

Noises Off

(Buena Vista)

Critics Rating: ★★★

Genre: Comedy—Director Peter Bogdanovich has brought the Tony Award-winning Broadway comedy of the same name to the screen with much success.

Plot: The story revolves around a theater company that takes its play, a sexual farce titled "Nothing On," on the road prior to opening on Broadway. When big egos, little rehearsal time and backstage romance are added to the mix, the slapstick comedy and high jinks take off. As the touring company travels from city to city, the back-stage infighting goes from bad to worse and eventually culminates in disaster, when the members of the troup declare war on one another, on stage, during their final performance.

MPAA Rating: PG-13

Cast

Lloyd Fellowes	Michael Caine
Dotty Otley/Mrs. Clackett	Carol Burnett
Poppy Taylor	Julie Hagerty
Garry Lejeune/Roger	John Ritter
Brooke Ashton/Vicki	Nicollette Sheridan
Frederick Dallas/Philip Brent	Christopher Reeve
Belinda Blair/Flavia Brent	Marilu Henner
Tim Allgood	Mark Linn-Baker
Selsdon Mowbray/The Burglar	Denholm Elliott

Credits

Executive Producers	Kathleen Kennedy, Peter Bogdanovich
Producer	Frank Marshall
Co-Producer	Steve Starkey
Associate Producers	Joan Bradshaw, L. B. Straten
Director	Peter Bogdanovich
Assistant Director	Jery Ketcham
2nd Unit Director	Frank Marshall
Director of Photography	Tim Suhrstedt
2nd Unit Camera	Don Burgess
Sound	James E. Webb
Editor	Lisa Day
Production Design	Norman Newberry
Art Direction	Daniel F. Maltese
Set Design	Richard F. McKenzie
Set Decoration	Jim Duffy
Costume Design	Betsy Cox
Screenplay	Marty Kaplan
Based on the play by	Michael Frayn
Music Adaptations	Phil Marshall

Film Facts

Running Time	104 minutes
Film	Technicolor
Sound	Dolby Stereo
Location	Los Angeles

Of Mice And Men
(MGM)

Critics Rating: ★★★
Genre: Drama—Based on the 1937 novel by John Steinbeck, the film is a finely performed and beautifully filmed remake of the classic.
Plot: Malkovich and Sinise play Lenny and George, two California drifters struggling together to stay alive during the great depression. The two men dream of one day owning some land together. Lenny is a lumbering man with the mind of a child, who relies on his strength to get by. Conversely, George is a small man who relies on his smarts. Each is dependent on the other. A woman (Fenn) who comes into their lives unintentionally sets the stage for the tragic events that follow. Misinterpreting her kindness and not knowing his own strength, Lenny forces the woman into a situation that turns deadly and kills the dream the men held together.
MPAA Rating: PG-13—For scenes of violence.
Trivia: Malkovich and Sinise originally played Lenny and George together in the 1980 Chicago stage version of the story.

Cast
Lennie	John Malkovich
George	Gary Sinise
Candy	Ray Walston
Curley	Casey Siemaszko
Curley's wife	Sherilyn Fenn
Slim	John Terry
Whitt	Alexis Arquette
Crooks	Joe Morton
Carlson	Richard Riehle
The Boss	Noble Willingham

Credits
Executive Producer	Alan C. Blomquist
Producers	Russ Smith, Gary Sinise
Director	Gary Sinise
Assistant Director	Cara Giallanza
Director of Photography	Kenneth MacMillan
2nd Unit Camera	Alan Caso
Sound	David Brownlow
Editor	Robert L. Sinise
Production Design	David Gropman
Art Direction	Dan Davis
Set Design	Cheryl T. Smith
Set Decoration	Karen Schulz
	Joyce Anne Gilstrap
Costume Design	Shay Cunliffe
Casting	Amanda Mackey, Cathy Sandrich
Screenplay	Horton Foote
Based on the novel by	John Steinbeck
Music	Mark Isham

Film Facts
Running Time	115 minutes
Soundtrack	Varese Sarabande
Film	Deluxe Color
Sound	Dolby Stereo
Location	Los Angeles; Northern California

Once Upon A Crime
(MGM)

Critics Rating: Not Rated.
Genre: Comedy—A screwball comedy featuring an ensemble cast of unlikely characters in a predictable, but enjoyable, whodunit murder-mystery.
Plot: Taking place in Monte Carlo, the action involves a group of strangers whose paths cross and crisscross, and lead to a dead body. Giancarlo Giannini plays the police inspector investigating the murder. His possible suspects include a gambler, a hustler, a schemer and a housewife, for starters. Not your typical murder-mystery, this one is played strictly for laughs.
MPAA Rating: PG

Cast
Augie Morosco	John Candy
Neil Schwary	James Belushi

Marilyn Schwary	Cybill Shepherd
Phoebe	Sean Young
Julian Peters	Richard Lewis
Elena Morosco	Ornella Muti
Inspector Bonnard	Giancarlo Giannini
Alfonso de la Pena	George Hamilton
Hercules Popodopoulos	Joss Ackland
Detective Toussaint	Roberto Sbaratto

Credits

Executive Producer	Martha De Laurentiis
Producer	Dino De Laurentiis
Line Producer	Lucio Trentini
Director	Eugene Levy
Assistant Director	Juan Carlos Rodero Lopez
Director of Photography	Giuseppe Rotunno
Sound	Ivan Sharrock
Editor	Patrick Kennedy
Production Design	Pier Luigi Basile
Set Decoration	Gianfranco Fumagalli
Costume Design	Molly Maginnis
Casting	Francesco Cinieri
Screenplay	Charles Shyer
	Nancy Meyers, Steve Kluger
Music	Richard Gibbs

Film Facts

Running Time	94 minutes
Film	Technicolor
Sound	Dolby Stereo
Location	Rome; Monte Carlo
Other Working Titles	*Troublemakers*;
	Returning Napoleon; *Criminals*

MPAA Rating: Not Rated.

Cast

Wong Fei-hung	Jet Li
Leung Foon	Yuen Biao
Buck Teeth Sol	Jacky Cheung
Aunt Yee	Rosamund Kwan
Porky Lang	Kent Cheng

Credits

Executive Producer	Tsui Hark
Producer	Raymond Chow
Associate Producer	David Lo
Director	Tsui Hark
Action Directors	Yuen Chong-yan
	Yuen Shun-yi, Lau Kar-wing
Directors of Photography	David Chung
	Bill Wong
	Arthur Wong, Lam Kwok-wah
	Chan Tung-chuen, Chan Pui-kai
Editor	Mak Chi-sin
Production Design	Lau Man-hung
Art Direction	Yee Chung-man
Costume Design	Yu Ka-on
Screenplay	Tsui Hark, Yuen Kai-chi
	Leung Yiu-ming, Tang Pik-yin
Music	James Wong

Film Facts

Country of Origin	Hong Kong
Language	Mandarin (Chinese/English subtitles)
Running Time	112 minutes
Film	Color
Sound	Stereo

Once Upon A Time In China

(Wong Fei-Hung)

(Golden Harvest)

Critics Rating: Not Rated.

Genre: Action—*China* is based in part on the life of martial-arts master Wong Hei-fung. An action-comedy, it takes the martial-arts genre film to a new level of sophistication.

Plot: This humorous tale revolves around Master Wong (Jet Li) a peaceful man who is forced repeatedly into battle. His enemies include Western traders, local mobs and other kung fu masters. Each provides him with an opportunity to show off his impressive skills.

One False Move

(I.R.S. Releasing)

Critics Rating: Not Rated.

Genre: Drama—A realistic-looking low-budget psychological drama that focuses its lens on a dark and violent world of drug dealing and deception.

Tag Line: "Nothing is as dangerous as the past."

Plot: Cynda Williams plays Fantasia/Lila, a troubled young woman from Arkansas, who has moved to Los Angeles to escape her past. Now living with a violent drug dealer named Ray (Billy Bob Thornton), she finds it impossible to forget the past and longs to return home to see the 5-year-old son she abandoned. To raise the money, she reluctantly joins Ray and a partner, Pluto (Michael

Beach), in a murder and cocaine theft. Following the particularly brutal and deadly Los Angeles murders, the three hit the road. Behind them, however, they leave a trail for the police to follow. When they finally arrive, the local sheriff (Bill Paxton, *The Dark Backward*) is anxiously waiting. Little does he know that his past is about to catch up to him as well.

Critics hailed this film as one of the most impressive small films of the year. Powerfully acted and realistic, it will appeal to serious hard drama fans. Paxton's performance alone is reason enough to see the film.

MPAA Rating: R—Contains strong language and extreme violence.

Cast

Dale (Hurricane) Dixon	Bill Paxton
Fantasia/Lila	Cynda Williams
Ray Malcolm	Billy Bob Thornton
Pluto	Michael Beach
Dud Cole	Jim Metzler
McFeely	Earl Billings
Cheryl Ann	Natalie Canerday
Charlie	Robert Ginnaven
Byron	Robert Anthony Bell
Ronnie	Kevin Hunter
Mrs. Walker	Phyllis Kirklin
Car salesman	Steven Reich

Credits

Executives in Charge of Production	Toni Phillips
	Steven Reich, Kevin Reidy
Executive Producers	Miles A. Copeland III
	Paul Colichman, Harold Welb
Producers	Jesse Beaton, Ben Myron
Line Producer	Tony To
Director	Carl Franklin
Assistant Director	Michael Grossman
Director of Photography	James L. Carter
Sound	Ken Segal
Editor	Carole Kravitz
Production Design	Gary T. New
Art Direction	Dana Torrey
Set Decoration	Troy Myers
Costume Design	Ron Leamon
Casting	Don Pemrick
Screenplay	Billy Bob Thornton
	Tom Epperson
Music	Peter Haycock
	Derek Holt

Orchestrated Underscore by	Terry Plumeri

Film Facts

Running Time	105 minutes
Soundtrack	I.R.S. Records
Film	Foto-Kem Color
Sound	Dolby Stereo
Location	Cotton Plant, Arkansas; Los Angeles

Out On A Limb

(Universal)

Critics Rating: Not Rated.

Genre: Comedy—A moronic comedy-adventure intended for a youthful sitcom audience.

Tag Line: "He's got 24 hours to find his missing wallet with a phone number worth a hundred million dollars. There's only one place he hasn't looked…"

Plot: The film is told in flashback by Marci (Courtney Peldon) to her classmates as "what I did on my summer vacation." The best thing about this film is the clever adolescent Siskel & Ebert look-alikes who discuss the merits of her story as she tells it.

Matthew Broderick stars as Bill, a financial hot-shot yuppie in the middle of a $140 million deal. Before the deal closes, however, he gets a call from his sister Marci, who is in trouble. It seems their stepfather's evil twin brother (played by Jeffrey Jones) has come to town bent on revenge.

Coming to the rescue, Bill returns to his hometown of Buzzsaw, only to be robbed of his car and clothing by a desperate young woman named Sally (Kling), who is on the run from the law. Sally is just one of the many oddball characters who populate this town. Bill's search for his clothing, his wallet and his stepfather leads him on one long, wild ride, and the destination is a happy ending.

MPAA Rating: PG—Contains male nudity from behind.

Cast

Bill Campbell	Matthew Broderick
Matt/Peter	Jeffrey Jones
Sally	Heidi Kling
Jim, Jr.	John C. Reilly
Marci	Courtney Peldon

Jim, Sr.	Michael Monks
Ann	Marian Mercer
Darren	Larry Hankin
Buchenwald	David Margulies
Cindy	Shawn Schepps

Credits

Executive Producers	Ted Field
	Scott Kroopf
	Robert W. Cort
Producer	Michael Hertzberg
Line Producer	Kelly Van Horn
Associate Producer	James Moll
Director	Francis Veber
Assistant Director	David Householter
2nd Unit Director	Glenn Randall, Jr.
Director of Photography	Donald E. Thorin
2nd Unit Camera	John Stephens
Sound	Darin Knight
Editor	Glenn Farr
Production Manager	Kelly Van Horn
Production Design	Stephen Marsh
Casting	Dianne Crittenden
Written by	Daniel Goldin
	Joshua Goldin
Music	Van Dyke Parks
Stunt Coordinator	Glenn Randall, Jr.
Special Visual Effects	Introvision International
Special Visual Effects Supervisor	Tim Donahue

Film Facts

Running Time	82 minutes
Film	Deluxe Color
Sound	Dolby Stereo
Location	Santa Cruz, California; Los Angeles
Other Working Titles	*Welcome To Buzzsaw*

The Ox
(Oxen)
(Castle Hill/First Run Features)

Critics Rating: ★★★
Genre: Drama—Nominated for a Best Foreign Language Film Academy Award for Best in 1991.

Academy-Award-winning cinematographer Sven Nykvist directed the film.

Plot: The film is based on a true story of a family facing starvation during Sweden's famine years of the 1860s. Stellan Skarsgard plays Helge, a desperate man who is turned in by his priest (von Sydow) for killing his employer's oxen. To the priest's astonishment, the man receives a sentence of life in prison. To make matters worse, Helge's wife (Ewa Froling), is forced into prostitution to feed herself and her child in her husband's absence. In the end this bleak story manages a happy ending.

MPAA Rating: Not Rated.

Cast

Helga	Stellan Skarsgard
Elfrida	Ewa Froling
Svenning	Lennart Hjulstrom
The vicar	Max von Sydow
Maria	Liv Ullmann
Flyckt	Bjorn Granath
Silver	Erland Josephson
Johannes	Rikard Wolff
Navvy	Helge Jordal

Credits

Executive Producer	Jaqui Safra
Co-Executive Producer	Klas Olofsson
Producer	Jean Doumanian
Director	Sven Nykvist
Director of Photography	Sven Nykvist
Sound	Bo Persson
	Stefan Ljungberg, Jan Erik Lundberg
Editor	Lasse Summanen
Production Design	Peter Hoimark
Set Decoration	Magnus Magnusson
Costume Design	Inger Pehrsson
Screenplay	Sven Nykvist
	Lasse Summanen
Music	Thomas Drescher

Film Facts

Country of Origin	Sweden
Running Time	91 minutes
Film	Color
Sound	Stereo

Painting The Town
(Padded Cell Pictures)

Critics Rating: Not Rated.
Genre: Documentary—Filmmakers Andrew Behar and Sara Sackner focus their lens on eccentric New York painter Richard Osterweil.
Plot: Charming, witty and ingenious, Osterweil is relatively unknown as a painter but has made a name for himself as the party crasher of the rich and famous. The film is made up primarily of interviews with this entertaining man as he describes his exploits and the many famous parties and funerals he has crashed.
MPAA Rating: Not Rated.
Cast
With Richard Osterweil.
Credits
Producer ....Sara Sackner
Associate Producer ....Sheila Szczepaniak
Director...Andrew Behar
2nd Unit Director ....Ron Honsa
Director of Photography ....Hamid Shams
Sound ....Edward Campbell, Chazz Menendez
Editors ....Sara Sackner, Andrew Behar
Production Design ....Sara Sackner
Screenplay ....Richard Osterweil
Music..Peter Fish
Film Facts
Running Time ....80 minutes
Film...DuArt Color
Sound ....Stereo

The Panama Deception
(Empowerment Project)

Critics Rating: Not Rated.

Genre: Documentary—Narrated by Elizabeth Montgomery.
Plot: Focusing on the 1989 Panama invasion by the Bush administration, the film explores the numerous events leading up to the attack. It also looks at the brutal aftermath of carnage and poverty. Without a doubt, the film is an indictment of the policies that led to the invasion. It is just as critical of the media for its alleged willingness to support the American agenda and its lack of critical assessment of the administration's policies.
MPAA Rating: Not Rated.
Cast
Narrator....................................Elizabeth Montgomery
Credits
Producers ....Barbara Trent
....Joanne Doroshow
.............................Nico Panigutti, David Kasper
Director..Barbara Trent
Directors of Photography ....Michael Dobo
....Manuel Becker
Editor ....David Kasper
Written by ....David Kasper
Music ....Chuck Wild
Film Facts
Running Time ....91 minutes
Film ....Color/Video
Sound ....Stereo

Passed Away
(Buena Vista)

Critics Rating: ★★★
Genre: Comedy—A light-hearted comedy about an Irish family coming together and falling apart during a three-day wake.
Tag Line: "Dad finally did the one thing that could bring his family together."
Plot: Jack Warden (*Problem Child*) plays dearly departed dad, who exerts nearly as much control over his family as a corpse as he did when he was alive. Bob Hoskins (*Roger Rabbit, Mermaids*) plays eldest son, Johnny, who is responsible for bringing his family together for the funeral. For this family, the solemn ceremony quickly turns into a circus, with Johnny the master of ceremonies.

MPAA Rating: PG-13

Cast

Johnny Scanlan	Bob Hoskins
Amy Scanlan	Blair Brown
Boyd Pinter	Tim Curry
Nora Scanlan	Frances McDormand
Frank Scanlan	William Petersen
Terry Scanlan	Pamela Reed
Peter Syracusa	Peter Riegert
Mary Scanlan	Maureen Stapleton
Cassie Slocombe	Nancy Travis
Jack Scanlan	Jack Warden
Aunt Maureen	Helen Lloyd Breed
Father Hallahan	Patrick Breen
Rachel Scanlan	Teri Polo

Credits

Producers	Larry Brezner
	Timothy Marx
Director	Charlie Peters
Assistant Director	Matt Earl Beesley
Director of Photography	Arthur Albert
Sound	John Pritchett
Editor	Harry Keramidas
Production Design	Catherine Hardwicke
Art Direction	Gilbert Mercier
Set Decoration	Gene Serdena
Costume Design	Jennifer Von Mayrhauser
Casting	Gail Levin
Casting (New York)	Julie Mossberg
	Rosalie Joseph
Casting (Pittsburgh)	Nancy A. Mosser
	Seddon C. Stolze
Written by	Charlie Peters
Music	Richard Gibbs

Film Facts

Running Time	96 minutes
Film	DuArt Color
Sound	Dolby Stereo
Location	Pittsburgh

Passenger 57

(Warner Bros.)

Critics Rating: ★★

Genre: Action—A fun, formula-driven, martial-arts, action-hero, high-energy film with a twist—the hero's an African-American, a rarity in motion pictures.

Tag Line: "He's an ex-cop with a bad mouth, a bad attitude, and a bad seat. For the terrorists on flight 163...he's very bad news."

Plot: Snipes stars as John Cutter, a former airline security expert who finds himself on a passenger plane being hijacked by a team of terrorists. The leader is played by the menacing and completely insane Charles Rane (Bruce Payne). The cops in this film are morons, while Cutter is a smart, witty, one-man SWAT team who single-handedly saves the day and wins the girl. Not exactly original, but as entertaining as one might expect. Also, like Willis, Seagal and Schwarzenegger, the one-liners come just as fast as the action.

MPAA Rating: R—For terrorist violence and language.

Trivia: Film buffs may remember villain Bruce Payne from the 1984 British comedy *Privates On Parade*. Payne played one of the Andrews Sisters in drag, as a soldier with the song-and-dance unit of the Army. This is an actor with quite a range.

Cast

John Cutter	Wesley Snipes
Charles Rane	Bruce Payne
Sly Delvecchio	Tom Sizemore
Marti Slayton	Alex Datcher
Stuart Ramsey	Bruce Greenwood
Dwight Henderson	Robert Hooks
Sabrina Ritchie	Elizabeth Hurley
Forget	Michael Horse
Vincent	Marc Macaulay
Chief Biggs	Ernie Lively

Credits

Executive Producer	Jonathan Sheinberg
Producers	Lee Rich
	Dan Paulson
	Dylan Sellers
Co-Producer	Robert J. Anderson
Director	Kevin Hooks
Assistant Director	Gary Marcus
Director of Photography	Mark Irwin
Sound	Robert Anderson, Jr.
Editor	Richard Nord
Production Design	Jaymes Hinkle
Art Direction	Alan Muraoka
Set Decoration	Don K. Ivey
Costume Design	Brad Loman
Casting	Shari Rhodes

Screenplay ....David Loughery
....Dan Gordon
Story by ....Stewart Raffill
....Dan Gordon
Music...Stanley Clarke
Stunt Coordinators..............................Glenn Wilder
....Jeff Ward

Film Facts
Running Time ....83 minutes
Soundtrack.........Slamm Dunk Records/Epic Records
Film....................................Technicolor
Sound...................................Dolby Stereo
Location..............................Orlando, Florida

Passion Fish
(Miramax)

Critics Rating: ★★★★

Genre: Drama—John Sayles explores the internal struggles and fateful meeting of two very different women in this heartfelt tale.

Tag Line: "May Alice left New York to join the human race. She's down on the bayou, where the days are hot and the nights are hotter." "Passion Fish—The future is in the palm of your hands."

Plot: Mary McDonnell plays May Alice, a New York soap-opera actress whose career is cut short by an accident that leaves her a paraplegic. Forced to return to her family home in Louisiana, she sinks into a bitter, alcohol-laced depression. Her rejection and anger are too much for a series of nurses sent to care for her, until Chantelle (Woodard) arrives. Chantelle, a former drug addict, is in many ways emotionally crippled herself. Battling her own demons, she forces her employer to confront hers. Over time, the two women come to trust one another, and a bond develops as they help each other overcome their tragedies. The strong lead performances give this often humorous, warmhearted story its driving force.

MPAA Rating: R—For language.

Cast
May Alice Culhane..........................Mary McDonnell
Chantelle...................................Alfre Woodard
Rennie.....................................David Strathairn
Dawn/Rhonda.................................Angela Bassett
Nurse Quick................................Lenore Banks
Sugar LeDoux...............................Vondie Curtis-Hall
Ti-Marie...................................Nora Dunn
Kim..Sheila Kelley
Reeves.....................................Leo Burmester
Precious...................................Mary Portser
Denita.....................................Shauntisa Willis
Dr. Blades.................................John Henry
Redwood Vance..............................Michael Laskin

Credits
Executive Producer........................John Sloss
Producers..................................Sarah Green
....Maggie Renzi
Director/Editor............................John Sayles
Assistant Director.........................Steve Apicella
Director of Photography....................Roger Deakins
Sound......................................John Sutton
Production Design..........................Dan Bishop
....Dianna Freas
Costume Design.............................Cynthia Flynt
Casting....................................Barbara Hewson Shapiro
Screenplay.................................John Sayles
Music......................................Mason Daring

Film Facts
Running Time ....138 minutes
Soundtrack.................................Daring/Rounder Records
Film.......................................DuArt Color
Sound......................................Dolby Stereo

Past Midnight
(Cinetel)

Critics Rating: Not Rated.

Genre: Thriller—Television director Jan Eliasber makes her feature directing debut. She was the first woman to have directed such male-oriented dramas as *Crime Story*, *Wiseguy* and *Miami Vice*.

Plot: Natasha Richardson plays Laura Mathews, a social worker living in a small Washington town. Rutger Hauer plays Ben Jordan, a convicted murderer on parole. Laura is assigned Ben's case and is responsible for helping him resettle. As she gets to know him, she is convinced of his innocence but she's the only one who is. Normally repressed and controlled in her personal life, she leaves herself open and vulnerable to Ben, and for the first time ever she becomes romantically involved with a client. This sets the stage for a series of events that very quickly turn the tranquility of Laura's life into an explosive nightmare.

MPAA Rating: R

Cast

Ben Jordan	Rutger Hauer
Laura Mathews	Natasha Richardson
Steve Lundy	Clancy Brown
Dorothy Coleman	Kibibi Monie
Lee Samuels	Tom Wright
Kathy Tudor	Dana Eskelson
Bill Tudor	Ted D'Arms
Larry Canipe	Paul Giamatti
Todd Canipe	Guy Boyd
Carlton Daniels	Charles Boswell
Dr. Zastoupil	Krisha Fairchild
Det. Allan Tobias	Ernie Lively
Gerrie Greymark	Sarah Magnuson

Credits

Executive Producer	Paul Hertzberg
Producer	Lisa M. Hansen
Co-Producer	Nancy Rae Stone
Associate Producer	Frank Norwood
Director	Jan Eliasberg
Assistant Director	Mary Ellen Woods
Director of Photography	Robert Yeoman
Sound Mixer	Robert Marts
Editor	Christopher Rouse
Art Direction	Daniel Self
Set Decoration	Michael Anderson
Casting (Seattle)	Alison Roth Casting
Screenplay	Frank Norwood
Music	Steve Bartek
Stunt Coordinators	Steve Lambert
	Spiro Razatos
Special Effects Makeup	KNB EFX Group

Film Facts

Running Time	100 minutes
Film	Foto-Kem Color
Sound	Stereo
Location	Seattle; Vashon Island, Washington

Patriot Games

(Paramount)

Critics Rating:

Genre: Action—Based on the Tom Clancy novel, *Patriot Games* is a smart, suspenseful, edge-of-your seat political-action thriller from start to finish.

Plot: A follow-up to *Hunt For Red October*, Harrison Ford stars as former CIA agent Jack Ryan. While on holiday in London with his family, he witnesses a terrorist attack on a member of the royal family. Without taking time to think, he jumps in and foils the attempt, killing a terrorist in the process. Seeking revenge for the killing, the terrorist's brother, Sean (Sean Bean), tracks Ryan back to the U.S. In *Cape Fear*-like psychopathic fashion, Sean stalks Ryan and his family relentlessly. Right up to the film's over-the-top, spectacular Hollywood climax, it is a gripping, fascinating and involving tale. All of this makes the ending forgivable.

MPAA Rating: R—For violence, sexuality and language.

Cast

Jack Ryan	Harrison Ford
Cathy Ryan	Anne Archer
Kevin O'Donnell	Patrick Bergin
Sean Miller	Sean Bean
Sally Ryan	Thora Birch
Admiral Greer	James Earl Jones
Paddy O'Neil	Richard Harris
Lord Holmes	James Fox
Robby	Samuel L. Jackson
Annette	Polly Walker
Marty Cantor	J. E. Freeman
Watkins	Hugh Fraser
Dennis Cooley	Alex Norton

Credits

Executive Producer	Charles H. Maguire
Producers	Mace Neufeld
	Robert Rehme
Associate Producer	Lis Kern
Director	Phillip Noyce
Assistant Director	Dennis Maguire
2nd Unit Director	David R. Ellis
2nd Unit Assistant Director	Christopher T. Gerrity
Director of Photography	Donald M. McAlpine
Directors of Photography (U.K.)	Stephen Smith
	James Devis
2nd Unit Camera	Michael A. Benson
Sound	Jack Solomon
Sound (U.K.)	Ivan Sharrock
Editors	Neil Travis
	William Hoy

Production Design ....Joseph Nemec III
Art Direction...................................Joseph P. Lucky
Art Direction (U.K.) ....Alan Cassie
Set Design...................................Walter P. Martishius
Set Decoration ....John M. Dwyer
Costume Design ....Norma Moriceau
Casting...Amanda Mackey
....Cathy Sandrich
Casting (U.K./Ireland) ....John Hubbard
....Ros Hubbard
Screenplay..W. Peter Iliff
....Donald Stewart
Based on the novel by............................Tom Clancy
Music ....James Horner
Stunt Coordinators ....David R. Ellis
....Steve Boyum
Stunt Coordinator (U.K.) ....Martin Grace
Special Effects Coordinator.................Dale L. Martin
Visual Effects/Video Displays ....Video Image

Film Facts
Running Time ....118 minutes
Soundtrack..RCA Records
Film ....Technicolor
Sound ....Dolby Stereo
Location ....London; Los Angeles; Maryland

Pepi, Luci, Bom And The Other Girls

(Pepi, Luci, Bom Y Otras Chicas Del Monton)
(Cinevista)

Critics Rating: Not Rated.
Genre: Drama—Spanish director Pedro Almodóvar *(Tie Me Up, Tie Me Down!)* brings to the screen an often disturbing and just as often humorous story of sexual exploits and exploitation.
Plot: Suffice it to say that the characters in this film go to extreme measures to push the boundaries of sexuality. Acting and technical credits take a back seat to the film's topic.
MPAA Rating: Not Rated—Contains homoerotic themes and sexuality.
Cast
With Carmen Maura, Eva Siva, Alaska, Felix Rotaeta and Concha.
Credits
Director ....Pedro Almodovar
Director of Photography ....Paco Femenia

Written by ....Pedro Almodovar
Film Facts
Country of Origin ....Spain
Running Time ....80 minutes
Film ....Color
Sound ....Stereo

Pet Sematary Two
(Paramount)

Critics Rating: Not Rated.
Genre: Horror
Tag Line: "Raise some hell."
Plot: Edward Furlong *(Terminator 2: Judgment Day, American Heart)* stars as Jeff Matthews. Witnessing at the start of the film the death of his mother naturally leaves him depressed and withdrawn. To leave the sad memories behind, his father, Chase (Anthony Edwards), packs up their belongings and they move to Ludlow, Maine. This just happens to be the setting of the original film. Chase, who also just happens to be a veterinarian, soon discovers that his patients are already dead. Not only are they the walking dead, they're the walking angry dead. Not the neighborly welcome they were expecting.
MPAA Rating: R—For strong horror violence; and sexuality and language.
Cast
Jeff Matthews ....Edward Furlong
Chase Matthews ....Anthony Edwards
Sheriff Gus Gilbert ....Clancy Brown
Clyde ....Jared Rushton
Renee Hallow...................................Darlanne Fluegel
Drew Gilbert.......................................Jason McGuire
Marjorie Hargrove ....Sarah Trigger
Amanda Gilbert.......................................Lisa Waltz
Credits
Producer...Ralph S. Singleton
Director...Mary Lambert
Assistant Director...............................Jeffrey Wetzel
2nd Unit Director................................Peter Chesney
Director of Photography ....Russell Carpenter
Sound ....Shirley Libby
Editor ....Tom Finan
Production Design...........................Michelle Minch
Art Direction ....Karen Steward

Set Decoration ....Susan Benjamin
Costume Design ....Marlene Stewart
Casting...Richard Pagano
....Sharon Bialy
....Debi Manwiller
Written by...Richard Outten
Music ....Mark Governor
Mechanical & Special Effects..............Peter Chesney
Special Effects Makeup/Animatronics.Steve Johnson
Dead Animal Effects ....Bill (Splat) Johnson

Film Facts
Running Time ....102 minutes
Film...DuArt Color
Sound..Dolby Stereo
Location...Atlanta, Georgia

Peter's Friends
(Samuel Goldwyn)

Critics Rating: Not Rated
Genre: Drama—Kenneth Branagh directs this intelligent and witty tale of a 10-year reunion among six college friends, similar in theme to *The Big Chill*.
Tag Line: "Kenneth Branagh's new comedy about love, friendship and other natural disasters."
Plot: Stephen Fry plays Peter, a wealthy English heir who invites his old friends for a reunion at his country estate to celebrate the 1992 New Year. The friends arrive with ten years' worth of failed relationships, unrealized dreams and personal tragedies. Each of the characters is a bit stereo-typical—Branagh plays Andrew, a recovering-alcoholic writer with an obnoxious wife (Rudner)—but they are all fully formed and sympathetic. The wit, charm, intelligence and fine acting all combine to set this apart from its predecessors.
MPAA Rating: Not Rated.

Cast
Andrew ....Kenneth Branagh
Maggie ....Emma Thompson
Roger ....Hugh Laurie
Mary ....Imelda Staunton
Peter..Stephen Fry
Sarah ....Alphonsia Emmanuel
Carol ....Rita Rudner
Vera ....Phyllida Law

Paul...Alex Lowe
Brian..Tony Slattery

Credits
Executive Producer ....Stephen Evans
Producer/Director ....Kenneth Branagh
Co-Producer ....Martin Bergman
Line Producer......................................David Parfitt
Assistant Director ....Chris Newman
Director of Photography ....Roger Lanser
Sound...David Crozier
Editor..Andrew Marcus
Production Design...................................Tim Harvey
Art Direction..Martin Childs
Costume Design ....Susan Coates
....Stephanie Collie
Screenplay ....Rita Rudner
....Martin Bergman

Film Facts
Country of Origin ....Great Britain
Running Time ....102 minutes
Soundtrack ....Epic Soundtrax
Film...Technicolor
Sound...Dolby Stereo
Location...London

Pictures From
A Revolution
(Kino International)

Critics Rating: Not Rated.
Genre: Documentary—Photographer-filmmaker Susan Mieselas focuses her lens on the aftermath of the Nicaraguan conflict.
Plot: A still photographer in Nicaragua in 1978, she returned to interview many of the people she originally captured. Both Contras and Sandinistas express their disappointment at the result of the revolution. Much of the blame is placed on the media and the pictures that were used to support whichever side needed supporting at the time.
MPAA Rating: Not Rated.

Credits
Producers/Directors ....Susan Meiselas
....Richard P. Rogers
....Alfred Guzzetti
Director of Photography................Richard P. Rogers
Sound ....Alfred Guzzetti

Music..William Eldridge
....Terry Riley
Photo Animation..................................Patricia Kelly
Research ....Abbie Fields
Film Facts
Running Time ....93 minutes
Film ....Color
Sound ....Stereo
Location..Nicaragua

A Place For Jazz
(Cineresearch)

Critics Rating: Not Rated.
Genre: Documentary—Filmmaker Richard Broadman focuses his lens on a popular Boston jazz club, known as the 1369.
Plot: In the 1980s it was the place to be. Today it is out of business and just a footnote in jazz history. Interviews with the musicians and club owners reveal the jazz tradition and how the art form is passed from one generation to another.
MPAA Rating: Not Rated.
Credits
Producers ....Richard Broadman
....Jay Hoffman, Bob Pollak
Director/Editor ....Richard Broadman
Associate Director ....Michael Haggerty
Director of Photography ....John Bishop
Sound ....Stephen Olech
Film Facts
Running Time ....68 minutes
Film ....Color (16mm)
Sound ....Stereo

The Playboys
(Samuel Goldwyn Co.)

Critics Rating: ★★★★
Genre: Drama—Cowritten by the author of *My Left Foot* (Shane Connaughton), *Playboys* is a gripping and dramatic tale of a tragic love triangle in 1950s Ireland.
Plot: Albert Finney (*Miller's Crossing, Tom Jones*) plays Hegarty, a small-town policeman in love with Tara (Robin Wright, *State Of Grace*), a beautiful young woman who has just given birth to a baby

out of wedlock. When a traveling troupe of actors known as "The Playboys" comes to town, Tara suddenly finds herself involved with one of the players. Tom (Aidan Quinn, *At Play In The Fields Of The Lord*) is equally smitten with Tara, but before their relationship can grow, a jealous Hegarty reveals the truth about the father of Tara's baby. His jealous obsession, however, eventually leads to his own self-destruction.
MPAA Rating: PG-13
Cast
Constable Hegarty ....Albert Finney
Tom ....Aidan Quinn
Tara...Robin Wright
Freddie...Milo O'Shea
Father Malone ....Alan Devlin
Brigid..Niamh Cusack
Cassidy...Ian McElhinney
Rachel..Stella McCusker
Denzil...Niall Buggy
Vonnie ....Anna Livia Ryan
Mick ....Adrian Dunbar
Credits
Producers..............William P. Cartlidge, Simon Perry
Director ....Gillies MacKinnon
Assistant Director ....Chris Carreras
Director of Photography ....Jack Conroy
Sound ....Peter Lindsay
Editor ....Humphrey Dixon
Production Design ....Andy Harris
Costume Design ....Consolata Boyle
Casting ....Pat Condron
Written by.................................Shane Connaughton
....Kerry Crabbe
Music ....Jean-Claude Petit
Film Facts
Country of Origin ...............................U.S./Ireland
Running Time ....108 minutes
Film ....Color
Sound ....Dolby Stereo
Location ....Ireland

The Player
(Fine Line Features)

Critics Rating: ★★★★★
Genre: Comedy—Director Robert Altman has

assembled an enormous and impressive cast of stars—from Julia Roberts and Whoopi Goldberg to Dean Stockwell and Bruce Willis—in this satirical and irreverent comedy. The story is about a back-stabbing, kill-your-way-to-the-top, Hollywood studio executive. Opening in April, one reviewer claimed that the film was the best American film released so far this year. Many other reviewers agreed.

Plot: Tim Robbins (*Bob Roberts*) stars as Griffin Mill, a studio-production VP afraid of losing his tenuous position to a "comer" (Peter Gallagher) being recruited from another studio. Simultaneously, a writer Mill has casually and callously rejected begins to threaten and harass him with postcards. Tracking down the writer, Mill unintentionally murders the man and then does his best to cover it up. At this point, the real fun begins, as the murder is investigated and Mill must lie his way through the rest of the film to hold onto his job. In a wicked twist of events, the murder turns out to be the best thing he could have done for his career and ensures a happy ending to this insightful and humorous tale about getting away with murder in Hollywood.

MPAA Rating: R—For language and some sensuality. Contains brief full frontal male nudity.

Cast

Griffin Mill	Tim Robbins
June Gudmundsdottir	Greta Scacchi
Walter Stuckel	Fred Ward
Detective Avery	Whoopi Goldberg
David Kahane	Vincent D'Onofrio
Tom Oakley	Richard E. Grant
Andy Civella	Dean Stockwell
Dick Mellen	Sydney Pollack
Larry Levy	Peter Gallagher
Joel Levison	Brion James
Bonnie Sherow	Cynthia Stevenson
Sandy	Leah Ayres
Frank Murphy	Frank Barhydt
Reg Goldman	Randall Batinkoff
Whitney Gersh	Gina Gershon
Jan	Angela Hall
Jimmy Chase	Paul Hewitt
Marty Grossman	Mike E. Kaplan
Det. DeLongpre	Lyle Lovett
Celia	Dina Merrill
Steve Reeves	Jeremy Piven
Gar Girard	Kevin Scannell

Cameos by Steve Allen, Richard Anderson, Rene Auberjonois, Harry Belafonte, Shari Belafonte, Karen Black, Michael Bowen, Gary Busey, Robert Carradine, Charles Champlin, Cher, James Coburn, Cathy Lee Crosby, John Cusack, Brad Davis, Paul Dooley, Thereza Ellis, Peter Falk, Felicia Farr, Kasia Figura, Louise Fletcher, Dennis Franz, Teri Garr, Leeza Gibbons, Scott Glenn, Jeff Goldblum, Elliott Gould, Joel Grey, David Alan Grier, Buck Henry, Anjelica Huston, Kathy Ireland, Steve James, Maxine John-James, Sally Kellerman, Sally Kirkland, Jack Lemmon, Marlee Matlin, Andie McDowell, Malcolm McDowell, Jayne Meadows, Martin Mull, Jennifer Nash, Nick Nolte, Alexandra Powers, Bert Remsen, Guy Remsen, Patricia Resnick, Burt Reynolds, Jack Riley, Julia Roberts, Mimi Rogers, Annie Ross, Alan Rudolph, Jill St. John, Susan Sarandon, Adam Simon, Rod Steiger, Joan Tewkesbury, Brian Tochi, Lily Tomlin, Robert Wagner, Ray Walston, Bruce Willis and Marvin Young.

Credits

Executive Producer	Cary Brokaw
Co-Executive Producer	William S. Gilmore
Producers	David Brown
	Michael Tolkin
	Nick Wechsler
Co-Producer	Scott Bushnell
Associate Producer	David Levy
Director	Robert Altman
Assistant Director	Allan Nichols
Director of Photography	Jean Lepine
Sound	John Pritchett
Editor	Geraldine Peroni
Production Design	Stephen Altman
Art Direction	Jerry Fleming
Set Decoration	Susan Emshwiller
Costume Design	Alexander Julian
Screenplay	Michael Tolkin
Based on the novel by	Michael Tolkin
Music	Thomas Newman

Film Facts

Running Time	123 minutes
Soundtrack	Varese Sarabande
Film	Deluxe Color
Sound	Ultra-Stereo
Location	Los Angeles

Poison Ivy

(New LIne Cinema)

Critics Rating: ★★★
Genre: Thriller
Tag Line: "Ivy thought her best friend had the perfect house, the perfect family, the perfect life. So she took them."
Plot: Similar to *The Hand That Rocks The Cradle* in plot—a young woman takes over a household with evil intent—critics and audiences were not as kind to this predictable melodrama. While performances are solid, the film lacks the necessary emotion and believability to make it worth the effort for audiences other than fans of the all-star cast.
MPAA Rating: R

Cast

Darryl Cooper	Tom Skerritt
Sylvie Cooper	Sara Gilbert
Georgie Cooper	Cheryl Ladd
Ivy	Drew Barrymore
Isabelle	Jeanne Sakata
Bob	Alan Stock

Credits

Executive Producers	Melissa Goddard
	Peter Morgan
Producer	Andy Ruben
Co-Producer	Rick Nathanson
Associate Producer	Jana Marx
Director	Katt Shea Ruben
Assistant Director	J. B. Rogers
Director of Photography	Phedon Papamichael
Sound	Bill Robbins
Editor	Gina Mittelman
Production Design	Virginia Lee
Art Direction	Hayden Yates
Set Decoration	Michele Munoz
Costume Design	Ellen Gross
Casting	Jeffrey Passero
Screenplay	Andy Ruben
	Katt Shea Ruben
Based on a story by	Peter Morgan
	Melissa Goddard
Music Supervisors	Bonnie Greenberg
	Jill Meyers
Music	Aaron Davies

Film Facts

Running Time	89 minutes
Film	Color
Sound	Dolby Stereo
Location	Los Angeles

Police Story III - Supercop

(Golden Harvest)

Critics Rating: Not Rated.
Genre: Action—A martial-arts actioner with subtitles.
Plot: Jackie Chan, a popular Chinese action star, plays Chen Chia-Chu, a super cop capable of single-handedly taking on all villains and bad guys—no stretch here. Just to make things interesting, he teams up with Fu-Sheng (Yang Gi-King) a beautiful, but equally deadly Hong Kong Security Force commander. Together they take on the international drug trade.
MPAA Rating: Not Rated.

Cast

Chen Chia-chu	Jackie Chan
Fu-Sheng	Yang Gi-King
May	Maggie Cheung
Director Yang	Michelle Yeaoh
Big Brother Wei	Tsang Kong
Panther	Yuen Wah
The General	Lo Lieh

Credits

Executive Producers	Leonard Ho, Jackie Chan
Producers	Tang King-Sung, Willie Chan
Director	Stanley Tong (Tong Kwei-Lai)
Director of Photography	Lam Kwok-Wah
Editors	Cheung Yae-Chung
	Cheung Kai Fei
Art Direction	Oliver Wong
Costume Design	Hung Wei-Chuk
Written by	Tang King-Sung
	Ma Mei-Ping
	Lee Wei-Yee
Music	Lee Chun Shing
Stunt Coordinator	Stanley Tong

Film Facts

Country of Origin	Hong Kong
Language	Cantonese (subtitled English/Chinese)
Running Time	100 minutes
Film	Color
Sound	Stereo

183

The Power Of One
(Warner Bros.)

Critics Rating: ★★★

Genre: Drama—Period film about a young white man who grows up to be the salvation of the oppressed black South Africans.

Plot: Stephen Dorff stars as Peter Keating (nicknamed PK), a young English boy raised in South Africa. At the age of 12, his mother dies, and he is raised by friends of the family doctor (Armin Mueller-Stahl) and Geel Piet (Morgan Freeman). Piet teaches the boy to box, and Keating turns out to be a natural. Eventually he uses his talents to take on the oppression of apartheid and is considered the "Rain Man" or savior of the people.

MPAA Rating: PG-13

Cast

P. K. (age 18)	Stephen Dorff
Geel Piet	Morgan Freeman
Headmaster St. John	John Gielgud
Doc	Armin Mueller-Stahl
P. K. (age 12)	Simon Fenton
Maria Marais	Fay Masterson
P. K. (age 7)	Guy Witcher
Sgt. Jaape Botha	Daniel Craig
Gideon Duma	Alois Moyo
Hoppie Gruenwald	Ian Roberts
Daniel Marais	Marius Weyers

Credits

Executive Producers	Steven Reuther
	Graham Burke
	Greg Coote
Producer	Arnon Milchan
Associate Producer	Doug Seeling
Director	John G. Avildsen
Assistant Director	Clifford Coleman
Director of Photography	Dean Semler
Sound	Clive Winter
Editor	John G. Avildsen
Production Design	Roger Hall
Art Direction	Les Tomkins
Set Decoration	Karen Brookes
Costume Design	Tom Rand
Casting	Caro Jones
Screenplay	Robert Mark Kamen
Based on the Novel by	Bryce Courtenay
Music	Hans Zimmer
Original Songs/African Music Supervisor	Johnny Clegg

Film Facts

Running Time	111 minutes
Soundtrack	Elektra Records
Film	Technicolor
Sound	Dolby Stereo
Location	Zimbabwe; England

Prelude To A Kiss
(20th Century Fox)

Critics Rating: ★★★

Genre: Comedy—Based on the successful Broadway play, *Kiss* is a quirky and complex contemporary fairy tale with a twist.

Tag Line: "It you can't believe your eyes, trust your heart."

Plot: Alec Baldwin and Meg Ryan star as Peter and Rita, two lonely people who find one another. On their wedding day, a mysterious old man (Walker) appears out of nowhere and asks to kiss the bride. During the kiss they exchange souls and Rita's body is taken over by the old man's. During the honeymoon the groom is confused and confounded by Rita's change in personality. When Peter realizes what has happened, he goes in search of the old man and Rita's soul. Many reviewers referred to the film as a sophisticated *Ghost*, this dark fairytale is about true love that transcends the body.

MPAA Rating: PG-13

Trivia: Critics by and large raved that veteran character actor Sydney Walker stole the film. Among his many roles, Walker played the Doctor who gave Ryan O'Neal the news that Ali McGraw had a terminal illness in *Love Story*.

Cast

Peter Hoskins	Alec Baldwin
Rita Boyle	Meg Ryan
Leah Blier	Kathy Bates
Dr. Boyle	Ned Beatty
Marion Boyle	Patty Duke
Julius	Sydney Walker
Taylor	Stanley Tucci
Tom	Rocky Carroll
Jerry Blier	Richard Riehle

Credits

Executive Producer	Jennifer Ogden
Producers	Michael Gruskoff
	Michael I. Levy
Co-Producers	Craig Lucas
	Norman Rene
Associate Producer	Deborah Schindler
Director	Norman Rene
Assistant Director	Michael Steele
Assistant Director (N.Y.)	Tony Adler
Director of Photography	Stefan Czapsky
Sound	Les Lazarowitz
Sound (Jamaica)	James Sabat
Editor	Stephen A. Rotter
Production Design	Andrew Jackness
Art Direction	W. Steven Graham
Art Direction (Jamaica)	Maxine Walters
Art Direction (N.Y.)	Ray Kluga
Set Design	Karen Fletcher
Set Decoration	Cindy Carr
Set Decoration (N.Y.)	Sue Raney
Costume Design	Walter Hicklin
Casting	Jason LaPadura
	Natalie Hart
Screenplay	Craig Lucas
Based on the play by	Craig Lucas
Music	Howard Shore

Film Facts

Running Time	105 minutes
Soundtrack	RCA Records
Film	DuArt Color
Sound	Dolby Stereo
Location	Chicago

Primary Motive
(Hemdale)

Critics Rating: Not Rated.

Genre: Drama—Trailing behind *Bob Roberts* in the political-drama department, the story follows a college graduate into the halls of power and corruption.

Plot: Judd Nelson stars as Andrew Blumenthal, the son of a congressman. Getting a job as press secretary to a gubernatorial candidate (Frank Converse), Andrew quickly sets about to destroy the candidacy of an opponent. With the help of his naive girlfriend (Justine Bateman), he digs up ample dirt on the corrupt politician. However, in the end it backfires.

MPAA Rating: R—For language.

Cast

Andrew Blumenthal	Judd Nelson
Darcy Link	Justine Bateman
Chris Poulas	Richard Jordan
Wallace Roberts	John Savage
John Eastham	Frank Converse
Paul Melton	Joe Grifasi
Helen Poulas	Sally Kirkland
Ken Blumenthal	Malachi Throne
Stephanie Poulas	Jennifer Youngs

Credits

Producers	Thomas Gruenberg
	Don Carmody
	Richard Rosenberg
Director	Daniel Adams
Assistant Director	Alan Goluboff
Director of Photography	John Drake
Sound	R. Trevor Black
Editor	Jaqueline Carmody
Production Design	Dan Yarhi
Costume Design	Julie Engelsman
Casting	Lynn Kressel
Screenplay	William Snowden
	Daniel Adams
Music	John Cale
Make-up	Bill Miller-Jones

Film Facts

Running Time	93 minutes
Film	Rank Color
Sound	Stereo
Location	Boston; Luxembourg

The Professional: Golgo 13
(Streamline)

Critics Rating: Not Rated.

Genre: Animated—An adult adventure film based on the popular Japanese comic series "Golgo 13" by Takao Saito.

Tag Line: "He shoots. He scores. He'll blow you away!"

Plot: Golgo 13 aka Duke Togo, the Professional, is an international killer for hire. Hired to kill the son of Leonard Dawson, a ruthless tycoon, Togo underestimates the power of vengence. Well-connected, Dawson gathers secret assassins from the FBI, the Pentagon and the CIA to help capture and kill Togo. Their secret weapon is a perverted killer named "Big Snake." This of course leads to all-out battle, wall-to-wall action and martial-arts destruction. Genre fans of both animation and action will appreciate this dark, adult entertainment.

MPAA Rating: Not Rated.

Cast

Voices:

Golgo 13	Greg Snegoff
Leonard Dawson	Michael McConnohie
Bragan	Mike Reynolds
Laura	Edie Mirman
Cindy	Joyce Kurtz
Rita	Diane Michelle
Pablo	Kerrigan Mahan
Garvin	David Povall
Jefferson	Ed Mannix
Young	Mike Forrest
Albert	Milt Jamin
Paco	Steve Kramer
Bishop Moretti	John Dantona
Informant	Jeff Winkless
Robert Dawson	Tony Oliver

Credits

Producers	Yutaka Fujioka
	Mataichiro Yamamoto
	Nobuo Inada
Director	Osamu Dezaki
Director of Photography	Hirokata Takahashi
Editor	Mitsuo Tsurubuchi
Based on the graphic novels by	Takao Saito
Adaption Producer/Director	Carl Macek
English Dialogue and Direction	Greg Snegoff
Music	Toshiyuki Omori

Film Facts

Running Time	95 minutes
Film	Color
Sound	Stereo

Proof

(Fine Line Features)

Critics Rating: Not Rated.
Genre: Drama—*Proof* is a moving and memorable psychological drama.

Plot: Hugo Weaving stars as Martin, a blind young man with psychological scars that keep him from trusting or getting close to anyone. He also has a very odd hobby for a blind man—photography. When a chance meeting with Andy (Russell Crowe) turns into a very close friendship, Martin is again set up for a fall. His housekeeper (Genevieve Picot) is secretly in love with him. Resenting his new intimacy with Andy, she begins to sabotage their friendship.

MPAA Rating: R—For sensuality and some language.

Cast

Martin	Hugo Weaving
Celia	Genevieve Picot
Andy	Russell Crowe
Martin's mother	Heather Mitchell
Young Martin	Jeffrey Walker
Vet	Frank Gallacher
Brian	Frankie J. Holden
Waitress	Saskia Post

Credits

Producer	Lynda House
Director	Jocelyn Moorhouse
Assistant Director	Tony Mahood
Director of Photography	Martin McGrath
Sound	Glenn Newnham
Editor	Ken Sallows
Production Manager	Catherine (Tatts) Bishop
Production Design	Patrick Reardon
Casting	Liz Millinar
	Greg Apps
Written by	Jocelyn Moorhouse
Music	Not Drowning, Waving

Film Facts

Country of Origin	Australia
Running Time	86 minutes
Film	Eastmancolor
Sound	Stereo

The Public Eye

(Universal)

Critics Rating: ★★★
Genre: Drama—Loosely based on the life of infamous 1940s New York crime photographer Weegee. Slickly photographed, the film glamorizes the gritty underworld he haunted.

Tag Line: "Murder. Scandal. Crime. No matter what he was shooting, The Great Bernzini never took sides, he only took pictures...Except once."

Plot: Joe Pesci stars as Bernzy, an ambitious loner who walks the city streets in the middle of the night with a camera. The best in the business at capturing the underbelly of the streets, he craves respectability. Seduced by a nightclub owner into spying for her, he becomes a witness to a mob massacre. Capturing these images unexpectedly brings him the notoriety and celebrity he longs for.

MPAA Rating: R—For violence.

Cast

Leon "Bernzy" Bernstein	Joe Pesci
Kay Levitz	Barbara Hershey
Danny the Doorman	Jared Harris
Sal Minetto	Stanley Tucci
Arthur Nabler	Jerry Adler
Conklin	Gerry Becker
Spoleto	Dominic Chianes
H. R. Rineman	Del Close
Farinelli	Richard Foronjy
Agent Chadwick	Tim Gamble
Older agent	Bob Gunton
Spoleto's lieutenant	Joe Guzaldo
Federal watchman	Peter Maloney
Officer O'Brien	Richard Riehle

Credits

Executive Producer	Robert Zemeckis
Producer	Sue Baden-Powell
Director	Howard Franklin
Director of Photography	Peter Suschitzky
Sound	Stephan Von Hase-Mihalik
Editor	Evan Lottman
Production Design	Marcia Hinds-Johnson
Art Direction	Bo Johnson
Art Direction (Chicago)	Dina Lipton
Set Decoration	Jan Bergstrom
Costume Design	Jane Robinson
Casting	Donna Isaacson
Screenplay	Howard Franklin
Music	Mark Isham
Special Effects	Industrial Light & Magic

Film Facts

Running Time	99 minutes
Soundtrack	Varese Sarabande
Film	Deluxe Color
Sound	Dolby Stereo
Location	Cincinnati; Chicago; Los Angeles

The Puerto Rican Mambo (Not A Musical)
(Cabriolet)

Critics Rating: Not Rated.

Genre: Comedy—A low-budget film featuring the humorous performance, skits and jokes of Caballero, a standup comedian. Caballero's message, while funny, is a serious one about prejudice against Puerto Ricans in America. Despite the social commentary, this is a very entertaining straightforward comic performance that will please its intended audience.

MPAA Rating: Not Rated.

Cast

With Luis Cabellero, Jeff Eyres, Susan Gaspar, Johnny Leggs, Sandy McFadden, Lucia Mendoza, Mike Robles, Carole M. Eckman, John Fulweiler, David Healy, Carolyn McDermott, Ben Model, Howard Arnesson and Mary Perez.

Credits

Producer/Director	Ben Model
Directors of Photography	Vincent Manes
	Rosemary Tomosky-Franco
	Paul Koestner
Sound	Alina Avila
Editor	Ben Model
Written by	Luis Caballero
Adapted for the screen by	Ben Model
Music	Eddie Palmieri

Film Facts

Running Time	90 minutes
Film	DuArt Color
Sound	Stereo

Pure Country
(Warner Bros.)

Critics Rating: ★★

Genre: Drama—A showcase for country-singing superstar George Strait. Country fans and nonfans alike will find this film Strait-forward and easy to enjoy.

Plot: Strait plays Dusty Wyatt Chandler, a country singer who burns out from the excesses of life in the fast lane. After his manager, Lula Rogers (Warren), pushes him to the edge, he leaves the show mid-tour. Dusty heads for home, his roots, and the simple life. While there, he gets involved with Harley (Glasser), who helps him forget his troubles and the pressures of his life. Before long, an old buddy (Doe), comes to warn him that his manager is using a stand-in to replace him and fool his fans.

MPAA Rating: PG—For some mild violence; and sensuality and language.

Cast

Dusty Wyatt Chandler ....George Strait
Lula Rogers ....Lesley Ann Warren
Harley Tucker..Isabel Glasser
Ernest Tucker ....Rory Calhoun
Buddy Jackson ....Kyle Chandler
Earl Blackstock..John Doe
Grandma Ivy Chandler ....Molly McClure

Credits

Executive Producer..................................R. J. Louis
Producer ....Jerry Weintraub
Associate Producer ....Susan Elkins
Director...Christopher Cain
Assistant Director ....Cliff Coleman
2nd Unit Director.........................Bobby J. Foxworth
Director of Photography ....Richard Bowen
Aerial Concert Camera ....Jerry Holway
Sound...Andy Wiskes
Editor..Jack Hofstra
Additional Editing ....Robin Katz
Production Design ....Jeffrey Howard
Set Decoration....................................Derek R. Hill
Casting ....Sharon Howard-Field
Written by ....Rex McGee
Music...Steve Dorff
Stunt Coordinator.........................Bobby J. Foxworth

Film Facts

Running Time ....112 minutes
Soundtrack..MCA Records
Film..Technicolor
Sound ....Dolby Stereo
Location ....Ft. Worth, Texas; Las Vegas

The Quarrel
(Apple & Honey)

Critics Rating: ★★★

Genre: Drama—Essentially a one-act play based on Yiddish writer Chaim Grade's "My Quarrel With Hersh Rasseyner."

Plot: Thompson and Rubinek play Chaim and Hersh, two childhood friends who accidentally meet after many years of estrangement. The year is 1948, and each man has lost his family to the holocaust. As a result, Chaim has forsaken his faith and become a writer. Hersh, on the other hand, has grown stronger in his faith, becoming an Orthodox Jew. While their reactions are opposite in the extreme, they share a bond of friendship that ties them together. Strong performances give this story its power and dramatic intensity.

MPAA Rating: Not Rated.

Cast

Hersh Rasseyner	Saul Rubinek
Chaim Kovler	R. H. Thomson
Joshua	Robert Haiat

Credits

Producers	David Brandes
	Kim Todd
Director	Eli Cohen
Director of Photography	John Berrie
Sound	Donald Cohen
Editor	Havelock Gradidge
Art Direction	Michael Joy
Screenplay	David Brandes
Based on a story by	Chaim Grade
Music	William Goldstein

Film Facts

Country of Origin	Canada
Running Time	88 minutes
Film	Color
Sound	Stereo
Location	Montreal, Quebec

189

Radio Flyer
(Columbia)

Critics Rating: ★★★

Genre: Drama—A film about child abuse and the way two young boys deal with the pain. This is a moving film dealing with a sensitive topic and will appeal more to a mature audience.

Plot: The story is told in flashbacks as the narrator describes his life when he was a child, to his own two boys. He explains that as a child his father had abandoned the family. When his mother remarried, it was to an alcoholic who cruelly beat the younger brother. In order to deal with the abuse, the boys retreat into an unusual fantasy world that allows them to escape.

MPAA Rating: PG-13

Cast

Mary	Lorraine Bracco
Daugherty	John Heard
Mike	Elijah Wood
Bobby	Joseph Mazzello
The King	Adam Baldwin
Geronimo Bill	Ben Johnson
Young Fisher	Sean Baca
Older Mike	Tom Hanks
Older Fisher	Robert Munic

Credits

Executive Producers	Michael Douglas
	Rick Bieber, David Mickey Evans
Co-Executive Producers	Richard Solomon
	Peter McAlevey
Producer	Lauren Shuler-Donner
Co-Producers	Jennie Lew Tugend
	Jim Van Wyck, Dale R. de la Torre
Associate Producers	Sherry Lynn Fadely
	Alexander Bernhardt Collett
Director	Richard Donner

Assistant Director	Jim Van Wyck
Director of Photography	Laszlo Kovacs
2nd Unit Camera	Bobby Byrne
Sound	Ronald Judkins
Editor	Stuart Baird
Production Design	J. Michael Riva
Art Direction	David Frederick Klassen
Set Decoration	Michael Taylor
Costume Design	April Ferry
Casting	Mike Fenton
	Judy Taylor, Valorie Massalas
Written by	David Mickey Evans
Music	Hans Zimmer
Visual Effects Supervisor	Peter Donen
Stunt Coordinator	Mic Rodgers
Radio Flyer Conceptualist	Michael Scheffe

Film Facts

Running Time	113 minutes
Soundtrack	Big Screen Music
Film	Technicolor/Black & White
Sound	Dolby Stereo
Location	Los Angeles; Northern California
	Washington, D.C.

Raise The Red Lantern
(Dahong Denglong Gaogao Gua)
(Orion Classics)

Critics Rating: ★★★★

Genre: Drama—Directed by Zhang Yimou (*Ju Dou*), this tragic drama is nevertheless laced with humor and warmth.

Plot: The film takes place in Northern China in the 1920s. Gong Li stars as 19-year-old Songlian, a young woman who leaves home to become the the newest of four wives of a wealthy older man. The competi-tion for the master's favor among the four women is fierce. (The film's title comes from the ritual of raising the red lantern in front of the home of the wife the master wishes to sleep with that night.) At first, Songlian proves to be a cunning and vicious opponent but eventually her life is ruined as a result of these bitter battles.

MPAA Rating: PG-13

Cast

Songlian	Gong Li
Chen Zuoqian	Ma Jingwu

Meishan ....He Caifei
Zhuoyun ....Cao Caifeng
Yan'er ....Kong Lin
Yuru..Jin Shuyuan

Credits
Executive Producers ....Hou Hsiao-hsien
....Zhang Wei
Producer...Chiu Fu-Sheng
Director...Zhang Yimou
Directors of Photography ....Zhao Pei
....Yang Lun
Editor..Du Yuan
Production Manager ....Feng Yiting
Art Direction.................Cao Jiuping, Dong Huamiao
Written by ....Ni Zhen
Based on the novel *Wives and
  Concubines* by ....Su Tong
Music...Zhao Jiping

Film Facts
Country of Origin ....China/HongKong/Taiwan
Language ....Chinese (subtitled)
Running Time ....125 minutes
Film ....Color
Sound ....Dolby Stereo

Raising Cain
(Universal)

Critics Rating: ★★
Genre: Thriller—No simple thriller, this experiment in terror is outlandishly humorous throughout. Critics were split in their reaction and appreciation of this added element to the genre.
Tag Line: "De Mented. De Ranged. De Ceptive. De Palma." "When Jenny cheated on her husband, he didn't leave...he split."
Plot: John Lithgow stars as Carter, a demented child psychologist with a very split personality. When he witnesses his wife Jenny (Lolita Davidovich) having an affair, he is pushed over the edge. Using children for his experiments, he kidnaps his own daughter and the terror really begins.
MPAA Rating: R—For sexuality, language and terror violence.
Cast
Carter/Cain/Dr. Nix/Josh/Margo..........John Lithgow

Jenny ....Lolita Davidovich
Jack ....Steven Bauer
Dr. Waldheim.....................Frances Sternhagen
Sgt. Cally ....Tom Bower
Sarah ....Mel Harris
Lt. Terri ....Gregg Henry
Also with Teri Austin, Kathleen Callan, Gabrielle Carteris, Barton Heyman and Amanda Pombo.

Credits
Producer ....Gale Anne Hurd
Co-Producer...........................Michael R. Joyce
Director.................................Brian De Palma
Assistant Director......................James Dyer
Director of Photography ....Stephen H. Burum
Sound ....Nelson Stoll
Editors ....Paul Hirsch
.........................Bonnie Koehler, Robert Dalva
Production Design ....Doug Kraner
Costume Design........................Bobbie Read
Casting ....Pam Dixon
Written by.............................Brian De Palma
Music ....Pino Donaggio

Film Facts
Running Time ....95 minutes
Soundtrack ....Milan Records
Film ....Deluxe Color
Sound ....Dolby Stereo
Location ....Northern California
Other Working Titles ....*Father's Day*

Rampage
(Miramax)

Critics Rating: ★★★
Genre: Thriller—The film was billed as William Friedkin's most provocative thriller since *The Exorcist*. Completed in 1987, the film was not released at the time because its studio, The De Laurentiis Entertainment Group, experienced financial difficulties.
Tag Line: "In modern America, the boy next door isn't what he appears to be. Now he's bringing the terror home."
Plot: Michael Biehn (*K2*) plays an assistant DA assigned to an especially gruesome mass-murder case. Alex MacArthur plays the psycho-killer who coldly and brutally murders the members of two

households for no apparent reason. For the most part, this is a run-of-the-mill film about a murder trial, laced with gory flashback interludes.

MPAA Rating: R

Cast

Anthony Fraser	Michael Biehn
Charles Reece	Alex McArthur
Albert Morse	Nicholas Campbell
Kate Fraser	Deborah Van Valkenburgh
Dr. Keddie	John Harkins
Mel Sanderson	Art Lafleur
Judge McKinsey	Billy Greenbush
Gene Tippetts	Royce D. Applegate
Naomi Reece	Grace Zabriskie

Also with Donald Hotton, Roy London and Andy Romano.

Credits

Producer	David Salven
Director	William Friedkin
Assistant Directors	Michael Daves
	Regina Gordon
Director of Photography	Robert Yeoman
Sound	David MacMillan
Editor	Jere Huggins
Production Design	Buddy Cone
Art Direction	Carol Clements
Set Decoration	Nancy Nye
Casting	Rick Montgomery
Screenplay	William Friedkin
Based on the book by	William P. Wood
Original Music	Ennio Morricone

Film Facts

Running Time	97 minutes
Film	Technicolor
Sound	Dolby Stereo

Rapid Fire
(20th Century Fox)

Critics Rating: ★★

Genre: Action—The son of cult-hero Bruce Lee, American-born Brandon Lee follows in his father's footsteps with this wall-to-wall actioner.

Plot: Lee stars as Jake Lo, a college art student and reluctant hero. Before he knows what has happened, he finds himself on the run from thugs, after he witnesses a mob killing. Reluctant or not, it

doesn't take long before Lee is splattering, blasting, kicking, smashing, chopping and generally pulverizing everyone from the FBI to the Chinese drug lords to the Chicago police.

MPAA Rating: R—For language, violence, and sensuality. Contains brief nudity.

Trivia: Lee's first feature film was the Hong-Kong-produced *Legacy Of Rage*.

Cast

Jake Lo	Brandon Lee
Mace Ryan	Powers Boothe
Antonio Serrano	Nick Mancuso
Agent Stuart	Raymond J. Berry
Carl Chang	Michael Paul Chan
Karla Withers	Kate Hodge
Brunner Gazzi	Tony Longo
Kinman Tau	Tzi Ma

Credits

Executive Producers	Gerald Olson
	John Fasano
Producer	Robert Lawrence
Associate Producer	Barry Berg
Director	Dwight H. Little
Assistant Director	Denis Stewart
2nd Unit Director	Gerald Olson
Director of Photography	Ric Waite
Sound	Rob Janiger
Editor	Gib Jaffe
Production Design	Ron Foreman
Art Direction	Charles Butcher
Set Design	Natalie Richards
Set Decoration	Leslie Frankenheimer
Costume Design	Erica Edell Phillips
Casting	Richard Pagano
	Sharon Bialy
	Debi Manwiller
Screenplay	Alan McElroy
Story by	Cindy Cirile
	Alan McElroy
Music	Christopher Young
Stunt Coordinator	Jeff Imada
Fight Choreography	Brandon Lee
	Jeff Imada

Film Facts

Running Time	95 minutes
Film	Deluxe Color
Sound	Dolby Stereo
Location	Chicago; Los Angeles

Raspad—Chernobyl: A Tale Of The Human Spirit
(MK2)

Critics Rating: ★★★★
Genre: Drama—A dramatization of the aftereffects of the nuclear accident.
Tag Line: "Chernobyl: A tale of the human spirit."
Plot: Sergei Shakurov plays Zhuralev, a man struggling to keep his family together, even though his wife is having an affair with a Party official. When the Chernobyl reactor explodes on April 25, 1986, a friend of Zhuralev is a witness to the catastrophe. Residents at first refuse to listen to his call to action or to accept the truth about what has happened. When they finally do, it is too late for many of them. Among the many tragedies, Zhuralev finds that his wife is leaving with her child and her lover. He decides there is no reason to live and volunteers for the the disaster cleanup committee.
MPAA Rating: Not Rated.

Cast

Zhuralev	Sergei Shakurov

Credits

Executive Producer	Mikhail Kistikowski
Director	Mikhail Belikov
Directors of Photography	Alexander Shagayev
	Piotr Trashevski
Sound	Tom Johnson
Screenplay	Mikhail Belikov
	Oleg Pridhodko

Film Facts

Country of Origin	U.S./Ukraine
Running Time	95 minutes
Film	Color/Black & White
Sound	Dolby Stereo
Location	Kiev

The Refrigerator
(Avenue D Films)

Critics Rating: Not Rated.
Genre: Horror—An entertaining, low-budget, tongue-in-cheek send-up of the horror genre by first-time director Nicholas Tony Jacobs.
Plot: David Simonds and Julia Mueller play Steve and Eileen, New York City newlyweds who move into an apartment. They discover that the former tenants have had a run-in with their evil refrigerator and that the refrigerator won. The fridge, it seems, is set on destroying this marriage as well. Eileen battles the evil appliance with the help of a flamenco-dancing plumber.
MPAA Rating: Not Rated.

Cast

Eileen Bateman	Julia Mueller
Steve Bateman	David Simonds
Juan (the plumber)	Angel Caban
Tanya	Phyllis Sanz

Credits

Producer	Christopher Oldcorn
Director	Nicholas Tony Jacobs
Director of Photography	Paul Gibson
Sound	Thomas Szabolcs
Editors	P. J. Pesce
	Suzanne Pillsbury
	Christopher Oldcorn
Art Direction	Therese Deprez
Written by	Nicholas Tony Jacobs
Music	Don Peterkofsy
	Chris Burke
	Adam Roth

Film Facts

Running Time	85 minutes
Film	Color
Sound	Stereo

Reservoir Dogs
(Miramax)

Critics Rating: ★★★★
Genre: Drama—Impressive, violent and bloody crime drama about a botched robbery and its aftermath by first-feature director Quentin Tarantino. Critics compared him to Scorsese and Kubrick.
Plot: Set in Los Angeles, the story is told in flashbacks. Tierney plays Joe Cabot, the mastermind of a jewelry-store diamond heist. Together with his son (Penn), he puts together a group of pros to pull it off. It looks like the perfect crime, except that the police have been tipped off and the robbery is a fiasco. The robbery ends in

death for two cops and two robbers, but this is only the beginning of a tragic tale that leads to a brutal and gory climax. Performances are top-notch from a strong ensemble cast.
MPAA Rating: R—For strong violence and language.
Cast

Mr. White	Harvey Keitel
Mr. Orange	Tim Roth
Nice Guy Eddie	Chris Penn
Mr. Pink	Steve Buscemi
Joe Cabot	Lawrence Tierney
Mr. Blonde	Michael Madsen
Mr. Blue	Eddie Bunker
Hostage policeman	Kirk Baltz
Mr. Brown	Quentin Tarantino

Also with Randy Brooks.
Credits

Executive Producers	Richard N. Gladstein
	Ronna B. Wallace
	Monte Hellman
Producer	Lawrence Bender
Co-Producer	Harvey Keitel
Director	Quentin Tarantino
Director of Photography	Andrzej Sekula
Editor	Sally Menke
Production Design	David Wasco
Costume Design	Betsy Heimann
Screenplay	Quentin Tarantino
Music Supervisor	Karyn Rachtman

Film Facts

Running Time	105 minutes
Soundtrack	MCA Records
Film	Foto-Kem Color
Sound	Stereo
Location	Los Angeles

The Restless Conscience
(Beller)

Critics Rating: Not Rated.
Genre: Documentary—Using archival footage, interviews with survivors and family photos, this powerful documentary examines the German resistance to Hitler throughout his reign of terror.
Plot: Often overlooked are the heroes of this period who gave their lives trying to end Hitler's. Most of

these individuals were executed during the war and their stories are told by relatives and acquaintances. The dissidents were primarily among the democratic politicians, the labor movement, the clergy and even the military officers.
MPAA Rating: Not Rated.
Credits

Producer/Director	Hava Kohav Beller
Directors of Photography	Volker Rodde
	Martin Schaer
	Gabor Bagyoni
Editors	Tonicka Janek
	Juliette Weber
	David Rogow
Written by	Hava Kohav Beller
Music	Elliot Sokolov
Consulting Historian	Prof. Peter Hoffman
Narrated by	John Dildine

Film Facts

Running Time	113 minutes
Film	Color/Black & White
Sound	Stereo

A River Runs Through It
(Columbia)

Critics Rating: ★★★★
Genre: Drama—Directed and narrated by Robert Redford (his directorial debut, *Ordinary People,* won Best Picture, Best Director and Best Supporting Actor in 1980), the story is based on the 1976 novella by Norman Maclean.
Tag Line: "The Classic story of an American family."
Plot: Set in Montana in the early 1900s, the story follows the lives of two brothers from childhood to manhood. Craig Sheffer (*Nightbreed, Instant Karma*) plays Norman, the older, more serious of the two. Brad Pitt (*Thelma & Louise, Cool World*) plays the easy-going, carefree Paul whose path takes a downhill course. The lives of both young men are affected profoundly by their parents, especially by their father (Skerritt), a stern Presbyterian minister. Norman goes to college, becomes a literature professor and marries, while Paul becomes a reporter, drinks, gambles, lands in jail once too often and eventually meets with a

tragic end. All the while, the river is the common thread that ties their lives together forever.

MPAA Rating: PG—Contains male and female nudity.

Trivia: Published in 1976, *A River Runs Through It* has sold more than 500,000 copies.

Cast

Norman Maclean	Craig Sheffer
Paul Maclean	Brad Pitt
Rev. Maclean	Tom Skerritt
Mrs. Maclean	Brenda Blethyn
Jessie Burns	Emily Lloyd
Mrs. Burns	Edie McClurg
Neal Burns	Stephen Shellen
Mabel	Nicole Burdette
Young Paul	Vann Gravage
Young Norman	Joseph Gordon-Levitt
Rawhide	Susan Traylor

Credits

Executive Producer	Jake Eberts
Producers	Robert Redford
	Patrick Markey
Co-Producers	Annick Smith
	William Kittredge
	Barbara Maltby
Director	Robert Redford
Assistant Director	J. Stephen Buck
2nd Unit Directors	Paul Ryan
	Steve Perry
Director of Photography	Philippe Rousselot
2nd Unit Camera	Paul Ryan
Sound	Hans Roland
Editors	Lynzee Klingman
	Robert Estrin
Production Design	Jon Hutman
Art Direction	Walter Martishius
Set Decoration	Gretchen Rau
Costume Design	Bernie Pollack
	Kathy O'Rear
Casting	Elisabeth Leustig
Screenplay	Richard Friedenberg
Based on the story by	Norman Maclean
Music	Mark Isham

Film Facts

Running Time	123 minutes
Film	Technicolor
Sound	Dolby Stereo
Location	Montana

Roadside Prophets
(Fine Line Features)

Critics Rating: ★★★

Genre: Comedy—"*Roadside Prophets* is little more than a soundtrack and an attitude in search of a film," exclaimed Brian Lowry of *Variety*. Abee Wool, who wrote *Sid & Nancy,* makes her directorial debut with this low-budget on-the-road buddy film.

Plot: John Doe, former member of the music group X, stars as Joe, a construction worker from Los Angeles on a motor-cycle mission to Nevada. Along the way, he meets up with Sam (Adam Horovitz of the Beastie Boys). Together they set out in search of reality. What they find is an oddball cast of lunatics and madmen.

MPAA Rating: R—For language and a scene of drug use.

Trivia: John Cusack makes a cameo appearance as a "crazy" in a roadside cafe. He also holds the year's record for most cameos in films released in the same month. Cusack appeared in Woody Allen's *Shadows And Fog* and in Robert Altman's *The Player*, all three films released in April.

Cast

Sam	Adam Horovitz
Joe Mosely	John Doe
Othello	David Carradine
Oscar	Bill Cobbs
Caspar	John Cusack
Harvey	Arlo Guthrie
Salvadore	Timothy Leary
Labia Mirage	Jennifer Balgobin
Sheriff Durango	Barton Heyman
Celeste	Lin Shaye

Credits

Executive Producer	Nancy Israel
Producers	Peter McCarthy
	David Swinson
Associate Producer	Bill Stankey
Director	Abbe Wool
Director of Photography	Tom Richmond
Editor	Nancy Richardson
Production Design	J. Rae Fox
Costume Design	Prudence Moriaty
Casting	Vickie Thomas
Written by	Abbe Wool
Based on an original idea by	David Swinson

Music ....Pray For Rain
Film Facts
Running Time ....96 minutes
Soundtrack ....Vanguard Records
Film...CFI Color
Sound ....Dolby Stereo

Rock-A-Doodle
(Samuel Goldwyn Co.)

Critics Rating: ★★★
Genre: Animated—This Don Bluth animated tale is an upbeat family feature about a young farm boy and his fantasy adventure.
Plot: When a little boy named Edmond (Toby Scott Granger) is knocked out during a storm on the farm, he dreams he is transported into the animated world of a favorite bedtime story about a rooster named Chanticleer. An evil owl has run Chanticleer out of town and forced him to earn a living as a rock 'n' roll singer. The same owl has turned Edmond into a kitten. He manages to escape, however and, aided by a group of animated characters, goes in search of Chanticleer.
MPAA Rating: G
Cast
Voices:
Edmond......................................Toby Scott Granger
Chanticleer.....................................Glen Campbell
Patou..Phil Harris
Grand Duke...........................Christopher Plummer
Peepers..Sandy Duncan
Goldie..Ellen Greene
Snipes..Eddie Deezen
Hunch ....Charles Nelson Reilly
Pinky..Sorrell Brooke
Credits
Executive Producers ....John Quested
....Morris F. Sullivan
Producers...Don Bluth
.............................Gary Goldman, John Pomeroy
Director ....Don Bluth
Co-Directors.....................................Gary Goldman
....Dan Kuenster
Screenplay ....David N. Weiss
Music ....Robert Folk
Original Songs.................................T. J. Kuenster

Film Facts
Running Time ....74 minutes
Soundtrack ....Liberty Records
Film...Color
Sound ....Dolby Stereo

Rock Soup
(First Run Features)

Critics Rating: Not Rated.
Genre: Documentary—Director, producer and editor Lech Kowalski focuses his camera on a soup kitchen that was run by the homeless in New York City and was shut down by City Hall.
Plot: Filmed in black and white, the focus is on the losing battle of these heroic figures to keep the kitchen open. Often painful and frustrating to witness, this is a powerful film that will appeal to an intelligent and socially conscious audience.
MPAA Rating: Not Rated.
Credits
Producer/Director/Editor.....................Lech Kowalski
Line Producer...Hilary White
Associate Producer.............................Gaetano Maida
Director of Photography ....Doron Schlair
Sound...Joshua Landis
Music..Chico Freeman
Film Facts
Running Time ....81 minutes
Film ....Black & White/16 mm
Sound ....Stereo

Romeo & Julia
(Intercontinental Releasing)

Critics Rating: Not Rated.
Genre: Comedy—Wildly humorous at times, this sweetly romantic, low-budget comedy is about two hapless people who meet on a bridge where each has gone to commit suicide. Instead fall in love.
Plot: Bob Koherr plays Romeo, an obnoxious practical joker. Ivana Kane plays Julia, a hypochondriac. Each has reason to believe that they have only limited time to live, so they decide to live it together.

MPAA Rating: Not Rated.
Cast

Romeo	Bob Koherr
Julia	Ivana Kane
Pop	Max Brandt
Jake	Patrick McGuinness
Tony	Willard Morgan
Stella	Karen Porter White
Dr. Neil/director	Donovan Dietz

Credits

Executive Producer	Sandy Ratcliffe
Producer/Director	Kevin Kaufman
Associate Producer	Alan Jacobs
Director of Photography	Patrick Darrin
Sound	Chris Schwartz
Editor/Associate Director	Peter Hammer
Art Direction	Deborah Dawson
Costume Design	Sunny Ralfini
Casting	Avy Kaufman
Written by	Kevin Kaufman
Music	Christian Hammer

Film Facts

Running Time	92 minutes
Film	Color
Sound	Stereo

Roy Rogers: King Of The Cowboys
(Scorpio Film)

Critics Rating: Not Rated.
Genre: Documentary
Plot: Dutch filmmaker Thys Ockersen's tribute to cowboy good-guy hero Roy Rogers is an entertaining journey down some nostalgicly happy trails. Making the trip from Amsterdam to Hollywood, Ockersen, a childhood fan of the king of cowboy films, takes a few fascinating detours before finally meeting his idol in the flesh. Along the way, he attends a Roy Rogers Convention, visits the Roy Rogers Museum, meets fellow fans and talks with former colleagues of the singing cowboy. But before the sun sets, the filmmaker's dreams come true, and he meets and interviews the star of his film, Roy Rogers and his wife and sidekick Dale Evans.
MPAA Rating: Not Rated.

Cast
With Roy Rogers, Dale Evans, Roy Rogers, Jr., William Witney, Trigger and the Sons of the Pioneers.

Credits

Producer	Kees Ryninks
Director	Thys Ockersen
Director of Photography	Peter Brugman
Editor	Stefan Kamp
Written by	Thys Ockersen

Film Facts

Country of Origin	Holland
Running Time	80 minutes
Film	Color
Sound	Stereo

Rubin & Ed
(I.R.S. Releasing)

Critics Rating: Not Rated.
Genre: Comedy—Mike Szymanski of the *New York Times Syndicate* called this film "a quirky comedy destined to become a cult classic." In essence it is the ultimate odd-couple-on-the-road film.
Plot: Howard Hesseman plays Ed Tuttle, a real estate salesman in search of recruits for a sales seminar. He convinces a very odd young man, Rubin Farr (Crispin Glover, *River's Edge, Little Voices*) to attend his seminar in return for a favor. Ed agrees to help Rubin bury his cat in the desert. Of course, his car breaks down in the middle of nowhere, which gives these two offbeat characters plenty of time to get to know one another.
MPAA Rating: PG-13

Cast

Rubin Farr	Crispin Glover
Ed Tuttle	Howard Hesseman
Rula	Karen Black
Mr. Busta	Michael Greene
Poster girl	Brittaney Lewis
Rubin's mom	Anna Louise Daniels
Ed's mom	Dorene Nielsen
Ed's dad	James Nielsen
Bob	Frank Magner
Ms. Bozzle	Diane St. Cyr
Jimbo	Michael Scott
Lacky	Patrick Michael Collins

Credits

Executive Producer.................................Tim Bevan
Producer...Paul Webster
Co-Producer ....David Stacey
Associate Producer...........................Damian Jones
Director...Trent Harris
1st Assistant Director ....John Cameron
2nd Assistant Director.....................Sarah Addington
Director of Photography ....Bryan Duggan
Sound..Rick Waddell
Editor...Brent Schoenfeld
Production Manager ....Elaine Dysinger
Production Design ....Clark Hunter
Set Decoration.............................Michele Spadoro
Costume Design ....Lawane Cole
Casting...Betsy Fels
Written by.......................................Trent Harris
Music ....Fredric Myrow

Film Facts

Running Time ....82 minutes
Film ....Alphacine Color
Sound..Ultra-Stereo

Ruby
(Triumph)

Critics Rating: ★★★

Genre: Drama—Following in the wake of last year's controversial *JFK*, director John Mackenzie presents a similar assassination-conspiracy story from a slightly different angle. Focusing on Jack Ruby's life, the film becomes a drama about the CIA, the mob and Ruby's place in both.

Plot: Danny Aiello plays Ruby, the owner of a Dallas strip-joint. The star of his show and his life is a stripper named Candy Cane (Sherilyn Fenn). As their relationship unfolds, so does the conspiracy. Ruby is coerced and recruited by the mob and the CIA, who are working together to assassinate Castro. But when Kennedy turns on the Cosa Nostra, they decide instead to have him killed. Ruby, betrayed by the mob, commits his last act in an effort to cast suspicion on the true assassins.

MPAA Rating: R—For language.

Cast

Jack Ruby.......................................Danny Aiello
Candy Cane ....Sherilyn Fenn
Maxwell ....Arliss Howard
Ferrie ....Tobin Bell
Louie Vitali.......................................Joe Cortese
Santos Alicante ....Marc Lawrence
Proby..Richard Sarafian
Sam Giancana ....Carmine Caridi
Officer Tippit.................................David Duchovny
Lee Harvey Oswald.............................Willie Garson
Joseph Valachi ....Joe Viterelli

Credits

Executive Producer...........................Michael Kuhn
Producers ....Sigurjon Sighvatsson
....Steve Golin
Co-Producer..Jay Roewe
Associate Producers.........................Richard Wright
....Lynn Weimer
Director..John Mackenzie
Assistant Director..........................Matthew Carlisle
Director of Photography ....Phil Meheux
Sound ....David Brownlow
Editor ....Richard Trevor
Production Design...........................David Brisbin
Art Direction ....Kenneth A. Hardy
Set Design ....Annie Mei-Ling Tien
Set Decoration ....Lauri Gaffin
Costume Design ....Susie DeSanto
Casting...Johanna Ray
Screenplay ....Stephen Davis
Based on the play "Love Field" by ......Stephen Davis
Music...John Scott

Film Facts

Running Time ....110 minutes
Soundtrack..Intrada
Film ....Deluxe Color
Sound..Dolby Stereo

Run Of The House
(Zoo Prods. Ltd.)

Critics Rating: Not Rated.

Genre: Comedy—Director James M. Felter makes his feature debut with a low-budget comedy about an encounter with a drag queen that turns one family home upside down.

Plot: The film centers on the troubled Felchbaum family. Mr. Felchbaum is a cab driver and the Mrs. is a homemaker suffering from pent-up sexual fantasies. Their niece, Tabby, is a wallflower desperate to bloom. When dear old dad falls for one of his fares, it turns out to be a drag queen on the run. Before long, he invites his new love back to meet the family, and that's when the real fun begins.

MPAA Rating: Not Rated.

Cast

Sady	Craig Alan Edwards
Tabby	Lisa-Marie Felter
Issy Felchbaum	Harry A. Winter
Barb Felchbaum	Susan Lynn Ross

Credits

Producer	Janice Holland
Director	James M. Felter
Director of Photography	Paul Ygelisias
Sound	Pauly Laurito
Editors	James M. Felter
	Rachel Sergi
Production Design	William Bordac
	Scott Simms
Written by	James M. Felter
Music	Russell Young

Film Facts

Running Time	109 minutes
Film	Color
Sound	Stereo

The Runestone

(Hyperion Pictures/Signature Communications)

Critics Rating: Not Rated.

Genre: Thriller—Murder and mayhem are unleashed on an unsuspecting New York City population in this sci-fi thriller when an archeological foundation takes possession of an enigmatic stone.

Plot: The mayhem is a result of an ancient and evil monster that has been unleashed by modern day scientists and is stalking the streets. Joan Severance and Tim Ryan play a husband and wife who are caught—along with Peter Riegert, a local cop—in the middle of this terror.

MPAA Rating: R

Cast

Capt. Gregory Fancucci	Peter Riegert
Marla Stewart	Joan Severance
Sigvaldson	Alexander Godunov
Lars Hagstrom	William Hickey
Sam	Tim Ryan
Martin Almquist	Mitchell Lawrence
Chief Richardson	Lawrence Tierney
Jacob	Chris Young

Credits

Executive Producers	Peter Strauss
	Frank Giustra
Producers	Harry E. Gould, Jr.
	Thomas L. Wilhite
Co-Producer	Joe-Michael Terry
Line Producer	David R. Cobb
Associate Producers	Maria C. Schaeffer
	Greg Everage
	Vicki Ellis
Director	Willard Carroll
Assistant Director	Phil Robinson
Director of Photography	Misha Suslov
Sound	Tony Smyles
Editor	Lynne Southerland
Production Design	Jon Gary Steele
Art Direction	Stella Wange
Costume Design	Terry Dresbach
Casting	Kevin Alber
	Jon Robert Samsel
Screenplay	Willard Carroll
Based on a novella by	Mark E. Rogers
Music	David Newman
Special Effects Makeup by	Lance Anderson
Special Visual Effects	Max W. Anderson

Film Facts

Running Time	98 minutes
Film	Color
Sound	Ultra-Stereo

Costume Design ....Stephen Chudey
Casting ....Linda Francis
Screenplay ....John Golden, Stephen LaRocque
Music ....Joel McNeely

Film Facts
Running Time ....100 minutes
Film...CFI Color
Sound...Ultra-Stereo

Samantha
(Academy Entertainment)

Critics Rating: Not Rated.
Genre: Comedy—An uneven bizarre and quirky dark comedy.
Plot: Martha Plimpton plays Samantha, an obnoxious, immature, self-indulgent 21-year-old woman who learns that she was adopted as an infant. The news has a profound effect on the woman and helps explain her unusual childhood. In her search for her biological parents, she manages to alienate and abuse those closest to her, including her adopted parents (Elizondo and Place) and her boyfriend (Mulroney).
MPAA Rating: PG

Cast
Samantha ....Martha Plimpton
Henry ....Dermot Mulroney
Walter...Hector Elizondo
Marilyn...Mary Kay Place
Elaine ....Ione Skye
Milos ....Marvin Silbersher
Father O'Rourke...................................I. M. Hobson
Mrs. Schtumer.......................................Bea Marcus
Also with Maryedith Burrell, Dody Goodman and Robert Picardo.

Credits
Executive Producers..........................Martin F. Gold
....Alan Somers
Producer ....Donald P. Borchers
Director...................................Stephen LaRocque
Assistant Director.................................Kris Krengle
Director of Photography........................Joey Forsyte
Sound ....Stewart Pearce
Editor..Lisa Churgin
Production Design........................Dorian Vernacchio
....Deborah Raymond

Sarafina!
(Buena Vista)

Critics Rating: ★★★
Genre: Musical—Based on Mbongeni Ngema's 1988 Broadway hit musical, *Sarafina!* is an imaginative, musical drama about the plight of blacks living under apartheid in South Africa.
Tag Line: "She was their teacher. They were her hope."
Plot: Filmed on location in the township of Soweto, the black struggle, horror and violence that took place in the '70s and '80s are seen through the eyes of Sarafina, played by Leleti Khumalo. Whoopi Goldberg plays a teacher and activist who inspires Sarafina and her other students to have hope and to persist in their struggles.
MPAA Rating: PG-13—For scenes of apartheid-driven violence.
Trivia: Khumalo was nominated for a Tony Award for her performance in the role on Broadway.

Cast
School teacher ....Whoopi Goldberg
Sarafina's mother..............................Miriam Makeba
Sarafina...Leleti Khumalo
Also with John Kani, Mbongeni Ngema and Sipho Kunen.

Credits
Executive Producers...........................Kirk D'Amico
..........Sudhir Pragjee, Helena Spring, Sanjeev Singh
Producer..Anant Singh
Producer (BBC) ....David Thompson
Director ....Darrell James Roodt
Director of Photography........................Mark Vicente
Editors ....Peter Hollywood, Sarah Thomas
Production Design................................David Barkham
Written by......William Nicholson, Mbongeni Ngema
Based on the play by ....Mbongeni Ngema

Music/Lyrics....................................Mbongeni Ngema
Additional Songs...............................Hugh Masekela
Music Score.......................................Stanley Myers
Choreography.....................................Michael Peters
....Mbongeni Ngema

Film Facts
Country of Origin.................................South Africa/
....United Kingdom/France
Running Time ....115 minutes
Soundtrack.....................................Qwest Records
Film...Color
Sound.......................................Dolby Stereo
Location ....Soweto, South Africa

Satan
(Satana)
(Russimpex Film)

Critics Rating: Not Rated.
Genre: Thriller—The Satan of this graphically chilling Soviet thriller is not only a sociopath bent on revenge, but the Soviet system itself.
Plot: Sergei Kupriyanov plays Vitali, a handsome and calculating young man who is one day rejected by his married lover. His lover, Aljona (Svetlana Bragarnik), holds a high ranking Soviet position. Seeking revenge, Vitali kidnaps Aljona's daughter and demands a ransom. He alone is aware that she has embezzled funds from her Party. When she discovers that he has murdered her daughter, he coldly invites her to turn him in and have her own crime exposed.
MPAA Rating: Not Rated.

Cast
Vitali ....Sergei Kupriyanov
Aljona.................................Svetlana Bragarnik
Aljona's husband................Veniamin Malotschevski
Armen ....Armen Nasikjan
Vera..Maria Averbach
Also with Margarita Alekseva, Anatoli Aristov, Anna Sagalovitch, Zhanna Schipkova and Mikhail Staroduboz.

Credits
Producers.................................Sergei Avrutin
....Valentina Goroschnikova
Director......................................Viktor Aristov
Assistant Director ....L. Schumjatchev

Director of Photography ....Juri Voronzov
Sound ....Nikolai Astachov
Editor...J. Vigdorshik
Production Manager ....G. Matjuschin
Production Design ....Vladimir Bannykh
Screenplay ....Viktor Aristov
Music ....Arkady Gagulaschvili

Film Facts
Country of Origin ....Soviet Union
Running Time ....106 minutes
Film..Sovcolor
Sound ....Stereo

Save And Protect
(Spasi I Sokhrani)
(International Film Circuit)

Critics Rating: Not Rated.
Genre: Drama—Soviet director Aleksandr Sokurov's sexual extravaganza contrasts a passion for life with the everyday struggles to survive.
Plot: Set in a nondescript, disease-ridden Soviet village, a bored and aging housewife begins a search for meaning in her life through an endless series of sexual encounters. She has affairs with both students and shopkeepers alike, and still she is unable to find meaning and happiness. She eventually loses her passion as well.
MPAA Rating: Not Rated.

Cast
With Daria Chpalikova, Viatcheslav Rogovoi, Aleksandr Tcherednik, Robert Vaab and Cecile Zervoudaki.

Credits
Director ....Aleksandr Sokurov
Director of Photography ....Sergei Yurisditski
Production Design ....Elena Amachinskaia
Screenplay ....Yuri Arabov
Based on the novel *Madame Bovary* by ....Gustave Flaubert
Music..Yuri Khanine

Film Facts
Country of Origin ....Soviet Union
Running Time ....165 minutes
Film...Color
Sound ....Stereo

Scent Of A Woman
(Universal)

Critics Rating: ★★★

Genre: Drama—Many critics described this film as *Dead Poets Society* meets *Rain Man*.

Tag Line: "Col. Frank Slade has a very special plan for the weekend. It involves travel, women, good food, fine wine, the tango, chauffeured limousines and a loaded forty-five. And he's bringing Charlie along for the ride."

Plot: In this morality tale, Al Pacino stars as Lt. Col. Frank Slade, a bitter, belligerent and blind veteran who lives with his niece's family in New England. To compensate for his disability he has become incredibly intuitive and psychologically astute. His abrupt and abrasive personality comes naturally. The family wants to go away for the Thanksgiving holiday. Franks niece hires Charlie (ODonnell, *School Ties*), a local prep school student, to look after him for the long weekend and keep him away from the bottle. Unbeknownst to Charlie, Frank has other plans. Taking Charlie to New York City, Frank plans to end it all after indulging in a blow-out, farewell weekend. Before the weekend is through, however, the two unlikely and very different men have helped one another confront the difficult life decisions they both face.

MPAA Rating: R—For language.

Cast
Lt. Col. Frank Slade	Al Pacino
Charlie Simms	Chris O'Donnell
Mr. Trask	James Rebhorn
Donna	Gabrielle Anwar
George Willis, Jr.	Philip S. Hoffman
W. R. Slade	Richard Venture
Randy	Bradley Whitford
Officer Gore	Ron Eldard
Christine Downes	Frances Conroy
Karen Rossi	Sally Murphy
Harry Havemeyer	Nicholas Sadler
Manny	Gene Canfield
Gretchen	Rochelle Oliver
Gail	Margaret Eginton
Garry	Tom Ris Farrell

Credits
Executive Producer	Ronald L. Schwary
Producer/Director	Martin Brest
Associate Producer	G. Mac Brown
Assistant Director	Amy Sayres
Director of Photography	Donald E. Thorin
Sound	Danny Michael
Editors	William Steinkamp
	Michael Tronick
	Harvey Rosenstock
Production Design	Angelo Graham
Art Direction	W. Steven Graham
Set Decoration	George DeTitta, Jr.
Costume Design	Aude Bronson-Howard
Casting	Ellen Lewis
Screenplay	Bo Goldman
Suggested by the film "Profumo Di Donna" by	Dino Risi
"Profumo Di Donna" Written by	Ruggero Maccari
	Dino Risi
Based on the novel *Il Buio E Il Miele* by	Giovanni Arpino
Music	Thomas Newman

Film Facts
Running Time	157 minutes
Soundtrack	MCA Records
Film	DuArt Color
Sound	Dolby Stereo
Location	New York

School Ties
(Paramount)

Critics Rating: ★★★

Genre: Drama—A tale of anti-Semitism at an Eastern prep school set in the 1950s. The film has many similarities to *Dead Poets Society* and *The Lords Of Discipline*.

Tag Line: "Just because you're accepted doesn't mean you belong."

Plot: Brendan Fraser (*Encino Man*) stars as David Greene, a high-school star quarterback from Scranton, Pennsylvania who is offered a scholarship to St. Matthew's, an elite, all-male boarding school. Advised to hide his Jewish heritage, he succeeds in fitting in, passing as a non-Jew even when it means denying his true self. When he is eventually exposed by a team rival named Dillon (Damon), he is ostracized and left alone to deal with anti-Semitic attacks. Just when things look as if they couldn't get any worse, he is set up as a scapegoat once again, by Dillon and the other students.

MPAA Rating: PG-13—For language. Contains male nudity.

Cast

David Greene	Brendan Fraser
Charlie Dillon	Matt Damon
Sally Wheeler	Amy Locane
Chris Reece	Chris O'Donnell
Rip Van Kelt	Randall Batinkoff
Jack Connors	Cole Hauser
McGivern	Andrew Lowery
Chesty Smith	Ben Affleck
McGoo	Anthony Rapp
Dr. Bartram	Peter Donat
Cleary	Zeljko Ivanek
Coach McDevitt	Kevin Tighe
Mr. Gierasch	Michael Higgins
Alan Greene	Ed Lauter

Credits

Executive Producer	Danton Rissner
Producers	Stanley R. Jaffe
	Sherry Lansing
Associate Producer	Michael Tadross
Director	Robert Mandel
Assistant Directors	Steve Danton
	Newton D. Arnold
2nd Unit Director	Buddy Joe Hooker
Director of Photography	Freddie Francis
Sound	Keith Wester
Editors	Jerry Greenberg
	Jacqueline Cambas
Production Design	Jeannine Claudia Oppewall
Art Direction	Steven Wolff
Set Decoration	Rosemary Brandenburg
Set Design	Marc Fisichella
Costume Design	Ann Roth
Casting	Pat McCorkle
	Lisa Beach
Screenplay	Dick Wolf
	Darryl Ponicsan
Story by	Dick Wolf
Music	Maurice Jarre
Stunt Coordinator	Buddy Joe Hooker

Film Facts

Running Time	107 minutes
Soundtrack	Big Screen Records
Film	Technicolor
Sound	Dolby Stereo
Location	Massachusettes; Pennsylvania

Secret Friends
(Briarpatch Films)

Critics Rating: Not Rated.

Genre: Drama—Abstract, bizarre and absurd best describe this film about a near-schizophrenic artist.

Plot: Alan Bates is the bright spot in this film. He portrays John, an illustrator who one day finds himself on a train with no knowledge of who he is, how he got there, or where he is going. This could be a metaphor for the film as well.

MPAA Rating: Not Rated.

Cast

John	Alan Bates
Helen	Gina Bellman
Angela	Frances Barber
Martin	Tony Doyle
Kate	Joanna David
First businessman	Ian McNeice
Second businessman	Davyd Harries

Also with Rowena Cooper and Colin Jeavons.

Credits

Executive Producers	Robert Michael Geisler
	John Roberdeau
Producer	Rosemarie Whitman
Associate Producer	Alison Barnett
Director	Dennis Potter
Assistant Director	Edward Brett
Director of Photography	Sue Gibson
Sound	John Midgley
Editor	Clare Douglas
Production Design	Gary Williamson
Art Direction	Sarah Horton
Costume Design	Sharon Lewis
Casting	Kathleen Mackie
Written by	Dennis Potter
Suggested by the novel *Ticket To Ride* by	Dennis Potter
Music	Nicholas Russell-Pavier

Film Facts

Running Time	97 minutes
Film	Metrocolor
Sound	Dolby Stereo
Location	London; Kent, England

Shadows And Fog
(Orion)

Critics Rating: ★★★

Genre: Comedy—Woody Allen's black and white comedy-drama boasts a stellar cast of big-name stars and tackles such heavy topics as the meaning of life, good and evil, and belief and nonbelief. Allen fans will find this philosophical film to be one of his more dark and ponderous works. The terrific ensemble cast is the brightest spot of the film.

Plot: Set in 1920s Germany, Allen stars as Kleinman, a "Kafkaesque" clerk who is chosen to help capture a murderer. As always, he is the re-luctant character sent out into the world. While his search for a lunatic is the catalyst that begins his journey, his encounters with a colorful group of performers in a circus, a mad doctor and a group of whores along the way make it possible for him to find himself.

MPAA Rating: PG-13

Cast
Kleinman	Woody Allen
Irmy	Mia Farrow
Clown	John Malkovich
Marie	Madonna
Doctor	Donald Pleasance
Prostitute	Lily Tomlin
Prostitute	Jodie Foster
Prositute	Kathy Bates
Student Jack	John Cusack
Eva	Kate Nelligan
Hacker's follower	Fred Gwynne
Alma	Julie Kavner
Magician	Kenneth Mars
Hacker	David Ogden Stiers
Mr. Paulsen	Philip Bosco
Priest	Josef Sommer
Vogel's follower	Kurtwood Smith
Hacker's follower	Robert Silver

Also with Eszter Balint, Robert Joy and Wallace Shawn.

Credits
Executive Producer	Robert Greenhut
Producers	Jack Rollins, Charles H. Joffe
Co-Producers	Helen Robin, Joseph Hartwick
Associate Producer	Thomas Reilly
Director	Woody Allen
Assistant Director	Thomas Reilly
Director of Photography	Carlos DiPalma
Sound	James Sabat
Editor	Susan E. Morse
Production Design	Santo Loquasto
Art Direction	Speed Hopkins
Set Decoration	George DeTitta, Jr.
	Amy Marshall
Costume Design	Jeffrey Kurland
Casting	Juliet Taylor
Written by	Woody Allen
Music	Kurt Weill

Film Facts
Running Time	86 minutes
Film	Black & White
Sound	Dolby Stereo
Location	New York

Shakes The Clown
(I.R.S. Releasing)

Critics Rating: Not Rated.

Genre: Comedy—Comedian Bobcat Goldthwait makes his directorial debut with this offbeat comedy about clowns on the skids. One reviewer described it as "The *Citizen Kane* of alcoholic-clown films."

Plot: Goldthwait stars as Shakes, an alcoholic clown who has been framed by a rival clown named Binky (Tom Kenny) for murder. The story takes place in a town called Palukaville, where all the residents are depressed and desperate clowns. While the humor is often zany and twisted, the story is just as often dark and intense.

When the film debuted early in the year, it sparked a controversy among parents, who objected to portraying characters that children look up to as deadbeats and alcoholics. Real-life clowns also objected to the portrayal.

MPAA Rating: R—For language and drug use.

Cast
Shakes the Clown	Bobcat Goldthwait
Judy	Julie Brown
Stenchy the Clown	Blake Clark
Jerry the Mime	Marty Fromage (Robin Williams)
Dink the Clown	Adam Sandler

Binky...Tom Kenny
Lucy ....Kathy Griffin
Owen Cheese ....Paul Dooley
Ty the Rodeo Clown.........................Bruce Baum
Officer Crony.................................Jack Gallagher
The unknown woman.................Florence Henderson
Hoho the Clown ....Paul Kozlowski
Detective Boar.........................Jeremy S. Kramer
Female clown barfly........................La Wanda Page
Boots the Clown............................Dan Spencer
Randi the Rodeo Clown ....Greg Travis
Dirthead in car................................Tom Villard
Male clown barfly ....Martin Charles Warner

Credits

Executive Producers.................Miles A. Copeland III
.................................Barry Krost, Harold Welb
Producers.......................Ann Luly, Paul Colichman
Line Producer...........................Michael Bennett
Associate Producers ....Melissa Cobb
....Steven Reich
Director.............................Bobcat Goldthwait
Assistant Director.........................Matthew Clark
Directors of Photography ....Elliot Davis
....Bobby Bukowski
Sound....................................Giovanni Di Simone
Editor..............................J. Kathleen Gibson
Production Design ....Pamela Woodbridge
Costume Design...........................Stephen Chudej
Casting......................................Don Pemrick
Written by.................................Bobcat Goldthwait
Music......................................Tom Scott

Film Facts

Running Time ....86 minutes
Film ....Foto-Kem Color
Sound....................................Dolby Stereo

Shaking The Tree
(Castle Hill)

Critics Rating: Not Rated.

Genre: Drama—The film follows the very different life directions of four high school buddies from Chicago 10 years after graduation.

Tag Line: "They're all looking for adventure, romance, happiness, friendship, success. But they'll settle for great sex."

Plot: Taking place in 1989, Steven Wilde plays lead character, Duke, a bartender with big

ambitions. His friends are Barry (Arye Gross), a real-estate broker, Sully (Gale Hansen), a gambler and an alcoholic, and Michael (Doug Savant), a struggling writer. The story is simply one of friends who are there for each other through the good and the bad as they make their way and their place in the world.

MPAA Rating: PG-13—Film was edited afted receiving an initial "R" rating.

Cast

Barry Goldberg...............................Arye Gross
John "Sully" Sullivan.............................Gale Hansen
Michael Thatcher ....Doug Savant
Terry "Duke" Keegan ....Steven Wilde
Kathleen Thatcher ....Courteney Cox
Nickel.......................................Michael Arabian
Grandpa Sullivan ....Nathan Davis
Duke's father ....Ron Dean
Michelle ....Christina Haag
The student ....Brittney Hansen
Bridgette ....Kristin Messner
Mr. Jack......................................Ned Schmidtke
Tony Villanova ....Mick Scriba
Richie......................................Joey Tomaska

Credits

Executive Producers..................Anthony J. Tomaska
.................................Richard Wagstaff
Producer....................................Robert J. Wilson
Director.......................................Duane Clark
Assistant Director................................Kris Krengel
Director of Photography ....Ronn Schmidt
Sound Mixer..................................Hans Roland
Editor.................................Martin L. Bernstein
Production Design ....Sean Mannion
Costume Design....................Susan Michel Kaufman
Casting.......................................Eddie Foy III
Written by.......................Steven Wilde, Duane Clark
Music ....David E. Russo

Film Facts

Film ....Color
Sound.......................................Ultra-Stereo

Shining Through
(20th Century Fox)

Critics Rating: ★★★

Genre: Drama—An old-fashioned, big-budget

Hollywood spy drama that takes place during World War II.

Plot: Melanie Griffith stars as Linda, a secretary who falls head-over-heels for her boss, Ed Leland, played by Michael Douglas. Ed as it turns out, is actually a spy who must sabotage the Germans before they complete a top-secret bomb. The best way to accomplish this task it seems is for Linda to infiltrate the enemy camp as a spy. This of course sets the scene for the predictable yet engaging action and drama that follow.

MPAA Rating: R—For language.

Cast

Ed Leland	Michael Douglas
Linda Voss	Melanie Griffith
Franze-Otto Dietrich	Liam Neeson
Margrete Von Eberstein	Joely Richardson
Sunflower	John Gielgud
Andrew Berringer	Francis Guinan
Fishmonger	Patrick Winczewski

Credits

Executive Producers	Sandy Gallin
	David Seltzer
Producers	Howard Rosenman
	Carol Baum
Co-Producer	Nigel Wooll
Director	David Seltzer
2nd Unit Director	Peter MacDonald
Assistant Director	Don French
Director of Photography	Jan De Bont
Sound	Ivan Sharrock
Editor	Craig McKay
Production Design	Anthony Pratt
Art Direction	Desmond Crowe
	Kevin Phipps
Set Decoration	Peter Howitt
Costume Design	Marit Allen
Casting	Simone Reynolds
	Mary Gail Artz, Barbara Cohen
Screenplay	David Seltzer
Based on the novel by	Susan Isaacs
Music	Michael Kamen
Special Effects Supervisor	Richard Conway

Film Facts

Running Time	127 minutes
Soundtrack	RCA Records
Film	Rank Film Laboratories Color
Sound	Dolby Stereo
Location	Berlin; England

The Silk Road
(Dun-Huang)
(Trimark)

Critics Rating: Not Rated.

Genre: Drama—Based upon the prize-winning novel *Dun Huang* by Yasushi Inoue, this epic tale of romance and warfare in ancient China unfolds like the Adian equivalent of a classic Hollywood adventure film,—like *Ivanhoe* or *The Black Rose*.

Plot: Koichi Sato stars as a scholarly young man who by circumstance finds himself caught in the middle of the war-torn Song Dynasty in the 11th century. As fate would have it, he finds that through all of his ordeals he is the one who must save the precious scrolls, the priceless record of Chinese culture from the destruction of war. Living up to his duty he hides the treasure in the Thousand Budda Cave. In 1900 the documents were discovered and it became one of the most important archeological finds of the 20th Century.

MPAA Rating: PG-13

Trivia: Koichi Sato who stars as Zhao Xingde is the son of famed Japanese actor Rentaro Mikuni (*Night Drum, Rikyu*). Sato made his debut in the 1981 film *The Gate Of Youth*.

Cast

Zhu Wangli	Toshiyuki Nishida
Zhao Xingde	Koichi Sato
Princess Tsurpia	Anna Nakagawa
Weichi Kuang	Daijiro Harada
Li Yuanhao	Tsunehiko Watase
Tsao Yanhui	Takahiro Tamura
Woman of Xixia	Yoshiko Mita

Credits

Executive Producers	Yasuyoshi Tokuma
	Gohei Kogure, Kazuo Haruna
Producers	Atsushi Takeda
	Yuzo Irie
Assistant Producers	Yo Tamamoto
	Shigeru Mori, Shingo Mori
Special Producers	Yoshihiro Yuki
	Ma Wang Liang, Masahiro Sato
Director	Junya Sato
Director of Photography	Akira Shizuka
Sound	Yasuo Hashimoto
Editor	Akira Suzuki
Art Direction	Hiroshi Tokuda

Screenplay	Junya Sato
	Tsuyoshi Yoshida
Based on the novel by	Yasushi Inoue
Music	Masaru Sato
Lighting	Shigeru Umetani
Prologue by	Saul Bass
	Elaine Bass
Title Calligraphy	Shunkei Iijima

Film Facts

Country of Origin	Japan
Running Time	126 minutes
Film	Color
Sound	Stereo
Location	China

Simple Men
(Fine Line)

Critics Rating: ★★★

Genre: Comedy—An offbeat comedy-drama about two brothers and their search for a father who is hiding out from the law. The story is really about their adventure and the quirky characters they meet along the way.

Plot: Robert Burke and William Sage play Bill and Dennis, two very different brothers with the same goal. Both men have decided to find their father, a former political radical who is wanted by the federal authorities. The one thing both men have in common is that they have been recently burned by women and are determined not to become emotionally involved again. It doesn't take long, however, before Bill has fallen in love with Kate (Sillas), a woman who runs the local inn where they are staying. Dennis also meets a woman (Lowensohn), but his relationship becomes a bit more complicated, since she is also his father's lover.

MPAA Rating: R—For language.

Cast

Bill McCabe	Robert Burke
Dennis McCabe	William Sage
Kate	Karen Sillas
Elina	Elina Lowensohn
The sheriff	Damian Young
Nun	Vivian Lanko
Martin	Martin Donovan

Mike	Mark Chandler Brailey
Ned Rifle	Jeffrey Howard

Credits

Executive Producers	Jerome Brownstein
	Bruce Weiss
Producers	Ted Hope, Hal Hartley
Director	Hal Hartley
Assistant Director	Greg Jacobs
Director of Photography	Michael Spiller
Sound	Jeff Pullman
Editor	Steve Hamilton
Production Design	Dan Ouellette
Art Direction	Theresa DePrez
Set Decoration	Jeff Hartmann
Costume Design	Alexandra Welker
Casting	Liz Kiegley
Screenplay	Hal Hartley
Music	Ned Rifle

Film Facts

Running Time	104 minutes
Film	Technicolor
Sound	Dolby Stereo

Single White Female
(Columbia)

Critics Rating: ★★★

Genre: Thriller—Director Barbet Schroeder's (*General Idi Amin Dada*, *Reversal Of Fortune*) psychological thriller is a masterwork of style and intelligence. It's hard to say which is more impressive, the first-rate technical credits or the outstanding lead performances—all are award-winning caliber.

Tag Line: "Living with a roommate can be deadly." "How do you lock the terror out, when you've already invited it in?"

Plot: Bridget Fonda plays Allison, a single, upper West Side New York fashion designer. Following a spat with her fiancee, Sam (Steven Weber, *Wings* TV series), she is fearful of living alone and advertises for a roommate. When Ally invites Hedra (Jennifer Jason Leigh), a meek and unassuming young woman, to move in, she has unknowingly opened her door to a monster. Hedra is really a mentally unstable woman who has never stopped blaming herself for her twin sister's death. In Ally she believes she has found her other half. When Ally decides to reconcile with Sam, Hedra begins to unravel at the psychological seams and turns all of their lives into a nightmare.

MPAA Rating: R—For language, violence and strong sexuality. Contains male and female nudity.

Cast

Allison Jones	Bridget Fonda
Hedra Carlson	Jennifer Jason Leigh
Sam Rawson	Steven Weber
Graham Knox	Peter Friedman
Myerson	Stephen Tobolowsky

Credits

Executive Producer	Jack Baran
Producer/Director	Barbet Schroeder
Co-Producer	Roger Joseph Pugliese
Associate Producer	Susan Hoffman
Assistant Director	Jack Baran
Director of Photography	Luciano Tovoli
Sound	Petur Hliddal
Sound Design	Gary Rydstrom
Editor	Lee Percy
Production Design	Milena Canonero
Art Direction	P. Michael Johnston
Set Decoration	Anne H. Ahrens
Casting	Howard Feuer
Screenplay	Don Roos
Based on the novel *SWF Seeks Same* by	John Lutz
Music	Howard Shore

Film Facts

Running Time	107 minutes
Film	Technicolor
Sound	Dolby Stereo
Location	Los Angeles; New York

Singles

(Warner Bros.)

Critics Rating: ★★★

Genre: Comedy—Contemporary romantic comedy about dating in the '90s, set in Seattle.

Plot: The story revolves around a group of singles who live together in the same apartment building. Each has their own story and occasionally they overlap in humorous ways. Kyra Sedgwick plays Linda, a young woman who is determined not to get burned in another romance. Campbell Scott plays Steve, a career-minded young man who doesnt have time for a serious relationship. Nevertheless, they meet and fall in love. At the same time their friends are also going through dating and relationship traumas that are just as painful and funny. This is a twenty- something tale set against the backdrop of Seattle's popular rock scene.

MPAA Rating: PG-13

Cast

Janet Livermore	Bridget Fonda
Steve Dunne	Campbell Scott
Linda Powell	Kyra Sedgwick
Cliff Poncier	Matt Dillon
Debbie Hunt	Sheila Kelley
David Bailey	Jim True
Dr. Jamison	Bill Pullman
Andy	James Le Gros
Ruth	Devon Raymond
Luiz	Camilo Gallardo
Pam	Ally Walker
Mime	Eric Stoltz
Doug Hughley	Jeremy Piven
Mayor Weber	Tom Skerritt
Boston doctor	Bill Smillie

Credits

Executive Producer	Art Linson
Producers	Cameron Crowe
	Richard Hashimoto
Co-Producer	Richard Chew
Associate Producer	Kelly Curtis
Director	Cameron Crowe
Assistant Director	Jerry Ziesmer
2nd Unit Director	Richard Chew
Director of Photography	Ueli Steiger
2nd Unit Camera	Billy O'Drobinak
Sound	Art Rochester
Editor	Richard Chew
Production Design	Stephen Lineweaver
Art Direction	Mark Haack
Set Design	Cosmas Demetriou
Set Decoration	Clay Griffith
Costume Design	Jane Ruhm
Casting	Marion Dougherty
Written by	Cameron Crowe
Music	Paul Westerberg

Film Facts

Running Time	99 minutes
Soundtrack	Epic Soundtrax
Film	Technicolor

Sound ....Dolby Stereo
Location...Seattle

Sister Act
(Buena Vista)

Critics Rating: ★★★
Genre: Comedy—Irreverent and witty, *Sister Act* is a fast-paced formula comedy that is blessed with the divinely outrageous Whoppi Goldberg.
Tag Line: "No Sex. No Booze. No Men. No Way."
Plot: Goldberg stars as Deloris, the lead singer in an all-girl lounge act. Before she can dump her boyfriend, a married man and a mobster, she accidentally walks in on him during a murder. She goes to the police and as part of a witness-protection plan, she is subsequently hidden in a convent. Predictably, casting this sinner in among the saints is a prescription for sure-fire laughs that works.
MPAA Rating: PG-13
Trivia: Singer Mary Wells, who sang Motown's first No. 1 hit "My Guy" died July 26 of cancer. The words "My Guy" were reworded "My God," and became one of the film's highlights.

Cast
Deloris..Whoopi Goldberg
Reverend Mother ....Maggie Smith
Vince LaRocca....................................Harvey Keitel
Lt. Eddie Souther ....Bill Nunn
Sister Mary Lazarus ....Mary Wickes
Sister Mary Robert..........................Wendy Makkena
Sister Mary Patrick ....Kathy Najimy
Willy ....Richard Portnow
Also with Pat Crawford Brown, Susan Browning, Georgia Creighton, Edith Diaz, Ellen Albertini Dow, Beth Fowler, Prudence Wright Holmes, Sherri Izzard, Susan Johnson, Ruth Kobart, Darlene Koldenhoven and Carmen Zapata.

Credits
Executive Producer....................................Scott Rudin
Producer ....Teri Schwartz
Co-Producer.......................................Mario Iscovich
Associate Producer...........................Cindy Gilmore
Director ....Emile Ardolino
Assistant Director ....Joe Camp III
Director of Photography ....Adam Greenberg

Sound ....Darin Knight
Editor ....Richard Halsey
Production Design ....Jackson DeGovia
Assistant Art Direction..............................Eve Cauley
Set Decoration............................Thomas L. Roysden
Set Design.....................Robert M. Beall, Ann Harris
Costume Design................................Molly Maginnis
Casting ....Judy Taylor, Lynda Gordon
....Johnson-Liff & Zerman
Written by ....Joseph Howard
Music ....Marc Shaiman
Musical Numbers Staged by ....Lester Wilson

Film Facts
Running Time ....100 minutes
Soundtrack..................................Hollywood Records
Film..Technicolor
Sound ....Dolby Stereo
Location ....Los Angeles; Reno; San Francisco

Sleeping Beauty
(Gemini Pictures)

Critics Rating: Not Rated.
Genre: Comedy—A straightforward, modern-day comedy about sexual repression.
Plot: Ainsley Kellar stars as Natalie, a sexually repressed wife, in this modern-day fable. Natalie is a file clerk, while husband Tom (Fred Tietz) works for the Sanitation Department. Tom is obsessed with cleanliness and is a bit obsessive. Together their life is neat, sanitized and without much life. Neither having an interest in sharing their lives with children nor having enough time or interest in sex, their lives are a bit passionless. That is, until Natalie wakes up from her dull existence and her sexual urges begin to blossom. Hubby, needless to say, is horrified and confused and spends the remainder of the film trying desperately to cure his wife of her newfound sexuality.
MPAA Rating: Not Rated.

Cast
Natalie...Ainsley Kellar
Tom..Fred Teitz
Betty Smith.........................Dianne Sherwood-Hood
John Smith...................................Edward Prince
Jane Smith ....Kathleen Rudum
Uncle Bob Smith ....Charlie Mahoney

Mule ....David Marks
Credits
Executive Producers ....Francis O'Brien
....Joan Sugerman
Producer ....Ralph Groemping
Associate Producer...............................Willa Taylor
Director...Joan Sugerman
Assistant Director ....Linsey Evans-Thomas
Director of Photography ....Chris Li
Sound...Jim Gilchrist
Editor..Deborah Peretz
Production Design ....Richard Montgomery
Costume Design...............................Paul Tazewell
Screenplay....................................Joan Sugerman
Music ....Cracked Actor
Film Facts
Running Time ....100 minutes
Film...DuArt Color
Sound ....Stereo
Location ....Washington, D. C.

Sneakers
(Universal)

Critics Rating: ★★★
Genre: Drama—A sharp, highly touted, mystery caper.
Tag Line: "A burglar, a spy, a fugitive, a delinquent, a hacker and a piano teacher...and these are the good guys."
Plot: Redford stars as Martin Bishop, a former counterculture radical still wanted on a warrant for computer misdeeds. A high-tech specialist, Bishop runs his own business. He and his team are hired by companies to test the vulnerability of their security systems. One day the National Security Agency shows up with a deal. They are willing to forget his warrant in return for a big favor. The agency wants his team to go undercover and penetrate the ultimate computer security-code decoder.
MPAA Rating: PG-13
Cast
Martin Bishop ....Robert Redford
Mother...Dan Aykroyd
Cosmo ....Ben Kingsley
Liz ....Mary McDonnell
Carl...River Phoenix

Crease..Sidney Poitier
Whistler...David Strathairn
Dick Gordon ....Timothy Busfield
Gregor..George Hearn
Buddy Wallace ....Eddie Jones
Dr. Gunter Janek....................................Donal Logue
Dr. Elena Rhyzkov ....Lee Garlington
Dr. Brandes................................Stephen Tobolowsky
Bernard Abbott.............................James Earl Jones
Cosmo (college-age) ....Jojo Marr
Bishop (college-age) ....Gary Hershberger
Credits
Executive Producer ....Lindsley Parsons, Jr.
Producers ....Walter F. Parkes, Lawrence Lasker
Associate Producer.........................William M. Elvin
Director ....Phil Alden Robinson
Assistant Director......................William M. Elvin
2nd Unit Director.....................Glenn H. Randall, Jr.
Director of Photography ....John Lindley
Sound ....Willie D. Burton
Editor ....Tom Rolf
Production Design.............Patrizia von Brandenstein
Art Direction...Dianne Wager
Set Design.............................James J. Murakami
....Keith B. Burns
Set Decoration........................Samara Schaffer
Costume Design ....Bernie Pollack
Casting ....Risa Bramon Garcia, Juel Bestrop
Written by ....Phil Alden Robinson
....Lawrence Lasker
....Walter F. Parkes
Music ....James Horner
Featuring...Branford Marsalis

Film Facts
Running Time ....121 minutes
Soundtrack ....Columbia Records
Film ....Deluxe Color
Sound ....Dolby Stereo
Location ....San Francisco; Los Angeles

Society
(Zecca Corp.)

Critics Rating: Not Rated.
Genre: Horror—In his directorial debut, the producer of *Re-Animator*, Brian Yuzna, brings to the screen an offbeat tale of horror.

Tag Line: "The rich have always fed off the poor. This time it's for real."

Plot: Billy Warlock stars as Bill Whitney, a popular Beverly Hills Academy senior who believes his family is really a group of aliens who feed off humans. In this simple plot, his investigations lead him to a very slimy and spectacular special-effects climax in an otherwise run-of-the-mill film.

MPAA Rating: R

Cast

Bill Whitney......................................Billy Warlock
Clarisa...Devin DeVasquez
Milo ....Evan Richards
Ferguson ....Ben Meyerson
Dr. Cleveland..................................Ben Slack
Blanchard..Tim Bartell
Also with Connie Danese, Heidi Holm, Charles Lucia, Patrice Jennings and David Wiley.

Credits

Executive in Charge of Production........Dean Ramser
Executive Producers ....Paul White
.................................Keizo Kabata, Terry Ogisu
Producer...Keith Walley
Director...Brian Yuzna
Director of Photography ....Rick Fichter
Sound ....William Fiege
Editor..Peter Teschner
Production Design..........................Mathew C. Jacobs
Art Direction ....Kelle DeForrest
Costume Design ....Robin Lewis
Written by ....Woody Keith, Rick Fry
Music ....Mark Ryder, Phil Davies
Special Makeup Effects Created by...........................
.................................Screaming Mad George
Stunt Coordinator ....Dan Bradley

Film Facts

Running Time ....99 minutes
Film ....Foto-Kem Color
Sound..Ultra-Stereo

South Central
(Warner Bros.)

Critics Rating: ★★★

Genre: Drama—Set in South Central Los Angeles, this is the story of one man's struggle to end the chain of drugs, gangs, violence and death in his own family.

Plot: Glenn Plummer stars as Bobby, a gang leader who is reformed, after having spent 10 years in prison. After being convicted of murder in 1981, Bobby spends his time in prison, studying Muslim teachings. There he learns to turn his life around. When he is released in 1991, he returns to the world he left, only to find his 11-year-old son a member of the gang that helped put Bobby in jail. Determined to save his son, he risks everything and stops at nothing to rescue the young boy from repeating his mistakes.

MPAA Rating: R—For gang violence, language and drug content.

Trivia: Following just four months on the heels of the Los Angeles riots, Warner Bros. decided to open the film in cities around the country, not in Los Angeles to avoid any potential controversy.

Cast

Bobby Johnson ....Glenn Plummer
Ray Ray ....Byron Keith Minns
Bear ....Lexie D. Bigham
Loco..Vincent Craig Dupree
Carole...LaRita Shelby
Genie Lamp....................................Kevin Best
Baby Jimmie ....Allan Hatcher, Alvin Hatcher
Jimmie (age 10) ....Christian Coleman
Willie Manchester.........................Ivory Ocean
Nurse Shelly..................................Starletta Dupois
Ali...Carl Lumbly

Credits

Executive Producer ....Oliver Stone
Co-Executive Producers ....Michael Spielberg
.................................Brad Gilbert
Producers...............Janet Yang, William B. Steakley
Co-Producer...................................Steve Anderson
Line Producer................................Lowell D. Blank
Director...Steve Anderson
Assistant Director..........................Phillip Christon
Director of Photography...............Charlie Lieberman
Sound ....Michael Florimbi
.................................Rick Ash, Dean Zupancic
Editor ....Steve Nevius
Production Design..........................David Brian Miller
.................................Marina Kieser
Art Direction ....Andrew D. Brothers
Set Decoration ....Caroline Stover
Costume Design.............................Mary Law Weir
Casting ....Jaki Brown
Written by......................................Steve Anderson

Based on the novel *Crips* by ....Donald Bakeer
Music ....Tim Truman
Stunt Coordinator ....Julius LeFlore

Film Facts
Running Time ....99 minutes
Soundtrack ....Hollywood Basic
Film ....Deluxe Color
Sound ....Dolby Stereo

Split Second
(Interstar Releasing)

Critics Rating: ★

Genre: Horror—There is a murderous creature on the loose in London, in this low-budget, science-fiction horror tale set in the year 2008.

Tag Line: "He's seen the future. Now he has to kill it."

Plot: Rutger Hauer (*Buffy The Vampire Slayer*) stars as Harley Stone, the cop assigned to track down the murderer. The monster is killing its victims as part of a satanic ritual, it seems, and leaving plenty of clues. Overall, the predictable story leads to a predictable climax.

MPAA Rating: R—For gore and language.

Cast
Harley Stone..................................Rutger Hauer
Michelle ....Kim Cattrall
Dick Durkin ....Neil Duncan
Rat Catcher ....Michael J. Pollard
Thrasher..................................Alun Armstrong
Jay Jay..Ian Dury
Robin..Roberta Eaton
Paulsen..............................Pete Postlethwaite
O'Donnell ....Tony Steedman

Credits
Executive in Charge of Production.....Susan Nicoletti
Executive Producers ....Keith Cavele
....Chris Hanley
Producer ....Laura Gregory
Line Producer ....Laurie Borg
Associate Producer..................Gary Scott Thompson
Director ....Tony Maylam
Director (Subway train/Additional
  Sequences ....Ian Sharp
Assistant Director ....Ray Corbett
2nd Unit Director/Camera..............Arthur Wooster
Director of Photography ....Clive Tickner

Sound ....Peter Glossop
Editor..Dan Rae
Production Design........................Chris Edwards
Costume Design ....Antoinette Gregory
Casting (U.K.)................................John Hubbard
....Ros Hubbard
Casting (U.S.)..............................Linda Francis
Written by..........................Gary Scott Thompson
Music Coordinators ....Chris Hanley
....Roberta Eaton
Music ....Stephen Parsons
....Francis Haines
Special Effects....................Ace Effects Ltd.
Creature Effects ....Stephen Norrington
....Kate Murray
....Ian Morce
....Cliff Wallace
Stunt Coordinator......................Colin Skeaping
Rat/Pigeon Wrangler....................David Corke

Film Facts
Country of Origin ....Great Britain
Running Time ....91 minutes
Soundtrack ....Milan-America Records
Film ....Metrocolor
Sound ....Dolby Stereo
Location ....London

The Station
(La Stazione)
(Aries)

Critics Rating: Not Rated.

Genre: Thriller—A small, but charming Italian story with subtitles about a simple man whose life is turned upside down by a beautiful and troubled young woman who briefly enters his life.

Plot: Director-actor Sergio Rubini plays Domenico, stationmaster at a train station in Italy. Bored out of his mind, he spends his free time timing how long it takes coffee to brew. One night a beautiful woman arrives at the station. Bringing a moment of joy to Domenico's life, she also brings her emotional baggage and troubled past.

MPAA Rating: Not Rated.

Cast
Domenico ....Sergio Rubini
Flavia..Margherita Buy
Danilo ....Ennio Fantastichini

Credits

Producer ....Domenico Procacci
Director..Sergio Rubini
Director of Photography ....Alessio Gelsini
Editor...Angelo Nicolini
Art Direction.................................Carolina Ferrara
....Luca Gobbi
Written by ....Umberto Marino
....Gianfilippo Ascione
....Sergio Rubini
Based on the play by ....Umberto Marino

Film Facts

Country of Origin ....Italy
Language...............................Italian (subtitled)
Running Time ....92 minutes
Film ....Color

Stay Tuned
(Warner Bros.)

Critics Rating: Not Rated.
Genre: Comedy—An imaginative and original satirical send up of television. This is essentially *The Running Man* played for laughs.
Tag Line: "Something weird's on the air. The Knables signed up for a cable system that's out of this world. A comedy adventure on the wrong side of the screen."
Plot: John Ritter plays Roy Knable, an underachieving couch potato. Pam Dawber plays his overachieving wife Helen. When Roy is offered an opportunity to try out a super 666-channel TV by an "evil" TV salesman (Jeffrey Jones), he sees this as an opportunity of a lifetime. What Roy doesn't realize is that he has sold his soul to the television devil. Sucked into the satellite dish in the backyard, Roy and Helen find themselves trapped in television hell. They must survive a series of deadly shows for 24 hours in order to go free. The shows have names like, "3 Men And Rosemary's Baby," Autopsies Of The Rich And Famous" and "Sadistic Hidden Video," to name a few.
MPAA Rating: PG

Cast

Roy Knable..John Ritter
Helen Knable ....Pam Dawber
Spike...Jeffrey Jones
Crowley ....Eugene Levy
Darryl Knable ....David Tom
Diane Knable ....Heather McComb
Murray Seidenbaum ....Bob Dishy
Mrs. Seidenbaum...........................Joyce Gordon
Pierce ....Eric King

Credits

Executive Producers ......Gary Barber, David Nicksay
Producer.....................................James G. Robinson
Co-Producer.....................................Arne Schmidt
Director..Peter Hyams
Assistant Director..............................Jack Sanders
Director of Photography ....Peter Hyams
Sound ....Ralph Parker
Editor ....Peter E. Berger
Production Design..............................Philip Harrison
Art Direction ....Richard Hudolin
....David Wilson
Set Decoration.........................Rose Marie McSherry
....Daniel Bradette
.............................Lin MacDonald, Annmarie Corbert
Costume Design ....Joe Thompkins
Casting..Lynn Stalmaster
Casting (Vancouver)..........................Michelle Allen
Casting (Toronto) ....Karen Hazzard
Screenplay ....Tom S. Parker, Jim Jennewein
Story by...Tom S. Parker
...............................Jim Jennewein, Richard Siegel
Music...Bruce Broughton
Animation Supervisor ....Chuck Jones
Animation Co-Supervisor ....Jeffrey DeGrandis
Visual Effects ....Rhythm & Hues
Visual Effects Supervisor ....John Nelson
Stunt Coordinator ....Gary Combs

Film Facts

Running Time ....82 minutes
Soundtrack............................Morgan Creek Records
Film ....Alpha Cine Color
Sound ....Dolby Stereo
Location.......................Vancouver, British Columbia

Steal America
(Tara)

Critics Rating: Not Rated.
Genre: Drama—An offbeat, low-budget, black-and-white drama about three illegal European immigrants in search of the American Dream. Unable to find it, they steal it.

Plot: Charlie Homo stars as Christophe, a parking lot attendant. His girlfriend Stella (Clara Bellino) works in a postcard shop. Christophe is attracted to Maria (Diviana Ingravallo), a coworker, while Stella is attracted to Jack (Kevin Haley), a regular customer. Christophe and Stella are dissatisfied with one another and with their own lives. When Christophe is fired from his job, he steals a car and picks up Stella. She, in turn, steals money from the shop, and together with Maria, they head off across the country in search of the their dreams and themselves.

MPAA Rating: Not Rated.

Cast

Stella	Clara Bellino
Christophe	Charlie Homo
Maria Maddelena	Diviana Ingravallo
Jack	Kevin Haley
Mickey	Liza Monjauze
Ace	Christopher Fisher

Credits

Executive Producers	Susan O'Connell
	Patricia Marshall
Producers	Liz Gazzanno, Lucy Phillips
Associate Producer	Patsy Shorr
Director	Lucy Phillips
Assistant Director	Liz Gazzano
Directors of Photography	Jim Barrett
	Glen Scantlebury
Editor	Glen Scantlebury
Production Manager	Liz Gazzano
Written by	Lucy Phillips, Glen Scantlebury
Music	Gregory Jones

Film Facts

Running Time	84 minutes
Film	Black & White
Sound	Stereo

Steeper And Deeper

(Warren Miller Entertainment)

Critics Rating: Not Rated.
Genre: Adventure
Plot: In his 43rd feature, Warren Miller, "King of the Sports Filmmakers," as he has been called, spans the globe to bring to the screen his annual ski spectacular.

From the slopes of Chile's new Valle Nevado resort to Mt. Buller in Australia, the locations are breathtaking and often treacherous. Whether the action focuses on snowboarders dropped from a helicopter into the Canadian mountains or the hilarious "Dummy Downhill" skiers, the action is nonstop and action-packed.

MPAA Rating: Not Rated.

Credits

Producers	Kurt Miller
	Peter Speek
Associate Producer	Max Bervy, Jr.
Director	Don Brolin
Principal Photography	Bill Heath
	Gary Nate
	Brian Sisselman
Editors	Katie Hedrick
	Kim Schneider
Written/Narrated by	Warren Miller
Original Music Score	Michael Gurley
	Billy Lincoln

Film Facts

Running Time	90 minutes
Soundtrack	I.R.S. Records
Film	Color
Sound	Stereo
Location	Australia; British Columbia; California
	Colorado; Chile; Idaho; Montana; New York
	Turkey; New Mexico; Hawaii; Japan; Vermont
	Pennsylvania; Switzerland; Utah

Step Across The Border

(Pro Helvetica)

Critics Rating: Not Rated.
Genre: Documentary—A film about an avant-garde British blues musician filmed in black and white.
Plot: The film, like the music, is unconventional. Following a band on tour through rehearsals and concerts, and through interviews, an unusual style of music is revealed.

MPAA Rating: Not Rated.

Cast
With Robert Frank, Jolia Judge, Jonas Mekas and Ted Milton.

Credits

Directors	Nicolas Humbert, Werner Penzel

Director of Photography ....Oscar Saigodo
Sound ....Jean Vapeur
Editor...Gisela Castronari
Written by..............Nicolas Humbert, Werner Penzel
Music...Fred Frith
.........................Joey Baron, Ciro Batista, Iva Bitova

Film Facts
Country of Origin ....Germany/Switzerland
Running Time ....90 minutes
Film...Black & White
Sound ....Stereo

Stephen King's Sleepwalkers
(Columbia)

Critics Rating: Not Rated.
Genre: Horror—Stephen King's first horror tale written directly for the screen is a quirky variation on the vampire theme.
Plot: Alice Krige (*See You In The Morning*) and Brian Krause (*Return To The Blue Lagoon*) star as modern-day mother-and-son vampires of sorts, who also happen to be lovers. Cats apparently are the only creatures able to recognize them as vampires. To survive, Krause must feed off young virgins and in turn feed his mother. Having recently claimed a victim in California, the two have moved to the Midwest in search of new victims. It isn't long before Krause sets his sights on the perfect victim (Madchen Amick)—only this victim isn't so willing.
MPAA Rating: R—For strong violence, sensuality and language.
Trivia: When the film opens in Bodega Bay, California (the location where Hitchcock filmed *The Birds*), hundreds of dead cats hang from a house, in one of the film's many visual inside references to other genre films and directors.

Cast
Charles Brady ....Brian Krause
Tanya Robertson.............................Madchen Amick
Mrs. Brady ....Alice Krige
Sheriff ....Jim Haynie
Andy Simpson...Dan Martin
Captain Soames ....Ron Perlman
Mrs. Robertson....................................Cindy Pickett

Mr. Robertson...Lyman Ward
Also with Monty Bane, Clive Barker, Joe Dante, Tobe Hooper, Stephen King, John Landis and Glenn Shadix.
Credits
Executive Producers ....Dimitri Logothetis
....Joseph Medawar
Producers...Mark Victor
.................................Michael Grais, Nabeel Zahid
Co-Producer ....Richard Stenta
Director..Mick Garris
Assistant Director ....Randall Badger
2nd Unit Directors.......Richard Stenta, Rexford Metz
Director of Photography ....Rodney Charters
Additional Camera....................................Bert Dunk
Sound....................................Don H. Matthews
Editor ....O. Nicholas Brown
Production Manager......................Richard Stenta
Production Design ....John DeCuir, Jr.
Casting......................Wendy Kurtzman, Lisa Mionie
Written by ....Stephen King
Music ....Nicholas Pike
Special Makeup Effects.....................Alterian Studios
Special Visual Effects ....Apogee Prods.
Film Facts
Running Time ....91 minutes
Soundtrack ....Milan Records
Film...Technicolor
Sound ....Dolby Stereo
Location ....Los Angeles

Stop! Or My Mom Will Shoot
(Universal)

Critics Rating: ★
Genre: Comedy—This is a goofy, old-fashioned, one-joke film with a couple of strong comic performances by Sylvester Stallone and Estelle Getty.
Plot: Stallone stars as bachelor Joe Bomowski, a Los Angeles cop whose personal and professional life is in disarray. When his mom (Getty) comes to visit, she decides to help him, or humiliate him, into getting his life in order. In the process she helps him solve a murder case, reconciles his relationship problems and provides some screwball humor along the way.

MPAA Rating: PG-13

Cast

Joe Bomowski	Sylvester Stallone
Tutti	Estelle Getty
Gwen Harper	JoBeth Williams
Parnell	Roger Rees
Lou	Al Fann
Paulie	Martin Ferraro
Munroe	Gailard Sartain
Tony	John Wesley
Mitchell	Dennis Burkley
Ross	J. Kenneth Campbell
McCabe	Ella Joyce

Credits

Executive Producers	Joe Wizan, Todd Black
Producers	Ivan Reitman
	Joe Medjuck, Michael C. Gross
Associate Producers	Art Levinson, Tony Munafo
Director	Roger Spottiswoode
Assistant Director	Art Levinson
Director of Photography	Frank Tidy
Sound	Thomas Causey
Editors	Mark Conte, Lois Freeman-Fox
Production Design	Charles Rosen
Art Direction	Diane Yates
Set Design	Robert Maddy
Set Decoration	Don Remacle
Costume Design	Marie France
Casting	Jackie Burch
Written by	Blake Snyder
	William Osborne, William Davies
Music	Alan Silvestri

Film Facts

Running Time	87 minutes
Film	Deluxe Color
Sound	Dolby Stereo
Location	Los Angeles
Other Working Title	*Stop Or My Mother Will Shoot*

Storyville
(20th Century Fox)

Critics Rating: ★★★

Genre: Drama—A political melodrama and big-screen directorial debut for Mark Frost, David Lynch's partner on the *Twin Peaks* TV series.

Tag Line: "A candidate's private moment can all too quickly become public record."

Plot: James Spader stars as Cray Fowler, a wealthy young man from a political family, running for Congress. Set in Storyville, Louisiana, Cray, already in the middle of a divorce, becomes involved in an affair and a murder, and he is being blackmailed. His father has also just committed suicide as a result of an investigation into shady family dealings. These problems are just for starters. The film is full of outrageous and mysterious plot twists and turns that lead to a surprising and satisfying climax.

MPAA Rating: R—For language, sensuality and a scene of violence.

Cast

Cray Fowler	James Spader
Natalie Tate	Joanne Whalley-Kilmer
Clifford Fowler	Jason Robards
Lee	Charlotte Lewis
Nathan Lefleur	Michael Warren
Constance Fowler	Piper Laurie
Abe Choate	Charles Haid
Pudge Herman	Chuck McCann
Michael Trevallian	Michael Parks

Also with Justine Arlin, Galyn Gorg, Jeff Perry, Woody Strode and Chino Fats Williams.

Credits

Executive Producers	John Davis, John Flock
Co-Executive Producers	Les Lithgow
	George Zecevic
Producers	David Roe, Edward R. Pressman
Co-Producer	Evzen Kolar
Associate Producer	Chappy Hardy
Director	Mark Frost
Assistant Director	Deepak Nayar
Director of Photography	Ron Garcia
Sound	Stephen Halbert
Editor	B. J. Sears
Production Design	Richard Hoover
Art Direction	Kathleen M. McDernin
Set Decoration	Brian Kasch
Costume Design	Louise Frogley
Casting	Johanna Ray
Screenplay	Mark Frost, Lee Reynolds
Based on the novel *Juryman* by	Frank Galbally
	Robert Macklin
Music	Carter Burwell

Film Facts

Running Time	111 minutes
Film	CFI Color
Sound	Ultra-Stereo
Location	New Orleans

Straight Talk
(Buena Vista)

Critics Rating: ★★
Genre: Comedy—Parton holds her own as the star of this predictable, but nevertheless entertaining, old-fashioned light comedy.
Tag Line: "A modern-day Cinderella story."
Plot: Parton plays Shirlee, a woman who has lost her job, left her insensitive boyfriend and has just moved to Chicago. Shortly after landing a job at a local radio station, she is mistaken for a radio psychologist and finds herself on the air. Since giving advice comes naturally and is the only thing she seems to do well, the show is a natural and she becomes a star. Things become complicated, however, when her past comes back to haunt her and her charade is exposed. But in a film like this a happy ending can't be too far away.
MPAA Rating: PG

Cast

Dr. Shirlee Kenyon	Dolly Parton
Jack Russell	James Woods
Alan Riegert	Griffin Dunne
Steve Labell	Michael Madsen
Lily	Deirdre O'Connell
Guy Girardi	John Sayles
Gene Perlman	Philip Bosco
Tony	Charles Fleischer
Dr. Erdman	Spalding Gray
Janice	Teri Hatcher
Milo Jacoby	Jerry Orbach
Zim Zimmerman	Jay Thomas
Gordon	Keith MacKechnie
Ann	Amy Morton

Credits

Executive Producers	Sandy Gallin
	Carol Baum, Howard Rosenman
Producers	Robert Chartoff, Fred Berner
Associate Producer	Lynn Hendee
Director	Barnet Kellman
Assistant Director	John T. Kretchmer
2nd Unit Director (Illinois)	Jeffrey Townsend
2nd Unit Director (Georgia)	Victor Hammer
2nd Unit Assistant Director (Illinois)	Tom Busch
Director of Photography	Peter Sova
2nd Unit Camera (Illinois)	Alan Thatcher
Sound	Glenn Williams
Editor	Michael Tronick
Production Design	Jeffrey Townsend
Art Direction	Michael T. Perry
Set Design	Suzan Wexler
Set Decoration	Daniel L. May
Costume Design	Jodie Tillen
Casting	Mary Gail Artz, Barbara Cohen
Screenplay	Craig Bolotin, Patricia Resnick
Story by	Craig Bolotin
Original Score - Adaptations	Brad Fiedel
Original Songs - Written/Performed	Dolly Parton

Film Facts

Running Time	91 minutes
Soundtrack	Hollywood Records
Film	Technicolor
Sound	Dolby Stereo
Location	Chicago

The Stranger
(Agantuk)
(National Film Development Corporation)

Critics Rating: Not Rated.
Genre: Drama—Indian director Satyajit Ray's second film to be released in the U.S. in 1992 tells a simple but dramatic moral tale about trust.
Plot: When a wealthy Calcutta family receives word that a long-lost uncle is coming for a visit, suspicions are raised. The family suspects that the man is only coming for money or that he may even be an impostor, since he is a virtual stranger. Soon after this stranger arrives he not only allays their fears but also enriches their lives by his presence.
MPAA Rating: Not Rated.

Cast

Sudhindra Bose	Deepankar De
Anila Bose	Mamata Shankar
Manomohan Mitra	Utpal Dutt
Satyaki Bose	Bikram Bhattacharya
Prithwish	Dhritiman Chatterji
Ranjan Rakshikt	Rabi Ghosh
Chanda Rakshikt	Subrata Chatterji

Credits

Director	Satyajit Ray
Director of Photography	Barun Raha
Sound	Sujit Sarkar
Editor	Dulal Dutt
Production Design	Ashoke Bose
Costume Design	Lalita Ray

Written by ....Satyajit Ray
Music ....Satyajit Ray
Film Facts
Country of Origin ....India
Language ....Indian (subtitled)
Running Time ....120 minutes
Film ....Color
Sound ....Stereo

A Stranger Among Us
(Buena Vista)

Critics Rating: ★★
Genre: Drama—Sidney Lumet's stranger-in-a-strange-land mystery drama leads a female cop undercover into New York's Hasidic community, to find a killer.
Plot: Melanie Griffith stars as Emily Eden, a tough-talking, hardened New York cop assigned to a missing-persons case. The missing person turns up murdered and the case leads Emily into the mysteriously traditional Hasidic Jewish culture. Before long, she has fallen for Ariel (Eric Thal), a strict Hasidic Jew who is unable to return her affections. She eventually uncovers the killer. More important, she discovers many things about herself and her lifestyle as a result of her experience.
MPAA Rating: PG-13—Film was edited; originally received an "R" rating for language.
Cast
Emily Eden ....Melanie Griffith
Ariel..Eric Thal
Levine...John Pankow
Mara..Tracey Pollan
Rebbe..Lee Richardson
Leah...Mia Sara
Nick...Jamey Sheridan
Yaakov Klausman................................Jake Weber
Mendel...Ro'ee Levi
Mr. Klausman ....David Rosenmbaum
Credits
Executive Producers ....Sandy Gallin
....Carol Baum
Producers..Steve Golin
...................................Sigurjon Sighvatsson
....Howard Rosenman
Line Producer ....Burtt Harris

Co-Producers ....Susan Tarr
....Robert J. Averech
Associate Producer ....Lilith Jacobs
Director..Sidney Lumet
Assistant Director ....Burtt Harris
Director of Photography ....Andrzej Bartkowiak
Editor ....Andrew Mondshein
Production Design.........................Philip Rosenberg
Costume Design..................................Gary Jones
....Ann Roth
Casting ....Joy Todd
Written by ....Robert J. Averech
Music ....Jerry Bock
Film Facts
Running Time ....111 minutes
Film ....Color
Sound ....Dolby Stereo
Location...New York
Other Working Titles ....*Close To Eden*

Swoon
(New Line Cinema)

Critics Rating: ★★★
Genre: Drama—A low-budget, highly stylized film shot in black and white on 16mm and blown up to 35mm.
Tag Line: "Leopold + Loeb. Love gone mad. History gone bad."
Plot: In this dramatization of the notorious 1924 Leopold and Loeb murder case, first-time feature director Tom Kalin probes the topic from a contemporary point of view. Daniel Schlachet and Craig Chester play the wealthy, Jewish, intellectually brilliant Richard Loeb and Nathan Leopold, Jr. As homosexual lovers, their contempt for society, mixed with feelings of superiority, lead the two young men on a crime spree. It ends with the cold-blooded murder of a young boy. Called the crime of the century, Clarence Darrow represented the pair during their trial.
MPAA Rating: Not Rated—Includes gay kissing scenes and simulated gay sex.
Trivia: Two previous films dealing with this topic are Alfred Hitchcock's *Rope* (1948) and Richard Fleischer's *Compulsion* (1959).

Cast

Richard Loeb	Daniel Schlachet
Nathan Leopold, Jr.	Craig Chester
State's Attorney Crowe	Ron Vawter
Det. Savage	Michael Kirby
Dr. Bowman	Michael Stumm
Germaine Reinhardt	Valda Z. Crabla

Credits

Executive Producers	Lauren Zalaznick
	James Schamus
Producer	Christine Vachon
Line Producer	Lauren Zalaznick
Co-Producer	Tom Kalin
Associate Producer	Peter Wentworth
Director	Tom Kalin
Director of Photography	Ellen Kuras
Sound	Neil Danziger
	Tom Paul
Editor	Tom Kalin
Production Design	Therese Deprez
Art Direction	Stacey Jones
Costume Design	Jessica Haston
Casting	Daniel Haughey
Screenplay	Tom Kalin
Collaborating writer	Hilton Als
Music	James Bennett
Hair/Makeup	Jim Crawford
	For Iindorato Artists

Film Facts

Running Time	85 minutes
Film	Alpha Cine Black & White
Sound	Stereo

A Tale Of Springtime
(Conte De Printemps)
(Orion Classics)

Critics Rating: ★★★★
Genre: Drama
Tag Line: "A film by Eric Rohmer."
Plot: Anne Teyssedre plays Jeanne, a philosophy teacher who by chance meets Natacha, an 18-year-old student and the two become friends. However, Natacha sees more than friendship on the horizon. A master manipulator, she would like nothing better than to arrange a relationship between Jeanne and her divorced father. Much of the film involves lengthy dialogue and philosophical conversations between cast members. This, in the Rohmer tradition, is, as always lively and entertaining.
MPAA Rating: Not Rated.

Cast
Jeanne	Anne Teyssedre
Igor	Hugues Quester
Natacha	Florence Durrell
Eve	Eloise Bennett
Gaelle	Sophie Robin

Credits
Producer	Margaret Menegoz
Director	Eric Rohmer
Director of Photography	Luc Pages
Sound	Pascal Ribier
Editor	Lisa Garcia
Production Manager	Francoise Etchegaray
Written by	Eric Rohmer
Music	Beethoven, Schumann

Film Facts
Country of Origin	France
Running Time	110 minutes
Film	Color
Sound	Stereo

Talons Of The Eagle
(Shapiro Glickenhaus Entertainment)

Critics Rating: Not Rated.
Genre: Action—By the numbers martial-arts actioner.
Plot: Blanks plays Tyler Wilson, a New York Drug Enforcement Agency official who is sent to Toronto on an undercover mission. Wilson teams up with local agents Reed (Merhi) and Cassandra (Barnes), and the trio target drug kingpin James Hong. Genre fans will enjoy the nonstop violence, fighting and general mayhem in the pursuit of justice.
MPAA Rating: R—For martial arts violence and sexuality.

Cast
Tyler Wilson	Billy Blanks
Michael Reed	Jalal Merhi
Mr. Li	James Hong
Cassandra	Priscilla Barnes
Khan	Matthias Hues
Master Pan	Pan Qing Fu
Bodyguard	Eric Lee
Niko	Harry Mok
Tara	Kelly Gallant

Credits
Producer	Jalal Merhi
Co-Producers	Curtis Petersen
	Dale Hildebrand
Line Producer	Dale Hildebrand
Associate Producers	J. Stephen Maunder
	Kevin Ward
Director	Michael Kennedy
Assistant Director	Ian Robertson
Director of Photography	Curtis Petersen
Sound	Jack Buchanan
Editor	Reid Dennison
Art Direction	Jasna Stefanovich
Screenplay	J. Stephen Maunder
Music	VaRouje
Fight Choreography	Jalal Merhi
	Billy Blanks

Film Facts
Country of Origin	Canada
Running Time	96 minutes
Film	Color
Sound	Stereo

Terminal Bliss
(Cannon)

Critics Rating: Not Rated.
Genre: Drama—Story of a group of self-indulgent teenagers from wealthy families who find their lives short on meaning and purpose. Materialistic pursuits, drugs and sex just aren't enough to fill the void in their lives.
Plot: Luke Perry, one of the teenage heart-throbs of the television series *Beverly Hills, 90210* (also see *Buffy, The Vampire Slayer*), stars as John. Timothy Owen is his lifelong pal Alex. The story revolves around a conflict between the two young men caused when John moves in on Alex's romantic interest. As a result, Alex goes over the edge and lands in a drug rehab program. From this point on, the characters work out their resentments and frustrations to the degree that they are able.
MPAA Rating: R

Cast
John	Luke Perry
Alex	Timothy Owen
Stevie	Estee Chandler
Kirsten	Sonia Curtis
Bucky	Micah Grant
Craig	Alexis Arquette
Tanya	Heather Jones Challenge
Judy	Susan Nichols
Jack	Bruce Taylor

Credits
Executive Producer	Anant Singh
Producer	Brian Cox
Associate Producers	Paul Janssen
Sudhir Pragjee, Sanjeev Singh, Mickey Nivelli	
Director	Jordan Alan
Assistant Director	Tom Willey
Director of Photography	Gregory Smith
Sound	Pawel Wdowczak
Editor	Bruce Sinofsky
Production Design	Catherine Tirr
Art Direction	David Poses
Casting	Linda Phillips Palo
Written by	Jordan Alan
Music	Frank W. Becker

Film Facts
Running Time	91 minutes
Film	Technicolor
Sound	Stereo

Tetsuo - The Iron Man
(Original Cinema)

Critics Rating: Not Rated.
Genre: Science Fiction—Written, directed, edited and costarring Shinya Tsukamoto, *Tetsuo* is an avant-garde, experimental science-fiction film about a terrifying futuristic world in which people are part flesh and part metal. Shot in black and white, this bizarre film pushes all the boundaries of cinema and will more than likely only appeal to film students and possibly science-fiction fans.
MPAA Rating: Not Rated.

Cast
Salaryman	Tomoroh Taguchi
Girlfriend	Kei Fujiwara
Woman in glasses	Nobu Kanaoko
Metals fetishist	Shinya Tsukamoto
Doctor	Naomasa Musaka
Tramp	Renji Ishibashi

Credits
Producer	Kaijyu Theatre
Director/Editor	Shinya Tsukamoto
Assistant Director	Kei Fujiwara
Directors of Photography	Shinya Tsukamoto
	Kei Fujiwara
Art Direction	Shinya Tsukamoto
Written by	Shinya Tsukamoto
Music	Chu Ishikawa

Film Facts
Country of Origin	Japan
Language	Japanese (subtitled)
Running Time	67 minutes
Film	Black & White/16mm
Sound	Stereo

Texas Tenor: The Illinois Jacquet Story
(Rhapsody Films)

Critics Rating: Not Rated.
Genre: Documentary—Filmmaker Arthur Elgort explores the life and work of minor jazz legend Illinois Jacquet in black-and-white. This entertaining documentary is the first in a planned series spotlighting American Heroes.
Plot: Spotlighting Jacquet in New York's Blue Note

club and on tour, the film captures the musician's unique Texas school solo style he helped to pioneer. Jacquet, a star who recorded hit records in the early 1940s, is now a big band leader.

MPAA Rating: Not Rated.

Credits

Executive Producer/Director	Arthur Elgort
Producer/Sound	Ronit Avneri
Associate Producer	Morten Sandtroen
Director of Photography	Morten Sandtroen
Editor	Paula Heredia

Film Facts

Running Time	81 minutes
Film	Black and White
Sound	Stereo

Thank You And Goodnight!

(Aries)

Critics Rating: ★★★

Genre: Documentary—Combines real events with staged re-creations in a tribute to the filmmaker's grandmother, Mae Joffe. Joffe was battling cancer as the film was being made.

Plot: Filmmaker Jan Oxenberg tells the story of her grandmother's life using old family home film footage, old photos and testimonials—real and fictionalized.

MPAA Rating: Not Rated.

Credits

Executive Producer	Lindsay Law
Producers	James Shamus
	Katie Hersh
Director/Writer	Jan Oxenberg
Director of Photography	John Hazard
Sound	Piero Mura
Editor	Lucy Winer
Art Direction	Pamela Woodbridge
Music	Mark Suozzo
Cutouts Creator	Paula De Koenigsberg

Film Facts

Running Time	77 minutes
Film	Color (16 mm)
Sound	Stereo

There Goes The Neighborhood

(Paramount)

Critics Rating: Not Rated.

Genre: Comedy—A silly, goofy, screwball comedy aimed at a select audience.

Plot: Jeff Daniels stars as Willis, a down-and-out prison shrink who learns of a stash of money buried in the basement of a New Jersey home. Willis convinces Jessie (OHara), the owner of the home, to help him in his search. In the process they become romantically involved. At the same time, two escapees from the prison are also in search of the money. The only problem is they have got the wrong address and are holding the next-door neighbors hostage while they too search for the buried treasure. It doesn't take much imagination to figure out how this one ends.

MPAA Rating: PG-13

Cast

Willis Embris	Jeff Daniels
Jessie	Catherine O'Hara
Norman	Hector Elizondo
Peedi	Judith Ivey
Jeffrey	Dabney Coleman
Lydia	Rhea Perlman
Convict	Harris Yulin

Credits

Producer	Stephen Friedman
Director	Bill Phillips
Director of Photography	Walt Lloyd
Editor	Sharyn L. Ross
Production Design	Dean Tschetter
Casting	Mary Jo Slater
Written by	Bill Phillips
Music	David Bell

Film Facts

Running Time	88 miuntes
Film	Color
Sound	Stereo

There's Nothing Out There

(Valkhn Film)

Critics Rating: Not Rated.

Genre: Horror—Twenty-year-old writer, director Rolfe Kanefsky has put together a highly original, low-budget, horror comedy.

Plot: The story follows seven high school friends planning to spend spring break in a house in the woods. When one of the students, Mike (Craig Peck), a horror-film buff, warns the group that they will all die on this trip, his warning is ignored. When they discover that there actually is an alien in the woods, the scene is set for terror and humor in equal measure.

MPAA Rating: Not Rated.

Cast

Mike	Craig Peck
Doreen	Wendy Bednarz
Stacy	Bonnie Bowers
Nick	John Carhart III
Jim	Mark Collver
David	Jeff Dachis
Janet	Claudia Flores
Sally	Lisa Grant

Credits

Executive Producer	Alice Glenn
Producer	Victor Kanefsky
Assoc. Producer	Michael Berlly
Director	Rolfe Kanefsky
Director of Photography	Ed Hershberger
Sound	Natalie Budelis
Editor	Victor Kanefsky
Casting	Bill Williams
Written by	Rolfe Kanefsky
Music	Christopher Thomas
Special Effects Supervisor	Scott Hart
Creature Design	Ken Quinn

Film Facts

Running Time	90 minutes
Film	Color
Sound	Stereo

35 Up

(Samuel Goldwyn Co.)

Critics Rating: ★★★★★

Genre: Documentary—Filmmaker Michael Apted (*Incident At Oglala*) began this series 28 years ago by following the lives of a number of British children, then age seven. He has gone on to revisit

and document his subjects every seven years thereafter. The previous films have been titled *Seven Up, Seven Plus Seven, Twenty One,* and *Twenty Eight Up.*

Plot: Through interviews and film from their everyday lives, Apted has managed to capture a moving portrait of these individuals, many of whom now have children themselves near the age of seven.

MPAA Rating: Not Rated.

Credits

Executive Producer	Rod Caird
Producer/Director	Michael Apted
Co-Producer	Claire Lewis
Director of Photography	George Jesse Turner
Sound	Nick Steer
Editor	Kim Horton, Claire Lewis
Written by	Michael Apted

Film Facts

Country of Origin	Great Britain
Running Time	128 minutes
Film	Color/Black & White
Sound	Stereo

This Is My Life

(20th Century Fox)

Critics Rating: ★★★★

Genre: Drama—Making her feature directorial debut, Nora Ephron brings to the screen a modestly budgeted, old-fashioned drama, about a woman's struggles to make her dreams come true.

Plot: Julie Kavner, in a smart and appealing performance, stars as Dottie Nelson, a single woman working to support herself and her two daughters. While dreaming of making it as a stand up comic in New York City, she sells cosmetics in a department store in Queens. When she unexpectedly receives an inheritance, she uses the money to move to Manhattan and pursue her dream.

MPAA Rating: PG-13

Cast

Dottie Ingels	Julie Kavner
Erica Ingels	Samantha Mathis
Opal Ingels	Gaby Hoffmann
Claudia Curtis	Carrie Fisher
Arnold Moss ("The Moss")	Dan Aykroyd
Jordan	Danny Zorn

Ed ....Bob Nelson
Mia Jablon.................................Marita Geraghty
Lynn...Welker White
Martha Ingels ....Caroline Aaron
Credits
Executive Producers.....................Patricia K. Meyer
......................................Carole Isenberg
Producer ....Lynda Obst
Co-Producer............................Michael R. Joyce
Director ....Nora Ephron
Assistant Director ....Henry Bronchtein
Director of Photography ....Bobby Byrne
Sound...Doug Ganton
Editor ....Robert Reitano
Production Design ....David Chapman
Art Direction................................Barbra Matis
Set Decoration ....Hilton Rosemarin, Jaro Dick
Costume Design ....Jeffrey Kurland
Casting ....Juliet Taylor
Screenplay...................................Nora Ephron
......................................Delia Ephron
Based on the novel *This Is Your
Life* by ....Meg Wolitzer
Music...Carly Simon
Film Facts
Running Time ....105 minutes
Film...Deluxe Color
Sound...Dolby Stereo
Location..........................Toronto, Ontario, Canada

3 Ninjas
(Buena Vista)

Critics Rating: ★★
Genre: Action
Tag Line: "America's Newest Heroes."
Plot: Michael Treanor, Chad Power and Max Elliott Slade star as three brothers recently trained by their Japanese grandfather (Victor Wong) in the art of Ninja fighting. Their dad (Alan McRae) is an undercover investigator who goes after the bad guy and in turn plans to kidnap the kids. The three kidnappers don't stand a chance, however, against the three young Ninjas.
MPAA Rating: PG
Cast
Grandpa..................................Victor Wong
Rocky ....Michael Treanor

Colt ....Max Elliott Slade
Tum Tum....................................Chad Power
Jessica Douglas ....Margarita Franco
Hammer..D. J. Harder
Hugo Snyder ....Rand Kingsley
Fester ....Patrick Labyorteaux
Sam Douglas ....Alan McRae
Marcus ....Race Nelson
Rushmore ....Toru Tanaka
Credits
Executive Producer ....Shunji Hirano
Co-Executive Producer ....James Kang
Producer.......................................Martha Chang
Co-Producers ....Hiroshi Kusu, Akio Shimizu
Line Producer ....Susan Stremple
Associate Producer ....Richard Park
Director.......................................Jon Turteltaub
Assistant Directors............J. B. Rogers, Scott Harris
2nd Unit Director ....Charlie Kao
Director of Photography ....Richard Michalak
Additional Camera ....Chris Faloona
Sound..Bill Robbins
Editor ....David Rennie
Production Design.......................Kirk Petruccelli
Art Direction ....Ken Kirchener, Greg Grande
Set Decoration ....Carol Pressman
Costume Design ....Mona May
Casting ....Kim Williams
Screenplay.................................Edward Emanuel
Story by.......................................Kenny Kim
Music ....Rick Marvin
Stunt Coordinator ....Rick Avery
Film Facts
Running Time ....87 minutes
Film...Technicolor
Sound.......................................Dolby Stereo

Thunderheart
(TriStar)

Critics Rating: ★★★
Genre: Drama—Director Michael Apted (*35 Up*, *Incident At Oglala*) brings to the screen an intense thriller about a murder on a South Dakota Indian reservation and the government's attempted cover-up.
Plot: Val Kilmer (*The Doors*) stars as Ray Levoi, an FBI agent and part indian, who is sent to a reser-

vation to investigate a murder. Already on the case is veteran agent Frank Coutelle (Sam Shepherd). Levoi soon suspects that an innocent man is being framed by the government for the crime. With the aid of a tribal policeman (Graham Greene, *Dances With Wolves*) he begins to dig dangerously deeper into the case and into himself at the same time. All of this leads to a very suspenseful and satisfying climax.

MPAA Rating: R—For language violence.

Trivia: This is the first film to be shot on the Pine Ridge Indian Reservation.

Cast

Ray Levoi	Val Kilmer
Frank Coutelle	Sam Shepard
Walter Crow Horse	Graham Greene
Jack Milton	Fred Ward
Dawes	Fred Dalton Thompson
Grandpa Sam Reaches	Chief Ted Thin Elk
Maggie Eagle Bear	Sheila Tousey
Jimmy Looks Twice	John Trudell
Richard Yellow Hawk	Julius Drum

Credits

Executive Producer	Michael Nozik
Producers	Robert De Niro
	Jane Rosenthal, John Fusco
Director	Michael Apted
Assistant Director	Chris Soldo
Director of Photography	Roger Deakins
Sound	Chris Newman
Editor	Ian Crafford
Production Design	Dan Bishop
Art Direction	Bill Ballou
Set Decoration	Dianna Freas
Costume Design	Susan Lyall
Casting	Lisa Clarkson
Written by	John Fusco
Music	James Horner

Film Facts

Running Time	118 minutes
Film	DuArt Color
Sound	Dolby Stereo
Location	South Dakota

Time Will Tell

(I.R.S. Releasing)

Critics Rating: Not Rated.

Genre: Documentary—The life and legend of reggae superstar Bob Marley is pieced together in this musical documentary.

Plot: Marley died of cancer in 1981, at age 36. The music, the images and the interviews he left behind make up this musical montage. While the footage is primarily composed of Marley and the Wailers performing in concert, additional footage helps to document his rise to stardom in Kingston, Jamaica.

MPAA Rating: Not Rated.

Credits

Executive Producers	Neville Garrick
	Malcolm Gerrie
Producer	Rocky Oldham
Associate Producer	Chris Phipps
Director	Declan Lowney
Editors	Peter Bensimon
	Tim Thornton-Allen
Music	Bob Marley Music, Inc.
Consultant	Adrian Irvine
Animation	Sue Young

Film Facts

Country of Origin	Great Britain
Running Time	89 minutes
Film	Color/Black & White
Sound	Stereo

To Render A Life

(James Agee Film Project)

Critics Rating: Not Rated.

Genre: Documentary—This film is about the struggles of a poor American family to survive their poverty.

Plot: Filmmaker Ross Spears contrasts the lives of families photographed and written about 50 years ago in James Agee and Walker Evans book *Let Us Now Praise Famous Men*, with the life of a poor American family today. The family in focus is the Glass family. Poor Virginia farmers, they lack medical benefits, running water and a proper diet, but they are determined survivors. In one of many ironic twists, the Glasses live just 20 miles from the richest man in America. This is a heartfelt and memorable glimpse into a depressing and difficult topic that will appeal to a select audience.

MPAA Rating: Not Rated.
Credits
Producers ....Ross Spears
....Silvia Kerusan
Director/Director of Photography ....Ross Spears
Written by..Silvia Kerusan
Film Facts
Running Time ....88 minutes
Film...Color
Sound ....Stereo
Location ....Virginia

Together Alone
(Frameline)

Critics Rating: Not Rated.
Genre: Drama—Highly stylized, low-budget, black-and-white gay-themed drama about unsafe sex, AIDS and sexual identity.
Plot: Terry Curry plays Brian, a gay man who has spent the night with another man. Todd Stites plays the other man, a married bisexual, also named Bryan. In the heat of the moment they neglect to practice safe sex. The next morning the realization of the possible consequences sinks in and they begin to discuss what they have done.

The entire film is a real-time conversation that takes place for the most part in a single room. Because of the terrific performances and imaginative camerawork, the story avoids being claustrophobic or static and remains compelling. It is for these reasons that it has won numerous festival awards both locally and abroad.
MPAA Rating: Not Rated.
Cast
Bryan...Todd Stites
Brian..Terry Curry
Credits
Producer/Director ....P. J. Castellaneta
Director of Photography ....David Dechant
Editors...Maria Lee
....P. J. Castellaneta
Music ....Wayne Alabardo
Film Facts
Running Time ....87 minutes
Film..Black & White
Sound ....Stereo

Totos Le Heros
(Toto The Hero)
(Triton)

Critics Rating: ★★★★★
Genre: Drama—This imaginative and entertaining feature film debut by writer-director Jaco van Dormael won the Camera d'Or award at Cannes. In French with subtitles, the drama revolves around a troubled man with a vivid imagination.
Plot: The hero of the story is Thomas, played by three separate actors, as his story is told from different stages in his life—jumping randomly back and forth in time. His lifelong enemy is Alfred (Peter Bohlke), a wealthy man whom Thomas believes has stolen his life—certain that they were switched as babies in the hospital. As an old man, Thomas plots to kill his rival and in doing so his imagination takes over.
MPAA Rating: PG-13
Cast
Thomas van Hasebroeck ....Michel Bouquet
Evelyne ....Gisela Uhlen
Evelyne (young woman)....................Mireille Perrier
Thomas (child) ....Thomas Godet
Alice ....Sandrine Blancke
Alfred ....Peter Bohlke
Alfred (young man)............................Didier Ferney
Alfred (child) ....Hugo Harold Harrison
Thomas (young man) ....Jo De Backer
Thomas' mother ....Fabienne Loriaux
Credits
Producers ....Pierre Drouot, Dany Geys
Director ....Jaco van Dormael
Assistant Director..............................Danilo Catti
Director of Photography ....Walther van den Ende
Sound ....Dominique Warnier
Editor ....Susana Rossberg
Art Direction.....................................Hubert Pouille
Costume Design ....An D'Huys
....Anne van Bree
Written by ....Jaco van Dormael
Music ....Pierre van Dormael
Song.......................................Charles Trenet
Film Facts
Country of Origin ....France/Germany/Belgium
Language...French (subtitled)
Running Time ....90 minutes

Film	Eastmancolor
Sound	Stereo

Tous Les Matins Du Monde
(All The Mornings Of The World)
(October Films)

Critics Rating: ★★★

Genre: Drama—A historical biography of musician Monsieur de Sainte Colombe, the film received seven French Oscars (Ceasars) including Best Picture.

Plot: Jean-Pierre Marielle plays Colombe, a 17th century composer who retreats from life and into his music following the sudden death of his wife. Told in flashbacks, Gerard Depardieu plays Marin Marias, a court composer who has failed to become the protégé of Colombe. Flashing back to the 1660s, Guillaume Depardieu plays Marias as a young man who studies under Colombe at his daughter Madeleine's (Brochet) insistence. When Marias relationship with Madeleine ends badly, his apprenticeship does also. Stunning visually, on the mark performances and a winning tale make this an art-house pleaser.

MPAA Rating: Not Rated—Contains profanity and nudity.

Cast

Marin Marias	Gerard Depardieu
Monsieur de Sainte Colombe	Jean-Pierre Marielle
Madeleine	Anne Brochet
Young Marin Marias	Guillaume Depardieu
Madame de Sainte Colombe	Caroline Sihol
Toinette	Carol Richert

Also with Myriam Boyer, Jean-Claude Dreyfus, Yves Gase, Violaine Lacroix, Yves Lambrecht and Nadege Teron.

Credits

Producer	Jean-Louis Livi
Director	Alain Corneau
Assistant Director	Jerome Navarro
Director of Photography	Yves Angelo
Sound	Gerard Lamps
	Anne Le Campion
Editor	Marie-Joseph Yoyotte
Set Design	Bernard Vezat
Costume Design	Corinne Jorry
Screenplay	Pascal Quignard, Alain Corneau
Based on the Novel by	Pascal Quignard
Music	Jordi Savall
Musical Consultant/Instructor	
	Jean-Louis Charbonnier

Film Facts

Country of Origin	France
Language	French (subtitled)
Running Time	114 minutes
Film	Color
Sound	Stereo

Toys
(20th Century Fox)

Critics Rating: ★★

Genre: Comedy—While a few critics believed the film was inspired, just as many dubbed it the biggest disappointment of the season.

Tag Line: "This Christmas laughter is a state of mind."

Plot: Robin Williams stars as Leslie Zevo, a childlike innocent who is heir to his dying father's (Donald O'Connor) toy factory. His father, however, believes his children are not mature enough to run the factory and instead leaves it to Leslie's uncle (Gambon), a former Army general. The General sets about turning the factory into a war machine and it is up to Leslie and his sister Alsatia (Cusack) to stop him. While this slow and simplistic satire may have its detractors, everyone agrees that the true stars of the film were the spectacularly impressive art direction and the special effects.

MPAA Rating: PG-13—For some language and sensuality.

Cast

Leslie Zevo	Robin Williams
The General	Michael Gambon
Alsatia Zevo	Joan Cusack
Gwen	Robin Wright
Patrick	LL Cool J
Kenneth Zevo	Donald O'Connor
Owens Owens	Arthur Malet
Zevo, Sr.	Jack Warden
Nurse Debbie	Debi Mazar

Credits

Producers ....Mark Johnson, Barry Levinson
Co-Producers ....Charles Newirth, Peter Giuliano
Director ....Barry Levinson
Assistant Director ....Peter Giuliano
Director of Photography ....Adam Greenberg
Sound ....Ron Judkins
Sound Design.....................................Richard Beggs
Editor..Stu Linder
Production Design ....Ferdinando Scarfiotti
Art Direction ....Edward Richardson
Set Decoration.................................Linda DeScenna
Costume Design....................................Albert Wolsky
Casting ....Ellen Chenowith
Screenplay ....Valerie Curtin, Barry Levinson
Music ....Hans Zimmer, Trevor Horn
Special Visual Effects...............Dream Quest Images
Special Effects Coordinator...............Clayton Pinney
Visual Effects Supervisor ....Mat Beck
Choreography ....Anthony Thomas

Film Facts

Running Time ....121 minutes
Soundtrack...DGC Records
Film ....CFI Color
Sound ....Dolby Stereo
Location ....Los Angeles

Traces Of Red

(Samuel Goldwyn)

Critics Rating: ★

Genre: Thriller—An erotic thriller with a few laughs—mostly unintentional.

Tag Line: "Two cops. One beautiful woman. A shocking murder. The ultimate mystery that will keep you guessing until the very last moment. No one is beyond suspicion."

Plot: James Belushi plays Jack, a Palm Beach, Florida, cop. His brother (Russ) is a local politician. When Jack gets assigned to a murder case, he finds himself a suspect in a series of prostitute slayings. Goldwyn plays the sidekick with his usual intensity. Before long, nearly everyone in the film becomes a suspect, including Jack's brother. Eventually the mystery is resolved with a very enjoyable twist ending.

MPAA Rating: R—For sexuality, language and violence.

Cast

Jack Dobson.......................................James Belushi
Ellen Schofield ....Lorraine Bracco
Steve Frayn...Tony Goldwyn
Michael Dobson..................................William Russ
Beth Frayn..Faye Grant
Morgan Cassidy ....Michelle Joyner
Lt. J. C. Hooks...Joe Lisi
Susan Dobson.....................................Victoria Bass
Amanda..Melanie Tomlin
Mr. Martyn..Jim Piddock
Emilio...Ed Amatrudo
Prosecutor Dan Ayaroff ....Daniel Tucker Kamin
Louis Dobson ....Harriet Grinnell
Nancy Frayn ....Lindsey Jayde Sapp
Tony Garidi ....Mario Ernesto Sanchez
Tommy Hawkins ....Will Knickerbocker
Ian Wicks ....Edgar Allen Poe IV

Credits

Executive Producer.........................David V. Picker
Producer ....Mark Gordon
Director ....Andy Wolk
Assistant Director ....David Sardi
Director of Photography ....Tim Suhrstedt
Additional Camera...............................Don Burgess
Sound..Steve C. Aaron
Editor...Trudy Ship
Production Design.............Dan Bishop, Dianna Freas
Art Direction ....Richard Fojo
Set Decoration.....................................Nancy Sivitz
Costume Design ....Hilary Rosenfeld
Casting ....Pam Dixon
Casting (Florida) ....Ellen Jacoby
Screenplay...Jim Piddock
Music ....Graeme Revell

Film Facts

Running Time ....104 minutes
Film ....Deluxe Color
Sound...Dolby Stereo
Location ....Palm Beach, Florida
Other Working Titles ....*Beyond Suspicion*

Trespass

(Universal)

Critics Rating: ★★★

Genre: Action—Originally titled *Looters*, the film was renamed and the release date postponed due to the Spring riots in Los Angeles.

Tag Line: "They all came to the wrong place at the wrong time."

Plot: Bill Paxton and William Sadler play Vince and Don, two firemen friends who go in search of buried gold. The gold (or loot) is reportedly buried in an abandoned factory in East St. Louis, Illinois. As bad luck would have it, the men arrive at the abandoned factory just in time to become witnesses to a gang murder. The remainder of this fast-paced film takes place within the confines of the burned-out building, as the witnesses are pursued by gang members Ice T and Ice Cube, all leading to a predictably gory and ultraviolent climax.

MPAA Rating: R—For violence and language.

Cast

Vince	Bill Paxton
King James	Ice T
Don	William Sadler
Savon	Ice Cube
Bradlee	Art Evans
Lucky	De'voreaux White
Raymond	Bruce A. Young
Luther	Glenn Plummer
Wickey	Stoney Jackson
Video	T. E. Russell
Cletus	Tiny Lister
Goose	John Toles-Bey
Moon	Byron Minns
Davis	Tico Wells

Credits

Executive Producers	Robert Zemeckis, Bob Gale
Producer	Neil Canton
Co-Producer	Michael S. Glick
Director	Walter Hill
Assistant Director	Barry K. Thomas
2nd Unit Director	Allan Graf
Director of Photography	Lloyd Ahern
Sound	Charles M. Wilborn
Editor	Freeman Davies
Production Design	Jon Hutman
Art Direction	Charles Breen
Set Design	Kathleen Sullivan
Set Decoration	Beth Rubino
Costume Design	Dan Moore
Casting	Reuben Cannon
Screenplay	Bob Gale, Robert Zemeckis
Music Supervision	Sharon Boyle
	Jorge Hinojosa
Music	Ry Cooder

Film Facts

Running Time	101 minutes
Soundtrack	Sire/Warner Bros. Records
Original Score	Sire/Warner Bros. Records
Film	Deluxe Color
Sound	Dolby Stereo
Location	Atlanta, Georgia; Memphis, Tennessee
Other Working Titles	*Looters*

Tribulation 99: Alien Anomalies Under America
(Other Cinema)

Critics Rating: Not Rated.

Genre: Documentary—Producers promoted this 49-minute film as a pseudo-documentary. It is a collection of pre-existing film footage edited into a bizarre and humorous tale of an alien conspiracy.

Plot: Filmmaker Craig Baldwin suggests that aliens have orchestrated our modern history and set it on a cataclysmic collision course. He uses film from cartoons, monster films, news footage, James Bond films and other sources to support his position.

MPAA Rating: Not Rated.

Credits

Director/Editor	Craig Baldwin
Director of Photography	Bill Daniel
Written by	Craig Baldwin
Music	Dana Hoover
Narrator	Sean Kilcoyne

Film Facts

Running Time	50 minutes
Film	Color (16mm)
Sound	Stereo

Triple Bogey On A Par Five Hole
(Poe Productions)

Critics Rating: Not Rated.

Genre: Drama—This black-and-white mystery drama, according to critics, was short on both.

Plot: Eric Mitchell stars as Remy Gravelle, a screenwriter working on a story about two famous thieves, Harry and Sally Levy, who were killed on a golf course following a robbery. Remy eventually turns up at the Triple Bogey, a yacht where the Levy's children live. From this point on, the film is a series of interviews with the three children as they remember their parents and discuss their unusual lives living together on this ship.

MPAA Rating: Not Rated.

Cast

Remy Gravelle	Eric Mitchell
Amanda Levy	Daisy Hall
Satch Levy	Jesse McBride
Nina Baccardi	Alba Clemente
Bree Levy	Angela Goethals
Arnstein	Tom Cohen
Steffano Baccardi	Robbie Coltrane

Credits

Producer/Director	Amos Poe
Co-Producer/Assistant Director	Dolly Hall
Line Producer	Benjamin Gruberg
Director of Photography	Joe De Salvo
Sound	Tom Szabolcs
Editor	Dana Congdon
Production Manager	Benjamin Gruberg
Casting	Ellen Parks
Written by	Amos Poe
Music	Anna Domino
	Michel Delory
	Mader, Chic Streetman

Film Facts

Running Time	88 minutes
Film	Color/Black & White
Sound	Stereo

The Tune
(October Films)

Critics Rating: ★★★

Genre: Animated—An imaginative musical cartoon by Bill Plympton.

Plot: The story revolves around Dell, a songwriter experiencing a block. His boss, Mr. Mega, has given him only 47 minutes to produce a hit or hit the road. Being eager to make it big and win over the apple of his eye, Didi, he goes in search of inspiration. Along the way he gets lost on the highway and winds up in a strange land known as Flooby Nooby. Here he meets an assortment of oddball musical characters who provide him with the inspiration he needs.

MPAA Rating: Not Rated.

Cast

Voices of:

Del	Daniel Neiden
Didi	Maureen McElheron
Mayor/Mr. Mega/Mrs. Mega	Marty Nelson
Dot	Emily Bindiger
Wiseone/Surfer/Tango Dancer/Note	Chris Hoffman
Cabbie	Jimmy Ceribello
Houndog	Ned Reynolds
Bellhop	Jeff Knight
Surfer/Note	Jennifer Senko

Credits

Producer/Director/Animator	Bill Plympton
Director of Photography	John Donnelly
Sound	Phil Lee
Editor	Merril Stern
Artistic Supervisor	Jessica Wolf-Stanley
Screenplay	Bill Plympton
	Maureen McElheron, P. C. Vey
Music	Maureen McElheron

Film Facts

Running Time	69 minutes
Film	Color
Sound	Stereo

Turtle Beach
(Warner Bros.)

Critics Rating: Not Rated.

Genre: Drama—Similar in theme to Peter Weir's *The Year Of Living Dangerously.*

Plot: Greta Scacchi plays Judith, an Australian journalist out to record the plight of the Vietnamese boat people in Malaysia. Joan Chen plays Lady Minou Hobday, a Vietnamese woman now married to the Australian ambassador (Kaye) stationed in Kuala Lumpur. Former friends, Judith and Minou have similar goals. Though Minou's search for her three children, whom she believes to be refugees, is a more personal quest, both women are equally obsessed and share a bond.

MPAA Rating: R—For sensuality, language and violence. Contains nudity.

Cast

Judith	Greta Scacchi
Lady Minou Hobday	Joan Chen
Ralph Hamilton	Jack Thompson
Kanan	Art Malik
Sir Adrian Hobday	Norman Kaye
Sancha Hamilton	Victoria Longley
Richard	Martin Jacobs

Credits

Executive Producers	Graham Burke, Greg Coote
Producer	Matt Carroll
Line Producer	Irene Dobson
Director	Stephen Wallace
Assistant Director	Colin Fletcher
Director of Photography	Russell Boyd
Sound	Ben Osmo
Supervising Editor	William Russell
Editors	Lee Smith, Louise Innes
Production Design	Brian Thomson
Costume Design	Roger Kirk
Casting	Alison Barrett
Screenplay	Ann Turner
Based on the novel by	Blanche d' Alpuget
Music	Chris Neal

Film Facts

Country of Origin	Australia
Running Time	85 minutes
Film	Color
Sound	Stereo

Twin Peaks - Fire Walk With Me
(New Line Cinema)

Critics Rating: Not Rated.

Genre: Drama—In an original screenplay, director David Lynch focuses his quirky eye on high school beauty Laura Palmer prior to her murder. (The investigation of Palmer's murder was the basic storyline of the controversial TV series.)

Tag Line: "In a town like Twin Peaks, no one is innocent."

Plot: Sheryl Lee plays a cocaine addicted, mentally unstable Laura Palmer. As her bizarre life unfolds, we learn of her traumatic family life and the incidents leading up to her murder. And like the TV series, in this dark and mysterious film reality and fantasy become interchangeable.

MPAA Rating: R—For language, strong violence, drug content and sex.

Trivia: While the film was reportedly booed at Cannes, it was a phenomenal success in Japan and became one of the year's biggest hits there.

Cast

Dale Cooper	Kyle MacLachlan
Sam Stanley	Kiefer Sutherland
Laura Palmer	Sheryl Lee
Donna Haywood	Moira Kelly
Norma Jennings	Peggy Lipton
Carl Rodd	Harry Dean Stanton
Sarah Palmer	Grace Zabriskie
Leland Palmer	Ray Wise
Phillip Jeffries	David Bowie
Chet Desmond	Chris Isaak
Gordon Cole	David Lynch
Shelly Johnson	Madchen Amick
Bobby	Dana Ashbrook
Sheriff Cable	Gary Bullock
Albert Rosenfeld	Miguel Ferrer
Teresa Banks	Pamela Gidley
Annie Blackburn	Heather Graham
James	James Marshall
Woodsman	Jurgen Prochnow

Credits

Executive Producers	David Lynch
	Mark Frost
Producer	Gregg Fienberg
Co-Producer	John Wentworth
Associate Producers	Johanna Ray, Tim Harbert
Director	David Lynch
Assistant Director	Deepak Nayar
Director of Photography	Ron Garcia
Sound	Jon Huck
Sound Design	David Lynch
Editor	Mary Sweeney
Production Design	Patricia Norris
Set Decoration	Leslie Morales
Costume Design	Patricia Norris
Casting	Johanna Ray
Screenplay	David Lynch
	Robert Engels
Music	Angelo Badalamenti

Film Facts

Running Time	135 minutes
Soundtrack	Warner Bros. Records
Film	CFI Color
Sound	Dolby Stereo
Location	Los Angeles; Washington

U

Ultraviolet
(Concorde)

Critics Rating: Not Rated.
Genre: Thriller—Thirty-six-year-old director Mark Griffiths (*A Cry In The Wild*), helms this Roger Corman action thriller.
Plot: Stephen Meadows (*The End Of Innocence*) and Patricia Healy (*Those Hands*), star as Sam and Kristen Halsey, a Los Angeles couple in the wrong place at the wrong time. On a weekend trip to Death Valley the couple stops to help another couple, whose motorhome has gone up in flames. Nick (Esai Morales, *La Bamba, Naked Tango*), the owner of the motorhome, turns out to be a psycho who kills his wife, shoots Sam and abducts Kristen. Sam lives, however, only to pursue the two endlessly through the desert and to a horrific climax.
MPAA Rating: R
Trivia: The director's first feature was titled *Lucky 13* and starred Eric Stoltz (*The Waterdance*).

Cast
Nick	Esai Morales
Kristen Halsey	Patricia Healy
Sam Halsey	Steven Meadows

Credits
Executive Producer	Roger Corman
Producer	Catherine Cyran
Co-Producer	Mike Elliot
Director	Mark Griffiths
Director of Photography	Gregg Heschong
Editor	Kevin Tent
Production Manager	Michele Weisler
Casting	Steven Rabiner
Written by	Gordon Cassidy
Music	Ed Tomney

Film Facts
Film	Color
Sound	Stereo
Location	Death Valley, California; Los Angeles

Under Siege
(Warner Bros.)

Critics Rating: ★★★
Genre: Action—A slick and entertaining formula-driven, suspense-filled good-guy-bad-guy actioner.
Tag Line: "In 1992, a battleship's been sabotaged by nuclear pirates out to steal its warhead. Now, surrounded by terrorists, a lone man stands with a deadly plan of attack."
Plot: Seagal plays Casey, a Navy Seal in disguise as a cook aboard the battleship USS Missouri. On its way to be decommissioned, the ship is hijacked by two corrupt military officers (Jones and Busey), who plan to sell its nuclear arsenal. What the men have not counted on was the Navy's secret weapon—Seagal.
MPAA Rating: R—For violence, language and brief nudity.
Trivia: Warner Bros. claimed that this was the biggest October and biggest Seagal opening ever at $14 million. Critics claimed that this is also his best film to date.

Cast
Casey Ryback	Steven Seagal
William Strannix	Tommy Lee Jones
Commander Krill	Gary Busey
Jordan Tate	Erika Eleniak
Captain Adams	Patrick O'Neal
Tom Breaker	Nick Mancuso
Admiral Bates	Andy Romano
Daumer	Colm Meany

Credits
Executive Producers	J. F. Lawton
	Gary Goldstein
Producers	Arnon Milchan
	Steven Seagal
	Steven Reuther
Co-Producers	Jack B. Bernstein
	Peter Macgregor-Scott
Director	Andrew Davis

Assistant Director......................................Tom Mack
Director of Photography ....Frank Tidy
Editors ....Robert A. Ferretti
....Dennis Virkler
....Don Brochu
....Dov Hoenig
Production Design...................................Bill Kenney
Art Direction ....Bill Hiney
Set Design..Al Manzer
Set Decoration ....Rick Gentz
Costume Design.................................Richard Bruno
Casting ....Pamela Basker
Written by ....J. F. Lawton
Music ....Gary Chang
Special Effects Coordinator ....Thomas L. Fisher
Stunt Coordinator ....Conrad E. Palmisano

Film Facts

Running Time ....102 minutes
Film...Technicolor
Sound..Dolby Stereo
Location ....Mobile, Alabama
Other Working Titles ....*Dreadnought*;
....*Last To Surrender*

Under Suspicion

(Columbia)

Critics Rating: ★★★

Genre: Thriller—A slow-moving film about sexual exploits and murder with few thrills.
Plot: Liam Neeson stars as Tony Aaron, an ex-cop-turned-private-eye gone bad. He earns his living primarily from setting up victims in adultery cases by using his wife as bait. When his wife and one of his victims turn up murdered in bed, he sets out to uncover the murderer. Angeline, the dead man's mistress (Laura San Giacomo, *Pretty Woman*) is the primary suspect. But when Tony falls for her, the plot gets complicated.
MPAA Rating: R

Cast

Tony Aaron ....Liam Neeson
Angeline......................................Laura San Giacomo
Frank...Kenneth Cranham
Selina ....Alphonsia Emmanuel
Also with Martin Grace, Kevin Moore, Stephen Moore, Maggie O'Neill, Malcolm Storry and Alan Talbot.

Credits

Executive Producers ....Nick Elliott
....Fred Turner
....George Helyer
Producer ....Brian Eastman
Associate Producer ....Vincent Winter
Director ....Simon Moore
Assistant Directors ....Terry Needham
....Simon Hinkley
Director of Photography (U. K.).........Vernon Layton
Director of Photography (U. S.)..........Ivan Strasburg
Sound...................................Christopher Ackland
....Ian Fuller
....Ken Weston
....Stan Fiferman
Editor ....Tariq Anwar
Production Design ....Tim Hutchinson
Art Direction ....Tony Reading
Set Decoration (U. K.)...............Stephenie McMillan
Set Decoration (U. S.) ....Joel Washnetz
Costume Design..Penny Rose
Casting (U. K.)...................................Anne Henderson
Casting (U. S.) ....Mike Fenton
Written by ....Simon Moore
Music Composed/Conducted by.........................
....Christopher Gunning
Special Effects Supervisor.....................David Harris
Special Effects ....Steve Hamilton

Film Facts

Country of Origin ....Great Britain
Running Time ....99 minutes
Film...Rank Color
Sound..Dolby Stereo

Unforgiven

(Warner Bros.)

Critics Rating: ★★★★★

Genre: Western—Despite its downbeat tone and message, producer, director and star, Clint Eastwood, managed to win over critics and audiences alike with this violent yet humorous film of great contrasts.
Plot: Clint Eastwood stars as Bill Munny, a farmer and reformed hired killer who is down on his luck and strapped for cash to feed his two children. Desperate, it doesn't take much to pull him back into his former occupation. He in turn calls on his

former partner Ned Logan (Morgan Freeman). Together with an upstart gunslinger (Jamiz Woolvett), they go in search of two young men who cut up a whore to cash in on the big reward being offered. What they find is an evil sheriff (Gene Hackman) and a few moral dilemmas along the way.

MPAA Rating: R—For violence, language and a scene of sexuality. Contains very brief male nudity from behind.

Trivia: *Unforgiven* earned the highest opening three-day gross of any Eastwood film. It also earned more than his other biggest western, *Pale Rider*, which earned more than $41 million at the box office.

Cast

Bill Munny	Clint Eastwood
Little Bill Daggett	Gene Hackman
Ned Logan	Morgan Freeman
English Bob	Richard Harris
The "Schofield Kid"	Jamiz Woolvett
Davey Bunting	Rob Campbell
Strawberry Alice	Frances Fisher
Skinny Dubois	Anthony James
Quick Mike	David Mucci
W. W. Beauchamp	Saul Rubinek
Delilah Fitzgerald	Anna Thomson

Credits

Executive Producer	David Valdes
Producer/Director	Clint Eastwood
Associate Producer	Julian Ludwig
Assistant Director	Scott Maitland
Director of Photography	Jack N. Green
Sound	Rob Young
Editor	Joel Cox
Production Design	Henry Bumstead
Art Direction	Rick Roberts
	Adrian Gorton
Set Design	James J. Murakami
Set Decoration	Janice Blackie-Goodine
Costume Design (Men)	Carla Hetland
Costume Design (Women)	Joanne Hansen
Casting	Phyllis Huffman
Casting (Canada)	Stuart Aikins
Written by	David Webb Peoples
Music	Lennie Niehaus

Film Facts

Running Time	125 minutes
Soundtrack	Varese Sarabande
Film	Technicolor
Sound	Dolby Stereo
Location	Alberta, Canada
Other Working Titles	*The William Munny Killings*

Universal Soldier
(TriStar)

Critics Rating: ★★

Genre: Action—Director Roland Emmerich (*Moon 44*) described this summer action thriller as a "modern retelling of the classic Frankenstein myth." Genre fans get twice as much for their money in this energetic action thriller.

Tag Line: "The Future Has A Bad Attitude." "Almost human. Almost perfect. Almost under control,"

Plot: Jean-Claude Van Damme and Dolph Lundgren star as Luc Devreux and Andrew Scott, members of a top secret military unit known as the Universal Soldiers. Having been killed in the Vietnam war, they are brought back to life. In this top-secret government experiment they have been transformed into the perfect soldiers with no memory of their lives beforehand. The trouble begins when their memory begins to return. When TV news reporter Veronica Roberts (Ally Walker, *The Seventh Coin*) discovers the true nature of the unit, her life is in jeopardy. Devreux escapes the unit, rescues Roberts and escapes across the desert, only to be pursued by Scott and the other UniSols.

MPAA Rating: R—For strong graphic violence and strong language. Van Damme appears nude from behind in an extended and quite humorous scene.

Trivia: In the film, the lush tropical jungle of Vietnam was actually a Cottonwood, Arizona, golf course transformed by Production Designer Holger Gross.

Cast

Luc Devreux	Jean-Claude Van Damme
Andrew Scott	Dolph Lundgren
Veronica	Ally Walker
Col. Perry	Ed O'Ross
Dr. Gregor	Jerry Orbach
Woodward	Leon Rippy
Garth	Tico Wells
GR76	Ralph Moeller

Motel owner ....Robert Trebor
Lieutenant..Gene Davis
Charles ....Drew Snyder
GR55..."Tiny" Lister, Jr.
GR61 ....Simon Rhee
GR86 ....Eric Norris
Also with Bradford Bancroft, Joanne Baron, Lilyan Chauvin, Rance Howard, Monty Laird, Joseph Malone, Jack Moore, Lupe Ontiveros, Thomas Rosales, John Storey and Michael Winther.

Credits
Executive Producer ....Mario Kassar
Producers ....Allen Shapiro
....Craig Baumgarten
....Joel B. Michaels
Co-Producer ....Oliver Eberle
Director...Roland Emmerich
1st Assistant Director ....Steve Love
2nd Assistant Director ....Robert Leveen
2nd Unit Director................................Vic Armstrong
Director of Photography ....Karl Walter Lindenlaub
Sound ....David Chornow
Editor..Michael J. Duthie
Unit Production Manager....................Donald Heitzer
Production Design ....Holger Gross
Art Direction...Nelson Coates
Set Decoration ....Alex Carle
Set Costumer ....Laureen Jacques
Costumers ....Elaine Balboni
....Deanne Smith
....Victoria Wendell
Assistant Costume Design................Theda DeRamus
Casting..Penny Perry
....Annette Benson
Written by ....Richard Rothstein
....Christopher Leitch
....Dean Devlin
Music ....Christopher Franke
Stunt Coordinator ....Vic Armstrong
Special Makeup Effects ....Larry R. Hamlin
....Michael Burnett
Special Effects Supervisor ....Kit West

Film Facts
Running Time ....104 minutes
Soundtrack ....Varese Sarabande
Film..Technicolor
Sound...Dolby Stereo
Location ....Grand Canyon; Hoover Dam
..........Ashfork, Cottonwood, and Prescott, Arizona

Unlawful Entry
(20th Century Fox)

Critics Rating: ★★★

Genre: Thriller—Director Jonathan Kaplan has managed to create a tight, smart, suspenseful, thriller in the tradition of *Fatal Attraction* and *Hand That Rocks The Cradle.*

Plot: The plot is a simple and terrifying one about a psycho cop intent on destroying a man's life in order to get to his wife. Kurt Russell and Madeleine Stowe play Michael and Karen Carr, a trendy young couple living in an upscale Los Angeles neighborhood. When their home is broken into, Ray Liotta, as Pete Davis, is one of the cops who shows up to take the report. Before long he manages to become friends with the couple. By the time Michael realizes that Pete is a bit deranged, it's too late. Pete has decided that Michael doesn't deserve Karen and sets out to destroy his life and win over his wife—and will stop at nothing to fulfill his plans.

MPAA Rating: R—For terror, violence, language and sexuality.

Trivia: Because of the Rodney King beating trial and subsequent L. A. riot, a gruesome beating scene (shot prior to the real-life incident) was edited down to a fraction of its actual length.

Cast
Michael Carr ....Kurt Russell
Officer Pete Davis...................................Ray Liotta
Karen Carr..................................Madeleine Stowe
Officer Roy Cole ....Roger E. Mosely
Captain Hayes ....Andy Romano
Leon ....Dino Anello
Jerome Lurie.............................Carmen Argenziano
Roger Graham ....Ken Lerner
Ernie Pike....................................Johnny Ray McGhee
Penny ....Deborah Offner

Credits
Producer......................................Charles Gordon
Line Producer...Gene Levy
Associate Producer ....Sulla Hamer
Director ....Jonathan Kaplan
Assistant Director ....D. Scott Easton
Director of Photography ....Jamie Anderson
Sound...Glenn Anderson

Editor...Curtiss Clayton
Production Design ....Lawrence G. Paull
Art Direction...Bruce Crone
Set Design ....Dawn Snyder
Set Decoration.................................Rick Simpson
Costume Design..April Ferry
Casting...Jackie Burch
Screenplay ....Lewis Colick
Story by...................................George D. Putnam
....John Katchmer
....Lewis Colick
Music ....James Horner

Film Facts
Running Time ....111 minutes
Soundtrack ....Intrada
Film ....Deluxe Color
Sound ....Dolby Stereo
Location ....Los Angeles

Used People
(20th Century Fox)

Critics Rating: ★★★

Genre: Drama—Based on *The Grandma Plays* by Todd Graff. The film is an actor's showcase, with quirky, humorous and memorable performances by an all-star ensemble cast.

Tag Line: "A story about love, family and other embarrassments. Life's tough so laugh a little."

Plot: Set in Queens, N.Y., this film stars Shirley MacLaine as Pearl, a bitter, repressed, 56-year-old Jewish housewife whose controlled world is turned upside-down when her husband dies. Learning of her husband's death, Joe (Mastroianni), a romantically smitten secret admirer tries to pick Pearl up after the funeral. Having spent her entire adult life in a loveless marriage, Pearl's pent-up emotions make her a walking time bomb. Her two grown daughters, Harden and Bates, are her nearest targets—that is, until Joe enters the picture. Harden is a standout and provides many of the laughs as a woman who finds it easier to live as a fictional character from the films than to face the realities of her own life.

Though complete opposites, Joe and Pearl's attraction and love eventually become the catalyst that heals this dysfunctional family.

MPAA Rating: PG-13

Cast
Pearl Berman...................................Shirley MacLaine
Bibby ....Kathy Bates
Freida ....Jessica Tandy
Joe Meledandri....................Marcello Mastroianni
Norma ....Marcia Gay Harden
Becky..Sylvia Sidney
Frank...Joe Pantoliano
Swee' Pea ....Mathew Branton
Jack Berman ....Bob Dishy
Paolo...Charles Cioffi
Uncle Normy ....Louis Guss
Uncle Harry ....Lee Wallace
Also with Helen Hanft, Irving Metzman and Doris Roberts.

Credits
Executive Producers ....Lloyd Levin
....Michael Barnathan
Producer...Peggy Rajski
Co-Producer.......................................Todd Graff
Director..Beeban Kidron
Assistant Director ....Tony Lucibello
Director of Photography ....David Watkin
Sound...Doug Ganton
Sound (New York).............................Dennis Maitland
Sound (New York)............................Tod Maitland
Editor...John Tintori
Production Manager ....David Coatsworth
Production Manager (New York) ....Diana Pokorny
Production Design............................Stuart Wurtzel
Costume Design ....Marilyn Vance-Straker
Casting.......................................Mary Colquhoun
Screenplay...Todd Graff
Based on "The Grandma Plays" by..........Todd Graff
Music ....Rachel Portman
Choreography...Pat Birch

Film Facts
Running Time ....115 minutes
Soundtrack ....Big Screen Records
Film..DuArt Color
Sound ....Dolby Stereo
Location............New York; Toronto, Ontario, Canada

The Vagrant
(MGM)

Critics Rating: Not Rated.

Genre: Thriller—A predictable, straightforward, low-budget psychological thriller with humorous moments.

Plot: Bill Paxton (*The Dark Backward*) stars as Graham, a businessman who moves into a house in the wrong part of town. Living nearby is a grotesque-looking vagrant who begins to stalk his new neighbor. Before long all of Graham's energies are being used to keep the vagrant locked up and out of sight. In the meantime, he loses his job, his girlfriend and even his house. If that weren't enough, the vagrant returns for one final and bloody confrontation.

MPAA Rating: R—For some sensuality and violence.

Cast
Graham Krakowski	Bill Paxton
Lt. Ralf Barfuss	Michael Ironside
The Vagrant	Marshall Bell
Edie Roberts	Mitzi Kapture
Judy Dansig	Colleen Camp
Mr. Feemster	Stuart Pankin
Doattie	Patrika Darbo
Chuck	Mark McClure
Det. Lackson	Derek Mark Loughran
Mrs. Howler	Mildred Brion

Also with Teddy Wilson.

Credits
Executive Producer	Mel Brooks
Producer	Gillian Richardson-Walas
Co-Producer	Randy Auerbach
Director	Chris Walas
Directors of Photography	Jack Wallner
	John J. Connor
Sound	Jennifer L. Ware
Editor	Jay Ignaszewski
Production Manager	Robert Warner
Production Design	Michael Bolton
Art Direction	Eric A. Fraser
Set Decorator	Andrew Bernard
Costume Design	Katherine Dover
Casting	Bill Shepard
Screenplay	Richard Jefferies
Music	Christopher Young
Stunt Coordinator	Robert King

Film Facts
Running Time	91 minutes
Film	Deluxe Color
Sound	Dolby Stereo
Location	Arizona

Van Gogh
(Sony Pictures Classics)

Critics Rating: ★★★

Genre: Drama—Breathtakingly beautiful French biography of painter Van Gogh centering on the last few months of his life.

Plot: Jacques Dutronc plays the tormented artist. When the film opens he has just arrived in a small village where he soon finds companionship, love and inspiration from the locals in an idyllic setting. He is nonetheless tormented and within months has taken his own life, this after many years of madness. At a little over three hours, the film is ambling and true to a slower, more peaceful age, but is nevertheless a bit of an endurance test.

MPAA Rating: R—For sexuality and nudity.

Trivia: Other directors to film the life of Van Gogh have included Vincente Minnelli, Paul Cox and Robert Altman.

Cast
Vincent Van Gogh	Jacques Dutronc
Marguerite Gachet	Alexandra London
Dr. Gachet	Gerard Sety
Theo Van Gogh	Bernard Le Coq
Jo	Corinne Bourdon
Cathy	Elsa Zylberstein
Adeline Ravoux	Leslie Azzoulai
Madame Chevalier	Chantal Barbarit
The piano teacher	Claudine Ducret

Madame Ravoux ....Lisa Lametrie
The idiot....................................Didier Barbier
Also with Jacques Vidal.

Credits

Producers ....Daniel Toscan du Plantier
....Sylvie Danton
Director.......................................Maurice Pialat
Directors of Photography...........Emmanuel Machuel
....Gilles Henri
....Jacques Loiseleux
Sound ....Jean-Pierre Duret
Editors..........................Yann Dedet, Nathalie Hubert
Production Design...........................Philippe Pallut
....Katia Vischkof
Costume Design ....Edith Vesperini
Casting ....Marie-Jeanne Pascal
Written by.....................................Maurice Pialat

Film Facts

Country of Origin................................France
Running Time ....175 minutes
Film..Color
Sound..Stereo

MPAA Rating: Not Rated.

Cast

Dean.......................................Henry Jaglom
Jeanne.....................................Nelly Alard
Peggy.....................................Melissa Leo
Carlotta ....Suzanne Bertish
Eve ....Daphna Kastner
Dylan ....David Duchovny

Credits

Producer....................................Judith Wolinsky
Director/Editor ....Henry Jaglom
Director of Photography ....Hanania Baer
Sound (U.S.)..................................Sunny Meyer
Sound (Italy) ....Vito Catenia
Screenplay...................................Henry Jaglom
Music ....Marshall Barer
....David Colin Ross

Film Facts

Running Time ....92 minutes
Film ....Deluxe Color
Sound ....Stereo
Location...................Venice, Italy; Venice, California

Venice/Venice
(Rainbow)

Critics Rating: ★★★

Genre: Drama—A film about films, in the tradition of *The Player* and *Mistress*. The film has the Jaglom trademark: low-budget, homemade look.

Tag Line: "Life is not a film. Love is not an illusion...or vice versa."

Plot: Jaglom stars as Dean, a maverick independent filmmaker, who finds himself the center of attention at the Venice Film Festival and something of a celebrity. At the same time he has begun an affair with an admiring French journalist named Jeanne (Nelly Alard) that becomes more of an entanglement. In the second half of the film the director is back in Venice, California casting for a new film titled *Happy Endings*. Popping up throughout the film are interviews with women who speak directly to the camera about real life and the films. Each of the women believes that they were misled by the films to expect images of romance, love and happy endings that rarely exist in the real world.

Via Appia
(Strand)

Critics Rating: Not Rated.

Genre: Drama—A low-budget, cinema-verite-style, film within a film format. Via Appia is the gay district of Rio de Janeiro.

Plot: Peter Senner plays Frank, a former airline attendant who has been diagnosed with AIDS. After having spent the night with a man named Mario, (Kleber), Frank awakened to find the following message: Welcome to the AIDS Club. Desperate to confront the man who intentionally infected him, he returns to the scene of the crime taking along a film crew to document his search.

In his attempt to locate Mario, he searches the gay bathhouses, discos, hotels and parks. Though the premise is solid, this slow-moving film is hampered by its technical limitations.

MPAA Rating: Not Rated—Contains numerous scenes of full frontal male nudity.

Cast

Frank......................................Peter Senner
Jose.............................Guilherme de Padua

Sergio.....................................Jose Carlos Berenguer
The director...................................Yves Jansen
Mario..Luiz Kleber
Ulieno..Gustavo Motta
Lucia.....................................Margarita Schmidt
Credits
Producer.............................Norbert Friedlander
Director ....Jochen Hick
Director of Photography .....Peter Christian Neumann
Sound.........................Marc van der Willigen
Editor ....Claudia Vogeler
Written by ....Jochen Hick
Music ....Charly Schoppner
Film Facts
Country of Origin.........................Germany
Running Time ....90 minutes
Film ....Color (16 mm)
Sound ....Stereo

Voices From The Front
(Frameline)

Critics Rating: Not Rated.
Genre: Documentary—The battle in this powerful documentary is between people afflicted with AIDS and an inhuman and seemingly uncaring bureaucracy.
Plot: The focus of this admittedly one-sided film is on the AIDS activist movement in America (the ACT-UP group especially) and how they are forcing the government into action. The enemy of these activists is red tape, politics, ignorance, foot dragging, hospital mistreatment of AIDS patients and an assortment of other heart-wrenching horrors perpetrated and perpetuated by a system that is out of touch with the needs of its people.
MPAA Rating: Not Rated.
Credits
Producers/Directors/Editors.....................Robyn Hutt
....Sandra Elgear
....David Meieran
Co-Producers..............................Hilery Joy Kipnis
....Durwood Wiggins
Consulting Producers...................Jean Carlomusto
....Phil Zwickler
Associate Producers..................Carl Michael George
....Marla Maggenti

Film Facts
Running Time ....88 minutes
Film...Color/16mm
Sound ....Stereo

Voyager
(Castle Hill)

Critics Rating: ★★★★
Genre: Drama—Based on the 1957 German classic *Homo Faber* by Max Frisch, about coincidence and fate.
Plot: Set in the 1950s, Sam Shepard plays Walter Faber, an American engineer and self-made man who believes he is in charge of his own destiny. On a fatefull business trip to Mexico, Faber coincidentally makes the acquaintance of the brother of a long-lost friend. This is the first of many chance encounters that lead this middle-aged man on a journey of self-discovery. His friend, it seems, married the woman he once loved but abandoned. Sometime later, on an ocean liner to Europe, Faber meets and becomes sexually involved with a young woman named Sabeth (Delpy). Only later does he discover that she is his daughter by the woman he abandoned years earlier. This shatters all of his previously held beliefs and forces him to reevaluate his life.
MPAA Rating: PG-13
Cast
Walter Faber ....Sam Shepard
Sabeth ....Julie Delpy
Hanna ....Barbara Sukowa
Herbert Henke............................Dieter Kirchlechner
Charlene ....Traci Lind
Lewin...Bill Dunn
Ivy...................................Deborah-Lee Furness
Kurt...Thomas Heinze
Joachim.....................................August Zirner
Credits
Executive Producer ....Bodo Scriba
Producer ....Eberhard Junkersdorf
Director ....Volker Schlondorff
Directors of Photography................Yorgos Arvanitis
....Pierre L'Homme
Editor ....Dagmar Hirtz
Production Manager ....Alexander von Eschwege

Production Design ....Nicos Perakis
Artistic Advisor..................................Suzanne Baron
Set Designer....................................Benedikt Herforth
Costume Design ....Barbara Baum
Screenplay.........Rudy Wurlitzer, Volker Schlondorff
Based on the novel *Homo Faber* by ....Max Frisch

Music ....Stanley Myers
Film Facts
Country of Origin................France/Germany/Greece
Running Time ....117 minutes
Film ....Color/Black & White
Sound ....Dolby Stereo

The War Against The Indians

(Canadian Broadcasting Corp./Societe Radio-Canada)

Critics Rating: Not Rated.
Genre: Documentary
Plot: Canadian filmmaker Harry Rasky takes a straightforward approach to the cultural and historical distortions still being waged against American and Canadian Indians by society. The films discussions, made up almost entirely of interviews with Indians, cover a broad range of issues. This is a fascinating and compelling film about a difficult and often controversial subject.
MPAA Rating: Not Rated.

Credits

Producer/Director/Writer	Harry Rasky
Directors of Photography	Ken Gregg
	Milan Cleple

Film Facts

Running Time	150 minutes
Film	Color
Sound	Stereo

The Waterdance

(Samuel Goldwyn Co.)

Critics Rating: ★★★★
Genre: Drama—Writer Neal Jimenez (*River's Edge, For The Boys*) makes his codirectorial debut in this semiautobiographical drama about a young man's struggle to survive an accident that leaves him a paraplegic.
Tag Line: "Sometimes, life happens by accident."
Plot: Eric Stoltz (*Mask*) plays Joel, a promising young writer who is left paralyzed following a hiking accident. In a hospital with fellow paraplegics Ray (Wesley Snipes, *White Men Can't Jump*) and Bloss (William Forsythe, *Dick Tracy*) they are forced to come to terms, individually and collectively, with their situation.
MPAA Rating: PG-13

Cast

Joel Garcia	Eric Stoltz
Raymond Hill	Wesley Snipes
Bloss	William Forsythe
Anna	Helen Hunt
Rosa	Elizabeth Pena
Les	William Allen Young
Victor	Tony Genaro
Pat	Grace Zabriskie
Alice	Kimberley Scott
Vernon	Casey Stengal
Cheryl Lynn	Susan Gibney

Credits

Executive Producer	Guy Riedel
Producers	Gale Anne Hurd, Marie Cantin
Directors	Neal Jimenez, Michael Steinberg
Assistant Director	Josh King
Director of Photography	Mark Plummer
Sound Mixer	Steve Nelson
Editor	Jeff Freeman
Production Design	Richard Ziembicki
Art Direction	Ted Berner
Set Decoration	Julie M. Anderson
Costume Design	Isis Mussenden
Casting	Pam Dixon
Written by	Neal Jimenez
Music Supervisor	Sharon Boyle
Music	Michael Convertino

Film Facts

Running Time	106 minutes
Film	Color
Sound	Dolby Stereo

Waterland

(Fine Line Features)

Critics Rating: ★★★
Genre: Drama—An intricate literary work adapted from the award-winning novel by Graham Swift.
Tag Line: "Listen students and I'll tell you a story...of long-kept secrets, sexual scandal, even murder. It's the story of my life."

Plot: Jeremy Irons plays Tom Crick, a middle-aged Englishman now teaching history in a Pittsburgh high school. After being challenged by his students to make his class relevant to their lives, he begins to make it personal by relating the story of his own life over the past thirty years. The story is told in flashbacks that center on growing up in an area called the Fens, a marshland on the North Sea. A sexual involvement between Tom, as a teenager, and his girlfriend that would lead to an abortion, murder and suicide. Tom manages to capture their attention as well as their imagination in this original and compelling tale.

MPAA Rating: R—For sexuality, an abortion scene and for language.

Cast

Tom Crick	Jeremy Irons
Mary Crick	Sinead Cusack
Young Tom	Grant Warnock
Young Mary	Lena Headey
Matthew Price	Ethan Hawke
Dick Crick	David Morrissey
Lewis Scott	John Heard
Judy Dobson	Cara Buono
Freddie Parr	Callum Dixon
Henry Crick	Peter Postlethwaite

Credits

Executive Producers	Nik Powell
	Stephen Woolley, Ira Deutchman
Producers	Katy McGuinness, Patrick Cassavetti
Director	Stephen Gyllenhaal
Assistant Director	David Brown
Director of Photography	Robert Elswit
Sound	Simon Okin
Editor	Lesley Walker
Production Design	Hugo Luczyc-Wyhowski
Art Direction	Helen Rayner
Costume Design	Lindy Hemming
Casting (U.S.)	Deborah Aquila
Casting (U.K.)	Susie Figgis
Screenplay	Peter Prince
Based on the novel by	Graham Swift
Music	Carter Burwell

Film Facts

Country of Origin	Great Britain/U. S.
Running Time	95 minutes
Film	Metrocolor
Sound	Dolby Stereo
Location	Pittsburgh; London

Wax, Or The Discovery Of Television Among The Bees
(Jasmine Tea)

Critics Rating: Not Rated.

Genre: Science Fiction—This is an experimental and unconventionally bizarre film whose only dialogue is spoken by a narrator.

Plot: The title refers to bees that implant a futuristic television inside the head of the film's lead. This is a science-fiction head trip that uses video, stock film footage and computer animation to tell a futuristic tale. It is recommended for genre buffs and the adventuresome.

MPAA Rating: Not Rated.

Cast

Jacob Maker	David Blair
Melissa Maker	Meg Savlov
Allellee Zillah	Florence Ormezzano
James (Hive) Maker	William Burroughs
Father Bessarion	Father Bessarion
Dr. Clyde Tombaugh	Dr. Clyde Tombaugh

Credits

Producer/Director	David Blair
Director of Photography	Mark Kaplan
Sound/Music	Beo Morales, Brooks Williamson
Editor	Florence Ormezzano
Written by	David Blair

Film Facts

Running Time	85 minutes
Film	Color/Black & White
Sound	Stereo

Wayne's World
(Paramount)

Critics Rating: ★★★

Genre: Comedy—Actors-comedians Mike Myers and Dana Carvey have transformed their popular Saturday Night Live comedy routine into a big-screen blockbuster.

Tag Line: "You'll laugh. You'll cry. You'll hurl."

Plot: Like the SNL routine, the film focuses on Wayne (Myers) and Garth (Carvey), two heavy-metal heads who operate a cable access show from their basement in Aurora, Illinois.

When producer Rob Lowe offers the team a big-time show, the duo sell out and go corporate. In their pursuit of babes and fame, in that order, the two manage to lampoon heavy-metal party dudes in a witty and totally entertaining send-up.

Sophisticated and imaginative in its sophomoric humor, *Wayne's World* is cut from the same cloth as comedies like *Bill And Ted's Excellent Adventure*. Adults will appreciate the intelligent humor while younger audiences will find this film "way cool" on a different level.

MPAA Rating: PG-13

Trivia: Becoming the year's first mega-hit, *Wayne's World* remained number one at the box-office for five consecutive weeks; an achievement not matched since 1991's *The Silence Of The Lambs*.

Cast

Wayne Campbell	Mike Myers
Garth Algar	Dana Carvey
Benjamin Oliver	Rob Lowe
Cassandra	Tia Carrere
Noah Vanderhoff	Brian Doyle-Murray
Stacy	Lara Flynn Boyle
Mrs. Vanderhoff	Colleen Camp
Russell	Kurt Fuller

Also with Dan Bell, Frederick Coffin, Alice Cooper, Michael DeLuise, Donna Dixon, Chris Farley, Meat Loaf, Ed O'Neill, Robert Patrick, Ione Skye, Sean Gregory Sullivan, and Lee Tergesen.

Credits

Executive Producer	Howard W. Koch, Jr.
Producer	Lorne Michaels
Associate Producers	Dinah Minot
	Barnaby Thompson
Director	Penelope Spheeris
2nd Unit Director	Allan Graf
Assistant Director	John E. Hockridge
Director of Photography	Theo Van de Sande
2nd Unit Camera	Bobby Stevens
Sound	Thomas Nelson
Editor	Malcolm Campbell
Additional Editing	Earl Ghaffari
Production Manager	Tony Brown
Production Design	Gregg Fonseca
Casting	Glenn Daniels
Written by	Mike Myers
	Bonnie Turner, Terry Turner
Based on characters created by	Mike Myers

Music	J. Peter Robinson
Stunt Coordinator	Allan Graf

Film Facts

Running Time	95 minutes
Soundtrack	Reprise Records
Film	Technicolor
Sound	Dolby Stereo
Location	Los Angeles

We're Talkin' Serious Money
(Cinetel Films)

Critics Rating: Not Rated.

Genre: Comedy—Mildly humorous comedy about a pair of small-time New York thieves who move to Los Angeles.

Tag Line: "They could risk their lives in the scam of the century, or they could get real jobs. Tough choice."

Plot: Dennis Farina and Leo Rossi star as Sal and Charlie, two East Coast crooks who have skipped out on a loan from the Mafia. In an attempt to pay back the money they owe, they unintentionally engage in a big-time heist.

MPAA Rating: PG-13

Cast

Sal	Dennis Farina
Charlie	Leo Rossi
Valerie	Fran Drescher
Connie	Cynthia Frost
Gino "the Grocer"	John La Motta
Frankie "the Beast"	Peter Iacangelo
Joey Eggs	Anthony Powers
Cops	Lou Bonacki, John Cade
Rosemarie	Catherine Paolone
Michael	Robert Costanzo
Rosemarie's son	John Josef Spencer
Rosemarie's daughter	Maria Cavaiani
Amelia	Jeanie Moore
Marty "the Greek"	John Kapelos

Credits

Executive Producer	Harold Welb
Producer	Paul Hertzberg
Co-Producers	Leo Rossi, Lisa M. Hansen
Line Producer	Guy Louthan
Associate Producer	Catalaine Knell
Director	James Lemmo

1st Assistant Director.........................Whitney Hunter
2nd Assistant Director.........Franklin Adreon Vallette
Director of Photography ....Jacques Haitkin
2nd Unit Camera..............................Zoran Hochstatter
Sound Mixer......................................William M. Fiege
Editor ....Steve Nevius
Art Direction...................................Susan Benjamin
Set Decoration..Mary Buri
Wardrobe Supervisor..........................Barbara Ayers
Written by..James Lemmo
....Leo Rossi
Music ....Scott Grusin
Stunt Coordinator ....Spiro Razatos
Additional Stunt Coordinator.................Dan Bradley

Film Facts

Running Time ....100 minutes
Film ....Foto-Kem Color
Sound...Ultra-Stereo

When The Party's Over
(WTPO Production)

Critics Rating: Not Rated.
Genre: Drama—Set in Los Angeles, *When The Party's Over* is a modern-day drama about a group of roommates struggling with their identities. It also explores the paths they will each take when it's time to grow up and move on.
Plot: The story takes place during a New Year's Eve party held by four roommates—three very different women and a struggling gay actor (Kris Kamm). Roommate M.J. (Rae Dawn Chong) provides the friction that ignites the spirits and emotions of this group through her manipulations. The group interactions and melodrama take over and keep the plot moving in all directions from there.
MPAA Rating: Not Rated.

Cast

Frankie ....Elizabeth Berridge
Amanda...Sandra Bullock
M. J...Rae Dawn Chong
Banks...Kris Kamm
Taylor...Brian McNamara
Alexander ....Fisher Stevens

Credits

Producers..James A. Holt
..................................Ann Wycoff, Matthew Irmas

Director..Matthew Irmas
Director of Photography ....Alicia Webber
Sound ....Oliver Moss
Editors ....Dean Goodhill, Jerry Bixman
Production Design.............................Jon Gary Steele
Costume Design................................Terry Dresbach
Screenplay...Ann Wycoff
Story by.......................Matthew Irmas, Ann Wycoff
Music ....

Film Facts

Running Time ....114 minutes
Film ....Color
Sound ....Stereo
Location ....Los Angeles

Where Angels Fear To Tread
(Fine Line Features)

Critics Rating: ★★★★
Genre: Drama—Adapted from the E.M. Forester novel, this romantic drama follows a young widow who abandons her stuffy life in England and begins a new life in Italy only to be followed by her past.
Plot: Helen Mirren plays the widow Lilia who leaves her in-laws and her daughter behind. To the shock of her in-laws, she travels to Italy where she meets and marries a younger Italian man (Giovanni Guidelli). When the in-laws follow her, their lives are also forever changed as a result of their journey. From here the plot twists and character conflicts carry the film to its inevitable end.
MPAA Rating: PG

Cast

Caroline Abbott ....Helena Bonham Carter
Harriet Herriton..Judy Davis
Phillip Herriton...................................Rupert Graves
Lilia Herriton......................................Helen Mirren
Gina Carella...................................Giovanni Guidelli
Mrs. Herriton....................................Barbara Jefford
Mr. Abbott...Vass Anderson
Mrs. Theobald......................................Sylvia Barter
Irma...Sophie Kullman
Mr. Kingcroft ....Thomas Wheatley

Credits

Executive Producers ....Jeffrey Taylor
..............................Kent Walwin, Nick Elliott
Producer ....Derek Granger

Co-Producer ....Giovanna Romagnoli
Associate Producer ....Olivia Stewart
Director ....Charles Sturridge
Assistant Director (Italy) ....John Dodds
Assistant Director (U. K.)..................Cordelia Hardy
Director of Photography..................Michael Coulter
Sound..Peter Sutton
....Hugh Strain, John Ireland
Editor ....Peter Coulson
Production Managers ....Walter Massi
....Lil Stirling
Production Design...............................Simon Holland
Art Direction (Italy).......................Luigi Marchione
Art Direction (U. K.) ....Marianne Ford
Costume Design....................................Monica Howe
Casting ....Joyce Gallie, Rita Forzano
Screenplay..Tim Sullivan
...........................Derek Granger, Charles Sturridge
Based on the novel by ....E. M. Forster
Music..Rachel Portman

Film Facts
Country of Origin ....Great Britain
Running Time ....113 minutes
Soundtrack ....Virgin Film Music
Film...Eastmancolor
Sound...Dolby Stereo

Where Are We? Our Trip Through America
(Telling Pictures)

Critics Rating: Not Rated.

Genre: Documentary—Going in search of America, of roots and answers to topical questions, Academy-Award-winning documentary filmmakers Jeffrey Friedman and Rob Epstein (*Common Threads* and *The Times Of Harvey Milk*) took a drive through the Deep South and brought along their camera.

Randomly asking questions of an assortment of unusual and unlikely individuals, the film is a collection of sketchy bits and pieces of an American consciousness.

MPAA Rating: Not Rated.
Credits
Producers/Directors.........................Jeffrey Freidman
....Rob Epstein

Associate Producers ....Sharon Wood
....Pam Moskow
Director of Photography.................Jean de Segonzac
Sound ....Mark Roy
Editor...Ned Bastille
Music...Daniel Licht
Film Facts
Running Time ....73 minutes
Film...Color
Sound..Stereo
Location..Southern U. S.

Where The Day Takes You
(New Line Cinema)

Critics Rating: ★★★★

Genre: Drama—An all-star cast of up-and-comers fill out this tragic drama about the life of street kids in Hollywood. This is a beautifully photographed film about a very ugly and down-beat topic.

Plot: Dermot Mulroney (*Bright Angel, Career Opportunities*) plays King, a 21-year-old leader of a group of homeless runaways and throw-aways who have banded together to survive on the streets. They survive by stealing, selling drugs and prostitution. Their means of survival, however, is eventually the very thing that tears this "family" apart.

MPAA Rating: R—For language, violence and drug use.

Trivia: Christian Slater appears in an uncredited cameo.

Cast
Greg ....Sean Astin
Heather...Lara Flynn Boyle
Tommy Ray ....Peter Dobson
Little J ....Balthazar Getty
Brenda ....Ricki Lake
Crasher ....James Le Gros
King ....Dermot Mulroney
Manny...Will Smith
Ted ....Kyle MacLachlan
Charles ....Stephen Tobolowsky
Black...Adam Baldwin
Interviewer......................................Laura San Giacomo
Cop...Christian Slater
Also with Nancy McKeon, Alyssa Milano and Rachel Ticotin.

Credits

Executive Producers	Lisa M. Hansen
	Marc Rocco
Co-Executive Producer	Don McKeon
Producer	Paul Hertzberg
Co-Producer	Philip McKeon
Director	Marc Rocco
Assistant Director	Scott Javine
Director of Photography	King Baggot
Sound	Bill Fiege
Editor	Russell Livingstone
Production Design	Kirk Petrucelli
Set Decoration	Greg Grande
Casting	Mary Jo Slater
Written by	Kurt Voss
	Marc Rocco

Film Facts

Running Time	92 minutes
Film	Color
Sound	Dolby Stereo
Location	Los Angeles

Whispers In The Dark

(Paramount)

Critics Rating: ★★

Genre: Thriller

Plot: Annabella Sciorra stars as Ann, a Manhattan psychiatrist in a loveless relationship. When Eve (Deborah Unger), a patient with a wild and kinky sex life is brutally murdered, Ann becomes unwittingly involved. A homicide detective (Anthony LaPaglia) investigates the numerous suspects in this erotic mystery and eventually unravels this psycho-sexual tale. Fine performances by all lift the film above pure exploitation.

MPAA Rating: R

Cast

Ann Hecker	Annabella Sciorra
Doug McDowell	Jamey Sheridan
Morgenstern	Anthony LaPaglia
Leo Green	Alan Alda
Sarah Green	Jill Clayburgh
Johnny C.	John Leguizamo
Eve Abergray	Deborah Unger
Mrs. McDowell	Jacqueline Brooks
Billy O'Meara	Gene Canfield
Paul	Anthony Heald

Credits

Executive Producers	Eric Freiser
	Richard Gitelson, William Link
Producers	Martin Bregman
	Michael S. Bregman
Co-Producer	Stephen F. Kesten
Director	Christopher Crowe
Assistant Director	Anthony H. Gittelson
2nd Unit Director	David Ellis
Director of Photography	Michael Chapman
Additional Camera	Richard J. Quinlan
2nd Unit Camera	Michael Benson
Sound	Allan Byer
Editor	Bill Pankow
Production Design	John Jay Moore
Set Decoration	Justin Scoppa, Jr.
Costume Design	John Dunn
Casting	Mary Colquhoun
Written by	Christopher Crowe
Music	Thomas Newman

Film Facts

Running Time	102 minutes
Soundtrack	Varese Sarabande
Film	DuArt Color
Sound	Dolby Stereo
Location	New York; North Carolina
Other Working Titles	*Sessions*

White Men Can't Jump

(20th Century Fox)

Critics Rating: ★★★★

Genre: Comedy—Wesley Snipes (*Jungle Fever, New Jack City*) and Woody Harrelson of *Cheers* star in this critically hailed comedy and surprise hit about two cons on the basketball court running a scam that backfires.

Plot: Harrelson plays Billy Hoyle, a naive appearing Southern hick who has just arrived in Southern California. Snipes plays Sidney Dean, a local black basketball player who rules the courts. When Sidney is taken in by Billy's scam (no one expects this white boy to be much of a player), he suggests that they join forces. Together they scam other players until the day Sidney turns the tables on Billy and gets even.

MPAA Rating: R—For language and sensuality.

Cast

Sidney Deane	Wesley Snipes
Billy Hoyle	Woody Harrelson
Gloria Clemente	Rosie Perez
Rhonda Deane	Tyra Ferrell
Zeke	Kevin Benton
Robert	Cylk Cozart
George	Ernest Harden, Jr.
Junior	Kadeem Hardison
Raymond	Marques Johnson
Walter	John Marshall Jones
Dwight "The Flight" McGhee	Nigel Miguel
T. J.	David Roberson

Credits

Executive Producer	Michele Rappaport
Producers	Don Miller, David Lester
Director	Ron Shelton
Assistant Director	Richard Wells
Director of Photography	Russell Boyd
Sound	Kirk Francis
Editor	Paul Seydor
Production Design	Dennis Washington
Art Direction	Robert Fortune
Set Decoration	Robert Benton
Costume Design	Francine Jamison-Tanchuck
Casting	Victoria Thomas
Written by	Ron Shelton
Music	Bernie Wallace
Stunt Coordinator	Julius LeFlore

Film Facts

Running Time	115 minutes
Soundtrack	EMI Records
Film	Deluxe Color
Sound	Dolby Stereo
Location	Los Angeles

White Sands
(Warner Bros.)

Critics Rating: ★★

Genre: Thriller—A very dark modern-day thriller about a small town sheriff who stumbles onto big-time trouble.

Plot: Willem Dafoe stars as deputy sheriff Ray Dolezal. When he happens upon a dead body and a half-million dollars in the desert, his troubles begin. Before he knows what has happened, he is attacked and the money is stolen. The money, it turns out, was originally stolen from the government just as it was being used in an FBI sting. As sheriff Ray goes undercover to retrieve the money, the FBI is hot on his tail, in this dark adventure.

MPAA Rating: R—For violence, language and a scene of sensuality.

Cast

Ray Dolezal	Willem Dafoe
Lane Bodine	Mary Elizabeth Mastrantonio
Gorman Lennox	Mickey Rourke
Greg Meeker	Samuel L. Jackson
Bert Gibson	M. Emmet Walsh
Roz	Beth Grant
Flynn	James Rebhorn
Molly Dolezal	Mimi Rogers
Noreen	Maura Tierney

Also with John P. Ryan and Fred Dalton Thompson.

Credits

Executive Producers	James G. Robinson
	David Nicksay, Gary Barber
Producers	William Sackheim, Scott Rudin
Associate Producer	David Wisnievitz
Director	Roger Donaldson
Assistant Director	Joel Segal
Director of Photography	Peter Menzies, Jr.
Sound	Richard Goodman
Editor	Nicholas Beauman
Unit Production Manager	David Wisnievitz
Production Design	John Graysmark
Art Direction	Michael Rizzo
Set Decoration	Michael Seirton
Costume Design	Deborah Everton
Casting	David Rubin
Screenplay	Daniel Pyne
Music	Patrick O'Hearn

Film Facts

Running Time	101 minutes
Soundtrack	Morgan Creek Records
Film	Eastmancolor
Sound	Dolby Stereo
Location	Estancia, Santa Fe, Taos, and Alamogordo, New Mexico

White Trash
(Fred Baker Film & Video Co.)

Critics Rating: Not Rated.

Genre: Drama—Shot on an 8mm video camera, this gritty look into the lives of Hollywood street hustlers and drug addicts qualifies as an underground venture.

Plot: The story takes place on the day of the funeral of a runaway street hustler played by Brian Patrick. We come to know him through the reflections of friends and family during the course of the day. Though this look at reality is powerful, it is also a hopeless and difficult topic. Combined with low technical achievements this is a film that will be accessible to a very limited audience.

MPAA Rating: Not Rated.

Cast

CC's father	Jack Betts
Percy	Wheaton James
CC's sister	Winnie Thexton
Casino	John Hartman
John ("Rio")	Sean Christiansen
"Rotten" Rita	Periel Marr
CC	Brian Patrick

Credits

Producer/Director	Fred Baker
Assistant Director	Niva Ruschell
Director of Photography	Fred Baker
Sound	Fred Baker
Editor	Robert Simpson
Art Direction	Steve Nelson
Costume Design	Rikki Roberts
Written by	Mel Clay
Based on the play by	Mel Clay
Music	Fred Baker, Mariano Rocca

Film Facts

Running Time	87 minutes
Film	Hi-8 Video Color (blown up to 35mm)
Sound	Stereo

Who Shot Pat?

(Castle Hill)

Critics Rating: Not Rated.

Genre: Drama—Set in the 1950s, this nostalgic drama focuses on a group of teens growing up in Brooklyn, New York.

Plot: David Knight stars as Bic Bickham, the leader of a pack of friends. The film follows the friends as they get into trouble, fall in love and experience the growing pains of this much more innocent age.

MPAA Rating: R—For language.

Cast

Bic Bickham	David Knight
Devlin Moran	Sandra Bullock
Freddie	Chris Cardona
Cougar	Aaron Ingram
Mark Bickham	Kevin Otto
Goldie	Michael Puzzo
Patakango	Brad Randall
Tony	Christopher Crann
Vinnie	Gregg Marc Miller
Mr. Donnelly	Damon Chandler
Mitsy	Bridget Fogle
Ricky (Dick)	Clint Jordan
Marianna	Ella Arolovi
Carmen	Nicholas Reiner
Detective Levy	Ben Digregorio
Detective Driskill	Marc Davenport
Mr. Bickham	Jim Flanagan
Mrs. Bickham	Joyce Ellen Hill
Paula	Allison Eikaran
Ellen	Colatta Jackson
Tish	Jessica Tuck
Francis	Gloria Darpino
Therese	Cheryl Hendricks

Credits

Producer	Halle Brooks
Associate Producers	Gaby Gerber
	Sidney Spencer
Director	Robert Brooks
Director of Photography	Robert Brooks
Editors	Robert Brooks, Halle Brooks
Art Direction	Lionel Driskill
Screenplay	Robert Brooks, Halle Brooks

Film Facts

Running Time	104 minutes
Film	Color
Sound	Stereo
Other Titles	*Who Shot Patakango?*

The Whole Truth

(Cinevista)

Critics Rating: Not Rated.

Genre: Comedy—An independent romantic comedy from first-time director Jonathan Smythe about a relationship that turns sour.

Plot: When Vanessa (Kane) and Dan (Cohen) meet through a dating service it seems to be a case of opposites attracting. However, Vanessa's attraction soon turns to repulsion and she ends the relationship. Dan, however, will not let go. She eventually must take him to court on harassment charges where each side plays out its side of the truth.

MPAA Rating: Not Rated.

Cast

Dan .... Dan Cohen
Vanessa .... Dyan Kane
Judge .... Jim Willig
Also with Paul Kahane and Pat Lemay.

Credits

Executive Producer .... Dan Cohen
Producer .... Richard Bree
Directors .... Dan Cohen, Jonathan Smythe
Director of Photography .... Dennis Michaels
Sound .... Doris Soraci
Editor .... Rick Derby
Art Direction .... Christine Itle
Costume Design .... Toni Karahalios, Aggy Tockett
Screenplay .... Dan Cohen
Music .... Bill Grabowski

Film Facts

Running Time .... 85 minutes
Film .... Color
Sound .... Stereo

Wild Orchid 2: Two Shades Of Blue

(Vision International)

Critics Rating: Not Rated.

Genre: Drama—The only relationship to the original is its erotic theme. In this sexy drama, a young woman is torn between two worlds. One involving sex, the other love.

Plot: Nina Siemaszko plays Blue, a 17-year-old girl on tour with her musician father (Tom Skerritt, *Poison Ivy*). When he dies of a drug overdoses, she is forced by her father's drug dealer into a life of prostitution. While sex becomes just a job, her love belongs to Josh (Brant Fraser) a local high school boy. When she tries to escape her past, it of course catches up to her, leaving her to confront it head on.

MPAA Rating: R—For strong sensuality, language and drug content.

Cast

Elle .... Wendy Hughes
Ham .... Tom Skerritt
Sully .... Robert Davi
Josh .... Brent Fraser
Blue .... Nina Siemaszko
Mona .... Liane Curtis
Jules .... Joe Dallesandro
Dixon .... Christopher McDonald
Col. Winslow .... Stafford Morgan

Credits

Executive Producer .... Mark Damon
Producers .... David Saunders, Rafael Eisenman
Co-Producer .... Howard Worth
Associate Producer .... Steve Kaminsky
Director .... Zalman King
Assistant Director .... Roger La Page
Director of Photography .... Marc Reshovsky
Additional Camera .... David Rudd
.... Peter Lyons Collister
Sound .... Stephen Halbert
Editors .... Marc Grossman
.... James Gavin
Production Design .... Richard Amend
Casting .... Ferne Cassel
Written by .... Zalman King
Music .... George S. Clinton

Film Facts

Running Time .... 107 minutes
Film .... Foto-Kem Color
Sound .... Ultra-Stereo
Other Working Titles .. *Wild Orchid II: The Seduction*

Wild Wheels

(Tara)

Critics Rating: ★★★★★

Genre: Documentary—16mm original film by director Harold Blank, son of filmmaker Les Blank.

Plot: A humorous and quirky trip across the country captures 45 unusual and incredible cars, along with their equally interesting owners. This is a fascinating and entertaining kitsch display of modern-day pop art on wheels.

MPAA Rating: Not Rated.

Credits
Producer/Director ....Harrod Blank
Directors of Photography ....Paul Cope
....Harrod Blank
....Les Blank
Additional Camera ....David Silberberg
....Liz Zivic
Sound...David Silberberg
Editor...Harrod Blank
Narration written/directed................David Silberberg

Film Facts
Running Time ....64 minutes
Film.......................................Color (16 mm)
Sound ....Stereo

Wind
(TriStar)

Critics Rating: ★★★

Genre: Drama—A fictional story of one man's greatest challenge and the obstacles that stand in his way. The film is based on the America's Cup races.

Tag Line: "There's one thing better than winning the America's Cup...to lose it, then win it back."

Plot: Matthew Modine stars as Will Parker, helmsman for the Americans as they sail against the Australians for the America's Cup. When America loses the Cup for the first time in the race's history, Will is determined to win it back. It is also a story about losing and winning in a relationship, as well. He enlists the help of his former girlfriend, Kate (Jennifer Grey). Together they find themselves plunging into a world where money, power, love and ambition are the driving forces.

MPAA Rating: PG-13—For some sensuality.

Trivia: The home of Cliff Robertson's character in the film is a mansion located in Newport, Rhode Island. The mansion has appeared in numerous films, including *The Betsy* and *Mr. North*.

Cast
Will Parker ....Matthew Modine
Kate Bass ....Jennifer Grey
Morgan Weld.....................................Cliff Robertson
Jack Neville ....Jack Thompson
Joe Heiser..Stellan Skarsgard
Abigail Weld ....Rebecca Miller
Charley Moore ....Ned Vaughn

TV commentator ....Peter Montgomery
Sarge...Elmer Ahlwardt
Butler..Saylor Creswell
George..James Rebhorn
Artemus..Michael Higgins
Tad..Ron Colbin
Swami...Ken Kensei
Danny...Bill Buell
Jeff...Tom Fervoy
Tony...Ron Palillo
Lyle..Matt Malloy

Credits
Executive Producers ....Francis Ford Coppola
....Fred Fuchs
Producers....................Mata Yamamoto, Tom Luddy
Associate Producer..............................Betsy Pollock
Director ....Carroll Ballard
1st Assistant Director.........................L. Dean Jones
2nd Assistant Director ....Drew Rosenberg
2nd Asst. Director (Australia).......Brendan Campbell
Director of Photography ....John Toll
First Assistant Camera.......................Paul Marbury
2nd Unit Camera ....Gary Capo
Aerial Cinematography ....Stan McClain
Sound ....Drew Kunin
Sound Design ....Alan Splet
Editor...Michael Chandler
Production Manager (U.S.)...................Diana Phillips
Production Manager (Australia)..................Grant Hill
Production Design ....Laurence Eastwood
Art Direction (Australia) ....Nick Bonham
Art Direction (Newport)....................Paul W. Gorfine
Art Direction (Utah) ....Roger S. Crandall
Set Decoration (Australia)..................Richard Hobbs
Set Decoration (Newport)..................Bobbie Frankel
Set Decoration (Utah) ....Brian Lives
Costume Design ....Marit Allen
Makeup.......................Sharon Ilson, Kirsten Veysey
Casting.................................Linda Phillips Palo
Screenplay...Rudy Wurlitzer
....Mac Gudgeon
Story by ....Jeff Benjamin
........................Roger Vaughan, Kimball Livingston
Music ....Basil Poledouris

Film Facts
Running Time ....123 minutes
Film..Technicolor
Sound ....Dolby Stereo
Location...............Australia; Newport, Rhode Island;
....Utah; Hawaii

Window Shopping
(World Artists)

Critics Rating: Not Rated.

Genre: Comedy—A send-up of the traditional musical, *Window Shopping* is a humorous love story that takes place entirely in a shopping mall.

Plot: Delphine Seyrig stars as Jeanne, the wife of a workaholic boutique owner. Jeanne's former lover comes to town one day and threatens her marriage. Elsewhere in the mall, the shops are full of men and women cheating on one another, plotting and scheming for love and money in this satirical look at the decade of the '80s.

MPAA Rating: Not Rated.

Cast

Jeanne	Delphine Seyrig
Robert	Nicolas Tronc
Eli	John Berry
Mado	Lio
Lili	Cottencon
M. Schwartz	Charles Denner
M. Jean	Jean-Francois Balmer
Sylvie	Myriam Boyer
Pascale	Pascale Salkin

Credits

Producer	Martine Marignac
Director	Chantal Akerman
Directors of Photography	Gilberto Azevedo
	Luc Benhamou
Sound	Henri Morelle
	Miguel Rejas
Editor	Francine Sandberg
Art Direction	Serge Marzloff
Costume Design	Pierre Albert
Screenplay	Pascal Bonitzer
	Henry Bean
	Chantal Akerman
	Jean Gruault
	Leora Barish
Music	Marc Herouet
Lyrics	Chantal Akerman

Film Facts

Country of Origin	France/Belgium/Switzerland
Running Time	96 minutes
Film	Fujicolor
Sound	Stereo

The Winter In Lisbon
(Castle Hill)

Critics Rating: Not Rated.

Genre: Thriller—Dizzy Gillespie makes his acting debut in this English and French romantic thriller with subtitles.

Plot: The story is a simple one. Gillespie plays Bill Swann, an American jazz player in San Sebastian, a resort in Spain. When Jim (Christian Vadim), one of the members of Bill's quartet, becomes sexually involved with a local woman, the intrigue begins. She just happens to be married to the local mobster, and before Jim knows what has happened he becomes involved in a murder-conspiracy.

MPAA Rating: Not Rated.

Cast

Bill Swann	Dizzie Gillespie
Jim Biralbo	Christian Vadim
Lucrecia	Helene de Saint-Pere
Morton	Michel Duperial
Malcolm	Fernando Guillen
Floro	Eusebio Poncela
Daphne	Aitzpea Goenaga
Ramires	Carlos Wallenstein
Oscar	Isidoro Fernandez
Silveira	Victor Norte
Rigoleto	Mikel Garmendia

Credits

Executive Producer	Tino Navarro
Director	Jose Antonio Zorrilla
Assistant Director	Joseba Salegi
Director of Photography	Jean Francis Gondre
Sound	Ricardo Steinberg
	Daniel Goldstein
Editors	Pablo G. Del Amo
	Ivan Aleso
Production Manager	Jose Antonio Gomez
Art Direction	Mario Alberto
Set Decoration	Augusto Mayer
Costume Design	Javier Artinano
Written by	Jose Antonio Zorrilla
	Mason M. Funk
Based on the novel by	Antonio Munoz Molina
French Dialogue Adaptation	Pierre Fabre
Music	Dizzy Gillespie
Musical Arranger	Slide Hampton
Additional Music	Danilo Perez

Film Facts

Country of Origin ....Spain/France/Portugal
Language ....English/French (subtitled)
Running Time ....104 minutes
Film ....Color
Sound ....Stereo

Wiping The Tears Of Seven Generations

(Kifaru)

Critics Rating: Not Rated.

Genre: Documentary

Plot: The film uses a memorial horseback ride by Lakota Indians to the 1890 Wounded Knee massacre site as a focal point to retell American history from the Indians' point of view. The filmmakers use photographs, paintings, historical documents and interviews with elder tribespeople to paint a moving portrait of a past filled with persecution, starvation and extermination. From the early European attempts to seize land to the final slaughter of unarmed Indians at Wounded Knee, this film is both passionate and powerful.

MPAA Rating: Not Rated.

Cast

Narrator........................Hanna Left Hand Bull Sixico

Credits

Producer...Gary Rhine
Associate Producer ....Fidel Moreno
Directors.........................Gary Rhine, Fidel Moreno
Directors of Photography.......................Gary Rhine
....Fidel Moreno
Editor..Laurie Schmidt
Written by ....Gary Rhine, Phil Cousineau
Music Supervisor...........................Robert La Bratte

Film Facts

Running Time ....60 minutes
Film ....Color (16mm)
Sound ....Stereo
Location ....South Dakota

Wisecracks

(Alliance Releasing)

Critics Rating: Not Rated.

Genre: Documentary—Director Gail Singer documents the powerfully funny female comics of today and yesterday.

Plot: From interviews with contemporary comedians like Whoopi Goldberg, to vintage TV clips of veteran comics Lucille Ball and Carol Burnett, the film explores a broad range of material in a very entertaining style. The majority of film, however, is made up of female performers, on stage performing their acts. Some of the performers are funnier than others. Some better than others. Each adds a strong feminist perspective, and sheds light on a woman's place in the profession and the world at large.

MPAA Rating: Not Rated.

Cast

With Joy Behar, The Clichettes, Ellen DeGeneres, Phyllis Diller, Faking It Three, Whoopi Goldberg, Geri Jewell, Maxine Lapiduss, Jenny Lecoat, Paula Poundstone, Sandra Shamas, Pam Stone, Deborah Theaker and Kim Wayans.

Credits

Executive Producers ....Rina Fraticelli
...................................Ginny Stikeman, Susan Cavan
Producers ....Gail Singer, Signe Johansson
Director...Gail Singer
Directors of Photography...........................Zoe Dirse
....Bob Fresco
Editor ....Gordon McClellan
Music ....Maribeth Solomon

Film Facts

Country of Origin.......................................Canada
Running Time ....93 minutes
Film ....Color
Sound ....Stereo

Woman, Demon, Human

(Ren, Gui, Qing)

(Jasmine Tea)

Critics Rating: Not Rated.

Genre: Drama—Filmed in 1987 and only now released in the U.S.

Plot: Told in flashback form, this is the story of Qui Yun, a Soochow Opera singer, and her lonely rise to stardom. Yun is portrayed by three different actresses in different stages of her life, spanning four decades, from the 1950s to the 1980s. Will appeal to sophisticated art-house and specialty audiences.

MPAA Rating: Not Rated.

Cast

With Xu Shouli, Li Baotian, Pei Yan-ling, Gong Lin, Wang Feifei and Ji Qilin.

Credits

Director ....Huang Shuqin
Directors of Photography ....Xia Lixing
....Ji Hongsheng
Art Direction.............................Zheng Changfu
Screenplay................................Huang Shuqin
....Li Ziyu
....Song Guoxum
Music..Yang Mao
Conducted by ....Wang Yongji

Film Facts

Country of Origin ....China
Running Time ....104 minutes
Film ....Color
Sound ....Stereo

A Woman, Her Man And Her Futon

(Walrus/Republic Pictures)

Critics Rating: Not Rated.

Genre: Drama—*Woman* is a drama about two aspiring Los Angeles screenwriters who have a difficult time making their relationship work.

Plot: Jennifer Rubin (*Delusions*, *Too Much Sun*) is a recently divorced young woman trying to put the pieces of her life back together. She also happens to be writing a semi-autobiographical screenplay. While working for a video company, she meets an aspiring filmmaker. The only problem is that they are both more interested in their work than their relationship.

MPAA Rating: R—For language and scenes of strong sexuality.

Trivia: An August 1992 article in *The Wall Street Journal* included this film among the many B films that were rushing to video, giving the majors a run for their money. Fans of the television drama *Melrose Place* will recognize Grant Show appearing as the character Randy.

Cast

Helen ....Jennifer Rubin
Donald.....................................Lance Edwards
Randy.......................................Grant Show
Paul..Michael Cerveris
Jimmy......................................Richard Gordon
Max..Robert Lipton
Gail..Delaune Michel

Credits

Executive Producer ....Roy McAree
Producers ....Dale Rosenbloom
....Mussef Sibay
Director ....Mussef Sibay
Assistant Director.....................Louie Lawless
Director of Photography ....Michael Davis
Sound ....Austin H. McKinney
....Marty Kasparian
Editor.......................................Howard Heard
Production Design ....Peter Paul Raubertas
Art Direction............................Florina Roberts
Costume Design ....Lothar Delgado
Casting.....................................Andrea Stone Guttfreund
....Laurel Smith
Written by ....Mussef Sibay
Music.......................................Joel Goldsmith
Visual Consultant ....Alexander Graves

Film Facts

Running Time ....90 minutes
Film..CFI Color
Sound ....Surround Stereo

World Apartment Horror

(Sony Music Entertainment)

Critics Rating: Not Rated.

Genre: Action—Japanese director Katsuhiro Otomo, best known for his cult hit *Akira*, approaches the topic of racial intolerance in this outrageously offbeat and humorous live-action feature.

Plot: Hiroki Tanaka stars as Itta, an aspiring gangster sent by his Yakuza boss to evict an apartment full of foreign immigrants so that the building can be torn down. This tough guy, however, is no match for these tenants and their supernatural powers.

MPAA Rating: Not Rated.

Cast

Itta ....Hiroki Tanaka
Chang ....Weng Huarong
Misaki ....Kimiko Nakagawa
Hide ....Yuji Nakamura
Kokubu ....Hiroshi Shimuzu
Mohammed ....Ahmed Abud Said

Credits

Producers ....Hiro Osaki
....Yasuhisa Kazama
Director ....Katsuhiro Otomo

Director of Photography....................Noboru Shinoda
Editor ....Kan Suzuki
Written by ....Katsuhiro Otomo
....Keiko Nobumoto
Music ....Kimio Nomura

Film Facts

Country of Origin ....Japan
Language.......................................Japanese (subtitled)
Running Time ....97 minutes
Film ....Color
Sound ....Stereo

Year Of The Comet
(Columbia)

Critics Rating: ★★★

Genre: Comedy—Predictable but nonetheless entertaining romantic comedy.

Plot: Penelope Ann Miller (*The Gun In Betty Lou's Handbag*) stars as Margaret Harwood, the daughter of a wine merchant. While going through the estate wine cellars she discovers a rare bottle of wine. Her father soon sells it for a tasty sum. An employee of the new owner of the wine, Oliver Plexico (Timothy Daly, *Love Or Money* and the TV sitcom *Wings*), is sent to retrieve it. The two, of course, are opposites and do what opposites usually do. But not before they outsmart an evil scientist who is in hot pursuit.

MPAA Rating: PG-13

Cast

Margaret Harwood	Penelope Ann Miller
Oliver Plexico	Tim Daly
Philippe	Louis Jourdan
Sir Mason Harwood	Ian Richardson
Richard Harwood	Timothy Bentinck
Nico	Art Malik
Doctor Roget	Jacques Mathou
Landlady	Julia McCarthy
Ian	Ian McNiece

Credits

Executive Producers	Phil Kellogg
	Alan Brown
Producers	Nigel Wooll
	Peter Yates
Director	Peter Yates
Assistant Director	Gerry Gavigan
Director of Photography	Roger Pratt
Sound	Ken Weston
Editor	Ray Lovejoy
Production Design	Anthony Pratt
Art Direction	Desmond Crowe
	Chris Seagers
Set Decoration	Stephenie McMillan
Costume Design	Marilyn Vance-Straker
Casting	Noel Davis
	Jeremy Zimmerman
	Pam Dixon
Written by	William Goldman
Music	Hummie Mann

Film Facts

Running Time	90 minutes
Soundtrack	Varese Sarabande
Film	Rank Color
Sound	Dolby Stereo
Location	Scotland; United Kingdom; France

Zebrahead
(Triumph)

Critics Rating: ★★★★
Genre: Drama—An energetic, stylish, teenage romance between a black girl and a white boy.
Tag Line: "It's about change...It's about time."
Plot: Michael Rapaport plays Zack, a Jewish boy attending a mostly black high school in Detroit. When he starts up a relationship with a black girl named Nikki (Wright), he starts a firestorm of protest. Not only do the parents object, but the otherwise hip fellow students are also hostile. On top of everything, Zack becomes his own worst enemy when he is overheard by Nikki telling a sexist, racist joke. Dialogue, performances and technical credits are first-rate.
MPAA Rating: R—For strong language.

Cast

Zack Glass	Michael Rapaport
Nikki	N'Bushe Wright
Otis Wimms	Paul Butler
Dee Wimms	DeShonn Castle
Marlene	Candy Ann Brown
Mr. Modell	Luke Reilly
Mr. Cimino	Dan Ziskie
Dominic	Kevin Corrigan
Saul	Martin Priest
Nut	Ron Johnson
Richard Glass	Ray Sharkey
Diane	Helen Shaver
Mrs. Wilson	Marsha Florence

Credits

Executive Producers	Oliver Stone
	Janet Yang
Co-Executive Producer	Peter Newman
Producers	Jeff Dowd
	Charles Mitchell, William Willett
Line Producer	Stan Wlodkowski
Associate Producer	Matthew Coppola
Director	Anthony Drazan
Assistant Director	Don Wilkerson
Director of Photography	Maryse Alberti
Sound	Paul Cote
Editor	Elizabeth Kling
Production Design	Naomi Shohan
Art Direction	Dan Whifler
Set Decoration	Penny Barrett
Costume Design	Carol Oditz
Casting	Deborah Aquila
Written by	Anthony Drazan
Music Supervision	M. C. Serch
Music	Taj Mahal

Film Facts

Running Time	100 minutes
Soundtrack	Ruffhouse/Columbia Records
Film	DuArt Color
Sound	Dolby Stereo
Location	Detroit

Zentropa
(Prestige)

Critics Rating: Not Rated.
Genre: Thriller—Shot mostly in black and white, Zentropa is a suspenseful and stylized political thriller set in Germany in 1945. Originally titled *Europa*.
Plot: Jean-Marc Barr stars as Leopold, an idealistic young American with dreams of building a better world. Working as an apprentice conductor on a train, he unwittingly becomes involved with a group of surviving Nazis intent on political sabotage. His involvement eventually leads to murder and a tragic end. With nods to many of Hollywood's classic thrillers, Zentropa is a dark and stylized film that will appeal to genre fans and art-house audiences alike.
MPAA Rating: Not Rated.

Cast

Leopold Kessler	Jean-Marc Barr
Katharina Hartmann	Barbara Sukowa
Lawrence Hartmann	Udo Kier
Max Hartmann	Jorgen Reenberg
Uncle Kessler	Ernst Hugo

Jaregard Pater ....Erik Mork
Col. Harris ....Eddie Constantine
Jew ....Lars Von Trier
Narrator ....Max Von Sydow

Credits
Executive Producers ....Gerard Mital
....Lars Kolvig
....Gerard Corbiau
....Philippe Guez
Producers ....Peter Aalbak Jensen
....Bo Christensen
Director ....Lars Von Trier
Assistant Director ....Tom Hedegaard
2nd Unit Director ....Tommy Gislason
Directors of Photography...............Henning Bendtsen
........................Edward Klosinky, Jean-Paul Meurisse

Sound...Per Streit Jensen
Editor...Herve Schneid
Production Design ....Henning Bahs
Costume Design ....Mann Rasmussen
Screenplay...Lars Von Trier
....Niels Vorsel
Music ....Joakim Holbek
Special Effects ....Dansk Special Effekt Service
Front-Projection Effects...............................Paul Witz
Special Makeup Effects...................Morten Jacobsen

Film Facts
Country of Origin ....France/Germany/Denmark
Running Time ....117 minutes
Film ....Black & White/Kodak Pathe Color
Sound ....Dolby Stereo
Other Titles ....*Europa*

257

1993
Academy Awards

The following are nominees and winners of the 65th annual Academy Awards for films released in 1992. The awards were presented March 29, 1993. Winners are indicated with a star.

Best Picture
The Crying Game
A Few Good Men
Howards End
Scent Of A Woman
★ *Unforgiven*
Best Director
Robert Altman, *The Player*
Martin Brest,
Scent Of A Woman
★ Clint Eastwood, *Unforgiven*
James Ivory, *Howards End*
Neil Jordan, *The Crying Game*
Best Actor
Robert Downey, Jr., *Chaplin*
Clint Eastwood, *Unforgiven*
★ Al Pacino, *Scent Of A Woman*
Stephen Rea,
The Crying Game
Denzel Washington,
Malcolm X
Best Actress
Catherine Deneuve, *Indochine*
Mary McDonnell,
Passion Fish
Michelle Pfeiffer, *Love Field*
Susan Sarandon,
Lorenzo's Oil
★ Emma Thompson,
Howards End
Best Supporting Actor
Jaye Davidson,
The Crying Game

★ Gene Hackman, *Unforgiven*
Jack Nicholson,
A Few Good Men
Al Pacino,
Glengarry Glen Ross
David Paymer,
Mr. Saturday Night
Best Supporting Actress
Judy Davis,
Husbands And Wives
Joan Plowright,
Enchanted April
Vanessa Redgrave,
Howards End
Miranda Richardson, *Damage*
★ Marisa Tomei,
My Cousin Vinny
Best Original Screenplay
Woody Allen,
Husbands And Wives
★ Neil Jordan, *The Crying Game*
George Miller and
Nick Enright, *Lorenzo's Oil*
David Webb Peoples,
Unforgiven
John Sayles, *Passion Fish*
Best Adapted Screenplay
Richard Friedenberg,
A River Runs Through It
Bo Goldman,
Scent Of A Woman
★ Ruth Prawer Jhabvala,
Howards End

Peter Barnes, *Enchanted April*
Michael Tolkin, *The Player*
Best Foreign Language Film
Close To Eden (Russia)
Daens (Belgium)
★ *Indochine* (France)
A Place In The World
(Uruguay)(Disqualified)
Schtonk (Germany)
Best Art Direction
Bram Stoker's Dracula,
Thomas Sanders, set
decoration-Garrett Lewis
Chaplin, Stuart Craig, set
decoration- Chris A. Butler
★ *Howards End,*
Luciana Arrighi, set
decoration-Ian Whittaker
Toys, Ferdinando Scarfiotti,
set decoration-Linda
DeScenna
Unforgiven, Henry Bumstead,
set decoration-Janice
Blackie-Goodine
Best Cinematography
Hoffa, Stephen H. Burnum
Howards End,
Tony Pierce-Roberts
The Lover, Robert Fraisse
★ *A River Runs Through It,*
Philippe Rousselot
Unforgiven,
Jack N. Green

Best Costume Design

★ *Bram Stoker's Dracula*,
   Eiko Ishioka
Enchanted April,
   Sheena Napier
Howards End, Jenny Beavan
   and John Bright
Malcolm X, Ruth Carter
Toys, Albert Wolsky

Best Film Editing

Basic Instinct,
   Frank J. Urioste
The Crying Game, Kant Pan
A Few Good Men,
   Robert Leighton
The Player, Geraldine Peroni
★ *Unforgiven*, Joel Cox

Best Documentary Feature

*Changing Our Minds: The
   Story Of Dr. Evelyn
   Hooker*, David Haugland,
   producer
Fires Of Kuwait,
   Sally Dundas, producer
*Liberators: Fighting On Two
   Fronts In World War II*,
   William Miles and Nina
   Rosenblum, producers
*Music For The Movies:
   Bernard Herman*,
   Margaret Smilov and
   Roma Baran, producers
★ *The Panama Deception*,
   Barbara Trent and
   David Kasper, producers

Best Documentary Short

*At The Edge Of Conquest:
   The Journey Of Chief
   Wai-Wai*, Geoffrey
   O'Connor, producer
*Beyond Imaging: Margaret
   Anderson And The
   Little Review*, Wendy L.
   Weinberg, producer
The Colours Of My Father:

*A Portrait Of Sam
   Borenstein*, Richard Elson
   and Sally Bochner,
   producers
★ *Educating Peter*, Thomas C.
   Goodwin and Gerardine
   Wurzburg, producers
*When Abortion Was Illegal:
   Untold Stories*, Dorothy
   Fadiman, producer

Best Makeup

Batman Returns, Ve Neill,
   Ronnie Specter and
   Stan Winston
★ *Bram Stoker's Dracula*,
   Greg Cannom, Michele
   Burke and Matthew W.
   Mungle
Hoffa, Greg Cannom and
   John Blake

Best Original Score

John Barry, *Chaplin*
Jerry Goldsmith,
   Basic Instinct
Mark Isham,
   A River Runs Through It
★ Alan Menken, *Aladdin*
Richard Robbins,
   Howards End

Best Original Song

"Beautiful Maria Of My
   Soul," *The Mambo Kings*
"Friend Like Me," *Aladdin*
"I Have Nothing,"
   The Bodyguard
"Run To You,"
   The Bodyguard
★ "A Whole New World,"
   Aladdin

Best Animated Short

★ *Mona Lisa Descending A
   Staircase*, Joan C. Gratz

Best Live Action Short

Contact, Jonathan Darby
   and Jana Sue Memel

The Lady In Waiting,
   Christian M. Taylor
★ *Omnibus*, Sam Karmann
Swan Song, Kenneth Branagh
Cruise Control, Matt Palmieri

Best Sound

Aladdin, Terry Porter,
   Mel Metcalfe, David J.
   Hudson and Doc Kane
A Few Good Men,
   Kevin O'Connell,
   Rick Kline and Bob Eber
★ *The Last Of The Mohicans*,
   Chris Jenkins, Doug
   Hemphill, Mark Smith and
   Simon Kaye
Under Siege, Don Mitchell,
   Frank A. Montano,
   Rick Hart and Scott Smith
Unforgiven, Les Fresholtz,
   Vern Poore, Dick
   Alexander and Rob Young

Best Sound Effects Editing

Aladdin, Mark Mangini
★ *Bram Stoker's Dracula*,
   Tom C. McCarthy and
   David E. Stone
Under Seige, John Leveque
   and Bruce Stambler

Best Visual Effects

Alien 3, Richard Edlund,
   Alec Gillis, Tom Woodruff
   Jr. and George Gibbs
Batman Returns, Michael
   Fink, Craig Barron, John
   Bruno and Dennis Skotak
★ *Death Becomes Her*,
   Ken Ralston, Doug Chiang,
   Doug Smythe and
   Tom Woodruff

Honorary Award

Federico Fellini

Jean Hersholt Award

Audrey Hepburn
Elizabeth Taylor

Prior Academy Awards

1991

Best Picture
  The Silence Of The Lambs

Best Actor
  Anthony Hopkins,
  The Silence Of The Lambs

Best Actress
  Jodie Foster,
  The Silence Of The Lambs

Best Supporting Actor
  Jack Palance, *City Slickers*

Best Supporting Actress
  Mercedes Ruehl,
  The Fisher King

Best Director
  Jonathan Demme,
  The Silence Of The Lambs

Original Song
  "Beauty And The Beast,"
  Beauty And The Beast

1990

Best Picture
  Dances With Wolves

Best Actor
  Jeremy Irons, *Reversal of Fortune*

Best Actress
  Kathy Bates, *Misery*

Best Supporting Actor
  Joe Pesci, *GoodFellas*

Best Supporting Actress
  Whoopi Goldberg, *Ghost*

Best Director
  Kevin Costner,
  Dances With Wolves

Original Song
  "Sooner or Later (I Always Get
  My Man)," *Dick Tracy*

1989

Best Picture
  Driving Miss Daisy

Best Director
  Oliver Stone,
  Born on the Fourth of July

Best Actor
  Daniel Day Lewis, *My Left Foot*

Best Actress
  Jessica Tandy,
  Driving Miss Daisy

Best Supporting Actor
  Denzel Washington, *Glory*

Best Supporting Actress
  Brenda Fricker, *My Left Foot*

Song
  "Under the Sea,"
  The Little Mermaid

1988

Best Picture
  Rain Man

Best Director
  Barry Levinson, *Rain Man*

Best Actor
  Dustin Hoffman, *Rain Man*

Best Actress
  Jodie Foster, *The Accused*

Best Supporting Actor
  Kevin Kline,
  A Fish Called Wanda

Best Supporting Actress
  Geena Davis,
  The Accidental Tourist

Song
  "Let the River Run,"
  Working Girl

1987

Best Picture
  The Last Emperor

Best Director
  Bernardo Bertolucci,
  The Last Emperor

Best Actor
  Michael Douglas, *Wall Street*

Best Actress
  Cher, *Moonstruck*

Best Supporting Actor
  Sean Connery, *The Untouchables*

Best Supporting Actress
  Olympia Dukakis, *Moonstruck*

Song
  "(I've Had) the Time of My Life,"
  Dirty Dancing

1986

Best Picture
  Platoon

Best Director
  Oliver Stone, *Platoon*

Best Actor
  Paul Newman,
  The Color of Money

Best Actress
  Marlee Matlin,

Children of a Lesser God

Best Supporting Actor
Michael Caine,
Hannah and Her Sisters

Best Supporting Actress
Dianne Wiest,
Hannah and Her Sisters

Song
"Take My Breath Away,"
Top Gun

1985

Best Picture
Out of Africa

Best Director
Sydney Pollack,
Out of Africa

Best Actor
William Hurt,
Kiss of the Spider Woman

Best Actress
Geraldine Page,
The Trip to Bountiful

Best Supporting Actor
Don Ameche, *Cocoon*

Best Supporting Actress
Anjelica Huston, *Prizzi's Honor*

Song
"Say You, Say Me," *White Nights*

1984

Best Picture
Amadeus

Best Director
Milos Forman, *Amadeus*

Best Actor
F. Murray Abraham,
Amadeus

Best Actress
Sally Field,
Places in the Heart

Best Supporting Actor
Haing S. Ngor,
The Killing Fields

Best Supporting Actress
Peggy Ashcroft,
A Passage to India

Song
"I Just Called to Say I Love You,"
The Woman in Red

1983

Best Picture
Terms of Endearment

Best Director
James L. Brooks,
Terms of Endearment

Best Actor
Robert Duvall,
Tender Mercies

Best Actress
Shirley MacLaine,
Terms of Endearment

Best Supporting Actor
Jack Nicholson,
Terms of Endearment

Best Supporting Actress
Linda Hunt,
The Year of Living Dangerously

Song
"Flashdance (What a Feeling!),"
Flashdance

1982

Best Picture
Gandhi

Best Director
Richard Attenborough, *Ghandi*

Best Actor
Ben Kingsley, *Gandhi*

Best Actress
Meryl Streep, *Sophie's Choice*

Best Supporting Actor
Louis Gossett, Jr.,
An Officer and a Gentleman

Best Supporting Actress
Jessica Lange,
Tootsie

Song
"Up Where We Belong,"
An Officer and a Gentleman

1981

Best Picture
Chariots of Fire

Best Director
Warren Beatty, *Reds*

Best Actor
Henry Fonda,
On Golden Pond

Best Actress
Katharine Hepburn,
On Golden Pond

Best Supporting Actor
John Gielgud, *Arthur*

Best Supporting Actress
Maureen Stapleton, *Reds*

Song
"Arthur's Theme (The Best that
You Can Do)," *Arthur*

1980

Best Picture
Ordinary People

Best Director
Robert Redford, *Ordinary People*

Best Actor
Robert De Niro, *Raging Bull*

Best Actress
Sissy Spacek,
Coal Miner's Daughter

Best Supporting Actor
Timothy Hutton, *Ordinary People*

Best Supporting Actress
Mary Steenburgen,
Melvin & Howard

Song
"Fame," *Fame*

1979

Best Picture
Kramer vs. Kramer

Best Director
Robert Benton,
Kramer vs. Kramer
Best Actor
Dustin Hoffman,
Kramer vs. Kramer
Best Actress
Sally Field, *Norma Rae*
Best Supporting Actor
Melvyn Douglas, *Being There*
Best Supporting Actress
Meryl Streep,
Kramer vs. Kramer
Song
"It Goes Like It Goes,"
Norma Rae

1978
Best Picture
The Deer Hunter
Best Director
Michael Cimino,
The Deer Hunter
Best Actor
Jon Voight, *Coming Home*
Best Actress
Jane Fonda, *Coming Home*
Best Supporting Actor
Christopher Walken,
The Deer Hunter
Best Supporting Actress
Maggie Smith,
California Suite
Song
"Last Dance,"
Thank God It's Friday

1977
Best Picture
Annie Hall
Best Director
Woody Allen,
Annie Hall

Best Actor
Richard Dreyfuss,
The Goodbye Girl
Best Actress
Diane Keaton,
Annie Hall
Best Supporting Actor
Jason Robards, *Julia*
Best Supporting Actress
Vanessa Redgrave, *Julia*
Song
"You Light Up My Life,"
You Light Up My Life

1976
Best Picture
Rocky
Best Director
John G. Avildsen, *Rocky*
Best Actor
Peter Finch, *Network*
Best Actress
Faye Dunaway, *Network*
Best Supporting Actor
Jason Robards,
All the President's Men
Best Supporting Actress
Beatrice Straight, *Network*
Song
"Evergreen," *A Star is Born*

1975
Best Picture
One Flew Over the Cuckoo's Nest
Best Director
Milos Forman,
One Flew Over the Cuckoo's Nest
Best Actor
Jack Nicholson,
One Flew Over the Cuckoo's Nest
Best Actress
Louise Fletcher,
One Flew Over the Cuckoo's Nest

Best Supporting Actor
George Burns, *The Sunshine Boys*
Best Supporting Actress
Lee Grant, *Shampoo*
Song
"I'm Easy," *Nashville*

1974
Best Picture
The Godfather, Part II
Best Director
Francis Ford Coppola,
The Godfather, Part II
Best Actor
Art Carney, *Harry and Tonto*
Best Actress
Ellen Burstyn,
Alice Doesn't Live Here Anymore
Best Supporting Actor
Robert DeNiro,
The Godfather, Part II
Best Supporting Actress
Ingrid Bergman,
Murder on the Orient Express
Song
"We May Never Love Like This
Again," *The Towering Inferno*

1973
Best Picture
The Sting
Best Director
George Roy Hill, *The Sting*
Best Actor
Jack Lemmon, *Save the Tiger*
Best Actress
Glenda Jackson, *A Touch of Class*
Best Supporting Actor
John Houseman,
The Paper Chase
Best Supporting Actress
Tatum O'Neill,
Paper Moon

Song
"The Way We Were,"
The Way We Were

1972

Best Picture
The Godfather
Best Director
Bob Fosse,
Cabaret
Best Actor
Marlon Brando,
The Godfather (refused)
Best Actress
Liza Minnelli, *Cabaret*
Best Supporting Actor
Joel Grey, *Cabaret*
Best Supporting Actress
Eileen Heckart,
Butterflies are Free
Song
"The Morning After,"
The Poseidon Adventure

1971

Best Picture
The French Connection
Best Director
William Friedkin,
The French Connection
Best Actor
Gene Hackman,
The French Connection
Best Actress
Jane Fonda, *Klute*
Best Supporting Actor
Ben Johnson,
The Last Picture Show
Best Supporting Actress
Cloris Leachman,
The Last Picture Show
Song
"Theme from Shaft,"
Shaft

1970

Best Picture
Patton
Best Director
Franklin Schaffner, *Patton*
Best Actor
George C. Scott, *Patton* (refused)
Best Actress
Glenda Jackson, *Women in Love*
Best Supporting Actor
John Mills, *Ryan's Daughter*
Best Supporting Actress
Helen Hayes, *Airport*
Song
"For All We Know,"
Lovers and Other Strangers

1969

Best Picture
Midnight Cowboy
Best Director
John Schlesinger,
Midnight Cowboy
Best Actor
John Wayne, *True Grit*
Best Actress
Maggie Smith,
The Prime of Miss Jean Brodie
Best Supporting Actor
Gig Young,
They Shoot Horses, Don't They?
Best Supporting Actress
Goldie Hawn, *Cactus Flower*
Song
"Raindrops Keep Fallin' on My Head," *Butch Cassidy and the Sundance Kid*

1968

Best Picture
Oliver!
Best Director
Sir Carol Reed,
Oliver!

Best Actor
Cliff Robertson, *Charly*
Best Actress (tie)
Katharine Hepburn,
The Lion in Winter
Barbara Streisand, *Funny Girl*
Best Supporting Actor
Jack Albertson,
The Subject Was Roses
Best Supporting Actress
Ruth Gordon, *Rosemary's Baby*
Song
"The Windmills of Your Mind,"
The Thomas Crown Affair

1967

Best Picture
In the Heat of the Night
Best Director
Mike Nichols, *The Graduate*
Best Actor
Rod Steiger,
In the Heat of the Night
Best Actress
Katharine Hepburn,
Guess Who's Coming to Dinner
Best Supporting Actor
George Kennedy,
Cool Hand Luke
Best Supporting Actress
Estelle Parsons, *Bonnie and Clyde*
Song
"Talk to the Animals,"
Dr. Doolittle

1966

Best Picture
A Man for All Seasons
Best Director
Fred Zinnemann,
A Man for All Seasons
Best Actor
Paul Scofield,
A Man for All Seasons

Best Actress
Elizabeth Taylor,
Who's Afraid of Virginia Woolf?
Best Supporting Actor
Walter Matthau,
The Fortune Cookie
Best Supporting Actress
Sandy Dennis,
Who's Afraid of Virginia Woolf?
Song
"Born Free," *Born Free*

1965

Best Picture
The Sound of Music
Best Director
Robert Wise, *The Sound of Music*
Best Actor
Lee Marvin, *Cat Ballou*
Best Actress
Julie Christie, *Darling*
Best Supporting Actor
Martin Balsam,
A Thousand Clowns
Best Supporting Actress
Shelley Winters, *A Patch of Blue*
Song
"The Shadow of Your Smile,"
The Sandpiper

1964

Best Picture
My Fair Lady
Best Director
George Cukor,
My Fair Lady
Best Actor
Rex Harrison, *My Fair Lady*
Best Actress
Julie Andrews, *Mary Poppins*
Best Supporting Actor
Peter Ustinov, *Topkapi*
Best Supporting Actress
Lila Kedrova, *Zorba the Greek*

Song
"Chim-Chim-Cher-ee,"
Mary Poppins

1963

Best Picture
Tom Jones
Best Director
Tony Richardson,
Tom Jones
Best Actor
Sidney Poitier,
Lilies of the Field
Best Actress
Patricia Neal, *Hud*
Best Supporting Actor
Melvyn Dougals, *Hud*
Best Supporting Actress
Margaret Rutherford, *The V.I.P.s*
Song
"Call Me Irresponsible,"
Papa's Delicate Condition

1962

Best Picture
Lawrence of Arabia
Best Director
David Lean,
Lawrence of Arabia
Best Actor
Gregory Peck,
To Kill a Mockingbird
Best Actress
Anne Bancroft,
The Miracle Worker
Best Supporting Actor
Ed Begley,
Sweet Bird of Youth
Best Supporting Actress
Patty Duke,
The Miracle Worker
Song
"Days of Wine and Roses,"
Days of Wine and Roses

1961

Best Picture
West Side Story
Best Director
Jerome Robbins, Robert Wise,
West Side Story
Best Actor
Maximilian Schell,
Judgment at Nuremberg
Best Actress
Sophia Loren,
Two Women
Best Supporting Actor
George Chakiris,
West Side Story
Best Supporting Actress
Rita Moreno,
West Side Story
Song
"Moon River," *Breakfast at Tiffany's*

1960

Best Picture
The Apartment
Best Director
Billy Wilder, *The Apartment*
Best Actor
Burt Lancaster, *Elmer Gantry*
Best Actress
Elizabeth Taylor, *Butterfield 8*
Best Supporting Actor
Peter Ustinov, *Spartacus*
Best Supporting Actress
Shirley Jones, *Elmer Gantry*
Song
"Never on Sunday,"
Never on Sunday

1959

Best Picture
Ben-Hur
Best Director
William Wyler, *Ben-Hur*

Best Actor
Charlton Heston, *Ben-Hur*

Best Actress
Simone Signoret,
Room at the Top

Best Supporting Actor
Hugh Griffith, *Ben-Hur*

Best Supporting Actress
Shelley Winters,
Diary of Anne Frank

Song
"High Hopes,"
A Hole in the Head

1958

Best Picture
Gigi

Best Director
Vincente Minnelli, *Gigi*

Best Actor
David Niven, *Separate Tables*

Best Actress
Susan Hayward,
I Want to Live

Best Supporting Actor
Burl Ives,
The Big Country

Best Supporting Actress
Wendy Hiller, *Separate Tables*

Song
"Gigi," *Gigi*

1957

Best Picture
The Bridge on the River Kwai

Best Director
David Lean,
The Bridge on the River Kwai

Best Actor
Alec Guinness,
The Bridge on the River Kwai

Best Actress
Joanne Woodward,
The Three Faces of Eve

Best Supporting Actor
Red Buttons, *Sayonara*

Best Supporting Actress
Miyoshi Umeki, *Sayonara*

Song
"All the Way,"
The Joker is Wild

1956

Best Picture
Around the World in 80 Days

Best Director
George Stevens, *Giant*

Best Actor
Yul Brynner, *The King and I*

Best Actress
Ingrid Bergman, *Anastasia*

Best Supporting Actor
Anthony Quinn, *Lust for Life*

Best Supporting Actress
Dorothy Malone,
Written on the Wind

Song
"Whatever Will Be, Will Be
(Que Sera Sera),"
The Man Who Knew Too Much

1955

Best Picture
Marty

Best Director
Delbert Mann, *Marty*

Best Actor
Ernest Borgnine, *Marty*

Best Actress
Anna Magnani, *The Rose Tattoo*

Best Supporting Actor
Jack Lemmon, *Mister Roberts*

Best Supporting Actress
Jo Van Fleet, *East of Eden*

Song
"Love Is a Many Splendored
Thing,"
Love Is a Many Splendored Thing

1954

Best Picture
On the Waterfront

Best Director
Elia Kazan, *On the Waterfront*

Best Actor
Marlon Brando,
On the Waterfront

Best Actress
Grace Kelly, *The Country Girl*

Best Supporting Actor
Edmund O'Brien,
The Barefoot Contessa

Best Supporting Actress
Eva Marie Saint,
On the Waterfront

Song
"Three Coins in the Fountain,"
Three Coins in the Fountain

1953

Best Picture
From Here to Eternity

Best Director
Fred Zinnemann,
From Here to Eternity

Best Actor
William Holden,
Stalag 17

Best Actress
Audrey Hepburn,
Roman Holiday

Best Supporting Actor
Frank Sinatra,
From Here to Eternity

Best Supporting Actress
Donna Reed,
From Here to Eternity

Song
"Secret Love," *Calamity Jane*

1952

Best Picture
Greatest Show on Earth

Best Director
John Ford, *The Quiet Man*
Best Actor
Gary Cooper, *High Noon*
Best Actress
Shirley Booth,
Come Back Little Sheba
Best Supporting Actor
Anthony Quinn, *Viva Zapata!*
Best Supporting Actress
Gloria Grahame,
The Bad and the Beautiful
Song
"High Noon (Do Not Forsake Me,
Oh My Darlin')," *High Noon*

1951
Best Picture
An American in Paris
Best Director
George Stevens,
A Place in the Sun
Best Actor
Humphrey Bogart,
The African Queen
Best Actress
Vivien Leigh,
A Streetcar Named Desire
Best Supporting Actor
Karl Malden,
A Streetcar Named Desire
Best Supporting Actress
Kim Hunter,
A Streetcar Named Desire
Song
"In the Cool, Cool, Cool of the
Evening," *Here Comes the Groom*

1950
Best Picture
All About Eve
Best Director
Joseph L. Mankiewicz,
All About Eve

Best Actor
Jose Ferrer,
Cyrano de Bergerac
Best Actress
Judy Holliday,
Born Yesterday
Best Supporting Actor
George Sanders,
All About Eve
Best Supporting Actress
Josephine Hull, *Harvey*
Song
"Mona Lisa," *Captain Carey*

1949
Best Picture
All the King's Men
Best Director
Joseph L. Mankiewicz,
Letter to Three Wives
Best Actor
Broderick Crawford,
All the King's Men
Best Actress
Olivia de Havilland,
The Heiress
Best Supporting Actor
Dean Jagger,
Twelve O'Clock High
Best Supporting Actress
Mercedes McCambridge,
All the King's Men
Song
"Baby, It's Cold Outside,"
Neptune's Daughter

1948
Best Picture
Hamlet
Best Director
John Huston,
Treasure of Sierra Madre
Best Actor
Laurence Olivier, *Hamlet*

Best Actress
Jane Wyman, *Johnny Belinda*
Best Supporting Actor
Walter Huston,
Treasure of Sierra Madre
Best Supporting Actress
Claire Trevor, *Key Largo*
Song
"Buttons and Bows," *Paleface*

1947
Best Picture
Gentleman's Agreement
Best Director
Elia Kazan,
Gentleman's Agreement
Best Actor
Ronald Colman,
A Double Life
Best Actress
Loretta Young,
The Farmer's Daughter
Best Supporting Actor
Edmund Gwenn,
Miracle on 34th Street
Best Supporting Actress
Celeste Holm,
Gentleman's Agreement
Song
"Zip-a-Dee-Doo-Dah,"
Song of the South

1946
Best Picture
The Best Years of Our Lives
Best Director
William Wyler,
The Best Years of Our Lives
Best Actor
Fredric March,
The Best Years of Our Lives
Best Actress
Olivia de Havilland,
To Each His Own

Best Supporting Actor
Harold Russell,
The Best Years of Our Lives

Best Supporting Actress
Anne Baxter, *The Razor's Edge*

Song
"On the Atchison, Topeka, and
the Santa Fe," *The Harvey Girls*

1945

Best Picture
The Lost Weekend

Best Director
Billy Wilder, *The Lost Weekend*

Best Actor
Ray Milland, *The Lost Weekend*

Best Actress
Joan Crawford, *Mildred Pierce*

Best Supporting Actor
James Dunn,
A Tree Grows in Brooklyn

Best Supporting Actress
Anne Revere, *National Velvet*

Song
"It Might as Well Be Spring,"
State Fair

1944

Best Picture
Going My Way

Best Director
Leo McCarey, *Going My Way*

Best Actor
Bing Crosby, *Going My Way*

Best Actress
Ingrid Bergman, *Gaslight*

Best Supporting Actor
Barry Fitzgerald, *Going My Way*

Best Supporting Actress
Ethel Fitzgerald,
None But the Lonely Heart

Song
"Swinging on a Star,"
Going My Way

1943

Best Picture
Casablanca

Best Director
Michael Curtiz, *Casablanca*

Best Actor
Paul Lukas, *Watch on the Rhine*

Best Actress
Jennifer Jones.
The Song of Bernadette

Best Supporting Actor
Charles Coburn,
The More the Merrier

Best Supporting Actress
Katina Paxinou,
For Whom the Bell Tolls

Song
"You'll Never Know,"
Hello, Frisco, Hello

1942

Best Picture
Mrs. Miniver

Best Director
William Wyler,
Mrs. Miniver

Best Actor
James Cagney,
Yankee Doodle Dandy

Best Actress
Greer Garson, *Mrs. Miniver*

Best Supporting Actor
Van Heflin, *Johnny Eager*

Best Supporting Actress
Teresa Wright, *Mrs. Miniver*

Song
"White Christmas," *Holiday Inn*

1941

Best Picture
How Green Was My Valley

Best Director
John Ford,
How Green Was My Valley

Best Actor
Gary Cooper,
Sergeant York

Best Actress
Joan Fontaine,
Suspicion

Best Supporting Actor
Donald Crisp,
How Green Was My Valley

Best Supporting Actress
Mary Astor, *The Great Lie*

Song
"Last Time I Saw Paris,"
Lady Be Good

1940

Best Picture
Rebecca

Best Director
John Ford,
The Grapes of Wrath

Best Actor
James Stewart,
The Philadelphia Story

Best Actress
Ginger Rogers, *Kitty Foyle*

Best Supporting Actor
Walter Brennan, *The Westerner*

Best Supporting Actress
Jane Darwell,
The Grapes of Wrath

Song
"When You Wish Upon a Star,"
Pinocchio

1939

Best Picture
Gone With the Wind

Best Director
Victor Fleming,
Gone With the Wind

Best Actor
Robert Donat,
Goodbye Mr. Chips

Best Actress
Vivien Leigh,
Gone With the Wind
Best Supporting Actor
Thomas Mitchell, *Stage Coach*
Best Supporting Actress
Hattie McDaniel,
Gone With the Wind
Song
"Over the Rainbow,"
The Wizard of Oz

1938
Best Picture
You Can't Take It With You
Best Director
Frank Capra,
You Can't Take It With You
Best Actor
Spencer Tracy, *Boys Town*
Best Actress
Bette Davis, *Jezebel*
Best Supporting Actor
Walter Brennan, *Kentucky*
Best Supporting Actress
Fay Bainter, *Jezebel*
Song
"Thanks for the Memory,"
The Big Broadcast of 1938

1937
Best Picture
Life of Emile Zola
Best Director
Leo McCarey, *The Awful Truth*
Best Actor
Spencer Tracy,
Captains Courageous
Best Actress
Luise Rainer,
The Good Earth
Best Supporting Actor
Joseph Schildkraut,
Life of Emile Zola

Best Supporting Actress
Alice Brady,
In Old Chicago
Song
"Sweet Leilani," *Waikiki Wedding*

1936
Best Picture
The Great Ziegfeld
Best Director
Frank Capra,
Mr. Deeds Goes to Town
Best Actor
Paul Muni,
Story of Louis Pasteur
Best Actress
Luise Rainer,
The Great Ziegfeld
Best Supporting Actor
Walter Brennan,
Come and Get It
Best Supporting Actress
Gale Sondergaard,
Anthony Adverse
Song
"The Way You Look Tonight,"
Swingtime

1935
Best Picture
Mutiny on the Bounty
Best Director
John Ford, *The Informer*
Best Actor
Victor McLaglen, *The Informer*
Best Actress
Bette Davis, *Dangerous*
Song
"Lullaby of Broadway,"
Gold Diggers of 1935

1934
Best Picture
It Happened One Night

Best Director
Frank Capra,
It Happened One Night
Best Actor
Clark Gable,
It Happened One Night
Best Actress
Claudette Colbert,
It Happened One Night
Song
"The Continental,"
The Gay Divorcee

1932-33
Best Picture
Cavalcade
Best Director
Frank Lloyd, *Cavalcade*
Best Actor
Charles Laughton,
Private Life of Henry VIII
Best Actress
Katharine Hepburn,
Morning Glory

1931-32
Best Picture
Grand Hotel
Best Director
Frank Borzage,
Bad Girl
Best Actor (tie)
Fredric March,
Dr. Jekyll and Mr. Hyde
Wallace Beery, *The Champ*
Special
Walt Disney, *Mickey Mouse*

1930-31
Best Picture
Cimarron
Best Director
Norman Taurog,
Skippy

Best Actor
Lionel Barrymore,
Free Soul

Best Actress
Marie Dressler, *Min and Bill*

1929-30

Best Picture
All Quiet on the Western Front

Best Director
Lewis Milestone,
All Quiet on the Western Front

Best Actor
George Arliss, *Disraeli*

Best Actress
Norma Shearer, *The Divorcee*

1928-29

Best Picture
Broadway Melody

Best Director
Frank Lloyd, *The Divine Lady*

Best Actor
Warner Baxter,
In Old Arizona

Best Actress
Mary Pickford,
Coquette

1927-28

Best Picture
Wings

Best Director (tie)
Frank Borzage,
Seventh Heaven
Lewis Milestone,
Two Arabian Knights

Best Actor
Emil Jannings,
The Way of All Flesh

Best Actress
Janet Gaynor,
Seventh Heaven

1992
Film Awards

All of the following awards were presented in 1993 to films released in 1992. The winner in each category is indicated with a star symbol. Wherever possible, both nominees and winners are included.

British Academy of Film and Television Arts Awards

Best Film
The Crying Game, Neil Jordan, Stephen Woolley
★ Howards End, Ismail Merchant, James Ivory
The Player, David Brown, Michael Tolkin, Nick Wexler, Robert Altman
Unforgiven, Clint Eastwood

David Lean Award For Direction
The Crying Game, Neil Jordan
Howards End, James Ivory
★ The Player, Robert Altman
Unforgiven, Clint Eastwood

Actor In A Leading Role
Daniel Day-Lewis, The Last Of The Mohicans
★ Robert Downey, Jr., Chaplin
Stephen Rea, The Crying Game
Tim Robbins, The Player

Actress In A Leading Role
Judy Davis, Husbands And Wives
Tara Morice, Strictly Ballroom
Jessica Tandy, Fried Green Tomatoes
★ Emma Thompson, Howards End

Actor In A Supporting Role
Jaye Davidson, The Crying Game
★ Gene Hackman, Unforgiven
Tommy Lee Jones, JFK

Samuel West, Howards End

Actress In A Supporting Role
Kathy Bates, Fried Green Tomatoes
Helena Bonham-Carter, Howards End
Miranda Richardson, The Crying Game
★ Miranda Richardson, Damage

Original Screenplay
The Crying Game, Neil Jordan
Hear My Song, Peter Chelsom, Adrian Dunbar
★ Husbands And Wives, Woody Allen
Unforgiven, David Webb Peoples

Adapted Screenplay
Howards End, Ruth Prawer Jhabvala
JFK, Oliver Stone, Zachary Sklar
★ The Player, Michael Tolkin
Strictly Ballroom, Baz Luhrmann, Craig Pearce

Original Film Music
Beauty And The Beast, Alan Menken, Howard Ashman
Hear My Song, John Altman
The Last Of The Mohicans, Trevor Jones, Randy Edelman
★ Strictly Ballroom, David Hirschfelder

Chicago Film Critics Awards

Best Picture
The Crying Game
★ Malcolm X
The Player
Reservoir Dogs
Unforgiven

Best Director
Neil Jordan, The Crying Game
Clint Eastwood, Unforgiven
★ Robert Altman, The Player
Spike Lee, Malcolm X
Quentin Tarantino, Reservoir Dogs

Best Actor
Al Pacino, Scent Of A Woman
Clint Eastwood, Unforgiven
Robert Downey, Jr., Chaplin
★ Denzel Washington, Malcolm X
Tim Robbins, The Player

Best Actress
Susan Sarandon, Lorenzo's Oil
★ Emma Thompson, Howards End
Sharon Stone, Basic Instinct
Rebecca De Mornay, The Hand That Rocks The Cradle
Jennifer Jason Leigh, Single White Female

Best Supporting Actor
★ Jack Nicholson, A Few Good Men

Al Pacino, *Glengarry Glen Ross*
Gene Hackman, *Unforgiven*
Al Freeman, Jr., *Malcolm X*
Jeff Goldblum, *Deep Cover*

Best Supporting Actress
★ Judy Davis, *Husbands And Wives*
Marcia Gay Harden, *Used People*
Rosie Perez,
    White Men Can't Jump
Miranda Richardson, *Damage*
Marisa Tomei, *My Cousin Vinny*

Best Foreign Film
★ *The Crying Game*
Howards End
Flirting
La Belle Noiseuse
Enchanted April

Best Screenplay
Neil Jordan, *The Crying Game*
David Mamet,
    Glengarry Glen Ross
Spike Lee and Arnold Perl,
    Malcolm X
★ Michael Tolkin, *The Player*
David Webb Peoples,
    Unforgiven

Best Cinematography
★ Michael Ballhaus,
    Bram Stoker's Dracula
Mikael Salomon, *Far And Away*
Dante Spinotti,
    The Last Of The Mohicans
Philippe Rousselot,
    A River Runs Through It
Jack Green, *Unforgiven*

Most Promising Actor
Jaye Davidson, *The Crying Game*
Brendan Fraser, *Encino Man,*
    School Ties
★ Chris O'Donnell, *School Ties,*
    Scent Of A Woman
Glen Plummer, *South Central*
Wes Studi,
    The Last Of The Mohicans

Most Promising Actress
Jaye Davidson, *The Crying Game*
Angela Bassett, *Malcolm X*
Rosie Perez, *White Men Can't*
    Jump and *Night On Earth*
★ Marisa Tomei, *Chaplin*
    and *My Cousin Vinny*
Cynda Williams, *One False Move*

D.W.Griffith Awards (National Board of Review)

Best Picture
★ *Howards End*

Best Director
★ James Ivory, *Howards End*

Best Actor
★ Jack Lemmon,
    Glengarry Glen Ross

Best Actress
★ Emma Thompson, *Howards End*

Best Supporting Actor
★ Jack Nicholson,
    A Few Good Men

Best Supporting Actress
★ Judy Davis, *Husbands And Wives*

Best Foreign Film
★ *Indochine*

Best Documentary
★ Joe Berlinger and
    Bruce Sinofsky, *Brother's Keeper*

Career Achievement Award
Shirley Temple

The 45th Annual Directors Guild of America Awards

Best Director
Robert Altman, *The Player*
★ Clint Eastwood, *Unforgiven*
James Ivory, *Howards End*
Neil Jordan, *The Crying Game*
Rob Reiner, *A Few Good Men*

50th Golden Globe Awards (Hollywood Foreign Press Association)

Best Picture (Drama)
A Few Good Men
The Crying Game
Howards End
★ *Scent Of A Woman*
Unforgiven

Best Picture (Musical/Comedy)
Aladdin
Enchanted April
Honeymoon In Vegas
★ *The Player*
Sister Act

Best Director
Rob Reiner, *A Few Good Men*
Robert Altman, *The Player*
James Ivory, *Howards End*
Robert Redford,
    A River Runs Through It
★ Clint Eastwood, *Unforgiven*

Best Actor (Drama)
Tom Cruise, *A Few Good Men*
Robert Downey, Jr., *Chaplin*
Jack Nicholson, *Hoffa*
★ Al Pacino, *Scent Of A Woman*
Denzel Washington, *Malcolm X*

Best Actress (Drama)
Mary McDonnell, *Passion Fish*
Michelle Pfeiffer, *Love Field*
Susan Sarandon, *Lorenzo's Oil*
Sharon Stone, *Basic Instinct*
★ Emma Thompson, *Howards End*

Best Actor (Musical/Comedy)
Billy Crystal, *Mr. Saturday Night*
Nicholas Cage,
    Honeymoon In Vegas
Marcello Mastroianni,
    Used People
Tim Robbins, *Bob Roberts*
★ Tim Robbins, *The Player*

Best Actress (Musical/Comedy)
Whoopi Goldberg, *Sister Act*

Geena Davis,
A League Of Their Own
Shirley MacLaine, *Used People*
★ Miranda Richardson,
Enchanted April
Meryl Streep, *Death Becomes Her*

Best Foreign Language Film
Close To Eden
★ *Indochine*
Like Water For Chocolate
Schtonk!
Tous Les Matins du Monde

Best Supporting Actor
★ Gene Hackman,*Unforgiven*
Jack Nicholson,
A Few Good Men
Al Pacino, *Glengarry Glen Ross*
Chris O'Donnell,
Scent Of A Woman
David Paymer,
Mr. Saturday Night

Best Supporting Actress
Geraldine Chaplin, *Chaplin*
Judy Davis, *Husbands And Wives*
★ Joan Plowright, *Enchanted April*
Miranda Richardson, *Damage*
Alfre Woodard, *Passion Fish*

Best Screenplay
★ Bo Goldman, *Scent Of A Woman*
Ruth Prawer Jhabvala,
Howards End
Aaron Sorkin, *A Few Good Men*
Michael Tolkin, *The Player*
David Webb Peoples, *Unforgiven*

Best Original Score
★ Alan Menken, *Aladdin*
John Barry, *Chaplin*
Jerry Goldsmith, *Basic Instinct*
Vangelis,
1942: Conquest Of Paradise
Trevor Jones and Randy Edelman
The Last Of The Mohicans

**Best Original Song,
Music And Lyrics**
Alan Menken and

Howard Ashman,
"Friend Like Me," *Aladdin*
Alan Menken and
Howard Ashman,
"Prince Ali," *Aladdin*
Robert Kraft and Arne Glimcher,
"Beautiful Maria Of My Soul,"
The Mambo Kings
Madonna and Shep Pettibone,
"This Used To Be By
Playground, " *A League Of
Their Own*
★ Alan Menken and Tim Rice,
"A Whole New World,"
Aladdin

Los Angeles Film Critics Association Achievement Awards

Best Picture
★ *Unforgiven*
Best Director
★ Clint Eastwood, *Unforgiven*
Best Actor
★ Clint Eastwood, *Unforgiven*
Best Actress
★ Emma Thompson, *Howards End*
Best Supporting Actor
★ Gene Hackman, *Unforgiven*
Best Supporting Actress
★ Judy Davis, *Husbands And Wives*
Best Screenplay
★ David Webb Peoples, *Unforgiven*
Best Cinematographer
★ Jack N. Green,
Unforgiven
Best Foreign Film
★ *The Crying Game*
Best Documentary
★ Robert Connolly and Robin
Anderson, *Black Harvest* and
★ Stefan Jarl, *The Threat*
Best Animated Film
★ *Aladdin*

New Generation Award
★ Carl Franklin, *One False Move*
Career Achievement Award
★ Budd Boetticher

The National Society Of Film Critics

Best Picture
★ *Unforgiven*
Best Director
★ Clint Eastwood, *Unforgiven*
Best Actor
★ Stephen Rea, *The Crying Game*
Best Actress
★ Emma Thompson, *Howards End*
Best Supporting Actor
★ Gene Hackman, *Unforgiven*
Best Supporting Actress
★ Judy Davis, *Husbands And Wives*
Best Screenplay
★ David Webb Peoples, *Unforgiven*
Best Cinematographer
★ Zhao Fei, *Raise The Red Lantern*
Best Documentary
★ *American Dream*, Barbara Kopple
Best Foreign Film
★ *Raise The Red Lantern*

New York Film Critics Circle

Best Picture
★ *The Player*
Best Director
★ Robert Altman, *The Player*
Best Actor
★ Denzel Washington,
Malcolm X
Best Actress
★ Emma Thompson,
Howards End
Best Supporting Actor
★ Gene Hackman, *Unforgiven*

Best Supporting Actress
★ Miranda Richardson, *The Crying Game, Enchanted April* and *Damage*
Best Screenplay
★ Neil Jordan, *The Crying Game*
Best Cinematographer
★ Jean Lepine, *The Player*
Best Foreign Language Film
★ *Raise The Red Langern*
Best Documentary
★ Joe Berlinger and Bruce Sinofsky, *Brother's Keeper*
Best New Director
★ Allison Anders, *Gas, Food, Lodging*

19th Annual People's Choice Awards
(Sponsored by the Gallup Poll)

Favorite Motion Picture
★ *A Few Good Men*
 Aladdin
 Malcolm X
Favorite Comedy Motion Picture
★ *Home Alone 2: Lost In New York*
★ *Sister Act*

The Distinguished Gentleman
Favorite Dramatic Motion Picture
★ *A Few Good Men*
 Malcolm X
 The Bodyguard
Favorite Motion Picture Actor
★ Kevin Costner
 Mel Gibson
 Jack Nicholson
Favorite Motion Picture Actress
★ Whoopi Goldberg
 Demi Moore
 Michelle Pfeiffer
Favorite Actor In A Comedy Motion Picture
★ Steve Martin
 Eddie Murphy
 Robin Williams
Favorite Actress In A Comedy Motion Picture
★ Whoopi Goldberg
 Goldie Hawn
 Bette Midler
Favorite Actor In A Dramatic Motion Picture
★ Kevin Costner
 Tom Cruise
 Jack Nicholson

Favorite Actress In A Dramatic Motion Picture
 Whitney Houston
★ Demi Moore
 Sharon Stone

45th Annual Writers Guild Of America Awards

Best Original Screenplay
★ Neil Jordan, *The Crying Game*
 Woody Allen, *Husbands And Wives*
 George Miller and Nick Enright, *Lorenzo's Oil*
 John Sayles, *Passion Fish*
 David Webb Peoples, *Unforgiven*

Best Screenplay Adaptation
 Peter Barnes, *Enchanted April*
 David Mamet, *Glengarry Glen Ross*
 Ruth Prawer Jhabvala, *Howards End*
★ Michael Tolkin, *The Player*
 Bo Goldman, *Scent Of A Woman*

1992
Obituaries

While many beloved music, television and theater entertainers died during the year, only those individuals with film credits are included in this volume. The chronological list that follows is predominantly made up of award-winning and - nominated actors, actresses, writers, directors and technicians.

JANUARY

M.J. (Mike) Frankovich
Producer
Died January 1 of pneumonia at age 83.

Frankovich received the Academy of Motion Picture Arts and Sciences Jean Hersholt Humanitarian Award in 1984.

FILM CREDITS: *Cat Ballou; Guess Who's Coming To Dinner; To Sir With Love; In Cold Blood; A Man For All Seasons, Bob & Carol & Ted & Alice; The Shootist, Marooned; Cactus Flower; There's A Girl In My Soup;* and *Butterflies Are Free.*

Dame Judith Anderson
Actress
Died January 3 in Santa Barbara, Calif., at age 93.

Longtime stage, screen and television actress, Anderson was nominated for an Academy Award in 1940 for her role in *Rebecca*.

FILM CREDITS: Include *Blood Money* (1933), *Rebecca* (1940), *Forty Little Mothers* (1940), *King's Row* (1941), *Free*

And Easy (1941), *Lady Scarface* (1941), *All Through The Night* (1942), *Edge Of Darkness* (1943), *Stage Door Canteen* (1943), *Laura* (1944), *And Then There Were None* (1945), *The Diary Of A Chambermaid* (1946), *The Strange Love Of Martha Ivers* (1946), *The Specter Of The Rose* (1946), *Tycoon* (1947), *The Red House* (1947), *Pursued* (1947), *The Furies* (1950), *Salome* (1953), *The Ten Commandments* (1956), *Cat On A Hot Tin Roof* (1958), *Cinderfella* (1960), *Don't Bother*

To Knock (1961), *A Man Called Horse* (1970), *Inn Of The Damned* (1974), and *Star Trek III: The Search For Spock* (1984).

Andrew Marton
Director
Died January 7 in Santa Monica, Calif., at age 87.

FILM CREDITS: Marton was best known as a second-unit director. His credits include *Two-Faced Woman, Mrs. Miniver, Cabin In The Sky, Dragon Seed, On The Town, The Red Badge Of Courage, Ben-Hur, Cleopatra, Catch 22, Up The Sandbox* and *Day Of The Jackal*. He codirected *King Solomon's Mines* and *The Longest Day*, and went on to direct a number of films including *Clarence, The Cross-eyed Lion.*

Steve Brodie
Actor
Died January 9 of cancer in West Hills, Calif., at age 72.

FILM CREDITS: *For The Boys* (1944), *Thirty Seconds Over Tokyo, A Walk In The Sun, Crossfire, Home Of The Brave, Win-*

chester 73, The Far Country, Return Of The Badmen, Out Of The Past, The Caine Mutiny, Blue Hawaii and Roustabout.

Bill Naughton
Writer

Died January 9 on the Isle of Man at age 81.

FILM CREDITS: Nominated for an Academy Award in 1966 for the screenplay adaptation of his book Alfie. Other films include Spring And Port Wine and The Family Way.

Robert R. Martin
Film sound mixer

Died January 16 in Arroyo Grande, Calif., at age 75.

FILM CREDITS: Nominated for an Academy Award in 1969 for Gaily, Gaily. Other films include Some Like It Hot, The Apartment, Irma La Douce, The Fortune Cookie, The Front Page, Marty, It's A Mad, Mad, Mad, Mad, World, Hawaii, The Hawaiians and Midway.

Ruby Levitt
Set decorator

Died January 18 in Woodland Hills, Calif., at age 83.

Levitt received Academy Award nominations for her work on Chinatown, Smash-up, The Story Of Woman and The Sound Of Music.

FILM CREDITS: Other films include I Can't Help Singing; Pillow Talk; The Andromeda Strain; New York, New York and A Star Is Born.

Freddie Bartholomew
(Frederick Llewellyn)
Actor

Died January 23 of emphysema in Bradenton, Florida at 67.

FILM CREDITS: Bartholomew was a leading child star of the '30s and '40s. His films include Fascination (1930), Anna Karenina (1935), David Copperfield (1935), Little Lord Fauntleroy (1936), Lloyd's Of London (1936), Captains Courageous (1937), The Swiss Family Robinson (1940), Tom Brown's School Days (1940), Naval Academy (1941), Cadets On Parade (1942), A Yank At Eton (1942), and St. Benny The Dip (1951).

Ian Wolfe
Character actor

Died February 23 of natural causes in Los Angeles, at 95.

FILM CREDITS: Appearing in his first Hollywood film in 1934, he went on to do over 150 films, including Mutiny On the

Bounty, You Can't Take It With You, Now, Voyager, Mrs. Miniver, Johnny Belinda, Rebel Without A Cause, A Place In The Sun, Reds and Dick Tracy.

Ken Darby
Composer

Died January 24 in Sherman Oaks, Calif., at age 82.

FILM CREDITS: Darby won three Oscars during his career: The King And I (1956), Porgy And Bess (1959) and Camelot (1967). In addition, while collaborating with Alfred Newman, he was nominated for Academy Awards for How The West Was Won (1963), South Pacific (1958) and Flower Drum Song (1961).

Jose Ferrer
Actor

Died January 26 in Coral Gables, Florida at 83.

Ferrer is probably best known for his title role in the film Cyrano de Bergerac, for which he won an Academy Award in 1950. His work on Broadway also earned

him Tony awards for best dramatic actor in 1947 and 1952.

FILM CREDITS: Include *Joan Of Arc* (1948), *The Moulin Rouge* (1952), *Miss Sadie Thompson* (1953), *The Caine Mutiny* (1954), *Lawrence Of Arabia* (1962), *The Greatest Story Ever Told* (1965), *Ship Of Fools* (1965), *Dune* (1984) and *Old Explorers* (1990).

FEBRUARY

John Dehner
Actor

Died February 4 of emphysema and diabetes in Santa Barbara, Calif., at age 76.

FILM CREDITS: Making his film debut in the 1944 film *Thirty Seconds Over Tokyo*, he went on to appear in nearly 100 films, including *State Fair*, *The Reluctant Dragon*, *The Boys From Brazil*, *Cheyenne Social Club*, *Day Of The Dolphin*, *The Right*

Stuff and *Jagged Edge*. Dehner had regular roles on such television shows as *The Baileys Of Balboa*, *The Doris Day Show* and *Young Maverick*.

Jack Kinney
Animation director

Died February 9 in Glendale, Calif., of natural causes at age 82.

Kinney directed dozens of Disney animated shorts and worked on such films as *Pinocchio*, *Dumbo*, *The Reluctant Dragon*, *The Three Caballeros*, *Melody Time* and *1,001 Arabian Nights*.

In 1942 he directed the Academy-Award-winning Disney short subject *Der Fuehrer's Face*.

Alex Haley
Author

Died February 10 of a heart attack in Seattle at age 70.

Best known as the author of *Roots*, the 1977 Pulitzer-Prize-winning novel that was translated into *Roots: The Saga of an American Family*, the highest rated American miniseries of its time. His first major work was *The Autobiography of Malcolm X*, which was published in 1965. The film version, adapted for the screen by James Baldwin and directed by Spike Lee, was released after Haley's death.

Robert W. Russell
Writer

Died February 11 of heart failure following a stroke in New York, N.Y., at age 79.

FILM CREDITS: Russell received an Academy Award nomination along with Frank Ross for

their screenplay *The More The Merrier*. Other writing credits include *The Well Groomed Bride*, *The Lady Says No*, *Come September* and *Walk, Don't Run*.

Angelique Pettyjohn
Actress

Died February 14 of cancer in Las Vegas at age 48.

FILM CREDITS: *Childish Things*, *Clambake*, *The President's Analyst*, *Heaven With A Gun*, *The Mad Doctor Of Blood Island*, *The Curious Female*, *Hell's Bells*, *Tell Me That You Love Me, Junie Moon* and the cult classic *Repo Man*.

Dick York
Actor

Died February 20 after suffering from emphysema and a degenerative spinal condition, in Grand Rapids, Michigan, at age 63.

York will best be remembered for his co-starring role with Elizabeth Montgomery in the ABC television situation comedy *Bewitched* from 1964-1969.

FILM CREDITS: Include *My Sister Eileen* and *Inherit The Wind*. He also appeared in the 1962-63 TV series based on the 1944 film *Going My Way*.

Jacquelyn Hyde
Actress

Died February 23 in Woodland Hills, Calif., at age 61.

FILM CREDITS: A stage, screen and television actress, Hyde made her film debut in Woody Allen's *Take The Money And Run* in 1969. Other roles include *They Shoot Horses, Don't They?*, *The Dark*, *Little Miss Marker* and *Hopscotch*.

MARCH

Sandy Dennis
Actress

Died March 1 from cancer in Westport, Connecticut, at age 54.

FILM CREDITS: Beginning her career on Broadway, she went on to win two Tony Awards. In film she was the winner of a 1966

Best Supporting Actress Academy Award for her role in *Who's Afraid Of Virginia Woolf?* Other films include *Splendor In The Grass* (1961), *Three Sisters* (1964), *The Fox* (1967), *Up The Down Staircase* (1967), *Sweet November* (1968), *That Cold Day In The Park* (1969), *The Out-of-Towners* (1970), *Mr. Sycamore* (1974), *God Told Me To* (1976), *Nasty Habits* (1976), *The Animals Film* (1981), *The Four Seasons* (1981), *Come Back To The Five And Dime, Jimmy Dean, Jimmy Dean* (1982), *976-EVIL* (1988), *Another Woman* (1988), *Parents* (1989) and *The Indian Runner* (1991).

William Clatworthy
Art director

Died March 2 after a brief illness at age 80.

Clatworthy spent 45 years as an art director and received an Academy Award in 1965 for *Ship Of Fools*.

FILM CREDITS: He went on to receive Oscar nominations for *A Touch Of Mink, Psycho, Inside Daisy Clover* and *Guess Who's Coming To Dinner*.

Samuel Marx
Producer

Died March 2 of congestive heart failure in Los Angeles, Calif., at age 90.

FILM CREDITS: While working for MGM studios Marx produced such important and memorable films as *Grand Hotel, Tarzan The Ape Man, The Thin Man, Mutiny On The Bounty,*

Goodbye, Mr. Chips, A Family Affair and *Lassie Come Home*. He later went into television and produced *December Bride, Those Whiting Girls, General Electric Hour, Broken Arrow, The Thin Man* and *Northwest Passage*.

Nestor Almendros
Cinematographer

Died March 4 of lymphoma in New York City, at age 61.

FILM CREDITS: Nominated for numerous Academy Awards during his career, he won an Oscar in 1979 for cinematography on *Days Of Heaven* starring Richard Gere. Other films include *Kramer vs. Kramer* (1979), *Sophie's Choice* (1982), *The Last Metro* (1981), *Still Of The Night* (1982), *Places In The Heart* (1984), *Improper Conduct* (1985) and *Billy Bathgate* (1991).

Andrew Samuels
Actor

Died March 5 in Colton, Calif., at age 82.

FILM CREDITS: Samuels was one of the original *Our Gang* kids appearing in only a few films, including *The Big Show, The Champeen* and *Boys To Board*.

Elvia Allman
Actress

Died March 6 of pneumonia in Santa Monica, Calif., at age 87.

FILM CREDITS: Beginning her career in radio, she went on to do the voice of Disney's Clarabelle the cow. Other film credits include *You Can't Run Away From It, The Pleasure Of His Company* and *Breakfast At*

Tiffany's. Allman also made numerous television appearances.

Richard Brooks
Director/screenwriter

Died March 11 of congestive heart failure in Beverly Hills, Calif., at age 79.

In 1960, Brooks received the Best Screenplay Academy Award for *Elmer Gantry*. He received a total of eight nominations during his career. In 1990 he became the first filmmaker to receive Lifetime Achievement awards from both the Writers Guild of America and the Directors Guild of America.

FILM CREDITS: With 36 films to his credit, his best known works include *Key Largo* (1948), *Take The High Ground* (1953), *The Last Time I Saw Paris* (1954), *The Blackboard Jungle* (1955), *The Brothers Karamazov* (1958), *Cat On A Hot Tin Roof* (1958), *Elmer Gantry* (1960), *Sweet Bird Of Youth* (1962), *Lord Jim* (1965), *In Cold Blood* (1967) and *Looking For Mr. Goodbar* (1977).

Jean Poiret
Writer/actor

Died March 14 of a heart attack in Paris, France, at age 65.

Poiret will best be remembered for writing and starring in the play *La Cage Aux Folles*.

FILM CREDITS: One of France's most popular actors, his roles include *The Last Metro*, *Chicken In Vinegar*, *Inspecteur Lavardin* and *The Miracle Cure*.

Helen Deutsch
Writer

Died March 15 of natural causes in New York City, at the age of 86.

FILM CREDITS: In 1953 she received an Academy Award nomination for best screenplay for *Lili*. Other screenplays include *National Velvet*, *The Glass Slipper*, *I'll Cry Tomorrow*, *The Unsinkable Molly Brown* and *The Valley Of The Dolls*.

Jack Arnold
Director

Died March 17 of arteriosclerosis in Woodland Hills, Calif., at age 75.

Beginning his career as a documentary filmmaker, he received an Academy Award nomination for *With These Hands*.

FILM CREDITS: Arnold will best be remembered for his science-fiction classic *Creature From The Black Lagoon*. Other features include *The Glass Web*, *Tarantula*, *Red Sundown*, *High School Confidential*, *Man In The Shadow*, *The Mouse That Roared*, *Bachelor In Paradise* and *A Global Affair*. He later went on to earn an Emmy for his work in television.

Gracie Lantz
Actress/voice over

Died March 17 of spinal cancer in Burbank, Calif., at the age of 88.

FILM CREDITS: Lantz is best remembered as the voice of Woody Woodpecker, created by her husband, Walter Lantz. Feature credits include *Dr. Socrates*, *Anthony Adverse*, *Confessions Of A Spy* and *Indianapolis Speedway*.

Georges Delerue
Composer

Died March 20 at age 67.

Delerue won an Academy Award for Best Original Soundtrack in 1979 for *A Little Romance*. He also received Oscar nominations for *Anne Of A Thousand Days* (1969), *The Day Of The Dolphin* (1973) and *Julia* (1977).

FILM CREDITS: Include *Hiroshima, Mon Amour*, *Shoot The Piano Player*, *Jules And Jim*, *Behold A Pale Horse*, *Women In Love*, *Day Of The Jackal*, *Silkwood*, *Mister Johnson*, *Curly Sue* and *Man Trouble*.

John Ireland
Actor

Died March 21 of leukemia in Santa Barbara, Calif., at age 78.

Ireland appeared in more than 200 films and received an Academy Award nomination in 1949 for Best Supporting Actor in *All The King's Men*.

FILM CREDITS: *A Walk In The Sun* (1945), *My Darling Clementine* (1946), *Joan Of Arc*

(1948), *Red River* (1948), *I Shot Jesse James* (1949), *The Return Of Jesse James* (1950), *Outlaw Territory* (1953), *The Good Die Young* (1954), *Southwest Passage* (1954), *Gunfight At The O.K. Corral* (1957), *Spartacus* (1960), *I Saw What You Did* (1965), *Farewell My Lovely* (1975), *The Shape Of Things To Come* (1979) and *Sundown, The Vampire In Retreat* (1989).

Nancy Walker
Actress

Died March 25 of lung cancer at age 69.

Beginning her career on Broadway, she began working in television in the '70s and is probably best remembered for her role as Ida Morgenstern on the television series *Rhoda*. The role earned her an Emmy nomination in 1975. She also received three Emmy nominations for her role as Mildred, on *McMillan and Wife*. Her most recent starring role was in the television series *True Colors*.

FILM CREDITS: *Stand Up And Be Counted* (1972), *Forty Carats* (1973) and *Murder By Death* (1976).

Anita Colby
Actress

Died March 27 in New York City, at age 77.

FILM CREDITS: Early in her career as a model, Colby became the most highly paid model in America. Her roles in film include *Mary Of Scotland, The Bride Walks Out, China Passage, Brute Force* and *Cover Girl*.

Wendell Mayes
Screenwriter

Died March 28 of cancer in Santa Monica, Calif., at age 72.

Mayes received an Academy Award nomination in 1959 for *Anatomy Of A Murder*.

FILM CREDITS: *The Spirit Of St. Louis, Anatomy Of A Murder, The Enemy Below, Go Tell The Spartans* and *Von Ryan's Express*.

Paul Henreid
(Paul George Julius von Henreid)
Actor/director

Died March 29 in Santa Monica, Calif., at age 84.

Henreid will best be remembered for his role as the resistance fighter, Victor Laszlo, in 1942's *Casablanca*, in which he played opposite Humphrey Bogart and Ingrid Bergman. In April 1992, just weeks after his death, the film was re-released in theaters around the country in celebration of its 50th anniversary.

FILM CREDITS: Henreid

appeared in over 45 films, spaning five decades. They include *Casablanca* (1942), *Now, Voyager* (1942), *Between Two Worlds* (1944), *The Conspirators* (1944), *Hollywood Canteen* (1944), *The Spanish Main* (1945), *Deception* (1946), *Devotion* (1946), *Of Human Bondage* (1946), *Last Of The Buccaneers* (1950), *The Four Horsemen Of The Apocalypse* (1962), *Exorcist II: The Heretic* (1977) and *On The Road To Hollywood* (1984).

He also directed such films as *For Men Only* (1951), *A Woman's Devotion* (1956), *Live Fast, Die Young* (1958) and *Dead Ringer* (1964).

APRIL

Karl Tunberg
Screenwriter

Died April 4 in London, at age 83.

FILM CREDITS: Nominated for an Academy Award in 1959 for *Ben-Hur*. Other writing credits include *Where Were You When The Lights Went Out?*, *The Seventh Dawn*, *Beau Brummel*, *Bring On The Girls*, *My Gal Sal* and *A Yank At Oxford*.

Isaac Asimov
Science-fiction author

Died April 6 of heart and kidney failure in New York City, at age 72.

FILM CREDITS: While influencing many of Hollywood's science-fiction filmmakers, few of his own books—nearly 500 in all— were translated into film. In 1966 he wrote the novelization of *Fantastic Voyage,* which won an Academy Award. In 1988, Roger Corman produced *Nightfall,* based on Asimov's popular short story of the same name.

Alix Talton
Actress

Died April 7 of lung cancer in Burbank, Calif., at age 72.

FILM CREDITS: *In A Lonely Place, Romanoff And Juliet* and Hitchcock's *The Man Who Knew Too Much.*

From 1953 to 1955 Talton co-starred in the television show *My Favorite Husband.*

Sam Kinison
Comedian

Died April 10 in an auto accident near Needles, Calif., at age 38.

Kinison was best known as the loud and controversial standup comic who recorded the song "Wild Thing," featuring Jessica Hahn in the music video.

FILM CREDITS: He costarred

on the Fox Broadcasting Company comedy series *Charlie Hoover.* Known primarily for his television sitcoms and specials, he also appeared with Rodney Dangerfield in *Back To School* (1986).

James Brown
Actor

Died April 11 of cancer in Woodland Hills, Calif., at age 72.

FILM CREDITS: Best remembered for his role in the TV series *The Adventures Of Rin Tin Tin*, Brown's numerous film roles include *Going My Way, Air Force* and *The Charge At Feather River.*

David Miller
Director

Died April 14 of cancer in Los Angeles, at age 82.

FILM CREDITS: In 1946 Miller won an Academy Award for the documentary short subject *Seeds Of Destiny.* He went on to direct over 20 features, including *Flying Tigers, Sudden Fear, Lonely Are The Brave, Midnight Lace, Captain Newman, M.D.* and *Executive Action.*

Morton W. Scott
Musical director

Died April 15 of heart failure in Santa Barbara, Calif., at age 80.

FILM CREDITS: As the musical director for Republic Pictures, Scott received two Academy Award nominations in 1945 for *Flame Of Barbary Coast* and *Hitchhike To Happiness.*

Neville Brand
Actor

Died April 16 of emphysema

in Sacramento, Calif., at age 71.

FILM CREDITS: Appearing in more than 40 films, he gained a reputation for playing screen toughs. Films include *D.O.A., Riot In Cell Block Eleven, Halls Of Montezuma, The Lonely Man, The Prodigal, The George Raft Story, That Darn Cat, The Desperados, Tora! Tora! Tora!, The Train Robbers, Alligator* and *Birdman Of Alcatraz.*

Brand will best be remembered, however, for his roles on the television series *The Untouchables* (1959 to 1963) and *Laredo* (1965 to 1967).

Benny Hill
(Alfred Hawthorn Hill)
Actor/comedian

Died April 20 in London at age 67.

FILM CREDITS: Gaining international attention with his British television comedy *The Benny Hill Show*, the popular comedian appeared in his first film, *Who Done It?* in 1956. Other films include *Light Up The Sky,*

Those Magnificent Men In Their Flying Machines, Chitty Chitty Bang Bang and *The Waiters* (short).

Satyajit Ray
Director

Died April 23 in Calcutta, at age 70.

A little more than a month before his death, Ray received an honorary Lifetime Achievement Academy Award. He accepted the award from his hospital bed.

FILM CREDITS: A giant in the international film industry, his 29 features include *Panther Panchali (The Song Of The Little Road*, 1955), *Aparajito (The Unvanquished*, 1956), *Apnur Sansar (The World Of Apu*, 1959), *Jalsaghar (The Music Room*, 1959), *Devi (The Goddess*, 1960), *Charulata (The Lonely Wife*, 1964), *Days And Nights In The Forest* (1970), *Ashani Sanket (Distant Thunder*, 1973), *Ghare Baire (The Home And The World*, 1984), *The Branches Of The Tree* (1990) and *The Stranger* (1991).

Mae Clarke
Actress

Died April 29 of cancer in Woodland Hills, Calif., at age 81.

FILM CREDITS: A leading lady in the '30s and '40s, Clarke appeared in over 80 films but is best remembered as the woman whom James Cagney hit in the face with a grapefruit in *Public Enemy* (1931). Other roles include *Big Time, Frankenstein, The Front Page, Waterloo Bridge, The Good Bad Girl, Men On Call, Reckless Living, Pat And Mike,*

Flying Tigers, Big Hand For The Little Lady, The Great Caruso, Annie Get Your Gun, Because Of You, Singin' In The Rain, Kitty, Magnificent Obsession, Thoroughly Modern Millie and *The Watermelon Man.*

MAY

George Murphy
Actor/senator

Died May 3 of leukemia in Palm Beach, Fla., at age 89.

In 1950 he received a special Academy Award for his work in the film industry.

FILM CREDITS: Murphy appeared in over 50 films for MGM, including *Kid Millions, This Is The Army, Broadway Melody, Little Miss Broadway, For Me And My Gal* and *It's A Big Country.*

In 1964 he was elected to the U.S. Senate. Longtime friend Ronald Reagan would enter politics shortly thereafter.

Marlene Dietrich
(Maria Magdalena Von Losch)
Actress

Died May 6 in Paris at age 90.

Nominated for an Academy Award for Best Actress in the 1931 film *Dishonored*, Dietrich came to symbolize the sexy, sultry femme fatale she so often played. Beyond her image, however, she will be remembered as one of a handful of Hollywood legends.

FILM CREDITS: Dietrich began her film career in 1923 with the German film *The Little Napoleon*. She made over a dozen films in Germany for director Max Reinhardt before being discovered by American director Josef von Sternberg and cast in *The Blue Angel* (1930). Other films include *Morocco* (1930), *Dishonored* (1931), *Shanghai Express* (1932), *Blonde Venus* (1932), *Song Of Songs* (1933), *The Scarlet Empress* (1934), *The Devil Is A Woman* (1935), *Desire* (1936), *The Garden Of Allah* (1936), *Knight Without Armor* (1937), *Angel* (1937), *Destry Rides Again*

(1939), *Seven Sinners* (1940), *The Flame Of New Orleans* (1941), *Manpower* (1941), *The Lady Is Willing* (1942), *The Spoilers* (1942), *Pittsburgh* (1942), *Follow The Boys* (1944), *Kismet* (1944), *The Room Upstairs* (1946), *Golden Earrings* (1947), *A Foreign Affair* (1948), *Stage Fright* (1950), *Rancho Notorious* (1952), *The Monte Carlo Story* (1956), *Around The World In 80 Days* (1956), *Witness For The Prosecution* (1957), *Judgment At Nuremberg* (1961), *Paris When It Sizzles* (1964) and *Just A Gigolo* (1978).

Richard Derr
Actor

Died May 8 of heart failure in Santa Monica, Calif., at age 74.

FILM CREDITS: Derr appeared on Broadway and in television but is best remembered as a leading man in numerous films, including *When Worlds Collide, Secret Heart, Luxury Liner, The Bride Goes Wild, Something To Live For* and *The Drowning Pool.*

John Lund
Actor

Died May 10 in Los Angeles, at age 81.

FILM CREDITS: A leading man in the '40s and '50s, Lund's films include *Dakota Incident, The Perils Of Pauline, The Mating Season, To Each His Own, A Foreign Affair, High Society, Miss Matlock's Millions, My Friend Irma, Duchess Of Idaho, Darling, How Could You?, Steel Town, Bronco Buster, The Woman They Almost Lynched, White Feather, Battle Stations, Affair In Reno,*

Chief Crazy Horse, The Wackiest Ship In The Army and *Night Has A Thousand Eyes.*

William A. Mueller
Sound engineer

Died May 12 of natural causes in Newport Beach, Calif., at 92.

FILM CREDITS: A pioneer in motion picture sound engineering, he received Academy Award nominations for *Calamity Jane* in 1953 and *Mister Roberts* in 1955. In 1927 he was a part of the team at Warner Brothers that produced the first talking picture, *The Jazz Singer* starring Al Jolson.

George Hurrell
Hollywood photographer

Died May 17 of cancer in Hollywood, at age 87.

A renowned Hollywood glamour photographer, Hurrell captured and immortalized all of the screen's legendary greats in images that have become as well known as the films they were intended to promote.

Beginning his Hollywood career in 1925, he continued to work until 1992.

Marshall Thompson
Actor

Died May 25 of congestive heart failure in Royal Oak, Michigan, at age 66.

FILM CREDITS: Marshall is best known for his role as Marsh Tracy on the television drama *Daktari* (1966-69). In addition, he appeared in more than 30 feature films, including *Battleground, They Were Expendable, Words And Music, Command Decision,*

To Hell And Back, My Six Convicts, Clarence, The Cross-eyed Lion and *The Turning Point.*

JUNE

Philip Dunne
Screenwriter

Died June 2 of cancer in Malibu, Calif., at age 84.

Dunne was a founder of the Writers Guild of America and received Academy Award nominations for *How Green Was My Valley* and *David And Bathsheba.*

FILM CREDITS: A director of 10 films, he is best remembered as a screenwriter. He wrote or co-wrote 36 films, including *The Count Of Monte Cristo* (1934), *The Last Of The Mohicans* (1936), *Suez* (1938), *How Green Was My Valley* (1941), *Forever Amber* (1947), *The Ghost And Mrs. Muir* (1947), *David And Bathsheba* (1951), *The Robe* (1953), *The View From Pompey's Head* (1955), *Hilda Crane* (1956), *Three Brave Men* (1956), *Blue Denim* (1959), *The Agony And The Ecstasy* (1965) and *Blindfold* (1966).

Robert Morley
British actor

Died June 3 following a stroke in Reading, England, at age 84.

Morley may best be remembered as the rotund spokesman for British Airways on American television commercials.

FILM CREDITS: Debuting on the London stage in 1929 he made his first Hollywood film, *Marie*

Antoinette, with Norma Shearer in 1938. He received an Academy Award nomination for the role.

He went on to roles in over 50 films, including *Major Barbara* (1941), *The African Queen* (1951), *Beat The Devil* (1953), *Beau Brummell* (1954), *The Good Die Young* (1954), *Around The World In 80 Days* (1956), *Oscar Wilde* (1960), *The Boys* (1962), *The Road To Hong Kong* (1962), *The Old Dark House* (1963), *Take Her, She's Mine* (1963), *Of Human Bondage* (1964), *Topkapi* (1964), *Genghis Khan* (1965), *The Loved One* (1965), *Life At The Top* (1965), *Those Magnificent Men In Their Flying Machines* (1965), *The Alphabet Murders* (1966), *Woman Times Seven* (1967), *Who Is Killing The Great Chefs Of Europe?* (1978), *Scavenger Hunt* (1979), *Oh Heavenly Dog* (1980), *The Great Muppet Caper* (1981) and *Istanbul: Keep Your Eyes Open* (1990).

Larry Riley
Actor

Died June 6 of AIDS related complications in Burbank, Calif., at age 39.

FILM CREDITS: Riley will best be remembered for his role as Frank Williams on the popular CBS television series *Knots Landing,* a role he held for the past five seasons.

In 1982 he received the Obie award for his role in *A Soldier's Play.* In 1984 he recreated the role in *A Soldier's Story,* directed by Norman Jewison. He also appeared in the film *Crackers.*

Serge Daney
French writer

Died June 11 of AIDS in Paris at age 48.

Daney was one of France's most respected writers about film. In 1968 he became editor of *Cahiers du Cinema.* He was also a critic for *Liberation.* In 1991, he launched *Trafic,* a new cinema quarterly.

Peter Allen
Singer/songwriter

Died June 18 of AIDS-related complications in San Diego, at the age of 48.

FILM CREDITS: Allen received an Academy Award in 1981, along with Burt Bacharach, Carole Bayer Sager and Christopher Cross for "Arthur's Theme" (Best That You Can Do), the theme from the film *Arthur.*

Allen, who was discovered by Judy Garland, had 11 albums to his credit, including the hit songs "I Honestly Love You," for Olivia Newton-John; "Don't Cry Out Loud," for Melissa Manchester and "You and Me (We Wanted It All)," for Frank Sinatra. He also appeared in concert and on Broadway.

Charles (Chuck) Mitchell
Actor

Died June 22 following abdominal surgery in Hollywood, at age 64.

FILM CREDITS: Mitchell is best remembered for his role as the rotund casino owner in the 1981 box-office hit *Porky's.* Other roles include *Porky's Revenge, Penitentiary, Don't Answer The Phone, The Hearse, Chopsticks, Goodbye Cruel World* and *California.*

He also had numerous roles in television and played Big Ralph on the daytime soap *General Hospital.*

Frederic I. Rinaldo
Screenwriter

Died June 22 of complications following surgery in Los Angeles, at age 78.

Rinaldo, and Robert Lees, were one of Hollywood's most renowned writing teams from 1934 to the early '50s. In 1941, they wrote the first of seven Abbott & Costello pictures. They would later write for Dean Martin and Jerry Lewis as well.

The team won Academy Awards for their shorts *How To Sleep* and *Penny Wisdom*.

FILM CREDITS: *Street Of Memories, The Invisible Woman, Hold That Ghost, Hit The Ice, Buck Privates Come Home, The Wistful Widow Of Wagon Gap, Abbott And Costello Meet Frankenstein, Abbot And Costello Meet The Invisible Man, Comin' Round The Mountain, No Time For Love, Crazy House, Holiday In Havana* and *Jumping Jacks*.

Renie
Costume designer

Died June 23 of natural causes in Pacific Palisades, Calif., at the age of 90.

Renie won an Oscar in 1963, along with Irene Sharaff and Vittorio Nino Novarese, for *Cleopatra*. She also received Academy Award nominations for her work on *The Model And The Marriage Broker, The President's Lady* and *The Big Fisherman*.

FILM CREDITS: *Kitty Foyle, Cat People, Tom, Dick And Harry, Mr. Lucky, The Sky's The Limit, None But The Lonely Heart, The Miracle Of The Bells, A Man Called Peter, The Three Faces Of Eve, The Sand Pebbles* and *Body Heat*.

Allan Jones
Actor/singer

Died June 27 of lung cancer in New York at age 84.

A leading man in the 1930s, he was also the father of singer Jack Jones.

FILM CREDITS: *A Night At The Opera, Show Boat, A Day At The Races, The Firefly, Rose Marie, Everybody Sing, Moonlight In Havana, The Boys From Syracuse, Larceny With Music, Rhythm Of The Islands* and *Stage To Thunder Rock*.

JULY

Franco Cristaldi
Italian producer

Died July 1 of cardiac arrest in Monte Carlo, France, at age 67.

Cristaldi produced more than 100 films during his career, including those of top filmmakers Federico Fellini, Giuseppe Tornatore and Luchino Visconte.

FILM CREDITS: Three of his films won Academy Awards for Best Foreign Language film: *Divorce American Style* (1961), *Amarcord* (1974) and *Cinema Paradiso* (1990).

In addition, his films won four Palm d'Ors at Cannes, three Golden Lions at Venice and eight Donatello David's, Italy's top film award.

Rudolf Ising
Animator

Died July 18 in Los Angeles, at age 88.

Ising began working with Walt Disney in 1922, before Mickey Mouse. He later went on to create the Looney Tunes series for Warner Bros.

In 1940, he received an Oscar for the the MGM cartoon *The Milky Way*.

Herman King
Producer

Died July 20 of complications following back surgery in Los Angeles, at age 77.

King, along with his brothers Maurice and Frank, produced many of the B films of the '40s, '50s and '60s.

FILM CREDITS: *The Brave One, Dillinger* (1945), *Suspense, The Ring, Carnival Story, When Strangers Marry, I Escaped From The Gestapo, Gorgo, Maya* and *Return Of The Gunfighter*.

Joe Shuster
Cartoonist

Died July 30 of congestive heart failure and hypertension in West Los Angeles, at age 78.

Shuster, along with writer Jerry Siegel, created the Superman comic book hero in the '30s.

FILM CREDITS: Besides the '50s television series, the Superman character has been portrayed in the films *Superman* (1978), *Superman II* (1980), *Superman III* (1983) and *Superman IV: The Quest For Peace* (1987).

Robert Peak
Movie poster artist

Died July 31 of a brain hemorrhage, in Carefree, Arizona at the age of 65.

A well-known, award-winning illustrator, Peak began creating movie posters in 1961, with *West Side Story*. Other film posters include *Camelot, Funny Girl, Apocalypse Now, Silverado, Hair, Superman* and *Reds*. He also illustrated five of the *Star Trek* movie posters.

AUGUST

John Sturges
Director

Died August 18 of a heart attack in San Luis Obispo, Calif., at age 82.

Received an Academy Award nomination in 1954 for *Bad Day At Black Rock*.

FILM CREDITS: *Thunderbolt, The Man Who Dared, The Best Man Wins, The Walking Hills, The Magnificent Yankee, Escape From Fort Bravo, Jeopardy, Backlash, Gunfight At The O.K. Corral, The Law And Jake Wade, The Magnificent Seven, Sergeants 3, The Great Escape, The Hallelujah Trail, Hour Of The Gun, Ice Station Zebra, Marooned, Joe Kidd, McQ,* and *The Eagle Has Landed*.

SEPTEMBER

Henry Ephron
Screenwriter/producer

Died September 6 in Woodland Hills, Calif. at age 81.

Writer and film director Nora Ephron (*Heartburn, Silkwood, This Is My Life*), and writers Delia and Amy Ephron are his surviving daughters.

FILM CREDITS: *The Jackpot* (1950), *What Price Glory?* (1952), *There's No Business Like Show Business* (1954), *Daddy Long Legs* (1955), *The Best Things In Life Are Free* (1956), *Carousel* (1956), *Desk Set* (1957) and *Captain Newman, M.D.* (1963).

Anthony Perkins
Actor/director

Died August 13 of AIDS complications, in Hollywood, at age 60.

Although nominated for an Academy Award in 1953 for his role in *Friendly Pesuasion*, he will best be remembered as Norman Bates, in Hitchcock's *Psycho*. Few actors have been so strongly identified with a role or film.

FILM CREDITS: *The Actress* (1953), *Friendly Persuasion* (1956), *The Lonely Man, Fear Strikes Out, The Tin Star* (1957), *Desire Under The Elms, This Angry Age, The Matchmaker* (1958), *Green Mansions, On The Beach* (1959), *Tall Story, Psycho* (1960), *Phaedra, Goodbye Again* (1961), *Five Miles To Midnight, The Trial* (1962), *The Fool Killer, Is Paris Burning?* (1965), *Pretty Poison* (1968), *WUSA, Catch 22* (1970), *Ten Days Wonder* (1971), *The Life And Times Of Judge Roy Bean, Play It As It Lays* (1972), *Lovin' Molly* (1973), *Murder On The Orient Express* (1974), *Mahogany* (1975), *Winter Kills* (1977), *Double Negative, The Horror Show, The Black Hole, Esther, Ruth And Jennifer* (1979), *Psycho II* (1983), *Crimes Of Passion* (1984), *Psycho 3* (1986) and *Destroyer* (1988).

Michael A. Luciano
Film editor

Died September 15 of a heart attack in Los Angeles, at age 82.

Luciano received Academy Award nominations for *Flight Of The Phoenix, What Ever Happened To Baby Jane?, The Dirty Dozen* and *Hush, Hush Sweet Charlotte*.

FILM CREDITS: *The Longest Yard, The Big Knife, Kiss Me Deadly, Apache, Attack!, Too Late The Hero, Autumn Leaves, Emperor Of The North Pole, The Killing Of Sister George, The Legend Of Lylah Clare, Twilight's Last Gleaming, Four For Texas, World For Ransom, The Last Sunset* and *The Grissom Gang*.

Herbert Spencer
Composer/arranger
and orchestrator

Died Sept. 18 of complications from pneumonia in Culver City, Calif., at age 87.

Received an Academy Award nomination in 1970 for his work on *Scrooge* and in 1973 for *Jesus Christ Superstar*.

FILM CREDITS: *Alexander's Ragtime Band, Tin Pan Alley, With A Song In My Heart, Gentlemen Prefer Blondes, There's No Business Like Show Business, The King And I, Hello, Dolly!, The Towering Inferno, The Eiger Sanction, M*A*S*H*, Jaws, Star Wars, Superman, Close Encounters Of The Third Kind, E.T., The Extra-Terrestrial, The Witches Of Eastwick* and *Home Alone*.

Bill Williams
Actor

Died Sept. 21 of a brain tumor in Burbank, Calif., at age 77.

Williams starred in the 1950s TV series *The Adventures Of Kit Carson*. He was married to actress

Barbara Hale, who played Della Street on the *Perry Mason* TV series.

FILM CREDITS: *Thirty Seconds Over Tokyo, Those Endearing Young Charms, Till The End Of Time, The Great Missouri Raid, Son Of Paleface, Bronco Buster, Rio Lobo, The Giant Spider Invasion* and *The Hallelujah Trail*.

Paul Jabara
Songwriter/actor

Died Sept. 29 following a long illness in Los Angeles, at age 44.

Jabara won an Academy Award in 1978 for Best Original Score for "Last Dance," from the film *Thank God It's Friday*. He made his acting debut in the original cast of *Hair* on Broadway. He later joined the original cast of *The Rocky Horror Show*.

Songwriting credits include "The Main Event," "Enough Is Enough," "Work That Body," "It's Raining Men" and "Two Lovers."

FILM CREDITS: *Midnight Cowboy, The Lords Of Flatbush, The Day Of The Locust, Honky Tonk Freeway, Star 80, Legal Eagles, The Ski Bum, Les Patterson Saves The World, Medea* and *Light Sleeper*.

Bill Rowe
Director of postproduction

Died Sept. 29 of a stroke in London.

Rowe won an Academy Award for his work on *The Last Emperor*.

FILM CREDITS: *Alien, The French Lieutenant's Woman, The Killing Fields, The Last Emperor, City Of Joy* and *Bitter Moon*.

OCTOBER

Denholm Elliot
British actor

Died October 6 of AIDS in Ibiza, Spain, at age 70.

Elliot was nominated for a Best Supporting Actor Academy Award in 1985 for *A Room With A View*.

FILM CREDITS: *Alfie* (1966), *The Night They Raided Minsky's* (1968), *The Apprenticeship Of Duddy Kravitz* (1974), *Voyage Of The Damned* (1976), *The Boys From Brazil* (1978), *Zulu Dawn* (1979), *Raiders Of The Lost Ark* (1981), *The Missionary* (1982), *Trading Places* (1983), *The Razor's Edge* (1984), *A Room With A View* (1985), *Maurice* (1987), *September* (1988), *Toy Soldiers* and *Noises Off* (1991).

John Hancock
Actor

Died October 13 of a heart attack in Los Angeles, at age 51.

FILM CREDITS: *A Soldier's Story* (1984), *Foul Play* (1978)

and *Bonfire Of The Vanities* (1990). At the time of his death he was co-starring in the CBS comedy *Love & War*. Television viewers will remember him as well for his recurring role on *L.A. Law*.

Shirley Booth (Thelma Ford)
Actress

Died October 16 of natural causes in Cape Cod, Mass., at the age of 94

Booth received an Academy Award in 1952 for Best Actress in *Come Back Little Sheba*.

FILM CREDITS: Although she won an Oscar, Booth will best be remembered for her starring role in the television sitcom *Hazel*, which ran from 1961 to 1966. Her films include *Come Back Little Sheba* (1952), *Main Street To Broadway* (1953), *About Mrs. Leslie* (1954), *Hot Spell* (1958) and *The Matchmaker* (1958).

Anna Johnstone
Costume designer

Died October 16 following a long illness, in Lenox, Mass., at the age of 79.

Johnstone received Academy Award nominations for her work in *The Godfather* and *Ragtime*.

FILM CREDITS: *The Group, On The Waterfront, East Of Eden, America, America, Baby Doll, Edge Of The City, A Face In The Crowd, Serpico, Dog Day Afternoon, The Wiz, Prince Of The City, The Verdict* and *Running On Empty*.

Cleavon Little
Actor

Died October 22 of colon cancer in Sherman Oaks, Calif., at age 53.

Little appeared on stage, television and in films. He won a 1971 Tony award for his role in *Purlie*, and an Emmy for an appearance on the television series *Dear John*.

FILM CREDITS: His most memorable performance was in the 1974 Mel Brooks comedy *Blazing Saddles*. Other roles include *Cotton Comes To Harlem* (1970), *Vanishing Point* (1971), *Greased Lightning* (1977), *FM* (1978), *Scavenger Hunt* (1979), *High Risk* (1981), *Toy Soldiers* (1984), *Arthur 2: On The Rocks* (1988), *Fletch Lives* (1989) and *Once Bitten* (1985).

Hal Roach
Producer

Died October 31 in Bel Air, Calif., at age 100.

Considered the last of the great film pioneers, Roach founded the Rolin Film Co. with Harold Lloyd in 1912. He went on to team up Laurel and Hardy as well as *Our Gang (Little Rascals)*.

FILM CREDITS: Over 100 shorts and feature-length films. He received four Academy Award nominations for Best Live Action Short Film for *The Music Box* (1932), *Tit For Tat* (1935), *There Goes My Heart* (1938) and *Flying With Music* (1942).

Other films include *Bumping Into Broadway* (1919), *Grandma's Boy* (1922), *From Soup To Nuts* (1928), *Topper* (1937), *Topper Takes A Trip* (1939) and *Topper Returns* (1941).

NOVEMBER

John H. Davis
Actor

Died November 3 of respiratory failure in Los Angeles, at the age of 78.

FILM CREDITS: Davis played the tough kid in 19 of the *Our Gang* films in the 1920s. He left acting to pursue a medical career.

Jack Kelly
Actor

Died November 7 of a stroke in Huntington Beach, Calif., at the age of 65.

Kelly will best be remembered as James Garner's co-star Bart Maverick in the popular ABC television western *Maverick* (1957 to 1962).

FILM CREDITS: *The Story Of Alexander Graham Bell, Fighting Men Of The West, Where Danger Lives, The Country Girl, Red Ball*

Express, Gunsmoke, Forbidden Planet, She-Devil, Love And Kisses, Drive A Crooked Road and *Young Billy Young.*

Chuck Connors
(Kevin Connors)
Actor

Died November 10 of lung cancer in Los Angeles, at age 71.

While Connors appeared in numerous films, he will best be remembered for his role as Lucas McCain on the popular ABC television western *The Rifleman* (1958 to 1963).

FILM CREDITS: *Pat And Mike* (1952), *South Sea Woman* (1953), *The Human Jungle* (1954), *Good Morning Miss Dove* (1955), *Tomahawk Trail* (1957), *Designing Woman* (1957), *Geronimo* (1962), *Move Over, Darling* (1963), *Synanon* (1965), *Support Your Local Gunfighter* (1971), *Soylent Green* (1973) and *Airplane II, The Sequel* (1982).

Diane Varsi
Actress

Died November 19 of a respiratory illness in Hollywood, at age 54.

FILM CREDITS: Varsi received an Academy Award nomination for her role as Allison MacKenzie in the 1957 film *Peyton Place.* Other film roles include *Ten North Frederick* (1958), *From Hell To Texas* (1959), *Compulsion* (1959), *Johnny Got His Gun* (1971) and *I Never Promised You A Rose Garden* (1977).

John Foreman
Producer

Died November 20 of a heart attack in Beverly Hills, Calif., at age 67.

FILM CREDITS: *Butch Cassidy And The Sundance Kid, They Might Be Giants, The Effect Of Gamma Rays On Man-In-The-Moon Marigolds, The Life And Times Of Judge Roy Bean, The Mackintosh Man , The Man Who Would Be King, Bobby Deerfield, The Great Train Robbery* and *Prizzi's Honor.*

Sterling Holloway
Charactor actor

Died November 22 in Los Angeles, at age 87.

FILM CREDITS: Appearing in over 100 films, Holloway will best be remembered as the voice of *Winnie The Pooh.* He also brought life to other Disney animated characters like the Cheshire cat in *Alice In Wonder-*

land, the stork in *Dumbo* and the snake in *The Jungle Book.*

Other films include *Meet John Doe; Gold Diggers Of 1933; International House; The Beautiful Blonde From Bashful Bend; Casey At The Bat; Hell Below; Life Begins At Forty; Professor Beware; The Bluebird; A Walk In The Sun; Shake, Rattle And Rock* and *Live A Little, Love A Little.*

He also appeared as a regular on the television series *The Life Of Riley* (1953-1958) and *The Baileys Of Balboa* (1964-1965).

Robert Shayne
(Robert Shaen Dawe)
Actor

Died November 29 of lung cancer in Woodland Hills, Calif.

FILM CREDITS: Shayne appeared on Broadway, in television and in over 100 films including *Keep 'Em Rolling, Hollywood Canteen, Mr. Skeffington, Rhapsody In Blue, Let's Live A Little, Tora! Tora! Tora!, Wife Wanted* and *The Million Dollar*

Duck.

Shayne played Inspector William Henderson on the television series *The Adventures Of Superman* (1952 to 1957).

DECEMBER

Vincent Gardenia
Actor

Died December 9 of a heart attack in Philadelphia at age 71.

FILM CREDITS: Gardenia received Academy Award nominations for his role in *Bang The Drum Slowly* (1973) and for *Moonstruck* (1987). Other film roles include *The Hustler, The Front Page, Heaven Can Wait, California Suite, Death Wish, Little Shop Of horrors* and *The Super.*

In addition, Gardenia appeared on Broadway and in television. He received a Tony for his performance in *The Prisoner Of Second Avenue* in 1972 and an Emmy in 1990 for *Age-old Friends.*

Dana Andrews
(Carver Dana Andrews)
Actor

Died December 17 of pneumonia in Los Alamitos, Calif., at age 83.

Andrews was a leading man in the '40s. His brother is actor Steve Forrest.

FILM CREDITS: *Lucky Cisco Kid* (1939), *The Westerner, Sailor's Lady, Kit Carson* (1940), *Tobacco Road, Belle Starr, Swamp Water, Ball Of Fire* (1941), *Berlin Correspondent, The Ox-Bow Incident* (1942), *December Seventh, Crash Dive, North Star* (1943), *The Purple Heart, Wing And A Prayer, Up In Arms, Laura* (1944), *State Fair, Fallen Angel, A Walk In The Sun* (1945), *The Best Years Of Our Lives* (1946), *Boomerang* (1947), *The Iron Curtain, Deep Waters* (1948), *Sword In The Desert* (1949), *My Foolish Heart, Edge Of Doom* (1950), *Sealed Cargo* (1951), *Elephant Walk* (1953), *Comanche, Beyond A Reasonable Doubt* (1956), *The Satan Bug* (1964), *In Harm's Way, The Loved One, Battle Of The Bulge* (1965), *Hot*

Rods To Hell (1967), *The Devil's Brigade* (1968), *Airport 1975* (1975), *The Last Tycoon* (1976), *Prince Jack* (1984).

Stella Adler
Actress and acting coach

Died December 21 of heart failure in Los Angeles, at age 91.

Adler studied under the legendary Stanislavsky and went on to promote his method acting. She gained attention in the '30s as a member of the Group Theater in New York. Her best-known students include Marlon Brando, Shelley Winters, Warren Beatty, Robert De Niro, Peter Bogdanovich and Candice Bergen.

FILM CREDITS *Love On Toast, Shadow Of The Thin Man* and she was the subject of the 1989 documentary *Stella Adler: Awake And Dream.*

Cast/Credit Index

INDEX

Carpenter, Vic, 140
Carpintieri, Renato, 92
Carquin, Denis, 46
Carr, Budd, 99
Carr, Cindy, 185
Carr, Cristen M., 121
Carr, Jackie, 69
Carra, Lucille, 118
Carradine, David, 75, 195
Carradine, Keith, 32, 61
Carradine, Robert, 182
Carrafa, John, 45
Carrasco, Carlos, 116
Carreras, Chris, 26, 181
Carrere, Tia, 243
Carrick, Lloyd, 79
Carriere, Mathieu, 54
Carroll, Gordon, 26
Carroll, Matt, 231
Carroll, Rocky, 85, 184
Carroll, Willard, 37, 199
Carrot, Bryan, 123
Carrus, Gerald, 118
Carter, Helena Bonham, 111, 244
Carter, Jack, 116
Carter, James L., 173
Carter, John, 44, 69, 129
Carter, Nell, 37
Carter, Reggie, 148
Carter, Rick, 69
Carter, Ruth, 150
Carteris, Gabrielle, 191
Cartlidge, William P., 181
Cartwright, Lynn, 134
Cartwright, Randy, 24
Cartwright, Veronica, 151
Carvalho, Betty, 151
Carvey, Dana, 243
Casados, Eloy, 140
Casale, Roberto, 94
Casella, Max, 166
Casey, Kimberley, 74
Casey, Michael R., 21
Casile, Genevieve, 130
Caso, Alan, 171
Casparian, Marty, 41
Cassavetti, Patrick, 242
Cassel, Ferne, 249
Cassel, Jean-Pierre, 85
Cassel, Seymour, 71, 116
Cassidy, Esther B., 28
Cassidy, Gordon, 232

Cassidy, Joanna, 143
Cassidy, William J., 45
Cassie, Alan, 163, 179
Castaldi, Jean-Pierre, 89
Castanedo, Rafael, 50
Castanon, Carlos, 50
Castellaneta, P. J., 226
Castellanos, Theodora, 150
Castellitto, Sergio, 25
Castile, Christopher, 38
Castle, Alien, 70
Castle, DeShonn, 256
Castro-Brechignac, Marie, 25
Castronari, Gisela, 215
Catenia, Vito, 238
Cathell, Cevin, 99
Catonne, Francois, 118
Catti, Danilo, 226
Cattrall, Kim, 212
Cauley, Eve, 85, 209
Causey, Thomas, 138, 216
Causey, Thomas D., 106
Cavaiani, Maria, 243
Cavan, Susan, 252
Cavanagh, Megan, 134
Cavanaugh, Tony, 84
Cave, Nick, 65, 124
Cavedon, Suzanne, 38
Cavele, Keith, 212
Cazenove, Christopher, 21
Caziot, Jean-Jacques, 170
Cecchi Gori, Mario, 91, 124, 154
Cecchi Gori, Vittorio, 91, 124, 151, 154
Cederna, Giuseppe, 154
Cehvit, Maurice, 102
Centonze, Alain, 25
Cepek, Petr, 79
Ceppi, Francois, 130
Cerami, Vincenzo, 124
Cercone, Janus, 135
Ceribello, Jimmy, 230
Cerveris, Michael, 253
Cesaretti, Gusmano, 132
Chabrol, Claude, 119
Chabrol, Matthieu, 119
Chadwick, Justin, 143
Chaimovitch, Samuel, 85
Chalfant, Kathleen, 125
Challenge, Heather Jones, 221

Chalou, Jerome, 58
Chambers, Patti, 164
Champlin, Charles, 182
Chan, Dennis, 127
Chan, Jackie, 183
Chan, Michael Paul, 192
Chan, Philip, 76
Chan, Willie, 183
Chandler, Damon, 248
Chandler, Estee, 221
Chandler, Kyle, 188
Chandler, Michael, 28, 250
Chang, Gary, 233
Chang, Martha, 224
Chang, William, 76
Changfu, Zheng, 253
Changwei, Gu, 138
Chaplin, Charles, 53
Chaplin, Geraldine, 52
Chaplin, Jane, 54
Chapman, David, 224
Chapman, Joan E., 91, 167
Chapman, Lanei, 115
Chapman, Matthew, 59
Chapman, Michael, 246
Chappelle, Aleta, 44, 158
Charbonneau, Jay, 59
Charbonneau, Patricia, 127
Charbonnet, Merideth Boswell, 101
Charbonnier, Jean-Louis, 227
Charles, Josh, 62
Charny, Ruth, 157
Charraborty, Lily, 46
Charters, Rodney, 215
Chartoff, Robert, 217
Chase, Chevy, 104, 155
Chase, Thomas, 141
Chatterjee, Soumitra, 46
Chatterji, Dhritiman, 217
Chatterji, Subrata, 217
Chau, Mai, 117
Chaudhri, Amin Q., 71
Chaulet, Emmanuelle, 27
Chauvin, Lilyan, 235
Chavanne, Brian, 126
Chaykin, Maury, 22, 104, 136
Cheeseman, Ken, 110
Chen, Joan, 231
Cheng, Kent, 172
Chenowith, Ellen, 139, 228

Cher, 182
Chereau, Patrice, 132
Chesney, Peter, 179, 180
Chesney, Peter M., 108
Chester, Craig, 219
Cheung, Carbon, 76
Cheung, Jacky, 172
Cheung, Maggie, 76, 183
Cheuviche, Jacques, 27
Chew, Richard, 208
Chi, 73
Chi-sin, Mak, 172
Chianes, Dominic, 187
Chiang, Peter, 94
Chiba, Sonny, 21
Childs, Martin, 62, 180
Chiles, Lois, 71
China Central TV, 123
Chiu, Mark, 76
Chobanian, Arthur, 117
Chong, Rae Dawn, 27, 244
Chong, Tommy, 86
Chong-yan, Yuen, 172
Chopelas, Tony, 136
Chornow, David, 140, 235
Chory, Jim, 161
Choudhury, Sarita, 157
Chouis, Del, 89
Chow, Raymond, 172
Chowdhry, Ranjit, 157
Chowdhury, Santu, 54
Chpalikova, Daria, 201
Christensen, Bo, 257
Christian, Victoria, 25
Christiansen, Sean, 248
Christon, Phillip, 140, 211
Christopher, Bojesse, 66, 152
Chubb, Caldecot, 106
Chudej, Stephen, 205
Chudey, Stephen, 200
Chung, David, 172
Chung-man, Yee, 172
Churgin, Lisa, 43, 200
Chvatal, Cindy, 103
Cibelli, Christopher, 104
Cidre, Cynthia, 150
Cinefex Workshop, 76
Cinema Research Corp., 106
Cinieri, Francesco, 32, 172
Cioffi, Charles, 166, 236
Cirile, Cindy, 192

297

Davenport, Marc, 248
Daves, Michael, 102, 192
Davey, Bruce, 93
Davi, Robert, 27, 52, 54, 249
David Stipes Prods., 121
David, Eleanor, 143
David, Joanna, 203
David, Keith, 30, 88
David, Pierre, 69, 70, 73
Davidovich, Lolita, 135, 191
Davidson, Jaye, 62
Davidson, Martin, 103
Davies, Aaron, 183
Davies, Freeman, 229
Davies, Phil, 211
Davies, Tom, 101, 146
Davies, William, 216
Davis, Andrew, 232
Davis, Battle, 138
Davis, Brad, 182
Davis, Catherine, 165
Davis, Dan, 63, 171
Davis, Deb, 59
Davis, Duane, 72
Davis, Elliot, 63, 205
Davis, Geena, 104, 134
Davis, Gene, 235
Davis, John, 216
Davis, John H., 288
Davis, Judy, 113, 244
Davis, Kaye, 148
Davis, Michael, 253
Davis, Mona, 77
Davis, Nathan, 205
Davis, Noel, 255
Davis, Ossie, 99, 149
Davis, Stephen, 198
Davis, Viveka, 151
Davis, Zack, 140
Davison, Steve, 155
Dawber, Pam, 213
Dawe, Tony, 26
Dawson, Deborah, 197
Day, Cora Lee, 67
Day, Dylan, 31
Day, Lisa, 170
Day-Lewis, Daniel, 132
DC Comics, 35
De Alexandre, Rodolfo, 153
de Almeida, Joaquim, 26
de Arminan, Jaime, 164
de Avila, Ann, 145

de Avila, Michael, 145
de Avila, Rolando, 145
De Backer, Jo, 226
De Bankole, Isaach, 169
de Bankole, Isaach, 170
de Blas, Manuel, 54
De Bont, Jan, 34, 138, 206
de Broca, Michelle, 85
de Castro, Tony, 28
de Cleremont-Tonnerre, Antoine, 85
De Concini, Ennio, 32
de Faria, Sylvana, 58
De Ganay, Thierry, 102
De Goros, Jean-Claude, 92
de Haviland, Consuelo, 58
De Jong, Ate, 106
de Keyzer, Bruno, 23, 130
De Koenigsberg, Paula, 222
De la Bouillerie, Hubert C., 158
de la Fontaine, Jeanne Marie, 169
De La Paz, Danny, 29
De La Pena, George, 45, 129
de la Torre, Dale R., 190
De la Touche, Adrian, 94
de Lancie, John, 102
De Laurentiis, Dino, 172
De Laurentiis, Martha, 172
De Luca, Michael, 69
de Luna, Alvara, 164
de Medeiros, Maria, 26
De Nesle, Yvone Sassinot, 130
De Niro, Robert, 157, 168, 225
de Padua, Guilherme, 238
De Palma, Brian, 191
de Passe, Suzanne, 55
de Saint-Pere, Helene, 251
De Salvo, Joe, 230
De Scenna, Linda, 109
de Segonzac, Jean, 133, 245
De Young, Cliff, 75
De, Deepankar, 46, 217
Deakins, Roger, 177, 225
Dean, Lisa, 43
Dean, Loren, 93
Dean, Rick, 42
Dean, Ron, 205
Dearborn, Richard, 88

DeCarlo, Mark, 49
Dechant, David, 226
Deckers, Jan, 123
DeCuir, John, Jr., 215
Dedet, Yann, 238
Dee, Patte, 115
Dee, Ruby, 58
Deezen, Eddie, 196
DeForrest, Kelle, 211
DeGeneres, Ellen, 252
DeGovia, Jackson, 209
DeGrandis, Jeffrey, 213
Deguy, Marie-Armelle, 130
Dehner, Durk, 64
Dehner, John, 277
Deja, Andreas, 24
Del Amo, Alvaro, 147
Del Amo, Pablo G., 251
Del Rosario, Linda, 22
Del Ruth, Thomas, 129, 156
Del Toro, Benicio, 54
del Toro, Guillermo, 50
Delany, Dana, 110, 139
Delerue, Georges, 151, 279
Delgado, Lothar, 253
Delia, Joe, 33
Dellar, Mel, 129
Delli Colli, Tonino, 120
Deloche, Carlos, 159
Delory, Michel, 230
Delpy, Julie, 239
DeLuise, Dom, 162
DeLuise, Michael, 81, 243
Delville, Bernard, 168
Demetral, Chris, 73
Demetrios, Eames, 99
Demetriou, Cosmas, 208
Demetriou, Cosmos A., 122
Deming, Peter, 44, 164
Demme, Jonathan, 61
DeMornay, Rebecca, 102
Dempsey, Mike, 145
Deneuve, Catherine, 117
Denis, Claire, 170
Denker, Lisa, 97
Dennehy, Brian, 99
Dennen, Barry, 140
Denner, Charles, 251
Dennis, Sandy, 278
Dennison, John, 29
Dennison, Reid, 220
Dennison, Sally, 129, 146
Depardieu, Gerard, 46, 93,

227
Depardieu, Guillaume, 227
DePrez, Theresa, 207
Deprez, Therese, 193, 219
Depusse, Jean, 119
Derakhshanian, Kayvon, 89
Derakhshanian, Mohummad, 89
DeRamus, Theda, 235
Derby, Rick, 249
Dern, Bruce, 72
Derr, Richard, 283
DeSalvo, Joe, 124
DeSantis, Stanley, 51
DeSanto, Susie, 198
Descas, Alex, 170
DeScenna, Linda, 228
DeShannon, Jackie, 37
Dessalles, Olivier, 168
DeTitta, George, Jr., 135, 202, 204
Detmers, Maruschka, 150
Detraz, Monique, 74
Deutch, Howard, 30
Deutchman, Ira, 242
Deutsch, Helen, 279
DeVasquez, Devin, 211
Devenney, Mary Jo, 66
Devine, Loretta, 55
Devine, Michael, 72
Devis, James, 178
DeVito, Danny, 35, 106
Devlin, Alan, 181
Devlin, Dean, 235
Devlin, Peter, 70
Devlin, Peter J., 54
DeWaay, Larry, 84
Dewhurst, Colleen, 38
Dezaki, Osamu, 186
Dharker, Ayesha, 54
Di Borgo, Valerie Pozzo, 70
di Giacomo, Franco, 89
Di Novi, Denise, 35
Di Palma, Carlo, 114
di Santo, Bymadette, 115
Di Simone, Giovanni, 205
Diamond, Gary, 39
Diamond, Keith, 75
Diarra, Helene, 89
Diaz, Edith, 209
DiBenedetto, Peter, 42
Dichter, Lee, 110
DiCillo, Tom, 124, 125